S T O C K
TRADER'S
A L M A N A C
2 O 1 8

Jeffrey A. Hirsch & Yale Hirsch

WILEY

www.stocktradersalmanac.com

This Fifty-First Edition is respectfully dedicated to:

Louis G. Navellier

Louie is Chairman and Founder of Navellier & Associates, Inc. In 1980 he began publishing *MPT Review*, a stock advisory newsletter for individuals that featured his quantitative analysis on growth stocks. In 1987 he started managing private accounts for high-net-worth individuals, and shortly thereafter for public plans. Since then, Navellier & Associates has guided thousands of investors and institutions by applying its disciplined, quantitative investment process to a broad range of equity products. Louie manages approximately $2 billion in assets. He also writes six investment newsletters focused on growth investing: *Blue Chip Growth, Emerging Growth, Dividend Growth, Family Trust, High Velocity Stocks* and *Platinum Growth*. His free Stock/ETF/Dividend Grader is super handy and his free *Weekly Marketmail* is nonpareil. Louie is always sharing his market outlook and analysis on Bloomberg, Fox News and CNBC. Louie has been an industry stalwart for nearly 40 years. He is a true believer in and user of seasonality and market cycles. His stocks, portfolios and funds rock and he has been a great friend.

INTRODUCTION TO THE FIFTY-FIRST EDITION

Once again we have the honor of introducing the Fifty-First Edition of the *Stock Trader's Almanac*. The *Almanac* provides you with the necessary tools to invest successfully in the twenty-first century.

J. P. Morgan's classic retort, "Stocks will fluctuate," is often quoted with a wink-of-the-eye implication that the only prediction one can make about the stock market is that it will go up, down, or sideways. Many investors agree that no one ever really knows which way the market will move. Nothing could be further from the truth.

We discovered that while stocks do indeed fluctuate, they do so in well-defined, often predictable patterns. These patterns recur too frequently to be the result of chance or coincidence. How else do we explain that since 1950 all the gains in the market were made during November through April, compared to a loss May through October? (See page 50.)

The *Almanac* is a practical investment tool. It alerts you to those little-known market patterns and tendencies on which shrewd professionals enhance profit potential. You will be able to forecast market trends with accuracy and confidence when you use the *Almanac* to help you understand:

- How our presidential elections affect the economy and the stock market—just as the moon affects the tides. Many investors have made fortunes following the political cycle. You can be sure that money managers who control billions of dollars are also political cycle watchers. Astute people do not ignore a pattern that has been working effectively throughout most of our economic history.

- How the passage of the Twentieth Amendment to the Constitution fathered the January Barometer. This barometer has an outstanding record for predicting the general course of the stock market each year, with only nine major errors since 1950, for an 86.6% accuracy ratio. (See page 16.)

- Why there is a significant market bias at certain times of the day, week, month, and year.

Even if you are an investor who pays scant attention to cycles, indicators, and patterns, your investment survival could hinge on your interpretation of one of the recurring patterns found within these pages. One of the most intriguing and important patterns is the symbiotic relationship between Washington and Wall Street. Aside from the potential profitability in seasonal patterns, there's the pure joy of seeing the market very often do just what you expected.

The *Stock Trader's Almanac* is also an organizer. Its wealth of information is presented on a calendar basis. The *Almanac* puts investing in a business framework and makes investing easier because it:

- Updates investment knowledge and informs you of new techniques and tools.
- Is a monthly reminder and refresher course.
- Alerts you to both seasonal opportunities and dangers.
- Furnishes a historical viewpoint by providing pertinent statistics on past market performance.
- Supplies forms necessary for portfolio planning, record keeping, and tax preparation.

 The WITCH icon signifies THIRD FRIDAY OF THE MONTH on calendar pages and alerts you to extraordinary volatility due to the expiration of equity and index options and index futures contracts. Triple-witching days appear during March, June, September, and December.

 The BULL icon on calendar pages signifies favorable trading days based on the S&P 500 rising 60% or more of the time on a particular trading day during the 21-year period January 1996 to December 2016.

 A BEAR icon on calendar pages signifies unfavorable trading days based on the S&P falling 60% or more of the time for the same 21-year period.

Also, to give you even greater perspective, we have listed next to the date of every day that the market is open the Market Probability numbers for the same 21-year period for the Dow (D), S&P 500 (S), and NASDAQ (N). You will see a "D," "S," and "N" followed by a number signifying the actual Market Probability number for that trading day, based on the recent 21-year period. On pages 121–128, you will find complete Market Probability Calendars, both long-term and 21-year for the Dow, S&P, and NASDAQ, as well as for the Russell 1000 and Russell 2000 indices.

Other seasonalities near the ends, beginnings, and middles of months—options expirations, around holidays, and other significant times—as well as all FOMC Meeting dates are noted for *Almanac* investors' convenience on the weekly planner pages. All other important economic releases are provided in the Strategy Calendar every month in our e-newsletter, *Almanac Investor*, available at our website, *www.stocktradersalmanac.com.*

One-year seasonal pattern charts for Dow, S&P 500, NASDAQ, Russell 1000, and Russell 2000 appear on pages 171 to 173. There are three charts each for Dow and S&P 500 spanning our entire database starting in 1901 and one each for the younger indices. As 2018 is a midterm election year, each chart contains typical midterm year performance compared to all years.

The Notable Events on page 6 provides a handy list of major events of the past year that can be helpful when evaluating things that may have moved the market. Over the past few years, our research had been restructured to flow better with the rhythm of the year. This has also allowed us more room for added data. Again, we have included historical data on the Russell 1000 and Russell 2000 indices. The Russell 2K is an excellent proxy for small and mid-caps, which we have used over the years, and the Russell 1K provides a broader view of large caps. Annual highs and lows for all five indices covered in the *Almanac* appear on pages 149–151, and we've tweaked the Best & Worst section.

In order to cram in all this material, some of our Record Keeping section was cut. We have converted many of these paper forms into computer spreadsheets for our own internal use. As a service to our faithful readers, we are making these forms available at our website, *www.stocktradersalmanac.com.*

Midterm election years have been the second worst year of the four-year cycle, while eighth years of decades have been the second best, so 2018 promises to be laced with cross-currents. The last nine eighth years of decades appear on page 24. You can find all the market charts of midterm elections since the Depression on page 26, "Midterm Election Years: Where Bottom Pickers Find Paradise" on page 30, "Prosperity More Than Peace Determines the Outcome of Midterm Congressional Races" on page 32, and "Why a 50% Dow Gain Is Possible From Its 2018 Low to Its 2019 High" on page 34.

Our "Super Boom Update: 2010 Forecast On Track for Dow 38820 By 2025" appears on page 40, followed by "Culturally Enabling Paradigm Shifting Technologies Poised to Fuel the Next Super Boom" on page 42. For the first time in the *Almanac* we show how "Summer Market Volume Doldrums Drives Worst Six Months" on page 42.

On page 76 is our Best Investment Book of the Year, *Relationship Investing: Stock Market Therapy for Your Money,* by Jeffrey S. Weiss, CMT (Skyhorse Publishing). Other top books are listed on page 116. Sector seasonalities include several consistent shorting opportunities and appear on pages 92–96.

We are constantly searching for new insights and nuances about the stock market and welcome any suggestions from our readers.

Have a healthy and prosperous 2018!

NOTABLE EVENTS

2016

Apr 3	Panama Papers detail 200K+ entities used for illegal purposes by noted personalities and heads of state
May 19	EgyptAir Flight 804 from Paris to Cairo crashes over Mediterranean killing all 66 people on board
Jun 1	Gotthard Base Tunnel, world's longest and deepest railway tunnel, opens after 2 decades work
Jun 7	Kurdish rebels bomb central Istanbul targeting a police bus killing 12, injuring 51
Jun 8	Kurdish rebel car bomb in Midyat targeting police office, 5 killed (2 police) 30 injured
Jun 12	Gunman kills 49 wounds 58 in Orlando Pulse nightclub terrorist/hate crime shooting after 3-hour standoff
Jun 23	UK votes in favor of Brexit referendum to leave the European Union
Jun 28	ISIL suspected in terror attack on Atatürk Airport, Istanbul, killing 45 injuring ~230
Jul 1	Latvia becomes 35th member of OECD
Jul 4	NASA's Juno spacecraft enters Jupiter's orbit begins 20-month survey of Jupiter
Jul 14	ISIS Bastille Day attack in Nice, France kills 77 when a truck plowed through a crowd
Jul 26	Solar Impulse 2 becomes the first solar-powered aircraft to circumnavigate the Earth
Aug 5-21	2016 Summer Olympics held in Rio de Janeiro, Brazil
Aug 31	Brazilian Senate votes 61–20 to impeach and remove President Dilma Rousseff from office
Sep 3	US & China (40% of world carbon emissions) formally join Paris climate agreement
Sep 8	NASA launches OSIRIS-REx, 1st asteroid sample return mission expected back with samples 2023
Sep 9	North Korea conducts 5th & reportedly largest nuclear test
Sep 30	2 Van Gogh paintings worth a combined $100 mil recovered after being stolen on Dec 7, 2002
Oct 13	Maldives withdraws from British Commonwealth of Nations
Nov 8	Donald J. Trump elected 45th President of the United States
Nov 24	Colombian government & FARC sign revised peace deal ending 50+-year conflict
Dec 19	Russian ambassador to Turkey Andrei Karlov is assassinated in Ankara
Dec 22	Study finds new Ebola virus vaccine 70–100% effective first proven vaccine against the disease
Dec 23	UN adopts resolution condemning Israeli settlements in Palestinian territories occupied since 1967
Dec 25	Russian jetliner crashes kills all 92 on board, including 64 members of Alexandrov Ensemble

2017

Jan 19	ECOWAS forces intervene in Gambia crisis to force President Yahya Jammeh to step down
Jan 21	Millions worldwide join Women's March in 588 marches largest single-day protest in history
Jan 26	Scientists at Harvard report 1st creation of metallic hydrogen in a laboratory
Jan 27	Trump executive order restricts travel from Iraq, Iran, Libya, Somalia, Sudan, Syria, Yemen
Feb 11	North Korea test fires a ballistic missile across the Sea of Japan
Mar 10	President of South Korea Park Geun-hye removed by Constitutional Court
	UN warns biggest humanitarian crisis since WWII 20 mil risk famine in Yemen, Somalia, S Sudan, Nigeria
Mar 22	Westminster Bridge attack, 5 dead, 49 injured
Mar 29	UK invokes Article 50 of the Treaty on European Union, beginning the formal EU withdrawal process
Mar 30	SpaceX conducts world's first reflight of an orbital class rocket
Apr 3	Saint Petersburg subway suicide bombing 15 dead, 64 injured
Apr 6	US launches 59 Tomahawk cruise missiles on Syrian airbase in response chemical weapons attack
Apr 7	Stockholm truck attack
Apr 20	Champs Elysees ISIS terror attack in Paris

2018 OUTLOOK

It's like déjà vu all over again. A new president is getting challenged from all angles on many fronts and having a difficult time implementing his agenda. However, for the first half of 2017 the market has rallied smartly on the promise of change, tax and healthcare reform, deregulation and a massive infrastructure buildout—but mostly on the fact that election uncertainty is over and nothing is happening in DC. So far little has been accomplished and although new highs have just been logged as of this writing, little ground has been gained since March 1.

If President Trump and the GOP agenda remain on the defensive midterm politics will likely rear its ugly head again in 2018. But midterm elections have a history of being a bottom picker's paradise. In the last 13 quadrennial cycles since 1961, 9 of the 17 bear markets bottomed in the midterm year. In the last 14 midterm election years, bear markets began or were in progress nine times—we experienced bull years in 1986, 2006, and 2010 while 1994 was flat.

However, this has provided excellent buying opportunities. By the third, pre-election, year the administrations' focus shifts to "priming the pump." Policies are enacted to improve the economic well-being of the country and its electorate. From the midterm low to the pre-election year high, the Dow has gained nearly 50% on average since 1914. With eighth years of decades being second best 2018 may be a wild ride that starts high and ends high with a bear in the middle.

After a near-term high around 22000 in July 2017 and a late-summer/early fall low around 20000–21000, we look for a yearend rally that runs all the way up to 23000–24000 in early 2018 before the impact of higher rates and new federal government policies and legislation reverberates through the stock market creating the potential for an old fashioned, cyclical 20–30% bear market—or a Ned Davis Research defined bear market in the 13–19.99% range, finding its low point near the midterm elections in 2018 or early in 2019.

—*Jeffrey A. Hirsch, June 23, 2017*

THE 2018 STOCK TRADER'S ALMANAC

CONTENTS

DIRECTORY OF TRADING PATTERNS AND DATABANK

STRATEGY PLANNING AND RECORD SECTION

2018 STRATEGY CALENDAR
(Option expiration dates circled)

	MONDAY	TUESDAY	WEDNESDAY	THURSDAY	FRIDAY	SATURDAY	SUNDAY
JANUARY	1 JANUARY New Year's Day	2	3	4	5	6	7
	8	9	10	11	12	13	14
	15 Martin Luther King Day	16	17	18	(19)	20	21
	22	23	24	25	26	27	28
	29	30	31	1 FEBRUARY	2	3	4
FEBRUARY	5	6	7	8	9	10	11
	12	13	14 ♥ Ash Wednesday	15	(16)	17	18
	19 President's Day	20	21	22	23	24	25
	26	27	28	1 MARCH	2	3	4
MARCH	5	6	7	8	9	10	11 Daylight Saving Time Begins
	12	13	14	15	(16)	17 ♣ St. Patrick's Day	18
	19	20	21	22	23	24	25
	26	27	28	29	30 Good Friday	31 Passover	1 APRIL Easter
APRIL	2	3	4	5	6	7	8
	9	10	11	12	13	14	15
	16	17	18	19	(20)	21	22
	23	24	25	26	27	28	29
	30	1 MAY	2	3	4	5	6
MAY	7	8	9	10	11	12	13 Mother's Day
	14	15	16	17	(18)	19	20
	21	22	23	24	25	26	27
	28 Memorial Day	29	30	31	1 JUNE	2	3
JUNE	4	5	6	7	8	9	10
	11	12	13	14	(15)	16	17 Father's Day
	18	19	20	21	22	23	24
	25	26	27	28	29	30	1 JULY

Market closed on shaded weekdays; closes early when half-shaded.

2018 STRATEGY CALENDAR

(Option expiration dates circled)

MONDAY	TUESDAY	WEDNESDAY	THURSDAY	FRIDAY	SATURDAY	SUNDAY	
2	3	4 Independence Day	5	6	7	8	JULY
9	10	11	12	13	14	15	
16	17	18	19	(20)	21	22	
23	24	25	26	27	28	29	
30	31	1 AUGUST	2	3	4	5	AUGUST
6	7	8	9	10	11	12	
13	14	15	16	(17)	18	19	
20	21	22	23	24	25	26	
27	28	29	30	31	1 SEPTEMBER	2	SEPTEMBER
3 Labor Day	4	5	6	7	8	9	
10 Rosh Hashanah	11	12	13	14	15	16	
17	18	19 Yom Kippur	20	(21)	22	23	
24	25	26	27	28	29	30	
1 OCTOBER	2	3	4	5	6	7	OCTOBER
8 Columbus Day	9	10	11	12	13	14	
15	16	17	18	(19)	20	21	
22	23	24	25	26	27	28	
29	30	31	1 NOVEMBER	2	3	4 Daylight Saving Time Ends	NOVEMBER
5	6 Election Day	7	8	9	10	11 Veterans' Day	
12	13	14	15	(16)	17	18	
19	20	21	22 Thanksgiving Day	23	24	25	
26	27	28	29	30	1 DECEMBER	2	DECEMBER
3 Chanukah	4	5	6	7	8	9	
10	11	12	13	14	15	16	
17	18	19	20	(21)	22	23	
24	25 Christmas	26	27	28	29	30	
31	1 JANUARY New Year's Day	2	3	4	5	6	

JANUARY ALMANAC

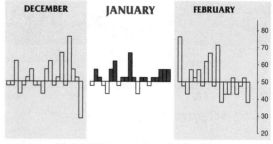

Market Probability Chart above is a graphic representation of the S&P 500 Recent Market Probability Calendar on page 124.

◆ January Barometer predicts year's course with .746 batting average (page 16) ◆ 10 of last 17 midterm election years followed January's direction ◆ Every down January on the S&P since 1950, *without exception,* preceded a new or extended bear market, a flat market, or a 10% correction (page 22) ◆ S&P gains in January's first five days preceded full-year gains 83.3% of the time, 8 of last 17 midterm election years followed first five days' direction (page 14) ◆ November, December, and January constitute the year's best three-month span, a 4.1% S&P gain (pages 48 & 147) ◆ January NASDAQ powerful 2.5% since 1971 (pages 56 & 148) ◆ "January Effect" now starts in mid-December and favors small-cap stocks (pages 108 & 110) ◆ 2009 has the dubious honor of the worst S&P 500 January on record.

January Vital Statistics

	DJIA		S&P 500		NASDAQ		Russell 1K		Russell 2K	
Rank	6		6		1		7		5	
Up	43		41		30		24		21	
Down	25		27		17		15		18	
Average % Change	0.9%		1.0%		2.6%		0.9%		1.4%	
Midterm Year	−0.9%		−1.0%		−0.7%		−1.3%		−0.9%	
Best & Worst January										
		% Change		% Change		% Change		% Change		% Change
Best	1976	14.4	1987	13.2	1975	16.6	1987	12.7	1985	13.1
Worst	2009	−8.8	2009	−8.6	2008	−9.9	2009	−8.3	2009	−11.2
Best & Worst January Weeks										
Best	01/09/76	6.1	01/02/09	6.8	01/12/01	9.1	01/02/09	6.8	01/09/87	7.0
Worst	01/08/16	−6.2	01/08/16	−6.0	01/28/00	−8.2	01/08/16	−6.0	01/08/16	−7.9
Best & Worst January Days										
Best	01/17/91	4.6	01/03/01	5.0	01/03/01	14.2	1/3/01	5.3	01/21/09	5.3
Worst	01/08/88	−6.9	01/08/88	−6.8	01/02/01	−7.2	1/8/88	−6.1	01/20/09	−7.0
First Trading Day of Expiration Week: 1980–2017										
Record (#Up – #Down)	25–13		22–16		20–18		20–18		20–18	
Current streak	D1		D1		D5		D5		D5	
Avg % Change	0.09		0.06		0.08		0.04		0.05	
Options Expiration Day: 1980–2017										
Record (#Up – #Down)	21–17		21–17		21–17		21–17		22–16	
Current streak	U7		U3		U3		U3		U3	
Avg % Change	−0.01		0.01		−0.04		−0.01		0.01	
Options Expiration Week: 1980–2017										
Record (#Up – #Down)	20–18		16–22		21–17		16–22		20–18	
Current streak	D1		D1		D1		D1		D1	
Avg % Change	−0.16		−0.06		0.25		−0.07		0.20	
Week After Options Expiration: 1980–2017										
Record (#Up – #Down)	21–17		24–14		22–16		24–14		26–12	
Current streak	U3		U3		U3		U3		U3	
Avg % Change	0.06		0.24		0.18		0.22		0.24	
First Trading Day Performance										
% of Time Up	28.8		48.5		55.3		43.6		46.2	
Avg % Change	0.25		0.16		0.18		0.15		0.04	
Last Trading Day Performance										
% of Time Up	55.9		60.3		63.8		56.4		74.4	
Avg % Change	0.21		0.25		29		0.32		0.29	

Dow & S&P 1950–April 2017, NASDAQ 1971–April 2017, Russell 1K & 2K 1979–April 2017.

20th Amendment made "lame ducks" disappear.
Now, "As January goes, so goes the year."

JANUARY 2018

1

Look for an impending crash in the economy when the best seller lists are filled with books on business strategies and quick-fix management ideas.
— Peter Drucker (Austrian-born pioneer management theorist, 1909–2005)

Small Caps Punished First Trading Day of Year   TUESDAY
Russell 2000 Down 16 of Last 28, But Up 6 of Last 9

D 61.9
S 47.6
N 66.7

2

There is only one side of the market and it is not the bull side or the bear side, but the right side.
— Jesse Livermore (Early 20th century stock trader and speculator, *How to Trade in Stocks,* 1877–1940)

Second Trading Day of the Year, Dow Up 18 of Last 26   WEDNESDAY
Santa Claus Rally Ends (Page 114)

D 66.7
S 57.1
N 47.6

3

I had an unshakable faith. I had it in my head that if I had to, I'd crawl over broken glass. I'd live in a tent—it was gonna happen. And I think when you have that kind of steely determination…people get out of the way.
— Rick Newcombe (Syndicator, *Investor's Business Daily*)

THURSDAY

D 47.6
S 52.4
N 47.6

4

Everyone wants to make the same three things: money, a name, and a difference. What creates diversity in the human race is how we prioritize the three.
— Roy H. Williams (*The Wizard of Ads*)

FRIDAY

D 47.6
S 47.6
N 52.4

5

A bull market tends to bail you out of all your mistakes. Conversely, bear markets make you PAY for your mistakes.
— Richard Russell (*Dow Theory Letters*)

SATURDAY

6

January Almanac Investor Sector Seasonalities: See Pages 92, 94 and 96   SUNDAY

7

JANUARY'S FIRST FIVE DAYS: AN EARLY WARNING SYSTEM

The last 42 up First Five Days were followed by full-year gains 35 times for an 83.3% accuracy ratio and a 13.6% average gain in all 42 years. The seven exceptions include flat 1994, 2011, 2015 and four related to war. Vietnam military spending delayed the start of the 1966 bear market. Ceasefire imminence early in 1973 raised stocks temporarily. Saddam Hussein turned 1990 into a bear. The war on terrorism, instability in the Mideast, and corporate malfeasance shaped 2002 into one of the worst years on record. The 25 down First Five Days were followed by 14 up years and 11 down (44.0% accurate) and an average gain of 1.4%.

In midterm years this indicator has a poor record. In the last 17 midterm years, 8 full years followed the direction of the First Five Days.

THE FIRST-FIVE-DAYS-IN-JANUARY INDICATOR

Chronological Data

	Previous Year's Close	January 5th Day	5-Day Change	Year Change
1950	16.76	17.09	2.0%	21.8%
1951	20.41	20.88	2.3	16.5
1952	23.77	23.91	0.6	11.8
1953	26.57	26.33	-0.9	-6.6
1954	24.81	24.93	0.5	45.0
1955	35.98	35.33	-1.8	26.4
1956	45.48	44.51	-2.1	2.6
1957	46.67	46.25	-0.9	-14.3
1958	39.99	40.99	2.5	38.1
1959	55.21	55.40	0.3	8.5
1960	59.89	59.50	-0.7	-3.0
1961	58.11	58.81	1.2	23.1
1962	71.55	69.12	-3.4	-11.8
1963	63.10	64.74	2.6	18.9
1964	75.02	76.00	1.3	13.0
1965	84.75	85.37	0.7	9.1
1966	92.43	93.14	0.8	-13.1
1967	80.33	82.81	3.1	20.1
1968	96.47	96.62	0.2	7.7
1969	103.86	100.80	-2.9	-11.4
1970	92.06	92.68	0.7	0.1
1971	92.15	92.19	0.04	10.8
1972	102.09	103.47	1.4	15.6
1973	118.05	119.85	1.5	-17.4
1974	97.55	96.12	-1.5	-29.7
1975	68.56	70.04	2.2	31.5
1976	90.19	94.58	4.9	19.1
1977	107.46	105.01	-2.3	-11.5
1978	95.10	90.64	-4.7	1.1
1979	96.11	98.80	2.8	12.3
1980	107.94	108.95	0.9	25.8
1981	135.76	133.06	-2.0	-9.7
1982	122.55	119.55	-2.4	14.8
1983	140.64	145.23	3.3	17.3
1984	164.93	168.90	2.4	1.4
1985	167.24	163.99	-1.9	26.3
1986	211.28	207.97	-1.6	14.6
1987	242.17	257.28	6.2	2.0
1988	247.08	243.40	-1.5	12.4
1989	277.72	280.98	1.2	27.3
1990	353.40	353.79	0.1	-6.6
1991	330.22	314.90	-4.6	26.3
1992	417.09	418.10	0.2	4.5
1993	435.71	429.05	-1.5	7.1
1994	466.45	469.90	0.7	-1.5
1995	459.27	460.83	0.3	34.1
1996	615.93	618.46	0.4	20.3
1997	740.74	748.41	1.0	31.0
1998	970.43	956.04	-1.5	26.7
1999	1229.23	1275.09	3.7	19.5
2000	1469.25	1441.46	-1.9	-10.1
2001	1320.28	1295.86	-1.8	-13.0
2002	1148.08	1160.71	1.1	-23.4
2003	879.82	909.93	3.4	26.4
2004	1111.92	1131.91	1.8	9.0
2005	1211.92	1186.19	-2.1	3.0
2006	1248.29	1290.15	3.4	13.6
2007	1418.30	1412.11	-0.4	3.5
2008	1468.36	1390.19	-5.3	-38.5
2009	903.25	909.73	0.7	23.5
2010	1115.10	1144.98	2.7	12.8
2011	1257.64	1271.50	1.1	-0.003
2012	1257.60	1280.70	1.8	13.4
2013	1426.19	1457.15	2.2	29.6
2014	1848.36	1837.49	-0.6	11.4
2015	2058.90	2062.14	0.2	-0.7
2016	2043.94	1922.03	-6.0	9.5
2017	2238.83	2268.90	1.3	??

Ranked by Performance

Rank	Year	5-Day Change	Year Change
1	1987	6.2%	2.0%
2	1976	4.9	19.1
3	1999	3.7	19.5
4	2003	3.4	26.4
5	2006	3.4	13.6
6	1983	3.3	17.3
7	1967	3.1	20.1
8	1979	2.8	12.3
9	2010	2.7	12.8
10	1963	2.6	18.9
11	1958	2.5	38.1
12	1984	2.4	1.4
13	1951	2.3	16.5
14	2013	2.2	29.6
15	1975	2.2	31.5
16	1950	2.0	21.8
17	2004	1.8	9.0
18	2012	1.8	13.4
19	1973	1.5	-17.4
20	1972	1.4	15.6
21	1964	1.3	13.0
22	2017	1.3	??
23	1961	1.2	23.1
24	1989	1.2	27.3
25	2011	1.1	-0.003
26	2002	1.1	-23.4
27	1997	1.0	31.0
28	1980	0.9	25.8
29	1966	0.8	-13.1
30	1994	0.7	-1.5
31	1965	0.7	9.1
32	2009	0.7	23.5
33	1970	0.7	0.1
34	1952	0.6	11.8
35	1954	0.5	45.0
36	1996	0.4	20.3
37	1959	0.3	8.5
38	1995	0.3	34.1
39	1992	0.2	4.5
40	1968	0.2	7.7
41	2015	0.2	-0.7
42	1990	0.1	-6.6
43	1971	0.04	10.8
44	2007	-0.4	3.5
45	2014	-0.6	11.4
46	1960	-0.7	-3.0
47	1957	-0.9	-14.3
48	1953	-0.9	-6.6
49	1974	-1.5	-29.7
50	1998	-1.5	26.7
51	1988	-1.5	12.4
52	1993	-1.5	7.1
53	1986	-1.6	14.6
54	2001	-1.8	-13.0
55	1955	-1.8	26.4
56	2000	-1.9	-10.1
57	1985	-1.9	26.3
58	1981	-2.0	-9.7
59	1956	-2.1	2.6
60	2005	-2.1	3.0
61	1977	-2.3	-11.5
62	1982	-2.4	14.8
63	1969	-2.9	-11.4
64	1962	-3.4	-11.8
65	1991	-4.6	26.3
66	1978	-4.7	1.1
67	2008	-5.3	-38.5
68	2016	-6.0	9.5

Based on S&P 500

JANUARY 2018

January's First Five Days Act as an "Early Warning" (Page 14)

MONDAY
D 38.1
S 42.9
N 52.4
8

The most important lesson in investing is humility.
— Sir John Templeton (Founder Templeton Funds, philanthropist, 1912–2008)

TUESDAY
D 47.6
S 57.1
N 57.1
9

Averaging down in a bear market is tantamount to taking a seat on the down escalator at Macy's.
— Richard Russell (*Dow Theory Letters*, 1984)

WEDNESDAY
D 52.4
S 61.9
N 66.7
10

If the winds of fortune are temporarily blowing against you, remember that you can harness them and make them carry you toward your definite purpose, through the use of your imagination.
— Napoleon Hill (Author, *Think and Grow Rich*, 1883–1970)

THURSDAY
D 57.1
S 47.6
N 47.6
11

The political problem of mankind is to combine three things: economic efficiency, social justice, and individual liberty.
— John Maynard Keynes (British economist, 1883–1946)

FRIDAY
D 52.4
S 52.4
N 47.6
12

Press on. Nothing in the world can take the place of persistence. Talent will not: nothing is more common than unrewarded talent. Education alone will not: the world is full of educated failures. Persistence alone is omnipotent.
— Calvin Coolidge (30th U.S. President, 1872–1933)

SATURDAY
13

SUNDAY
14

THE INCREDIBLE JANUARY BAROMETER (DEVISED 1972): ONLY NINE SIGNIFICANT ERRORS IN 67 YEARS

Devised by Yale Hirsch in 1972, our January Barometer states that as the S&P 500 goes in January, so goes the year. The indicator has registered **only nine major errors since 1950 for an 86.6% accuracy ratio**. Vietnam affected 1966 and 1968; 1982 saw the start of a major bull market in August; two January rate cuts and 9/11 affected 2001; the anticipation of military action in Iraq held down the market in January 2003; 2009 was the beginning of a new bull market; the Fed saved 2010 with QE2; QE3 likely staved off declines in 2014; and global growth fears sparked selling in January 2016. (*Almanac Investor* newsletter subscribers receive full analysis of each reading as well as its potential implications for the full year.)

Including the eight flat-year errors (less than +/– 5%) yields a 74.6% accuracy ratio. A full comparison of all monthly barometers for the Dow, S&P, and NASDAQ can be seen in the January 3, 2017 Alert at *www.stocktradersalmanac.com*. Bear markets began or continued when Januarys suffered a loss (*see page 22*). Full years followed January's direction in 10 of the last 17 midterm years. *See page 18 for more.*

AS JANUARY GOES, SO GOES THE YEAR

	Market Performance in January						January Performance by Rank			
	Previous Year's Close	January Close	January Change	Year Change		Rank	Year	January Change	Year's Change	
1950	16.76	17.05	1.7%	21.8%		1	1987	13.2%	2.0%	flat
1951	20.41	21.66	6.1	16.5		2	1975	12.3	31.5	
1952	23.77	24.14	1.6	11.8		3	1976	11.8	19.1	
1953	26.57	26.38	-0.7	-6.6		4	1967	7.8	20.1	
1954	24.81	26.08	5.1	45.0		5	1985	7.4	26.3	
1955	35.98	36.63	1.8	26.4		6	1989	7.1	27.3	
1956	45.48	43.82	-3.6	2.6	flat	7	1961	6.3	23.1	
1957	46.67	44.72	-4.2	-14.3		8	1997	6.1	31.0	
1958	39.99	41.70	4.3	38.1		9	1951	6.1	16.5	
1959	55.21	55.42	0.4	8.5		10	1980	5.8	25.8	
1960	59.89	55.61	-7.1	-3.0	flat	11	1954	5.1	45.0	
1961	58.11	61.78	6.3	23.1		12	2013	5.0	29.6	
1962	71.55	68.84	-3.8	-11.8		13	1963	4.9	18.9	
1963	63.10	66.20	4.9	18.9		14	2012	4.4	13.4	
1964	75.02	77.04	2.7	13.0		15	1958	4.3	38.1	
1965	84.75	87.56	3.3	9.1		16	1991	4.2	26.3	
1966	92.43	92.88	0.5	-13.1	X	17	1999	4.1	19.5	
1967	80.33	86.61	7.8	20.1		18	1971	4.0	10.8	
1968	96.47	92.24	-4.4	7.7	X	19	1988	4.0	12.4	
1969	103.86	103.01	-0.8	-11.4		20	1979	4.0	12.3	
1970	92.06	85.02	-7.6	0.1	flat	21	2001	3.5	-13.0	X
1971	92.15	95.88	4.0	10.8		22	1965	3.3	9.1	
1972	102.09	103.94	1.8	15.6		23	1983	3.3	17.3	
1973	118.05	116.03	-1.7	-17.4		24	1996	3.3	20.3	
1974	97.55	96.57	-1.0	-29.7		25	1994	3.3	-1.5	flat
1975	68.56	76.98	12.3	31.5		26	1964	2.7	13.0	
1976	90.19	100.86	11.8	19.1		27	2006	2.5	13.6	
1977	107.46	102.03	-5.1	-11.5		28	1995	2.4	34.1	
1978	95.10	89.25	-6.2	1.1	flat	29	2011	2.3	-0.003	flat
1979	96.11	99.93	4.0	12.3		30	1972	1.8	15.6	
1980	107.94	114.16	5.8	25.8		31	1955	1.8	26.4	
1981	135.76	129.55	-4.6	-9.7		32	2017	1.8	??	
1982	122.55	120.40	-1.8	14.8	X	33	1950	1.7	21.8	
1983	140.64	145.30	3.3	17.3		34	2004	1.7	9.0	
1984	164.93	163.41	-0.9	1.4	flat	35	1952	1.6	11.8	
1985	167.24	179.63	7.4	26.3		36	2007	1.4	3.5	flat
1986	211.28	211.78	0.2	14.6		37	1998	1.0	26.7	
1987	242.17	274.08	13.2	2.0	flat	38	1993	0.7	7.1	
1988	247.08	257.07	4.0	12.4		39	1966	0.5	-13.1	X
1989	277.72	297.47	7.1	27.3		40	1959	0.4	8.5	
1990	353.40	329.08	-6.9	-6.6		41	1986	0.2	14.6	
1991	330.22	343.93	4.2	26.3		42	1953	-0.7	-6.6	
1992	417.09	408.79	-2.0	4.5	flat	43	1969	-0.8	-11.4	
1993	435.71	438.78	0.7	7.1		44	1984	-0.9	1.4	flat
1994	466.45	481.61	3.3	-1.5	flat	45	1974	-1.0	-29.7	
1995	459.27	470.42	2.4	34.1		46	2002	-1.6	-23.4	
1996	615.93	636.02	3.3	20.3		47	1973	-1.7	-17.4	
1997	740.74	786.16	6.1	31.0		48	1982	-1.8	14.8	X
1998	970.43	980.28	1.0	26.7		49	1992	-2.0	4.5	flat
1999	1229.23	1279.64	4.1	19.5		50	2005	-2.5	3.0	flat
2000	1469.25	1394.46	-5.1	-10.1		51	2003	-2.7	26.4	X
2001	1320.28	1366.01	3.5	-13.0	X	52	2015	-3.1	-0.7	flat
2002	1148.08	1130.20	-1.6	-23.4		53	2014	-3.6	11.4	X
2003	879.82	855.70	-2.7	26.4	X	54	1956	-3.6	2.6	flat
2004	1111.92	1131.13	1.7	9.0		55	2010	-3.7	12.8	X
2005	1211.92	1181.27	-2.5	3.0	flat	56	1962	-3.8	-11.8	
2006	1248.29	1280.08	2.5	13.6		57	1957	-4.2	-14.3	
2007	1418.30	1438.24	1.4	3.5	flat	58	1968	-4.4	7.7	X
2008	1468.36	1378.55	-6.1	-38.5		59	1981	-4.6	-9.7	
2009	903.25	825.88	-8.6	23.5	X	60	1977	-5.1	-11.5	
2010	1115.10	1073.87	-3.7	12.8	X	61	2000	-5.1	-10.1	
2011	1257.64	1286.12	2.3	-0.003	flat	62	2016	-5.1	9.5	X
2012	1257.60	1312.41	4.4	13.4		63	2008	-6.1	-38.5	
2013	1426.19	1498.11	5.0	29.6		64	1978	-6.2	1.1	flat
2014	1848.36	1782.59	-3.6	11.4	X	65	1990	-6.9	-6.6	
2015	2058.90	1994.99	-3.1	-0.7	flat	66	1960	-7.1	-3.0	flat
2016	2043.94	1940.24	-5.1	9.5	X	67	1970	-7.6	0.1	flat
2017	2238.83	2278.87	1.8	??		68	2009	-8.6	23.5	X

X = major error   Based on S&P 500

Martin Luther King Jr. Day *(Market Closed)*

I really do inhabit a system in which words are capable of shaking the entire structure of government, where words can prove mightier than ten military divisions.
— Vaclav Havel (Czech dramatist, essayist, political leader and president, 1936–2011)

First Trading Day of January Expiration Week, Dow Up 17 of Last 25

TUESDAY

D 52.4
S 52.4
N 38.1

16

Sell stocks whenever the market is 30% higher over a year ago.
— Eugene D. Brody (Oppenheimer Capital)

January Expiration Week, Dow Down 11 of Last 19
Average Dow Loss: –1.1%

WEDNESDAY

D 57.1
S 66.7
N 71.4

17

I have learned as a composer chiefly through my mistakes and pursuits of false assumptions, not by my exposure to founts of wisdom and knowledge.
— Igor Stravinsky (Russian composer, 1882–1971)

THURSDAY

D 42.9
S 52.4
N 61.9

18

If you could kick the person in the pants responsible for most of your trouble, you wouldn't sit for a month.
— Theodore Roosevelt (26th U.S. President, 1858–1919)

January Expiration Day Improving Since 2009, Dow Up 8 of Last 9

FRIDAY

D 38.1
S 42.9
N 38.1

19

Of a stock's move, 31% can be attributed to the general stock market, 12% to the industry influence, 37% to the influence of other groupings, and the remaining 20% is peculiar to the one stock.
— Benjamin F. King (Market and Industry Factors in Stock Price Behavior, Journal of Business, January 1966)

SATURDAY
20

SUNDAY
21

JANUARY BAROMETER IN GRAPHIC FORM SINCE 1950

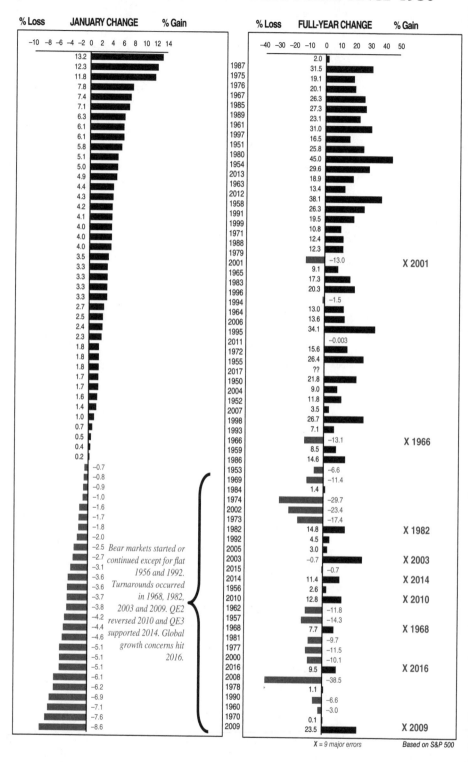

% Loss	JANUARY CHANGE	% Gain		% Loss	FULL-YEAR CHANGE	% Gain

-10 -8 -6 -4 -2 0 2 4 6 8 10 12 14

January	Year	Full-Year
13.2		
12.3	1987	2.0
11.8	1975	31.5
7.8	1976	19.1
7.4	1967	20.1
7.1	1985	26.3
6.3	1989	27.3
6.1	1961	23.1
6.1	1997	31.0
5.8	1951	16.5
5.1	1980	25.8
5.0	1954	45.0
4.9	2013	29.6
4.4	1963	18.9
4.3	2012	13.4
4.2	1958	38.1
4.1	1991	26.3
4.0	1999	19.5
4.0	1971	10.8
4.0	1988	12.4
3.5	1979	12.3
3.3	2001	-13.0 → X 2001
3.3	1965	9.1
3.3	1983	17.3
3.3	1996	20.3
2.7	1994	-1.5
2.5	1964	13.0
2.4	2006	13.6
2.3	1995	34.1
1.8	2011	-0.003
1.8	1972	15.6
1.8	1955	26.4
1.7	2017	??
1.7	1950	21.8
1.6	2004	9.0
1.4	1952	11.8
1.0	2007	3.5
0.7	1998	26.7
0.5	1993	7.1
0.4	1966	-13.1 → X 1966
0.2	1959	8.5
-0.7	1986	14.6
-0.8	1953	-6.6
-0.9	1969	-11.4
-1.0	1984	1.4
-1.6	1974	-29.7
-1.7	2002	-23.4
-1.8	1973	-17.4
-2.0	1982	14.8 → X 1982
-2.5	1992	4.5
-2.7	2005	3.0
-3.1	2003	-0.7 → X 2003
-3.6	2015	-0.7 → X 2014
-3.6	2014	11.4
-3.7	1956	2.6
-3.8	2010	12.8 → X 2010
-4.2	1962	-11.8
-4.4	1957	-14.3
-4.6	1968	7.7 → X 1968
-5.1	1981	-9.7
-5.1	1977	-11.5
-5.1	2000	-10.1
-6.1	2016	9.5 → X 2016
-6.2	2008	-38.5
-6.9	1978	1.1
-7.1	1990	-6.6
-7.6	1960	-3.0
-8.6	1970	0.1
	2009	23.5 → X 2009

Bear markets started or continued except for flat 1956 and 1992. Turnarounds occurred in 1968, 1982, 2003 and 2009. QE2 reversed 2010 and QE3 supported 2014. Global growth concerns hit 2016.

X = 9 major errors   Based on S&P 500

18

MONDAY

D 38.1
S 52.4
N 42.9

22

A good trader has to have three things: a chronic inability to accept things at face value, to feel continuously unsettled, and to have humility.
— Michael Steinhardt (Financier, philanthropist, political activist, chairman WisdomTree Investments, b. 1940)

TUESDAY

D 47.6
S 52.4
N 47.6

23

Never will a man penetrate deeper into error than when he is continuing on a road that has led him to great success.
— Friedrich von Hayek (*Counterrevolution of Science*, 1899–1992)

January Ends "Best Three-Month Span" (Pages 48, 56, 147 and 148)

WEDNESDAY

D 38.1
S 47.6
N 57.1

24

I invest in people, not ideas; I want to see fire in the belly and intellect.
— Arthur Rock (First venture capitalist, b. 1926)

THURSDAY

D 57.1
S 52.4
N 47.6

25

Things may come to those who wait, but only the things left by those who hustle.
— Abraham Lincoln (16th U.S. President, 1809–1865)

FRIDAY

D 61.9
S 52.4
N 76.2

26

Technology will gradually strengthen democracies in every country and at every level.
— William H. Gates (Microsoft founder, b. 1955)

SATURDAY

27

February Almanac Investor Sector Seasonalities: See Pages 92, 94 and 96

SUNDAY

28

FEBRUARY ALMANAC

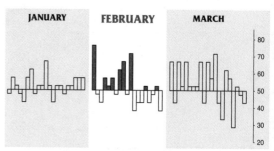

FEBRUARY							MARCH						
S	M	T	W	T	F	S	S	M	T	W	T	F	S
					1	2	3					1	2	3
4	5	6	7	8	9	10	4	5	6	7	8	9	10
11	12	13	14	15	16	17	11	12	13	14	15	16	17
18	19	20	21	22	23	24	18	19	20	21	22	23	24
25	26	27	28				25	26	27	28	29	30	31

Market Probability Chart above is a graphic representation of the S&P 500 Recent Market Probability Calendar on page 124.

♦ February is the weak link in "Best Six Months" (pages 48, 50 & 147) ♦ RECENT RECORD: S&P up 10, down 5, average change 0.6% last 15 years ♦ Fourth best NASDAQ month in midterm election years, average gain 1.0%, up 6 down 5 (page 157), #6 Dow, up 12 down 5 and #5 S&P, up 10, down 7 (pages 153 & 155) ♦ Day before Presidents' Day weekend S&P down 17 of 26, 11 straight 1992–2002, day after up 7 of last 8 (see pages 88 & 133) ♦ Many technicians modify market predictions based on January's market.

February Vital Statistics

	DJIA		S&P 500		NASDAQ		Russell 1K		Russell 2K	
Rank	8		9		7		9		7	
Up	41		38		26		24		23	
Down	27		30		21		15		16	
Average % Change	0.3%		0.1%		0.7%		0.4%		1.2%	
Midterm Year	1.0%		0.7%		1.0%		1.3%		1.9%	
Best & Worst February										
	% Change		% Change		% Change		% Change		% Change	
Best	1986	8.8	1986	7.1	2000	19.2	1986	7.2	2000	16.4
Worst	2009	−11.7	2009	−11.0	2001	−22.4	2009	−10.7	2009	−12.3
Best & Worst February Weeks										
Best	02/01/08	4.4	02/06/09	5.2	02/04/00	9.2	02/06/09	5.3	02/01/91	6.6
Worst	02/20/09	−6.2	02/20/09	−6.9	02/09/01	−7.1	02/20/09	−6.9	02/20/09	−8.3
Best & Worst February Days										
Best	02/24/09	3.3	02/24/09	4.0	02/11/99	4.2	02/24/09	4.1	02/24/09	4.5
Worst	02/10/09	−4.6	02/10/09	−4.9	02/16/01	−5.0	02/10/09	−4.8	02/10/09	−4.7
First Trading Day of Expiration Week: 1980–2017										
Record (#Up – #Down)	23–15		27–11		22–16		27–11		23–15	
Current streak	U3		U4		U4		U4		U4	
Avg % Change	0.31		0.27		0.10		0.24		0.14	
Options Expiration Day: 1980–2017										
Record (#Up – #Down)	19–19		16–22		16–22		17–21		18–20	
Current streak	U1		U1		U3		U1		U4	
Avg % Change	−0.05		−0.12		−0.23		−0.12		−0.07	
Options Expiration Week: 1980–2017										
Record (#Up – #Down)	23–15		21–17		21–17		21–17		25–13	
Current streak	U3		U3		U4		U8		U8	
Avg % Change	0.42		0.23		0.15		0.24		0.32	
Week After Options Expiration: 1980–2017										
Record (#Up – #Down)	18–20		18–20		22–16		18–20		20–18	
Current streak	U2		U2		U4		U2		D1	
Avg % Change	−0.23		−0.16		−0.14		−0.12		−0.05	
First Trading Day Performance										
% of Time Up	61.8		61.8		72.3		66.7		64.1	
Avg % Change	0.14		0.15		0.33		0.19		0.32	
Last Trading Day Performance										
% of Time Up	48.5		54.4		48.9		53.8		53.8	
Avg % Change	−0.01		−0.02		−0.09		−0.07		0.04	

Dow & S&P 1950–April 2017, NASDAQ 1971–April 2017, Russell 1K & 2K 1979–April 2017.

Either go short, or stay away the day before Presidents' Day.

20

JANUARY/FEBRUARY 2018

MONDAY

D 57.1
S 57.1
N 61.9
29

The greatest lie ever told: Build a better mousetrap and the world will beat a path to your door.
— Yale Hirsch (Creator of Stock Trader's Almanac, b. 1923)

FOMC Meeting (2 Days)

TUESDAY

D 52.4
S 57.1
N 52.4
30

A market is the combined behavior of thousands of people responding to information, misinformation and whim.
— Kenneth Chang (NY Times journalist)

"January Barometer" 86.6% Accurate (Page 16)
Almanac Investor Subscribers Emailed Official Results (See Insert)

WEDNESDAY

D 52.4
S 57.1
N 52.4
31

What is it that attracts me to the young? When I am with mature people I feel their rigidities, their tight crystallizations.
They have become...like the statues of the famous. Achieved. Final.
— Anaïs Nin (The Diaries of Anaïs Nin, Vol. IV, 1903–1977)

First Day Trading in February, Dow and S&P Up 12 of Last 15

THURSDAY

D 71.4
S 76.2
N 81.0
1

When someone told me "We're going with you guys because no one ever got fired for buying Cisco (products)."
That's what they used to say in IBM's golden age.
— Mark Dickey (Former Cisco sales exec, then at SmartPipes, Fortune 5/15/00).

FRIDAY

D 42.9
S 47.6
N 52.4
2

When Amercia sneezes, the rest of the word catches cold.
— Anonymous (circa 1929)

SATURDAY

3

SUNDAY

4

DOWN JANUARYS: A REMARKABLE RECORD

In the first third of the 20th century, there was no correlation between January markets and the year as a whole (page 24). Then, in 1972, Yale Hirsch discovered that the 1933 "Lame Duck" Amendment to the Constitution changed the political calendar, and the January Barometer was born—its record has been quite accurate (page 16).

Down Januarys are harbingers of trouble ahead, in the economic, political, or military arenas. Eisenhower's heart attack in 1955 cast doubt on whether he could run in 1956—a flat year. Two other election years with down Januarys were also flat (1984 & 1992). Thirteen bear markets began, and ten continued into second years with poor Januarys. 1968 started down, as we were mired in Vietnam, but Johnson's "bombing halt" changed the climate. Imminent military action in Iraq held January 2003 down before the market triple-bottomed in March. After Baghdad fell, pre-election and recovery forces fueled 2003 into a banner year. 2005 was flat, registering the narrowest Dow trading range on record. 2008 was the worst January on record and preceded the worst bear market since the Great Depression. A negative reading in 2015 and 2016 preceded an official Dow bear market declaration in February 2016.

Unfortunately, bull and bear markets do not start conveniently at the beginnings and ends of months or years. Though some years ended higher, **every down January since 1950 was followed by a new or continuing bear market, a 10% correction, or a flat year. Down Januarys were followed by substantial declines averaging** *minus* **12.9%,** providing excellent buying opportunities later in most years.

FROM DOWN JANUARY S&P CLOSES TO LOW NEXT 11 MONTHS

Year	January Close	% Change	11-Month Low	Date of Low	Jan Close to Low %	% Feb to Dec	Year % Change	
1953	26.38	−0.7%	22.71	14-Sep	−13.9%	−6.0%	−6.6%	bear
1956	43.82	−3.6	43.42	14-Feb	−0.9	6.5	2.6	FLAT/bear
1957	44.72	−4.2	38.98	22-Oct	−12.8	−10.6	−14.3	Cont. bear
1960	55.61	−7.1	52.30	25-Oct	−6.0	4.5	−3.0	bear
1962	68.84	−3.8	52.32	26-Jun	−24.0	−8.3	−11.8	bear
1968	92.24	−4.4	87.72	5-Mar	−4.9	12.6	7.7	−10%/bear
1969	103.01	−0.8	89.20	17-Dec	−13.4	−10.6	−11.4	Cont. bear
1970	85.02	−7.6	69.20	26-May	−18.6	8.4	0.1	Cont. bear
1973	116.03	−1.7	92.16	5-Dec	−20.6	−15.9	−17.4	bear
1974	96.57	−1.0	62.28	3-Oct	−35.5	−29.0	−29.7	Cont. bear
1977	102.03	−5.1	90.71	2-Nov	−11.1	−6.8	−11.5	bear
1978	89.25	−6.2	86.90	6-Mar	−2.6	7.7	1.1	Cont. bear/bear
1981	129.55	−4.6	112.77	25-Sep	−13.0	−5.4	−9.7	bear
1982	120.40	−1.8	102.42	12-Aug	−14.9	16.8	14.8	Cont. bear
1984	163.42	−0.9	147.82	24-Jul	−9.5	2.3	1.4	Cont. bear/FLAT
1990	329.07	−6.9	295.46	11-Oct	−10.2	0.4	−6.6	bear
1992	408.79	−2.0	394.50	8-Apr	−3.5	6.6	4.5	FLAT
2000	1394.46	−5.1	1264.74	20-Dec	−9.3	−5.3	−10.1	bear
2002	1130.20	−1.6	776.76	9-Oct	−31.3	−22.2	−23.4	bear
2003	855.70	−2.7	800.73	11-Mar	−6.4	29.9	26.4	Cont. bear
2005	1181.27	−2.5	1137.50	20-Apr	−3.7	5.7	3.0	FLAT
2008	1378.55	−6.1	752.44	20-Nov	−45.4	−34.5	−38.5	bear
2009	825.88	−8.6	676.53	9-Mar	−18.1	35.0	23.5	Cont. bear
2010	1073.87	−3.7	1022.58	2-Jul	−4.8	17.1	12.8	−10%/no bear
2014	1782.59	−3.6	1741.89	3-Feb	−2.3	15.5	11.4	−10% intraday
2015	1994.99	−3.1	1867.61	25-Aug	−6.4	2.5	−0.7	bear
2016	1940.24	−5.1	1829.08	11-Feb	−5.7	15.4	9.5	Cont. bear
				Totals	−348.8%	32.3%	−76.0%	
				Average	−12.9%	1.2%	−2.8%	

FEBRUARY 2018

D 47.6
S 42.9
N 38.1

The thing you do obsessively between age 13 and 18, that's the thing you have the most chance of being world class at.
— William H. Gates (Microsoft founder, *Charlie Rose* interview 2/22/2016, b. 1955)

TUESDAY
6

D 57.1
S 57.1
N 57.1

It wasn't raining when Noah built the ark.
— Warren Buffett (CEO Berkshire Hathaway, investor & philanthropist, b. 1930)

Week Before February Expiration Week, NASDAQ Down 10 of Last 17,
2010 Up 2.0%, 2011 Up 1.5%, 2014 Up 2.9%, 2015 Up 3.2%

WEDNESDAY
7

D 52.4
S 52.4
N 52.4

When a falling stock becomes a screaming buy because it cannot conceivably drop further, try to buy it 30 percent lower.
— Al Rizzo (1986)

THURSDAY
8

D 47.6
S 57.1
N 57.1

Buy when you are scared to death; sell when you are tickled to death.
— Market Maxim (*The Cabot Market Letter*, April 12, 2001)

FRIDAY
9

D 57.1
S 47.6
N 42.9

The words "I am…" are potent words; be careful what you hitch them to. The thing you're claiming has a way of reaching back and claiming you.
— A. L. Kitselman (Author, math teacher, 1914–1980)

SATURDAY
10

SUNDAY
11

THE EIGHTH YEAR OF DECADES

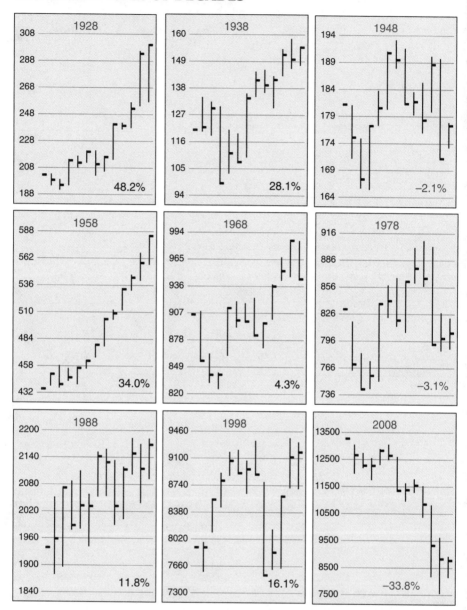

Based on Dow Jones Industrial Average monthly ranges and closing

First Trading Day of February Expiration Week Dow Down 7 of Last 13,
But Up Three Straight

MONDAY
D 52.4
S 61.9
N 57.1
12

Under capitalism man exploits man: under socialism the reverse is true.
— Polish proverb

TUESDAY
D 61.9
S 66.7
N 66.7
13

If buying equities seem the most hazardous and foolish thing you could possibly do, then you are near the
bottom that will end the bear market.
— Joseph E. Granville (American financial writer and speaker, 1923–2013)

Valentine's Day ♥
Ash Wednesday

WEDNESDAY
D 47.6
S 47.6
N 66.7
14

Develop interest in life as you see it; in people, things, literature, music—the world is so rich, simply throbbing with rich
treasures, beautiful souls and interesting people. Forget yourself.
— Henry Miller (American writer, *Tropic of Cancer, Tropic of Capricorn*, 1891–1980)

THURSDAY
D 66.7
S 71.4
N 57.1
15

No one ever claimed that managed care was either managed or cared.
— Anonymous

February Expiration Day, NASDAQ Down 12 of Last 18
Day Before Presidents' Day Weekend, S&P Down 17 of Last 26

FRIDAY
D 42.9
S 38.1
N 47.6
16

Chance favors the informed mind.
— Louis Pasteur (French chemist, founder of microbiology, 1822–1895)

SATURDAY
17

SUNDAY
18

MARKET CHARTS OF MIDTERM ELECTION YEARS

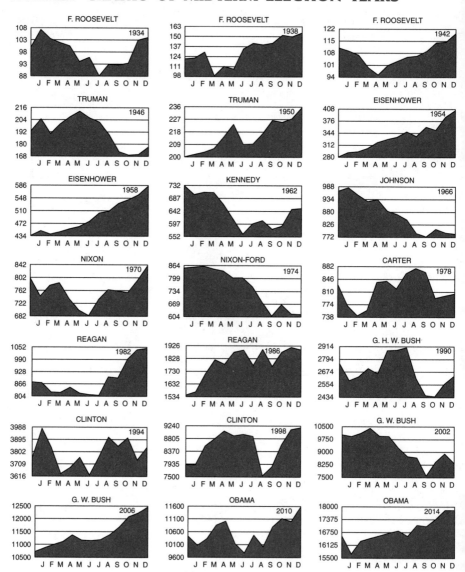

Based on Dow Jones Industrial Average monthly closing prices

Presidents' Day *(Market Closed)*

If I had eight hours to chop down a tree, I'd spend six sharpening my axe.
— Abraham Lincoln (16th U.S. President, 1809–1865)

*Day After Presidents' Day, NASDAQ Down 14 of Last 23,
But Up Five Straight*

TUESDAY

D 38.1
S 42.9
N 47.6

20

Follow the course opposite to custom and you will almost always do well.
— Jean-Jacques Rousseau (Swiss philosopher, 1712–1778)

Week After February Expiration Week, Dow Down 11 of Last 19

WEDNESDAY

D 47.6
S 42.9
N 42.9

21

*Benjamin Graham was correct in suggesting that while the stock market in the short run may be a voting mechanism,
in the long run it is a weighing mechanism. True value will win out in the end.*
— Burton G. Malkiel (Economist, April 2003 Princeton Paper, *A Random Walk Down Wall Street*, b. 1932)

THURSDAY

D 47.6
S 52.4
N 61.9

22

*Vietnam, the original domino in the Cold War, now faces the prospect of becoming, in the words of political scientist Sunai
Phasuk of Chulalongkorn University in Bangkok, one of the new "dominos of democracy."*
— Quoted by Seth Mydans (*NY Times*, Jan. 6, 2001)

End of February Miserable in Recent Years (Pages 20 and 133)

FRIDAY

D 38.1
S 42.9
N 57.1

23

*Institutions tend to dump stock in a single transaction and buy, if possible, in smaller lots, gradually accumulating a position.
Therefore, many more big blocks are traded on downticks than on upticks.*
— Justin Mamis (Author, *The Mamis Letter, WhenTo Sell*, b. 1929)

SATURDAY

24

March Almanac Investor Sector Seasonalities: See Pages 92, 94 and 96

SUNDAY

25

MARCH ALMANAC

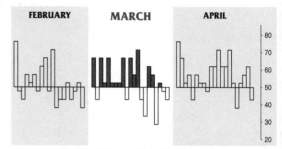

FEBRUARY   MARCH   APRIL

MARCH						
S	M	T	W	T	F	S
				1	2	3
4	5	6	7	8	9	10
11	12	13	14	15	16	17
18	19	20	21	22	23	24
25	26	27	28	29	30	31

APRIL						
S	M	T	W	T	F	S
1	2	3	4	5	6	7
8	9	10	11	12	13	14
15	16	17	18	19	20	21
22	23	24	25	26	27	28
29	30					

Market Probability Chart above is a graphic representation of the S&P 500 Recent Market Probability Calendar on page 124.

◆ Mid-month strength and late-month weakness are most evident above ◆ RECENT RECORD: S&P 13 up, 8 down, average gain 1.8%, third best ◆ Rather turbulent in recent years with wild fluctuations and large gains and losses ◆ March has been taking some mean end-of-quarter hits (page 134), down 1469 Dow points March 9–22, 2001 ◆ Last three or four days Dow a net loser 18 out of last 28 years ◆ NASDAQ hard hit in 2001, down 14.5% after 22.4% drop in February ◆ Third best NASDAQ month during midterm election years, average gain 1.7%, up 7, down 4 ◆ Third Dow month to gain more than 1000 points in 2016.

March Vital Statistics

	DJIA	S&P 500	NASDAQ	Russell 1K	Russell 2K
Rank	5	4	6	4	4
Up	44	44	30	26	28
Down	24	24	17	13	11
Average % Change	1.1%	1.2%	0.9%	1.2%	1.5%
Midterm Year	1.3%	1.3%	0.7%	2.0%	2.8%
Best & Worst March					
	% Change	% Change	% Change	% Change	% Change
Best	2000 7.8	2000 9.7	2009 10.9	2000 8.9	1979 9.7
Worst	1980 −9.0	1980 −10.2	1980 −17.1	1980 −11.5	1980 −18.5
Best & Worst March Weeks					
Best	03/13/09 9.0	03/13/09 10.7	03/13/09 10.6	03/13/09 10.7	03/13/09 12.0
Worst	03/16/01 −7.7	03/06/09 −7.0	03/16/01 −7.9	03/06/09 −7.1	03/06/09 −9.8
Best & Worst March Days					
Best	03/23/09 6.8	03/23/09 7.1	03/10/09 7.1	03/23/09 7.0	03/23/09 8.4
Worst	03/02/09 −4.2	03/02/09 −4.7	03/12/01 −6.3	03/02/09 −4.8	03/27/80 −6.0
First Trading Day of Expiration Week: 1980–2017					
Record (#Up – #Down)	25–13	25–13	19–19	23–15	20–18
Current streak	D1	U1	U5	U1	U1
Avg % Change	0.19	0.07	−0.25	0.02	−0.30
Options Expiration Day: 1980–2017					
Record (#Up – #Down)	20–18	22–16	19–19	20–18	18–19
Current streak	D1	D1	U3	D1	U3
Avg % Change	0.09	0.03	−0.03	0.03	0.001
Options Expiration Week: 1980–2017					
Record (#Up – #Down)	27–10	26–12	24–14	25–13	22–16
Current streak	U6	U6	U6	U6	U6
Avg % Change	0.92	0.77	0.11	0.71	0.30
Week After Options Expiration: 1980–2017					
Record (#Up – #Down)	16–22	12–26	18–20	12–26	17–21
Current streak	D3	D5	D5	D7	D6
Avg % Change	−0.29	−0.21	−0.04	−0.21	−0.16
First Trading Day Performance					
% of Time Up	67.6	64.7	63.8	61.5	66.7
Avg % Change	0.19	0.20	0.29	0.19	0.27
Last Trading Day Performance					
% of Time Up	41.2	39.7	63.8	46.2	82.1
Avg % Change	−0.10	−0.01	0.16	0.08	0.39

Dow & S&P 1950–April 2017, NASDAQ 1971–April 2017, Russell 1K & 2K 1979–April 2017.

March has Ides and St. Patrick's Day;
Begins bullishly, then fades away.

FEBRUARY/MARCH 2018

MONDAY
D 47.6
S 47.6
N 57.1
26

Wall Street has a uniquely hysterical way of thinking the world will end tomorrow but be fully recovered in the long run, then a few years later believing the immediate future is rosy but that the long term stinks.
— Kenneth L. Fisher (*Wall Street Waltz*, b. 1950)

TUESDAY
D 47.6
S 52.4
N 57.1
27

Corporate guidance has become something of an art. The CFO has refined and perfected his art, gracefully leading on the bulls with the calculating grace and cunning of a great matador.
— Joe Kalinowski (I/B/E/S)

WEDNESDAY
D 38.1
S 38.1
N 23.8
28

He who knows how will always work for he who knows why.
— David Lee Roth (Lead singer of Van Halen, b. 1954)

First Trading Day in March, Dow Up 15 of Last 22

THURSDAY
D 66.7
S 66.7
N 61.9
1

Nothing has a stronger influence psychologically on their environment and especially on their children than the unlived life of the parent.
— C.G. Jung (Swiss psychiatrist, 1875–1961)

FRIDAY
D 47.6
S 42.9
N 38.1
2

I have always picked people's brains. That's the only way you can grow. Ninety percent of the information I throw out immediately; five percent I try and discard; and five percent I retain.
— Tiger Woods (Top-ranked golfer, on his swing, April 2004, b. 1975)

SATURDAY
3

SUNDAY
4

MIDTERM ELECTION YEARS: WHERE BOTTOM PICKERS FIND PARADISE

American presidents have danced the Quadrennial Quadrille over the past two centuries. After the midterm congressional election and the invariable seat loss by his party, the president during the next two years jiggles fiscal policies to get federal spending, disposable income and social security benefits up and interest rates and inflation down. By Election Day, he will have danced his way into the wallets and hearts of the electorate and, hopefully, will have choreographed four more years in the White House for his party.

After the Inaugural Ball is over, however, we pay the piper. Practically all bear markets began and ended in the two years after presidential elections. Bottoms often occurred in an air of crisis: the Cuban Missile Crisis in 1962, tight money in 1966, Cambodia in 1970, Watergate and Nixon's resignation in 1974, and threat of international monetary collapse in 1982. But remember, the word for "crisis" in Chinese is composed of two characters: the first, the symbol for danger; the second, opportunity. In the last 14 quadrennial cycles since 1961, 9 of the 17 bear markets bottomed in the midterm year. *See pages 131–132 for further detail.*

THE RECORD SINCE 1914

1914	Wilson (D)	Bottom in July. War closed markets.
1918	Wilson (D)	**Bottom 12 days prior to start of year.**
1922	Harding (R)	**Bottom 4½ months prior to start of year.**
1926	Coolidge (R)	Only drop (7 wks, −17%) ends Mar. 30.
1930	Hoover (R)	**'29 Crash continues through 1930. No bottom.**
1934	Roosevelt (D)	1st Roosevelt bear, Feb to July 26 bottom (−23%).
1938	Roosevelt (D)	Big 1937 break ends in March, DJI off 49%.
1942	Roosevelt (D)	World War II bottom in April.
1946	Truman (D)	Market tops in May, bottoms in October.
1950	Truman (D)	June 1949 bottom, June 1950 Korean War outbreak causes 14% drop.
1954	Eisenhower (R)	**September 1953 bottom, then straight up.**
1958	Eisenhower (R)	**October 1957 bottom, then straight up.**
1962	Kennedy (D)	Bottoms in June and October.
1966	Johnson (D)	Bottom in October.
1970	Nixon (R)	Bottom in May.
1974	Nixon, Ford (R)	December Dow bottom, S&P bottom in October.
1978	Carter (D)	March bottom, despite October massacre later.
1982	Reagan (R)	Bottom in August.
1986	Reagan (R)	**No bottom in 1985 or 1986.**
1990	Bush (R)	Bottom October 11 (Kuwaiti Invasion).
1994	Clinton (D)	Bottom April 4 after 10% drop.
1998	Clinton (D)	October 8 bottom (Asian currency crisis, hedge fund debacle).
2002	Bush, GW (R)	October 9 bottom (Corp malfeasance, terrorism, Iraq).
2006	Bush, GW (R)	**No Bottom in 2006** (Iraq success, credit bubble).
2010	Obama (D)	**No Bear**, July low, −13.6% from April high.
2014	Obama (D)	**No Bear, No Bottom** (Fed QE).

Bold = *No bottom in midterm election year*

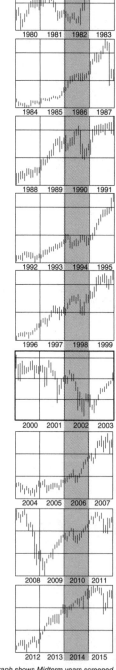

Graph shows Midterm years screened.
Based on Dow Jones Industrial Average monthly ranges.

🦬 **MONDAY**

D 57.1
S 66.7
N 66.7

5

Amongst democratic nations, each generation is a new people.
— Alexis de Tocqueville (Author, *Democracy in America*, 1840, 1805–1859)

March Historically Strong Early in the Month (Pages 28 and 134)

TUESDAY

D 47.6
S 52.4
N 42.9

6

The common denominator. Something that matters! Something that counts! Something that defines! Something that is imbued with soul. And with life!
— Tom Peters (referring to projects, *Reinventing Work*, 1999, b. 1942)

🦬 **WEDNESDAY**

D 66.7
S 66.7
N 42.9

7

Financial genius is a rising stock market.
— John Kenneth Galbraith (Canadian-American economist and diplomat, 1908–2006)

THURSDAY

D 47.6
S 52.4
N 47.6

8

The difference between life and the movies is that a script has to make sense, and life doesn't.
— Joseph L. Mankiewicz (Film director, writer, producer, 1909–1993)

Dow Down 1469 Points March 9–22 in 2001

FRIDAY

D 57.1
S 52.4
N 42.9

9

There are very few instances in history when any government has ever paid off debt.
— Walter Wriston (Retired CEO of Citicorp and Citibank, 1919–2005)

SATURDAY

10

Daylight Saving Time Begins

SUNDAY

11

PROSPERITY MORE THAN PEACE DETERMINES OUTCOME OF MIDTERM CONGRESSIONAL RACES

Though the stock market in presidential election years very often is able to predict if the party in power will retain or lose the White House, the outcome of congressional races in midterm years is another matter entirely. Typically, the President's party will lose a number of House seats in these elections (1934, 1998 and 2002 were exceptions). It is considered a victory for the President when his party loses a small number of seats, and a repudiation of sorts when a large percentage of seats is lost.

The table below would seem to indicate that there is no relationship between the stock market's behavior in the ten months prior to the midterm election and the magnitude of seats lost in the House. Roaring bull markets preceded the elections of 1954 and 1958, yet Republicans lost few seats during one, and a huge number in the other.

If the market does not offer a clue to the outcome of House races, does anything besides the popularity and performance of the Administration? Yes! In the two years prior to the elections in the first eleven midterm years listed, no war or major recession began. As a result, the percentage of House seats lost was minimal. A further observation is that the market gained ground in the last seven weeks of the year, except 2002.

Our five major wars began under four Democrats and one Republican in the shaded area. The percentage of seats lost was greater during these midterm elections. But the eight worst repudiations of the President are at the bottom of the list. These were preceded by: the sick economy in 1930, the botched health proposals in 1994, the severe recession in 1937, the post-war contraction in 1946, the recession in 1957, financial crisis and the second worst bear market in history from 2007 to 2009, Watergate in 1974, and rumors of corruption (Teapot Dome) in 1922. **Obviously, prosperity is of greater importance to the electorate than peace!**

LAST 25 MIDTERM ELECTIONS RANKED BY
% LOSS OF SEATS BY PRESIDENT'S PARTY

	% Seats Gained or Lost	Year	President	Dow Jones Industrials Jan 1 to Elec Day	Dow Jones Industrials Elec Day to Dec 31	Year's CPI % Change
1	3.6 %	2002	R: G.W. Bush	−14.5 %	−2.7 %	1.6 %
2	2.9	1934	D: Roosevelt	−3.8	8.3	1.5
3	2.4	1998	D: Clinton	10.1	5.5	1.6
4	−1.5	1962	D: Kennedy	−16.5	6.8	1.3
5	−2.7	1986	R: Reagan	22.5	0.1	1.1
6	−4.0	1926	R: Coolidge	−3.9	4.4	−1.1
7	−4.6	1990	R: G.H.W. Bush	−9.1	5.3	6.1
8	−5.1	1978	D: Carter	−3.7	0.6	9.0
9	−6.3	1970	R: Nixon	−5.3	10.7	5.6
10	−6.5	2014	D: Obama	7.3	3.5	0.8
11	−8.1	1954	R: Eisenhower	26.0	14.2	−0.7
12	−9.0	1918	D: Wilson (WW1)	15.2	−4.1	20.4
13	−11.0	1950	D: Truman (Korea)	11.2	−5.8	5.9
14	−12.9	2006	R: G.W. Bush (Iraq)	13.4	2.5	2.6
15	−13.5	1982	R: Reagan	14.9	4.1	3.8
16	−15.9	1966	D: Johnson (Vietnam)	−17.2	−2.1	3.5
17	−16.9	1942	D: Roosevelt (WW2)	3.4	4.1	9.0
18	−18.4	1930	R: Hoover	−25.4	−11.2	−6.4
19	−20.9	1994	D: Clinton	1.5	0.7	2.7
20	−21.3	1938	D: Roosevelt	28.2	−0.1	−2.8
21	−22.6	1946	D: Truman	−9.6	1.6	18.1
22	−23.9	1958	R: Eisenhower	25.1	7.1	1.8
23	−24.6	2010	D: Obama	7.3	3.5	1.5
24	−25.0	1974	R: Ford	−22.8	−6.2	12.3
25	−25.0	1922	R: Harding	21.4	0.3	−2.3

Cumulative Growth Chart (1/1/2008 – 7/31/2017)

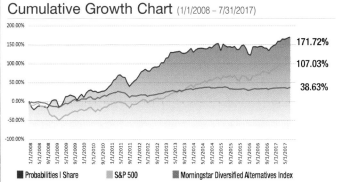

171.72%
107.03%
38.63%

■ Probabilities I Share   ■ S&P 500   ■ Morningstar Diversified Alternatives Index

Past Performance is no indication of future returns. Since inception, January 1, 2008 to present. The Morningstar Diversified Alternatives Index is comprised of seven alternative asset classes that broadly represent the alternative landscape, hedge funds, long/short equity, merger arbitrage, managed futures, breakeven Inflation, global Infrastructure, and listed private equity. The hypothetical scenario does not take into account federal, state or municipal takes. If taxes were taken into account, the hypothetical values shown would have been lower.

Using historical trends and patterns to obtain dynamic exposure to the US stock market.

Statistical Analysis vs S&P 500

	Probabilities I Share	MDAI	S&P 500
Cumulative Performance	171.72%	38.63%	107.03%
Annualized Alpha	7.35%	0.29%	0.00%
Beta	0.48	0.35	1.00
Sharpe Ratio	0.71	0.49	0.55
Standard Deviation	16.23%	6.66%	15.37%
Maximum Drawdown	-22.29%	—	-48.45%
Correlation	0.46	0.81	1.00
Up Capture of S&P 500	81.78%	38.77%	100%
Down Capture of S&P 500	57.35%	37.00%	100%

Standardized Returns As of 6/30/2017 (Greater than one year, annualized)

Updated Quarterly	YTD	1 Year	3 Years	5 Years	Since Inception
Probabilities Fund I Share (Inception 01/01/2008)	8.70%	9.54%	3.94%	8.25%	11.00%
Probabilities Fund A at NAV (Inception 01/16/2014)	8.67%	9.30%	3.70%	N/A	3.24%
Probabilities Fund A at Maximum Load	2.45%	3.01%	1.67%	N/A	1.48%
Probabilities Fund C (Inception 01/16/2014)	8.28%	8.49%	2.91%	N/A	2.47%
S&P 500 Total Return	9.34%	17.90%	9.61%	14.63%	7.74%

Historical Performance (PROTX)

	Jan	Feb	Mar	Apr	May	Jun	Jul	Aug	Sep	Oct	Nov	Dec	YTD	MDAI*	S&P 500
2017	1.05%	4.26%	-0.27%	2.27%	0.18%	0.98%	0.79%						9.56%	2.17%	11.59%
2016	-6.02%	-1.36%	9.89%	0.19%	-0.48%	0.78%	0.10%	-1.64%	-0.39%	-2.85%	3.74%	1.95%	3.16%	2.31%	11.96%
2015	-7.56%	7.58%	-1.95%	-1.14%	0.29%	-0.95%	1.35%	-3.61%	0.39%	3.83%	1.04%	-3.93%	-5.35%	-3.66%	1.38%
2014	-4.46%	2.98%	1.35%	0.19%	0.10%	-0.47%	0.00%	1.62%	-0.66%	2.27%	1.85%	0.61%	5.30%	3.04%	13.69%
2013	5.91%	0.53%	6.57%	-0.24%	0.62%	0.28%	0.71%	-2.23%	-0.35%	0.71%	2.53%	2.61%	18.73%	8.64%	32.39%
2012	6.19%	5.83%	2.04%	2.38%	-2.80%	0.18%	4.19%	1.77%	-0.26%	0.70%	5.13%	0.07%	28.07%	6.82%	16.00%
2011	4.16%	7.75%	2.12%	6.09%	0.81%	-3.26%	-0.49%	-8.86%	-6.67%	5.79%	4.38%	2.54%	13.65%	-3.67%	2.11%
2010	-6.75%	10.41%	4.41%	2.16%	-3.56%	0.62%	-2.97%	1.22%	1.70%	0.62%	3.09%	5.45%	16.43%	11.83%	15.06%
2009	-0.94%	-15.90%	1.44%	10.98%	15.15%	0.75%	3.01%	-1.84%	-1.82%	-7.96%	8.31%	5.76%	13.88%	21.73%	26.46%
2008	1.68%	-15.28%	-8.28%	5.59%	6.07%	-0.61%	-0.07%	-2.56%	-2.33%	10.19%	11.65%	2.30%	5.27%	-12.21%	-37.00%

Morningstar Diversified Alternatives Index.

Important Disclosures

Investors should carefully consider the investment objectives, risks, charges and expenses of the Probabilities Fund. This and other importantinformation about the Fund is contained in the Prospectus, which can be obtained by contacting your financial advisor, or by calling 1.888.868.9501. The Prospectus should be read carefully before investing. Probabilities Fund is distributed by Northern Lights Distributors, LLC member FINRA/SIPC. Probabilities Fund Management, LLC and Northern Lights Distributors are not affiliated.

Performance shown before the inception date of the mutual fund, December 12, 2013, is for the Fund's predecessor limited partnership. The prior performance is net of management fee and other expenses, including the effect of the performance fee. The Fund's investment goals, policies, guidelines and restrictions are similar to the predecessor limited partnership. From its inception date, the predecessor limited partnership was not subject to certain investment restrictions,diversification requirements and other restrictions of the Investment Company Act of 1940 which if they had been applicable, it might have adversely affected its performance. In addition, the predecessor limited partnership was not subject to sales loads that would have adversely affected performance. Performance of the predecessor fund is not an indicator of future results.

Mutual Funds involve risk including the possible loss of principal.

ETFs are subject to investment advisory and other expenses, which will be indirectly paid by the Fund. As a result, your cost of investing in the Fund will behigher than the cost of investing directly in the ETFs and may be higher than other mutual funds that invest directly in stocks and bonds. Each ETF is subject to specific risks, depending on its investments. Leveraged ETFs employ leverage, which magnifies the changes in the value of the Leveraged ETFs, which could result in significant losses to the Fund. The Fund invests in Leveraged ETFs in an effort to deliver daily performance at twice the rate of the underlying index and if held over long periods of time, particularly in volatile markets, the ETFs may not achieve their objective and may, in fact, perform contrary to expectations. Inverse ETFs are designed to rise in price when stock prices are falling.

Inverse ETFs tend to limit the Fund's participation in overall market-wide gains. Accordingly, their performance over longer terms can perform very differently than underlying assets and benchmarks, and volatile markets can amplify this effect.

The advisor's judgment about the attractiveness, value and potential appreciation of particular security or derivative in which the Fund invests or sells short may prove to be incorrect and may not produce the desired results. Equity prices can fall rapidly in response to developments affecting a specific company or industry, or to changing economic, political or market conditions. A higher portfolio turnover may result in higher transactional and brokerage costs. The indices shown are for informational purposes only and are not reflective of any investment. As it is not possible to invest in the indices, the data shown does not reflect or compare features of an actual investment, such as its objectives, costs and expenses, liquidity, safety, guarantees or insurance, fluctuation of principal or return, or tax features. Past performance does not guaranteed future results. The S&P 500 Index is an unmanaged composite of 500 large capitalization companies. This index is widely used by professional investors as a performance benchmark for large-cap stocks.

Alpha is a measure of the excess return of a fund over an index. Beta is a measure of a fund's volatility relative to market movements. Sharpe Ratio is a measure of risk adjusted performance calculated by subtracting the risk-free rate from the rate of return of the portfolio and dividing the result by the standard deviation of the portfolio returns. The 3 month T-Bill rate was used in the calculation.

Standard Deviation is a statistical measurement of volatility risk based on historical returns. Maximum Drawdown represents the largest peak-to-trough decline during a specific period of time. Correlation is a statistical measure of how two investments move inrelation to each other.

Up and Down Capture ratios reflect how a particular investment performed when a specific index has either risen or fallen. Long positions entail buying asecurity such as a stock, commodity or currency, with the expectation that the asset will rise in value. Short positions entail a sale that is completed by thedelivery of a security borrowed by the seller. Short sellers assume they will be able to buy the stock at a lower amount that the price at which they sold short.

Monday Before March Triple Witching, Dow Up 22 of Last 30

MONDAY

D 57.1
S 52.4
N 42.9

12

Today we deal with 65,000 more pieces of information each day than did our ancestors 100 years ago.
— Dr. Jean Houston (A founder of the Human Potential Movement, b. 1937)

TUESDAY

D 57.1
S 66.7
N 66.7

13

A man should always hold something in reserve, a surprise to spring when things get tight.
— Christy Mathewson (MLB Hall of Fame Pitcher, first 5 elected, 3rd most wins, 1880–1925)

WEDNESDAY

D 61.9
S 42.9
N 47.6

14

[Look for companies] where the executives have a good ownership position—not only options, but outright ownership—so that they will ride up and down with the shareholder.
— George Roche (Chairman, T. Rowe Price, *Barron's* 12/18/06, 1935–2006)

THURSDAY

D 71.4
S 66.7
N 47.6

15

Around the world, red tape is being cut. Whether it's telecom in Europe, water in South America, or power in Illinois, governments are stepping back, and competition is thriving where regulated monopolies once dominated.
— *(Fortune, 12/20/99)*

March Triple-Witching Day Mixed Last 28 Years, but Dow Down 6 of Last 9

FRIDAY

D 52.4
S 57.1
N 57.1

16

What's going on…is the end of Silicon Valley as we know it. The next big thing ain't computers…it's biotechnology.
— Larry Ellison (Oracle CEO, quoted in *The Wall Street Journal*, 4/8/03, b.1944)

St. Patrick's Day

SATURDAY

17

SUNDAY

18

WHY A 50% GAIN IN THE DOW IS POSSIBLE FROM ITS 2018 LOW TO ITS 2019 HIGH

Normally, major corrections occur sometime in the first or second years following presidential elections. In the last 14 midterm election years, bear markets began or were in progress nine times—we experienced bull years in 1986, 2006, 2010 and 2014, while 1994 was flat.

The puniest midterm advance, 14.5% from the 1946 low, was during the industrial contraction after World War II. The next five smallest advances were: 2014 (tepid global growth) 19.1%, 1978 (OPEC–Iran) 21.0%, 1930 (economic collapse) 23.4%, 1966 (Vietnam) 26.7%, and 2010 (European debt) 32.3%.

Since 1914 the Dow has gained 47.4% on average from its midterm election year low to its subsequent high in the following pre-election year. A swing of such magnitude is equivalent to a move from 10000 to 15000 or from 21000 to 31500.

POST-ELECTION HIGH TO MIDTERM LOW: –20.4%

Conversely, since 1913 the Dow has dropped –20.4% on average from its post-election-year high to its subsequent low in the following midterm year. At press-time the Dow's 2017 post-election year high is 21206.29. A 20.4% decline would put the Dow back at 16880.20 at the 2018 midterm bottom. Persistently sluggish global growth and the Fed tightening monetary policy make a decline back to this level or lower certainly not out of the question. Whatever the level, the rally off the 2018 midterm low could be another great buying opportunity.

Pretty impressive seasonality! There is no reason to think the quadrennial Presidential Election/Stock Market Cycle will not continue. Page 130 shows how effectively most presidents "managed" to have much stronger economies in the third and fourth years of their terms than in their first two.

% CHANGE IN DOW JONES INDUSTRIALS BETWEEN THE MIDTERM YEAR LOW AND THE HIGH IN THE FOLLOWING YEAR

			Midterm Year Low			Pre-Election Year High		
		Date of Low		Dow	Date of High		Dow	% Gain
1	Jul	30	1914*	52.32	Dec	27	1915	99.21	89.6%
2	Jan	15	1918**	73.38	Nov	3	1919	119.62	63.0
3	Jan	10	1922**	78.59	Mar	20	1923	105.38	34.1
4	Mar	30	1926*	135.20	Dec	31	1927	202.40	49.7
5	Dec	16	1930*	157.51	Feb	24	1931	194.36	23.4
6	Jul	26	1934*	85.51	Nov	19	1935	148.44	73.6
7	Mar	31	1938*	98.95	Sep	12	1939	155.92	57.6
8	Apr	28	1942*	92.92	Jul	14	1943	145.82	56.9
9	Oct	9	1946	163.12	Jul	24	1947	186.85	14.5
10	Jan	13	1950**	196.81	Sep	13	1951	276.37	40.4
11	Jan	11	1954**	279.87	Dec	30	1955	488.40	74.5
12	Feb	25	1958**	436.89	Dec	31	1959	679.36	55.5
13	Jun	26	1962*	535.74	Dec	18	1963	767.21	43.2
14	Oct	7	1966*	744.32	Sep	25	1967	943.08	26.7
15	May	26	1970*	631.16	Apr	28	1971	950.82	50.6
16	Dec	6	1974*	577.60	Jul	16	1975	881.81	52.7
17	Feb	28	1978*	742.12	Oct	5	1979	897.61	21.0
18	Aug	12	1982*	776.92	Nov	29	1983	1287.20	65.7
19	Jan	22	1986	1502.29	Aug	25	1987	2722.42	81.2
20	Oct	11	1990*	2365.10	Dec	31	1991	3168.84	34.0
21	Apr	4	1994	3593.35	Dec	13	1995	5216.47	45.2
22	Aug	31	1998*	7539.07	Dec	31	1999	11497.12	52.5
23	Oct	9	2002*	7286.27	Dec	31	2003	10453.92	43.5
24	Jan	20	2006	10667.39	Oct	9	2007	14164.53	32.8
25	Jul	2	2010**	9686.48	Apr	29	2011	12810.54	32.3
26	Feb	3	2014	15372.80	May	19	2015	18312.39	19.1

*Bear Market ended   ** Bear previous year   **Average   47.4%**

MONDAY
D 66.7
S 71.4
N 66.7
19

In most admired companies, key priorities are teamwork, customer focus, fair treatment of employees, initiative, and innovation. In average companies the top priorities are minimizing risk, respecting the chain of command, supporting the boss, and making budget.
— Bruce Pfau (*Fortune*)

FOMC Meeting (2 Days)

TUESDAY
D 57.1
S 42.9
N 61.9
20

The game is lost only when we stop trying.
— Mario Cuomo (Former NY Governor, *C-SPAN*, 1932–2015)

Week After Triple Witching, Dow Down 20 of Last 30, 2000 Up 4.9%, 2007 Up 3.1%, 2009 Up 6.8%, 2011 Up 3.1%, Down 5 Last 6

WEDNESDAY
D 38.1
S 33.3
N 52.4
21

Our firm conviction is that, sooner or later, capitalism will give way to socialism... We will bury you.
— Nikita Khrushchev (Soviet leader 1953–1964, 1894–1971)

THURSDAY
D 38.1
S 61.9
N 57.1
22

Short-term volatility is greatest at turning points and diminishes as a trend becomes established.
— George Soros (Financier, philanthropist, political activist, author and philosopher, b. 1930)

March Historically Weak Later in the Month (Pages 28 and 134)

FRIDAY
D 61.9
S 57.1
N 66.7
23

In my experience, selling a put is much safer than buying a stock.
— Kyle Rosen (Boston Capital Mgmt., *Barron's* 8/23/04)

SATURDAY
24

SUNDAY
25

APRIL ALMANAC

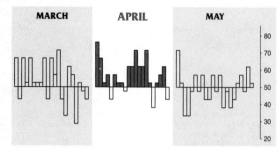

Market Probability Chart above is a graphic representation of the S&P 500 Recent Market Probability Calendar on page 124.

◆ April is still the best Dow month (average 1.9%) since 1950 (page 50) ◆ April 1999 first month ever to gain 1000 Dow points, 856 in 2001, knocked off its high horse in 2002 down 458, 2003 up 488 ◆ Up twelve straight, average gain 2.5% ◆ Prone to weakness after mid-month tax deadline ◆ Stocks anticipate great first-quarter earnings by rising sharply before earnings are reported, rather than after ◆ Rarely a dangerous month, recent exceptions are 2002, 2004, and 2005 ◆ "Best Six Months" of the year end with April (page 50) ◆ Midterm election year Aprils mixed since 1950 (Dow 0.8%, S&P 0.2%, NASDAQ 0.1%) ◆ End of April NASDAQ strength (pages 125 & 126).

April Vital Statistics

	DJIA		S&P 500		NASDAQ		Russell 1K		Russell 2K	
Rank	1		3		4		2		3	
Up	46		48		30		27		24	
Down	22		20		17		12		15	
Average % Change	1.9%		1.5%		1.4%		1.5%		1.5%	
Midterm Year	0.8%		0.2%		−0.1%		−0.1%		0.7%	
	Best & Worst April									
	% Change		% Change		% Change		% Change		% Change	
Best	1978	10.6	2009	9.4	2001	15.0	2009	10.0	2009	15.3
Worst	1970	−6.3	1970	−9.0	2000	−15.6	2002	−5.8	2000	−6.1
	Best & Worst April Weeks									
Best	04/11/75	5.7	04/20/00	5.8	04/12/01	14.0	04/20/00	5.9	04/03/09	6.3
Worst	04/14/00	−7.3	04/14/00	−10.5	04/14/00	−25.3	04/14/00	−11.2	04/14/00	−16.4
	Best & Worst April Days									
Best	04/05/01	4.2	04/05/01	4.4	04/05/01	8.9	04/05/01	4.6	04/09/09	5.9
Worst	04/14/00	−5.7	04/14/00	−5.8	04/14/00	−9.7	04/14/00	−6.0	04/14/00	−7.3
	First Trading Day of Expiration Week: 1980–2017									
Record (#Up − #Down)	23–15		21–17		20–18		20–18		17–21	
Current streak	U1		U1		U1		U1		U1	
Avg % Change	0.20		0.12		0.11		0.11		0.001	
	Options Expiration Day: 1980–2017									
Record (#Up − #Down)	24–14		24–14		21–17		24–14		24–14	
Current streak	D4		D3		D3		D3		D1	
Avg % Change	0.17		0.16		−0.04		0.15		0.18	
	Options Expiration Week: 1980–2017									
Record (#Up − #Down)	30–8		27–11		25–13		25–13		28–10	
Current streak	U2		U2		U2		U2		U2	
Avg % Change	1.06		0.87		0.93		0.85		0.84	
	Week After Options Expiration: 1980–2017									
Record (#Up − #Down)	26–12		26–12		27–11		26–12		26–12	
Current streak	U3		U3		U1		U3		U3	
Avg % Change	0.48		0.46		0.73		0.47		0.87	
	First Trading Day Performance									
% of Time Up	58.8		61.8		46.8		59.0		48.7	
Avg % Change	0.17		0.15		−0.09		0.17		−0.07	
	Last Trading Day Performance									
% of Time Up	50.0		54.4		63.8		53.8		64.1	
Avg % Change	0.07		0.06		0.13		0.04		0.03	

Dow & S&P 1950–April 2017, NASDAQ 1971–April 2017, Russell 1K & 2K 1979–April 2017.

April "Best Month" for Dow since 1950;
Day-before-Good Friday gains are nifty.

MARCH/APRIL 2018

MONDAY

D 28.6
S 28.6
N 28.6

26

News on stocks is not important. How the stock reacts to it is important.
— Michael L. Burke (*Investors Intelligence*)

TUESDAY

D 52.4
S 52.4
N 52.4

27

The first panacea for a mismanaged nation is inflation of the currency; the second is war. Both bring a temporary prosperity; both bring a permanent ruin. But both are the refuge of political and economic opportunists.
— Ernest Hemingway (*American writer, 1954 Nobel Prize, 1899–1961*)

Start Looking for the Dow and S&P MACD SELL Signal (Pages 50 and 52)

WEDNESDAY

D 57.1
S 47.6
N 57.1

28

Every great advance in natural knowledge has involved the absolute rejection of authority.
— Thomas H. Huxley (British scientist and humanist, defender of Darwinism, 1825–1895)

Last Day of March, Dow Down 18 of Last 28, Russell 2000 Up 17 of Last 24
NASDAQ Up 16 of Last 17 Days Before Good Friday

THURSDAY

D 38.1
S 42.9
N 57.1

29

640K ought to be enough for anybody.
— William H. Gates (Microsoft founder, 1981—try running Microsoft Vista on less than a gig, b. 1955)

Good Friday *(Market Closed)*

FRIDAY

30

Never doubt that a small group of thoughtful, committed citizens can change the world: indeed it's the only thing that ever has.
— Margaret Mead (American anthropologist, 1901–1978)

Passover

SATURDAY

31

Easter
April Almanac Investor Sector Seasonalities: See Pages 92, 94 and 96

SUNDAY

1

THE DECEMBER LOW INDICATOR: A USEFUL PROGNOSTICATING TOOL

When the Dow closes below its December closing low in the first quarter, it is frequently an excellent warning sign. Jeffrey Saut, Managing Director, Chief Investment Strategist at Raymond James, brought this to our attention a few years ago. The December Low Indicator was originated by Lucien Hooper, a *Forbes* columnist and Wall Street analyst back in the 1970s. Hooper dismissed the importance of January and January's first week as reliable indicators. He noted that the trend could be random or even manipulated during a holiday-shortened week. Instead, said Hooper, "Pay much more attention to the December low. If that low is violated during the first quarter of the New Year, watch out!"

Twenty of the 34 occurrences were followed by gains for the rest of the year—and 18# full-year gains—after the low for the year was reached. For perspective we've included the January Barometer readings for the selected years. Hooper's "Watch Out" warning was absolutely correct, though. All but two of the instances since 1952 experienced further declines, as the Dow fell an additional 10.5% on average when December's low was breached in Q1.

Only three significant drops occurred (not shown) when December's low was not breached in Q1 (1974, 1981 and 1987). Both indicators were wrong seven times and nine years ended flat. If the December low is not crossed, turn to our January Barometer for guidance. It has been virtually perfect, right nearly 100% of these times (view the complete results at *www.stocktradersalmanac.com.*)

YEARS DOW FELL BELOW DECEMBER LOW IN FIRST QUARTER

Year	Previous Dec Low	Date Crossed	Crossing Price	Subseq. Low	% Change Cross-Low	Rest of Year % Change	Full Year % Change	Jan Bar
1952	262.29	2/19/52	261.37	256.35	−1.9%	11.7%	8.4%	1.6%[2]
1953	281.63	2/11/53	281.57	255.49	−9.3	−0.2	−3.8	−0.7[3]
1956	480.72	1/9/56	479.74	462.35	−3.6	4.1	2.3	−3.6[1, 2, 3]
1957	480.61	1/18/57	477.46	419.79	−12.1	−8.7	−12.8	−4.2
1960	661.29	1/12/60	660.43	566.05	−14.3	−6.7	−9.3	−7.1
1962	720.10	1/5/62	714.84	535.76	−25.1	−8.8	−10.8	−3.8
1966	939.53	3/1/66	938.19	744.32	−20.7	−16.3	−18.9	0.5[1]
1968	879.16	1/22/68	871.71	825.13	−5.3	8.3	4.3	−4.4[1, 2, 3]
1969	943.75	1/6/69	936.66	769.93	−17.8	−14.6	−15.2	−0.8
1970	769.93	1/26/70	768.88	631.16	−17.9	9.1	4.8	−7.6[2, 3]
1973	1000.00	1/29/73	996.46	788.31	−20.9	−14.6	−16.6	−1.7
1977	946.64	2/7/77	946.31	800.85	−15.4	−12.2	−17.3	−5.1
1978	806.22	1/5/78	804.92	742.12	−7.8	0.01	−3.1	−6.2[3]
1980	819.62	3/10/80	818.94	759.13	−7.3	17.7	14.9	5.8[2]
1982	868.25	1/5/82	865.30	776.92	−10.2	20.9	19.6	−1.8[1, 2]
1984	1236.79	1/25/84	1231.89	1086.57	−11.8	−1.6	−3.7	−0.9[3]
1990	2687.93	1/15/90	2669.37	2365.10	−11.4	−1.3	−4.3	−6.9[3]
1991	2565.59	1/7/91	2522.77	2470.30	−2.1	25.6	20.3	4.2[2]
1993	3255.18	1/8/93	3251.67	3241.95	−0.3	15.5	13.7	0.7[2]
1994	3697.08	3/30/94	3626.75	3593.35	−0.9	5.7	2.1	3.3[2, 3]
1996	5059.32	1/10/96	5032.94	5032.94	NC	28.1	26.0	3.3[2]
1998	7660.13	1/9/98	7580.42	7539.07	−0.5	21.1	16.1	1.0[2]
2000	10998.39	1/4/00	10997.93	9796.03	−10.9	−1.9	−6.2	−5.1
2001	10318.93	3/12/01	10208.25	8235.81	−19.3	−1.8	−7.1	3.5[1]
2002	9763.96	1/16/02	9712.27	7286.27	−25.0	−14.1	−16.8	−1.6
2003	8303.78	1/24/03	8131.01	7524.06	−7.5	28.6	25.3	−2.7[1, 2]
2005	10440.58	1/21/05	10392.99	10012.36	−3.7	3.1	−0.6	−2.5[3]
2006	10717.50	1/20/06	10667.39	10667.39	NC	16.8	16.3	2.5
2007	12194.13	3/2/07	12114.10	12050.41	−0.5	9.5	6.4	1.4[2]
2008	13167.20	1/2/08	13043.96	7552.29	−42.1	−32.7	−33.8	−6.1
2009	8149.09	1/20/09	7949.09	6547.05	−17.6	31.2	18.8	−8.6[1, 2]
2010	10285.97	1/22/10	10172.98	9686.48	−4.8	13.8	11.0	−3.7[1, 2]
2014	15739.43	1/31/14	15698.85	15372.80	−2.1	13.5	7.5	−3.6[1, 2]
2016	17128.55	1/6/2016	16906.51	15660.18	−7.4	16.9	13.4	−5.1[1, 2]
				Average Drop	−10.5%			

[1]January Barometer wrong. [2]December Low Indicator wrong. [3]Year Flat.

APRIL 2018

First Trading Day in April, Dow Up 17 of Last 23
Day After Easter, Second Worst Post-Holiday (Page 88)

MONDAY
D 76.2
S 76.2
N 66.7
2

But how do we know when irrational exuberance has unduly escalated asset values, which then become subject to unexpected and prolonged contractions as they have in Japan over the past decade?
— Alan Greenspan (Fed Chairman 1987–2006, 12/5/96 speech to American Enterprise Institute, b. 1926)

TUESDAY
D 66.7
S 66.7
N 61.9
3

The mind is like the stomach. It is not how much you put into it that counts, but how much it digests — if you try to feed it with a shovel you get bad results.
— Albert Jay Nock (Libertarian writer and social theorist, 1873–1945)

April is the Best Month for the Dow, Average 1.9% Gain Since 1950

WEDNESDAY
D 42.9
S 52.4
N 66.7
4

There is a habitual nature to society and human activity. People's behavior and what they do with their money and time bears upon economics and the stock market.
— Jeffrey A. Hirsch (Editor, *Stock Trader's Almanac*, b. 1966)

THURSDAY
D 61.9
S 57.1
N 57.1
5

On Wall Street, to know what everyone else knows is to know nothing.
— Newton Zinder (Investment advisor and analyst, E.F. Hutton, b. 1927)

April is 3rd Best Month for S&P, 4th Best for NASDAQ (Since 1971)

FRIDAY
D 42.9
S 42.9
N 33.3
6

The first human being to live to 150 years of age is alive today, but will he get Social Security for 85 years of his longer life span, more than twice the number of years he worked?
— John Mauldin (Millennium Wave Advisors, 2000wave.com, 2/2/07)

SATURDAY
7

SUNDAY
8

SUPER BOOM UPDATE:
2010 FORECAST ON TRACK FOR DOW 38820 BY 2025

When we first released this forecast in our newsletter in May 2010 and published it in the *Stock Trader's Almanac 2011* with the Dow around 10,000 it was received with a great deal of incredulity. Since then the market has tracked it in principle yet outpaced our initial expectations. This extraordinary forecast was and is based upon the seminal research and reports our founder Yale Hirsch undertook and published back in the mid-seventies when he discovered this iconic market cycle, which led him to the greatest market call in history for a 500% move in the market from the 1974 low to 1990.

This pattern as illustrated below shows how the market failed to make any sustained advance while the world was embroiled in a significant conflagration. Once the war ended, inflation caused by government spending kicked in and the stock market made 500+% moves between all of the major wars the U.S. has been involved in. All three previous secular bear markets associated with the three major wars of the 20th Century were also affected by crisis that required a great deal of non-war-related spending.

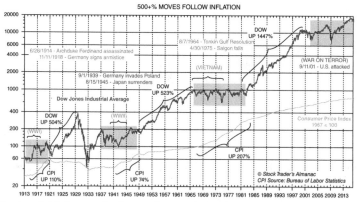

As we developed this forecast further we discovered the other variables of the Boom Equation. In addition to war and inflation several factors came into alignment that ignited prior Super Booms and Secular Bull Markets, including a properly functioning government that is in synch with the private sector, stimulating innovation and robust economic growth. The final factor is what we call a culturally enabling paradigm shifting technology—something that changes the world by touching and impacting the lives of humans individually across the planet (page 42).

We now believe that the final tactical bear of the next Super Boom has occurred. The outcome of the recent U.S. presidential election may be the start of a shift in political stagnation. Sure the market has tripled since the 2009 low, but we think the next big move is around the corner. Back in 1983 when folks started to realize the last boom was underway the market had already more than doubled. We appear to be on a similar path with the February 2016 bear market low equating to the August 1982 bear market low.

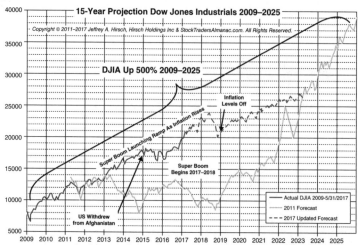

APRIL 2018

If you are not willing to study, if you are not sufficiently interested to investigate and analyze the stock market yourself, then I beg of you to become an outright long-pull investor, to buy good stocks, and hold on to them; for otherwise your chances of success as a trader will be nil.
— Humphrey B. Neill (Investor, analyst, author, *Tape Reading and Market Tactics*, 1931, 1895–1977)

More people and increased income cause resources to become scarcer in the short run. Heightened scarcity causes prices to rise. The higher prices present opportunity and prompt investors to search for solutions. These solutions eventually lead to prices dropping lower than before the scarcity occurred.
— Julian Simon (Businessman, Professor of Business Administration, *The Ultimate Resource*, 1996, 1932–1998)

April 1999 First Month Ever to Gain 1000 Dow Points

We spend $500 million a year just in training our people. We've developed some technology that lets us do simulations. Think of Flight Simulation. What we've found is that the retention rate from simulation is about 75%, opposed to 25% from classroom work.
— Joe Forehand (CEO, Accenture, *Forbes*, 7/7/03)

Banking establishments are more dangerous than standing armies; and that the principle of spending money to be paid by posterity, under the name of funding, is but swindling futurity on a large scale.
— Thomas Jefferson (3rd U.S. President, 1743–7/4/1826, 1816 letter to John Taylor of Caroline)

An autobiography must be such that one can sue oneself for libel.
— Thomas Hoving (Museum Director, 1931–2009)

CULTURALLY ENABLING PARADIGM SHIFTING TECHNOLOGY POISED TO FUEL THE NEXT SUPER BOOM

"Another factor contributing to productivity is technology, particularly the rapid introduction of new microcomputers based on single-chip circuits....The results over the next decade will be a second industrial revolution."—Yale Hirsch (Creator of *Stock Trader's Almanac*, *Smart Money* Newsletter 9/22/1976, b. 1923)

The final factor of our Super Boom Forecast (page 40) is the next breakthrough technologies that will drive humanity to the new frontier. When global military entanglements are at bay and political functionality fosters increased business and economic activity, healthy inflation quickens innovations. This opens the floodgates for new inventions and creations that will fuel decades if not centuries of growth and the expansion of civilization. When these new technologies, methodologies and contraptions explode on the scene they push the overall market up 500% or more with new industries that spawn future mega-cap companies that rule the world.

We make no assertion that we can identify even which discipline the next big thing will come from. In fact it may come from several fields simultaneously and/or be an amalgamation of several technologies and industries in one new product or realm (such as how the microprocessor, programming language and TCP/IP conspired to create computers, the internet, cell phones and the information revolution). But we do know some new devices or mechanisms will change the world and catalyze the next economic boom and advancement of civilization as they have throughout history, from the earliest stone tools to the smartphone.

In our search for what may be the next "culturally enabling paradigm shifting technology" poised to fuel the next Super Boom, we sought out things that would revolutionized society by impacting individuals separately and collectively worldwide, by touching nearly every person on the planet in a massive way that changes how people live like those that came before: the printing press, compass, paper currency, steel, the electric light, domestication of the horse, transistors, magnifying lenses, the telegraph, antibiotics, the steam engine, indoor plumbing, telephone, automobile, air travel, TV, microprocessor, TCP/IP protocol, programming language.

Current areas that appear to us to possess the greatest potential to produce technology and innovation that will change the world and fuel the next Super Boom are: genetics, energy tech, nanotech, robotics, 3D printing, blockchain/cryptocurrency and quantum computing. Since we first made this forecast on May 27, 2010 (https://www.stocktradersalmanac.com/NL_Archive/2010/2010_06.pdf) we have long believed that this breakthrough "will come from Energy Technology and/or Biotechnology."

Initially we were skeptical of 3D printing, but much progress has been made there. In May 2017 3D-printed ovaries allowed infertile mice to mate, give birth to healthy litters and lactate naturally, demonstrating embedded follicles produced normal levels of hormones. CRISPR/Cas genome editing has shown recent promise with many potential applications and was *AAAS's* 2015 breakthrough of the year. Advanced energy tech, storage, better batteries, fuel cells or some sort of personal unlimited power plant seem to be at the forefront of what the world needs now, with everything we use requiring limitless power.

Robotics has already changed industry immeasurably. If it can touch us all implicitly that could be revolutionary. Nanotech is already imbedded in many places and could easily be an instrumental part of transformative inventions. Blockchain/cryptocurrency could create a new monetary system like paper money did 500–1000 years ago helping pull us out of the dark ages. And, finally quantum computing could increase computational power exponentially across the spectrum of all fields, disciplines and industries.

We understand that we may have overlooked some areas and be off base on others. This conversation and quest for the next big things is far from over. Please send us your ideas, comments, questions and reflections and get ready for the Next Super Boom.

APRIL 2018

Monday Before Expiration, Dow Up 19 of Last 29, Mixed Last 13 Years 🖐️ **MONDAY**
D 66.7
S 61.9
N 47.6 **16**

Innovation can't depend on trying to please the customer or the client. It is an elitist act by the inventor who acts alone and breaks rules.
— Dean Kamen (Inventor, President of DEKA R&D, *Business Week*, Feb. 12, 2001)

Income Tax Deadline 🖐️ **TUESDAY**
D 61.9
S 71.4
N 61.9 **17**

If I owe a million dollars I am lost. But if I owe $50 billion the bankers are lost.
— Celso Ming (Brazilian journalist)

April Prone to Weakness After Tax Deadline (Pages 36 and 134) 🖐️ **WEDNESDAY**
D 57.1
S 61.9
N 52.4 **18**

English stocks…are springing up like mushrooms this year…forced up to a quite unreasonable level and then, for most part, collapse. In this way, I have made over 400 pounds…[Speculating] makes small demands on one's time, and it's worth while running some risk in order to relieve the enemy of his money.
— Karl Marx (German social philosopher and revolutionary, in an 1864 letter to his uncle, 1818–1883)

🖐️ **THURSDAY**
D 66.7
S 61.9
N 61.9 **19**

Buy when others are despondently selling and sell when others are greedily buying.
— Mark Mobius (Fund manager, Templeton Investments, on investing in foreign countries, b. 1936)

April Expiration Day Dow Up 14 of Last 21 🕊️🖐️ **FRIDAY**
D 66.7
S 71.4
N 66.7 **20**

Let me tell you the secret that has led me to my goal. My strength lies solely in my tenacity.
— Louis Pasteur (French chemist, founder of microbiology, 1822–1895)

SATURDAY
21

SUNDAY
22

SUMMER MARKET VOLUME DOLDRUMS DRIVE WORST SIX MONTHS

In recent years, Memorial Day weekend has become the unofficial start of summer. Not long afterwards trading activity typically begins to slowly decline (barring any external event triggers) towards a later summer low. We refer to this summertime slow-down in trading as the doldrums due to the anemic volume and uninspired trading on Wall Street. The individual trader, if they are looking to sell a stock, is generally met with disinterest from The Street. It becomes difficult to sell a stock at a good price. That is also why many summer rallies tend to be short lived and are quickly followed by a pullback or correction.

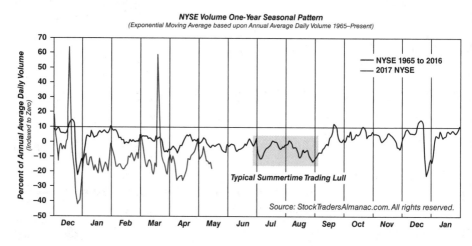

NYSE Volume One-Year Seasonal Pattern
(Exponential Moving Average based upon Annual Average Daily Volume 1965–Present)

Typical Summertime Trading Lull

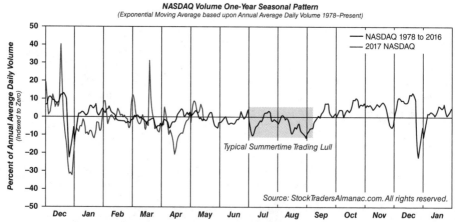

NASDAQ Volume One-Year Seasonal Pattern
(Exponential Moving Average based upon Annual Average Daily Volume 1978–Present)

Typical Summertime Trading Lull

Above are plotted the one-year seasonal volume patterns since 1965 for the NYSE and since 1978 for NASDAQ against the annual average daily volume moving average for 2017 as of the close on May 17, 2017. The typical summer lull is highlighted in blue. A prolonged surge in volume during the typically quiet summer months, especially when accompanied by gains, can be an encouraging sign that the bull market will continue. However, should traders lose their conviction and participate in the annual summer exodus from The Street, a market pullback or correction could quickly unfold.

APRIL 2018

MONDAY

D 57.1
S 52.4
N 52.4

23

Marketing is our No. 1 priority…A marketing campaign isn't worth doing unless it serves three purposes.
It must grow the business, create news, and enhance our image.
— James Robinson III (Former American Express CEO, b. 1935)

TUESDAY

D 42.9
S 38.1
N 52.4

24

Whoso neglects learning in his youth, loses the past and is dead for the future.
— Euripides (Greek tragedian, *Medea*, 485–406 BC)

WEDNESDAY

D 57.1
S 52.4
N 38.1

25

A government which robs Peter to pay Paul can always depend on the support of Paul.
— George Bernard Shaw (Irish dramatist, 1856–1950)

THURSDAY

D 71.4
S 57.1
N 52.4

26

Don't compete. Create. Find out what everyone else is doing and then don't do it.
— Joel Weldon

FRIDAY

D 66.7
S 61.9
N 71.4

27

Today's generation of young people holds more power than any generation before it to make a positive impact on the world.
— William J. Clinton (42nd U.S. President, Clinton Global Initiative, b. 1946)

SATURDAY

28

May Almanac Investor Sector Seasonalities: See Pages 92, 94 and 96

SUNDAY

29

MAY ALMANAC

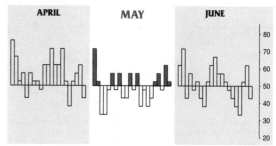

Market Probability Chart above is a graphic representation of the S&P 500 Recent Market Probability Calendar on page 124.

◆ "May/June disaster area" between 1965 and 1984 with S&P down 15 out of 20 Mays ◆ Between 1985 and 1997 May was the best month with 13 straight gains, gaining 3.3% per year on average, up 12, down 8 since ◆ Worst six months of the year begin with May (page 50) ◆ A $10,000 investment compounded to $975,223 for November–April in 67 years compared to a $116 loss for May–October ◆ Dow Memorial Day week record: up 12 years in a row (1984–1995), down 13 of the last 22 years ◆ Since 1950, midterm election year Mays rank poorly: #9 Dow, #10 S&P, and #9 NASDAQ.

May Vital Statistics

	DJIA		S&P 500		NASDAQ		Russell 1K		Russell 2K	
Rank	9		8		5		6		6	
Up	35		39		28		26		25	
Down	32		28		18		12		13	
Average % Change	−0.02%		0.2%		0.9%		1.0%		1.3%	
Midterm Year	−0.7%		−0.9%		−1.2%		−0.1%		−1.9%	
Best & Worst May										
		% Change		% Change		% Change		% Change		% Change
Best	1990	8.3	1990	9.2	1997	11.1	1990	8.9	1997	11.0
Worst	2010	−7.9	1962	−8.6	2000	−11.9	2010	−8.1	2010	−7.7
Best & Worst May Weeks										
Best	05/29/70	5.8	05/02/97	6.2	05/17/02	8.8	05/02/97	6.4	05/14/10	6.3
Worst	05/25/62	−6.0	05/25/62	−6.8	05/07/10	−8.0	05/07/10	−6.6	05/07/10	−8.9
Best & Worst May Days										
Best	05/27/70	5.1	05/27/70	5.0	05/30/00	7.9	05/10/10	4.4	05/10/10	5.6
Worst	05/28/62	−5.7	05/28/62	−6.7	05/23/00	−5.9	05/20/10	−3.9	05/20/10	−5.1
First Trading Day of Expiration Week: 1980–2017										
Record (#Up − #Down)	24−14		25−13		21−17		23−15		20−18	
Current streak	U2		U2		U2		D2		U4	
Avg % Change	0.19		0.19		0.18		0.16		0.04	
Options Expiration Day: 1980–2017										
Record (#Up − #Down)	19−19		22−16		19−19		22−16		19−19	
Current streak	U5		U5		U2		U5		U2	
Avg % Change	−0.07		−0.07		−0.07		−0.05		0.04	
Options Expiration Week: 1980–2017										
Record (#Up − #Down)	19−19		19−19		20−18		18−20		20−18	
Current streak	D2		D1		D1		D1		D1	
Avg % Change	0.05		0.03		0.18		0.03		−0.14	
Week After Options Expiration: 1980–2017										
Record (#Up − #Down)	21−17		24−14		26−12		24−14		28−10	
Current streak	U2		U4		U4		U4		U4	
Avg % Change	0.05		0.20		0.30		0.22		0.40	
First Trading Day Performance										
% of Time Up	57.4		58.8		63.8		59.0		61.5	
Avg % Change	0.21		0.24		0.34		0.27		0.27	
Last Trading Day Performance										
% of Time Up	59.7		61.2		67.4		55.3		65.8	
Avg % Change	0.18		0.26		0.19		0.20		0.32	

Dow & S&P 1950–April 2017, NASDAQ 1971–April 2017, Russell 1K & 2K 1979–April 2017.

May's new pattern, a smile or a frown,
Odd years UP and even years DOWN.

APRIL/MAY 2018

End of "Best Six Months" of the Year (Pages 50, 52, 54 and 147)

MONDAY
D 33.3
S 42.9
N 57.1

30

One thing John Chambers (Cisco CEO) does well is stretch people's responsibilities and change the boxes they are in. It makes our jobs new all the time.
— Mike Volpi (Senior VP of business development and alliances at Cisco, *Fortune*)

FOMC Meeting (2 Days)
First Trading Day in May, Dow Up 14 of Last 20

TUESDAY
D 71.4
S 71.4
N 76.2

1

The time to buy is when blood is running in the streets.
— Baron Nathan Rothschild (London Financier, 1777–1836)

WEDNESDAY
D 61.9
S 52.4
N 57.1

2

There is a perfect inverse correlation between inflation rates and price/earnings ratios... When inflation has been very high...P/E has been [low].
— Liz Ann Sonders (Chief Investment Strategist, Charles Schwab, June 2006)

THURSDAY
D 28.6
S 33.3
N 42.9

3

Men, it has been well said, think in herds; it will be seen that they go mad in herds, while they only recover their senses slowly, and one by one.
— Charles Mackay (Scottish poet, journalist, author, anthologist, novelist, and songwriter, *Extraordinary Popular Delusions and the Madness of Crowds*, 1814–1889)

FRIDAY
D 38.1
S 33.3
N 42.9

4

On [TV financial news programs], if the stock is near its high, 90% of the guests like it, if it is near its lows, 90% of the guests hate it.
— Michael L. Burke (*Investors Intelligence*, May 2002)

SATURDAY

5

SUNDAY

6

TOP PERFORMING MONTHS PAST 67⅓ YEARS:
STANDARD & POOR'S 500 AND DOW JONES INDUSTRIALS

Monthly performance of the S&P and the Dow are ranked over the past 67⅓ years. NASDAQ monthly performance is shown on page 56.

April, November, and December still hold the top three positions in both the Dow and the S&P. March has reclaimed the fourth spot on the S&P. Disastrous Januarys in 2008, 2009, and 2016 knocked January into sixth. This, in part, led to our discovery in 1986 of the market's most consistent seasonal pattern. You can divide the year into two sections and have practically all the gains in one six-month section and very little in the other. September is the worst month on both lists. (See "Best Six Months" on page 50.)

MONTHLY % CHANGES (JANUARY 1950–APRIL 2017)

Standard & Poor's 500					Dow Jones Industrials				
Month	Total % Change	Avg. % Change	# Up	# Down	Month	Total % Change	Avg. % Change	# Up	# Down
Jan	64.6%	1.0%	41	27	Jan	58.2%	0.9%	43	25
Feb	6.8	0.1	38	30	Feb	18.9	0.3	41	27
Mar	83.4	1.2	44	24	Mar	77.0	1.1	44	24
Apr	99.7	1.5	48	20	Apr	128.9	1.9	46	22
May	14.5	0.2	39	28	May	−1.4	−0.02	35	32
Jun	−2.1	−0.03	35	32	Jun	−21.1	−0.3	31	36
Jul	68.1	1.0	37	30	Jul	78.7	1.2	42	25
Aug	−6.1	−0.1	36	31	Aug	−12.2	−0.2	37	30
Sep*	−34.3	−0.5	29	37	Sep	−50.6	−0.8	26	41
Oct	60.4	0.9	40	27	Oct	42.4	0.6	40	27
Nov	102.4	1.5	45	22	Nov	104.5	1.6	45	22
Dec	108.5	1.6	50	17	Dec	111.1	1.7	47	20
% Rank					**% Rank**				
Dec	108.5%	1.6%	50	17	Apr	128.9%	1.9%	46	22
Nov	102.4	1.5	45	22	Dec	111.1	1.7	47	20
Apr	99.7	1.5	48	20	Nov	104.5	1.6	45	22
Mar	83.4	1.2	44	24	Jul	78.7	1.2	42	25
Jul	68.1	1.0	37	30	Mar	77.0	1.1	44	24
Jan	64.6	1.0	41	27	Jan	58.2	0.9	43	25
Oct	60.4	0.9	40	27	Oct	42.4	0.6	40	27
May	14.5	0.2	39	28	Feb	18.9	0.3	41	27
Feb	6.8	0.1	38	30	May	−1.4	−0.02	35	32
Jun	−2.1	−0.03	35	32	Aug	−12.2	−0.2	37	30
Aug	−6.1	−0.1	36	31	Jun	−21.1	−0.3	31	36
Sep*	−34.3	−0.5	29	37	Sep	−50.6	−0.8	26	41
Totals	**565.9%**	**8.4%**			**Totals**	**534.4%**	**8.0%**		
Average		**0.70%**			**Average**		**0.67%**		

*No change 1979

Anticipators, shifts in cultural behavior, and faster information flow have altered seasonality in recent years. Here is how the months ranked over the past 15⅓ years (184 months) using total percentage gains on the S&P 500: March 29.3, April 26.0, October 25.2, November 17.6, December 15.3, July 12.7, February 7.0, May 7.0, August −4.7, September −7.3, January −17.9 and June −19.5.

During the last 15⅓ years front-runners of our Best Six Months may have helped push October into the number-three spot. January has declined in 10 of the last 18 years. Sizeable turnarounds in "bear killing" October were a common occurrence from 1999 to 2007. Recent big Dow losses in the period were: September 2001 (9/11 attack), off 11.1%; September 2002 (Iraq war drums), off 12.4%; June 2008, off 10.2%; October 2008, off 14.1%; and February 2009 (financial crisis), off 11.7%.

MONDAY

D 52.4
S 47.6
N 42.9

7

A generation from now, Americans may marvel at the complacency that assumed the dollar's dominance would never end.
— Floyd Norris (Chief financial correspondent, *NY Times*, 2/2/07)

TUESDAY

D 66.7
S 57.1
N 76.2

8

If you can ever buy with a P/E equivalent to growth, that's a good starting point.
— Alan Lowenstein (co-portfolio manager, John Hancock Technology Fund, *TheStreet.com* 3/12/2001)

WEDNESDAY

D 52.4
S 47.6
N 47.6

9

We like what's familiar, and we dislike change. So, we push the familiar until it starts working against us big-time—a crisis. Then, MAYBE we can accept change.
— Kevin Cameron (Journalist, *Cycle World,* April 2013)

THURSDAY

D 66.7
S 57.1
N 47.6

10

The difference between great people and others is largely a habit—a controlled habit of doing every task better, faster and more efficiently.
— William Danforth (Ralston Purina founder, 1870–1955)

Friday Before Mother's Day, Dow Up 15 of Last 23

FRIDAY

D 42.9
S 42.9
N 52.4

11

Some men see things as they are and say "why?" I dream things that never were and say "why not?"
— George Bernard Shaw (Irish dramatist, 1856–1950)

SATURDAY

12

Mother's Day

SUNDAY

13

"BEST SIX MONTHS": STILL AN EYE-POPPING STRATEGY

Our Best Six Months Switching Strategy consistently delivers. Investing in the Dow Jones Industrial Average between November 1st and April 30th each year and then switching into fixed income for the other six months has produced reliable returns with reduced risk since 1950.

The chart on page 147 shows November, December, January, March, and April to be the top months since 1950. Add February, and an excellent strategy is born! These six consecutive months gained 20790.89 Dow points in 67 years, while the remaining May-through-October months lost 64.71 points. The S&P gained 2420.72 points in the same best six months versus 264.31 points in the worst six.

Percentage changes are shown along with a compounding $10,000 investment. The November–April $975,223 gain overshadows May–October's $116 loss. (S&P results $705,504 to $8,615.) Just three November–April losses were double-digit: April 1970 (Cambodian invasion), 1973 (OPEC oil embargo), and 2008 (financial crisis). Similarly, Iraq muted the Best Six and inflated the Worst Six in 2003. When we discovered this strategy in 1986, November–April outperformed May–October by $88,163 to minus $1,522. Results improved substantially these past 30 years, $877,060 to $1,406. A simple timing indicator triples results (page 52).

SIX-MONTH SWITCHING STRATEGY

	DJIA % Change May 1–Oct 31	Investing $10,000	DJIA % Change Nov 1–Apr 30	Investing $10,000
1950	5.0%	$10,500	15.2%	$11,520
1951	1.2	10,626	−1.8	11,313
1952	4.5	11,104	2.1	11,551
1953	0.4	11,148	15.8	13,376
1954	10.3	12,296	20.9	16,172
1955	6.9	13,144	13.5	18,355
1956	−7.0	12,224	3.0	18,906
1957	−10.8	10,904	3.4	19,549
1958	19.2	12,998	14.8	22,442
1959	3.7	13,479	−6.9	20,894
1960	−3.5	13,007	16.9	24,425
1961	3.7	13,488	−5.5	23,082
1962	−11.4	11,950	21.7	28,091
1963	5.2	12,571	7.4	30,170
1964	7.7	13,539	5.6	31,860
1965	4.2	14,108	−2.8	30,968
1966	−13.6	12,189	11.1	34,405
1967	−1.9	11,957	3.7	35,678
1968	4.4	12,483	−0.2	35,607
1969	−9.9	11,247	−14.0	30,622
1970	2.7	11,551	24.6	38,155
1971	−10.9	10,292	13.7	43,382
1972	0.1	10,302	−3.6	41,820
1973	3.8	10,693	−12.5	36,593
1974	−20.5	8,501	23.4	45,156
1975	1.8	8,654	19.2	53,826
1976	−3.2	8,377	−3.9	51,727
1977	−11.7	7,397	2.3	52,917
1978	−5.4	6,998	7.9	57,097
1979	−4.6	6,676	0.2	57,211
1980	13.1	7,551	7.9	61,731
1981	−14.6	6,449	−0.5	61,422
1982	16.9	7,539	23.6	75,918
1983	−0.1	7,531	−4.4	72,578
1984	3.1	7,764	4.2	75,626
1985	9.2	8,478	29.8	98,163
1986	5.3	8,927	21.8	119,563
1987	−12.8	7,784	1.9	121,835
1988	5.7	8,228	12.6	137,186
1989	9.4	9,001	0.4	137,735
1990	−8.1	8,272	18.2	162,803
1991	6.3	8,793	9.4	178,106
1992	−4.0	8,441	6.2	189,149
1993	7.4	9,066	0.03	189,206
1994	6.2	9,628	10.6	209,262
1995	10.0	10,591	17.1	245,046
1996	8.3	11,470	16.2	284,743
1997	6.2	12,181	21.8	346,817
1998	−5.2	11,548	25.6	435,602
1999	−0.5	11,490	0.04	435,776
2000	2.2	11,743	−2.2	426,189
2001	−15.5	9,923	9.6	467,103
2002	−15.6	8,375	1.0	471,774
2003	15.6	9,682	4.3	492,060
2004	−1.9	9,498	1.6	499,933
2005	2.4	9,726	8.9	544,427
2006	6.3	10,339	8.1	588,526
2007	6.6	11,021	−8.0	541,444
2008	−27.3	8,012	−12.4	474,305
2009	18.9	9,526	13.3	537,308
2010	1.0	9,621	15.2	619,071
2011	−6.7	8,976	10.5	684,073
2012	−0.9	8,895	13.3	775,055
2013	4.8	9,322	6.7	826,984
2014	4.9	9,779	2.6	848,486
2015	−1.0	9,681	0.6	853,577
2016	2.1	$9,884	15.4	$985,223
Average/Gain	0.4%	($116)	7.6%	$975,223
# Up/Down	40/27		53/14	

Monday After Mother's Day, Dow Up 15 of Last 23
Monday Before May Expiration, Dow Up 23 of Last 30, Average Gain 0.4%

MONDAY

D 52.4
S 42.9
N 42.9

14

Methodology is the last refuge of a sterile mind.
— Marianne L. Simmel (Psychologist)

TUESDAY

D 57.1
S 57.1
N 52.4

15

Cooperation is essential to address 21st-century challenges; you can't fire cruise missiles at the global financial crisis.
— Nicholas D. Kristof (*NY Times* columnist, 10/23/2008)

WEDNESDAY

D 47.6
S 47.6
N 52.4

16

Inflation is the modern way that governments default on their debt.
— Mike Epstein (MTA, MIT/Sloan Lab for Financial Engineering)

THURSDAY

D 57.1
S 57.1
N 61.9

17

Whoso would be a man, must be a non-conformist...Nothing is at last sacred but the integrity of your own mind.
— Ralph Waldo Emerson (American author, poet and philosopher, *Self-Reliance*, 1803–1882)

May Expiration Day Mixed, Dow Down 14 of Last 28

FRIDAY

D 38.1
S 38.1
N 33.3

18

There's a lot of talk about self-esteem these days. It seems pretty basic to me. If you want to feel good about yourself, you've got to do things that you can be proud of.
— Oseola McCarty (American author, *Simple Wisdom for Rich Living*, 1908–1999)

SATURDAY

19

SUNDAY

20

MACD-TIMING TRIPLES "BEST SIX MONTHS" RESULTS

Using the simple MACD (Moving Average Convergence Divergence) indicator developed by our friend Gerald Appel to better time entries and exits into and out of the Best Six Months (page 52) period nearly triples the results. Several years ago, Sy Harding (R.I.P.) enhanced our Best Six Months Switching Strategy with MACD triggers, dubbing it the "best mechanical system ever." In 2006, we improved it even more, achieving similar results with just four trades every four years (page 60).

Our *Almanac Investor eNewsletter* (see ad insert) implements this system with quite a degree of success. Starting October 1, we look to catch the market's first hint of an uptrend after the summer doldrums, and beginning April 1, we prepare to exit these seasonal positions as soon as the market falters.

In up-trending markets, MACD signals get you in earlier and keep you in longer. But if the market is trending down, entries are delayed until the market turns up, and exit points can come a month earlier.

The results are astounding, applying the simple MACD signals. Instead of $10,000 gaining $975,223 over the 67 recent years when invested only during the Best Six Months (page 50), the gain nearly tripled to $2,825,010. The $116 loss during the Worst Six Months expanded to a loss of $6,594.

Impressive results for being invested during only 6.3 months of the year on average! For the rest of the year consider money markets, bonds, puts, bear funds, covered calls, or credit call spreads.

Updated signals are e-mailed to our *Almanac Investor eNewsletter* subscribers as soon as they are triggered. Visit *www.stocktradersalmanac.com*, or see the ad insert for details and a special offer for new subscribers.

BEST SIX-MONTH SWITCHING STRATEGY+TIMING

	DJIA % Change May 1–Oct 31*	Investing $10,000	DJIA % Change Nov 1–Apr 30*	Investing $10,000
1950	7.3%	$10,730	13.3%	$11,330
1951	0.1	10,741	1.9	11,545
1952	1.4	10,891	2.1	11,787
1953	0.2	10,913	17.1	13,803
1954	13.5	12,386	16.3	16,053
1955	7.7	13,340	13.1	18,156
1956	−6.8	12,433	2.8	18,664
1957	−12.3	10,904	4.9	19,579
1958	17.3	12,790	16.7	22,849
1959	1.6	12,995	−3.1	22,141
1960	−4.9	12,358	16.9	25,883
1961	2.9	12,716	−1.5	25,495
1962	−15.3	10,770	22.4	31,206
1963	4.3	11,233	9.6	34,202
1964	6.7	11,986	6.2	36,323
1965	2.6	12,298	−2.5	35,415
1966	−16.4	10,281	14.3	40,479
1967	−2.1	10,065	5.5	42,705
1968	3.4	10,407	0.2	42,790
1969	−11.9	9,169	−6.7	39,923
1970	−1.4	9,041	20.8	48,227
1971	−11.0	8,046	15.4	55,654
1972	−0.6	7,998	−1.4	54,875
1973	−11.0	7,118	0.1	54,930
1974	−22.4	5,524	28.2	70,420
1975	0.1	5,530	18.5	83,448
1976	−3.4	5,342	−3.0	80,945
1977	−11.4	4,733	0.5	81,350
1978	−4.5	4,520	9.3	88,916
1979	−5.3	4,280	7.0	95,140
1980	9.3	4,678	4.7	99,612
1981	−14.6	3,995	0.4	100,010
1982	15.5	4,614	23.5	123,512
1983	2.5	4,729	−7.3	114,496
1984	3.3	4,885	3.9	118,961
1985	7.0	5,227	38.1	164,285
1986	−2.8	5,081	28.2	210,613
1987	−14.9	4,324	3.0	216,931
1988	6.1	4,588	11.8	242,529
1989	9.8	5,038	3.3	250,532
1990	−6.7	4,700	15.8	290,116
1991	4.8	4,926	11.3	322,899
1992	−6.2	4,621	6.6	344,210
1993	5.5	4,875	5.6	363,486
1994	3.7	5,055	13.1	411,103
1995	7.2	5,419	16.7	479,757
1996	9.2	5,918	21.9	584,824
1997	3.6	6,131	18.5	693,016
1998	−12.4	5,371	39.9	969,529
1999	−6.4	5,027	5.1	1,018,975
2000	−6.0	4,725	5.4	1,074,000
2001	−17.3	3,908	15.8	1,243,692
2002	−25.2	2,923	6.0	1,318,314
2003	16.4	3,402	7.8	1,421,142
2004	−0.9	3,371	1.8	1,446,723
2005	−0.5	3,354	7.7	1,558,121
2006	4.7	3,512	14.4	1,782,490
2007	5.6	3,709	−12.7	1,556,114
2008	−24.7	2,793	−14.0	1,338,258
2009	23.8	3,458	10.8	1,482,790
2010	4.6	3,617	7.3	1,591,034
2011	−9.4	3,277	18.7	1,888,557
2012	0.3	3,287	10.0	2,077,413
2013	4.1	3,422	7.1	2,224,909
2014	2.3	3,501	7.4	2,389,552
2015	−6.0	3,291	4.9	2,506,640
2016	3.5	3,406	13.1	2,835,010
Average	**−1.1%**		**9.3%**	
# Up	**36**		**58**	
# Down	**31**		**9**	
67-Year Gain (Loss)	**($6,594)**			**$2,825,101**

*MACD generated entry and exit points (earlier or later) can lengthen or shorten six-month periods.

MAY 2018

D 47.6
S 47.6
N 57.1

21

What is conservatism? Is it not adherence to the old and tried, against the new and untried?
— Abraham Lincoln (16th U.S. President, 1809–1865)

TUESDAY

D 28.6
S 38.1
N 42.9

22

If you destroy a free market you create a black market. If you have ten thousand regulations you destroy all respect for the law.
— Winston Churchill (British statesman, 1874–1965)

WEDNESDAY

D 38.1
S 42.9
N 47.6

23

If you can buy more of your best idea, why put [the money] into your 10th-best idea or your 20th-best idea? The more positions you have, the more average you are.
— Bruce Berkowitz (Fairholme Fund, Barron's 3/17/08)

THURSDAY

D 47.6
S 52.4
N 42.9

24

Any human anywhere will blossom in a hundred unexpected talents and capacities simply by being given the opportunity to do so.
— Doris Lessing (Iranian-born British writer, 2007 Nobel Prize in Literature, 1919–2013)

Friday Before Memorial Day Tends to Be Lackluster with Light Trading, Dow Down 10 of Last 18, Average –0.2%

FRIDAY

D 52.4
S 57.1
N 52.4

25

Anyone who believes that exponential growth can go on forever in a finite world is either a madman or an economist.
— Kenneth Ewart Boulding (Economist, activist, poet, scientist, philosopher, cofounder General Systems Theory, 1910–1993)

SATURDAY

26

June Almanac Investor Sector Seasonalities: See Pages 92, 94 and 96

SUNDAY

27

JUNE ALMANAC

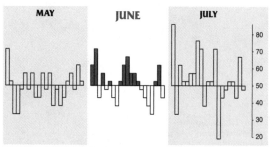

JUNE							JULY						
S	M	T	W	T	F	S	S	M	T	W	T	F	S
					1	2					1	2	3	4	5	6	7
3	4	5	6	7	8	9	8	9	10	11	12	13	14
10	11	12	13	14	15	16	15	16	17	18	19	20	21
17	18	19	20	21	22	23	22	23	24	25	26	27	28
24	25	26	27	28	29	30	29	30	31				

Market Probability Chart above is a graphic representation of the S&P 500 Recent Market Probability Calendar on page 124.

♦ The "summer rally" in most years is the weakest rally of all four seasons (page 70) ♦ Week after June Triple-Witching Day Dow down 23 of last 26 (page 78) ♦ RECENT RECORD: S&P up 12, down 9, average loss 0.3%, ranks ninth ♦ Stronger for NASDAQ, average gain 0.7% last 21 years ♦ Watch out for end-of-quarter "portfolio pumping" on last day of June, Dow down 17 of last 26, NASDAQ up 6 straight ♦ Midterm election year Junes: #12 S&P and Dow, #10 NASDAQ ♦ June ends NASDAQ's Best Eight Months.

June Vital Statistics

	DJIA	S&P 500	NASDAQ	Russell 1K	Russell 2K
Rank	11	10	8	11	8
Up	31	35	25	22	23
Down	36	32	21	16	15
Average % Change	−0.3%	−0.03%	0.7%	0.2%	0.6%
Midterm Year	−1.7%	−1.9%	−1.6%	−1.4%	−1.6%
Best & Worst June					
	% Change	% Change	% Change	% Change	% Change
Best	1955 6.2	1955 8.2	2000 16.6	1999 5.1	2000 8.6
Worst	2008 −10.2	2008 −8.6	2002 −9.4	2008 −8.5	2010 −7.9
Best & Worst June Weeks					
Best	06/07/74 6.4	06/02/00 7.2	06/02/00 19.0	06/02/00 8.0	06/02/00 12.2
Worst	06/30/50 −6.8	06/30/50 −7.6	06/15/01 −8.4	06/15/01 −4.2	06/09/06 −4.9
Best & Worst June Days					
Best	06/28/62 3.8	06/28/62 3.4	06/02/00 6.4	06/10/10 3.0	06/02/00 4.2
Worst	06/26/50 −4.7	06/26/50 −5.4	06/24/16 −4.1	06/24/16 −3.6	06/04/10 −5.0
First Trading Day of Expiration Week: 1980–2016					
Record (#Up – #Down)	19–18	21–16	16–21	19–18	14–22
Current streak	D2	D2	D2	D2	D2
Avg % Change	−0.04	−0.11	−0.26	−0.13	−0.35
Options Expiration Day: 1980–2016					
Record (#Up – #Down)	22–15	23–14	20–17	23–14	21–16
Current streak	D2	D2	D2	D2	D2
Avg % Change	−0.05	0.03	−0.03	−0.01	0.01
Options Expiration Week: 1980–2016					
Record (#Up – #Down)	21–16	19–18	16–21	17–20	17–20
Current streak	D1	D1	D1	D1	D1
Avg % Change	−0.08	−0.11	−0.32	−0.17	−0.26
Week After Options Expiration: 1980–2016					
Record (#Up – #Down)	11–26	17–20	21–16	17–20	19–19
Current streak	D3	D3	D2	D3	D2
Avg % Change	−0.47	−0.20	0.10	−0.17	−0.11
First Trading Day Performance					
% of Time Up	55.2	53.7	58.7	60.5	63.2
Avg % Change	0.14	0.11	0.11	0.06	0.12
Last Trading Day Performance					
% of Time Up	53.7	50.7	69.6	52.6	68.4
Avg % Change	0.06	0.11	0.34	0.05	0.43

Dow & S&P 1950–April 2017, NASDAQ 1971–April 2017, Russell 1K & 2K 1979–April 2017.

Last Day of June not hot for the Dow;
Down 17 of 26, WOW!

Memorial Day (Market Closed)

Never tell people how to do things. Tell them what to do and they will surprise you with their ingenuity.
— General George S. Patton, Jr. (U.S. Army field commander WWII, 1885–1945)

Day After Memorial Day, Dow Up 21 of Last 32
Memorial Day Week Dow Down 13 of Last 22, Up 12 Straight 1984–1995

TUESDAY
D 47.6
S 47.6
N 61.9
29

Imagination is more important than knowledge.
— Albert Einstein (German-American physicist, 1921 Nobel Prize, 1879–1955)

WEDNESDAY
D 61.9
S 61.9
N 71.4
30

Don't worry about people stealing your ideas. If the ideas are any good, you'll have to ram them down people's throats.
— Howard Aiken (U.S. computer scientist, 1900–1973)

First Trading Day in June, Dow Up 23 of Last 30
Down 2008/2010 –1.1%, 2011/12 –2.2%

THURSDAY
D 42.9
S 52.4
N 52.4
31

A cynic is a man who knows the price of everything and the value of nothing.
— Oscar Wilde (Irish-born writer and wit, 1845–1900)

Start Looking for NASDAQ MACD Sell Signal on June 1 (Page 60)
Almanac Investor Subscribers Emailed When It Triggers (See Insert)

FRIDAY
D 66.7
S 61.9
N 52.4
1

The reason the market did so well in the last several years is because the Federal Reserve drove interest rates down to extraordinary low levels like 1%.
— George Roche (Chairman, T. Rowe Price, Barron's 12/18/06)

SATURDAY
2

SUNDAY
3

TOP PERFORMING NASDAQ MONTHS PAST 46⅓ YEARS

NASDAQ stocks continue to run away during three consecutive months, November, December, and January, with an average gain of 6.0% despite the slaughter of November 2000, −22.9%, December 2000, −4.9%, December 2002, −9.7%, November 2007, −6.9%, January 2008, −9.9%, November 2008, −10.8%, January 2009, −6.4%, January 2010, −5.4%, and January 2016, −7.9%. Solid gains in November and December 2004 offset January 2005's 5.2% Iraq-turmoil-fueled drop.

You can see the months graphically on page 148. January by itself is impressive, up 2.6% on average. April, May, and June also shine, creating our NASDAQ Best Eight Months strategy. What appears as a Death Valley abyss occurs during NASDAQ's bleakest months: July, August, and September. NASDAQ's Best Eight Months seasonal strategy using MACD timing is displayed on page 58.

MONTHLY % CHANGES (JANUARY 1971–APRIL 2017)

NASDAQ Composite*					Dow Jones Industrials				
Month	Total % Change	Avg. % Change	# Up	# Down	Month	Total % Change	Avg. % Change	# Up	# Down
Jan	119.9%	2.6%	30	17	Jan	48.5%	1.0%	29	18
Feb	34.4	0.7	26	21	Feb	24.5	0.5	29	18
Mar	42.7	0.9	30	17	Mar	55.8	1.2	31	16
Apr	64.2	1.4	30	17	Apr	97.9	2.1	31	16
May	43.4	0.9	28	18	May	12.0	0.3	25	21
Jun	31.1	0.7	25	21	Jun	−3.9	−0.1	23	23
Jul	16.1	0.4	24	22	Jul	35.2	0.8	26	20
Aug	5.4	0.1	25	21	Aug	−14.9	−0.3	25	21
Sep	−24.3	−0.5	25	21	Sep	−46.7	−1.0	16	30
Oct	34.4	0.7	25	21	Oct	31.0	0.7	28	18
Nov	74.5	1.6	31	15	Nov	60.5	1.3	31	15
Dec	84.8	1.8	27	19	Dec	74.8	1.6	32	14
% Rank					% Rank				
Jan	119.9%	2.6%	30	17	Apr	97.9%	2.1%	31	16
Dec	84.8	1.8	27	19	Dec	74.8	1.6	32	14
Nov	74.5	1.6	31	15	Nov	60.5	1.3	31	15
Apr	64.2	1.4	30	17	Mar	55.8	1.2	31	16
May	43.4	0.9	28	18	Jan	48.5	1.0	29	18
Mar	42.7	0.9	30	17	Jul	35.2	0.8	26	20
Feb	34.4	0.7	26	21	Oct	31.0	0.7	28	18
Oct	34.4	0.7	25	21	Feb	24.5	0.5	29	18
Jun	31.1	0.7	25	21	May	12.0	0.3	25	21
Jul	16.1	0.4	24	22	Jun	−3.9	−0.1	23	23
Aug	5.4	0.1	25	21	Aug	−14.9	−0.3	25	21
Sep	−24.3	−0.5	25	21	Sep	−46.7	−1.0	16	30
Totals	526.6%	11.3%			Totals	374.7%	8.1%		
Average		0.94%			Average		0.68%		

*Based on NASDAQ composite; prior to Feb. 5, 1971 based on National Quotation Bureau indices.

For comparison, Dow figures are shown. During this period, NASDAQ averaged a 0.94% gain per month, 38.2 percent more than the Dow's 0.68% per month. Between January 1971 and January 1982, NASDAQ's composite index doubled in 12 years, while the Dow stayed flat. But while NASDAQ plummeted 77.9% from its 2000 highs to the 2002 bottom, the Dow only lost 37.8%. The Great Recession and bear market of 2007–2009 spread its carnage equally across Dow and NASDAQ. Recent market moves are increasingly more correlated.

JUNE 2018

🦫 **MONDAY**
D 52.4
S 71.4
N 66.7
4

Companies which do well generally tend to report (their quarterly earnings) earlier than those which do poorly.
— Alan Abelson (Financial journalist and editor, *Barron's*)

TUESDAY
D 47.6
S 42.9
N 47.6
5

The first stocks to double in a bull market will usually double again.
— Michael L. Burke (*Investors Intelligence*)

June Ends NASDAQ's "Best Eight Months" (Pages 56, 58 and 148)　　**WEDNESDAY**
D 57.1
S 57.1
N 57.1
6

The very purpose of existence is to reconcile the glowing opinion we hold of ourselves with the appalling things that other people think about us.
— Quentin Crisp (Author, performer, 1908–1999)

THURSDAY
D 66.7
S 47.6
N 42.9
7

What lies behind us and what lies before us are tiny matters, compared to what lies within us.
— Ralph Waldo Emerson (American author, poet and philosopher, *Self-Reliance*, 1803–1882)

2008 Second Worst June Ever, Dow −10.2%, S&P −8.6%,　　**FRIDAY**
Only 1930 Was Worse, NASDAQ −9.1%, June 2002 −9.4%
D 57.1
S 52.4
N 42.9
8

The market can stay irrational longer than you can stay solvent.
— John Maynard Keynes (*British economist*, 1883–1946)

SATURDAY
9

SUNDAY
10

GET MORE OUT OF NASDAQ'S "BEST EIGHT MONTHS" WITH MACD TIMING

NASDAQ's amazing eight-month run from November through June is hard to miss on pages 56 and 148. A $10,000 investment in these eight months since 1971 gained $644,914 versus a loss of $938 during the void that is the four-month period July–October (as of June 2, 2017).

Using the same MACD timing indicators on the NASDAQ as is done for the Dow (page 52) has enabled us to capture much of October's improved performance, pumping up NASDAQ's results considerably. Over the 46 years since NASDAQ began, the gain on the same $10,000 nearly doubles to $1,683,015 and the loss during the four-month void increases to $6,604. Only four sizeable losses occurred during the favorable period, and the bulk of NASDAQ's bear markets were avoided including the worst of the 2000–2002 bear.

Updated signals are e-mailed to our monthly newsletter subscribers as soon as they are triggered. Visit *www.stocktradersalmanac.com,* or see ad insert for details and a special offer for new subscribers.

BEST EIGHT MONTHS STRATEGY + TIMING

MACD Signal Date	Worst 4 Months July 1–Oct 31* NASDAQ	% Change	Investing $10,000	MACD Signal Date	Best 8 Months Nov 1–June 30* NASDAQ	% Change	Investing $10,000
22-Jul-71	109.54	−3.6	$9,640	4-Nov-71	105.56	24.1	$12,410
7-Jun-72	131.00	−1.8	9,466	23-Oct-72	128.66	−22.7	9,593
25-Jun-73	99.43	−7.2	8,784	7-Dec-73	92.32	−20.2	7,655
3-Jul-74	73.66	−23.2	6,746	7-Oct-74	56.57	47.8	11,314
11-Jun-75	83.60	−9.2	6,125	7-Oct-75	75.88	20.8	13,667
22-Jul-76	91.66	−2.4	5,978	19-Oct-76	89.45	13.2	15,471
27-Jul-77	101.25	−4.0	5,739	4-Nov-77	97.21	26.6	19,586
7-Jun-78	123.10	−6.5	5,366	6-Nov-78	115.08	19.1	23,327
3-Jul-79	137.03	−1.1	5,307	30-Oct-79	135.48	15.5	26,943
20-Jun-80	156.51	26.2	6,697	9-Oct-80	197.53	11.2	29,961
4-Jun-81	219.68	−17.6	5,518	1-Oct-81	181.09	−4.0	28,763
7-Jun-82	173.84	12.5	6,208	7-Oct-82	195.59	57.4	45,273
1-Jun-83	307.95	−10.7	5,544	3-Nov-83	274.86	−14.2	38,844
1-Jun-84	235.90	5.0	5,821	15-Oct-84	247.67	17.3	45,564
3-Jun-85	290.59	−3.0	5,646	1-Oct-85	281.77	39.4	63,516
10-Jun-86	392.83	−10.3	5,064	1-Oct-86	352.34	20.5	76,537
30-Jun-87	424.67	−22.7	3,914	2-Nov-87	328.33	20.1	91,921
8-Jul-88	394.33	−6.6	3,656	29-Nov-88	368.15	22.4	112,511
13-Jun-89	450.73	0.7	3,682	9-Nov-89	454.07	1.9	114,649
11-Jun-90	462.79	−23.0	2,835	2-Oct-90	356.39	39.3	159,706
11-Jun-91	496.62	6.4	3,016	1-Oct-91	528.51	7.4	171,524
11-Jun-92	567.68	1.5	3,061	14-Oct-92	576.22	20.5	206,686
7-Jun-93	694.61	9.9	3,364	1-Oct-93	763.23	−4.4	197,592
17-Jun-94	729.35	5.0	3,532	11-Oct-94	765.57	13.5	224,267
1-Jun-95	868.82	17.2	4,140	13-Oct-95	1018.38	21.6	272,709
3-Jun-96	1238.73	1.0	4,181	7-Oct-96	1250.87	10.3	300,798
4-Jun-97	1379.67	24.4	5,201	3-Oct-97	1715.87	1.8	306,212
1-Jun-98	1746.82	−7.8	4,795	15-Oct-98	1611.01	49.7	458,399
1-Jun-99	2412.03	18.5	5,682	6-Oct-99	2857.21	35.7	622,047
29-Jun-00	3877.23	−18.2	4,648	18-Oct-00	3171.56	−32.2	421,748
1-Jun-01	2149.44	−31.1	3,202	1-Oct-01	1480.46	5.5	444,944
3-Jun-02	1562.56	−24.0	2,434	2-Oct-02	1187.30	38.5	616,247
20-Jun-03	1644.72	15.1	2,802	6-Oct-03	1893.46	4.3	642,746
21-Jun-04	1974.38	−1.6	2,757	1-Oct-04	1942.20	6.1	681,954
8-Jun-05	2060.18	1.5	2,798	19-Oct-05	2091.76	6.1	723,553
1-Jun-06	2219.86	3.9	2,907	5-Oct-06	2306.34	9.5	792,291
7-Jun-07	2541.38	7.9	3,137	1-Oct-07	2740.99	−9.1	724,796
2-Jun-08	2491.53	−31.3	2,155	17-Oct-08	1711.29	6.1	769,009
15-Jun-09	1816.38	17.8	2,539	9-Oct-09	2139.28	1.6	781,313
7-Jun-10	2173.90	18.6	3,011	4-Nov-10	2577.34	7.4	839,130
1-Jun-11	2769.19	−10.5	2,695	7-Oct-11	2479.35	10.8	929,756
1-Jun-12	2747.48	9.6	2,954	6-Nov-12	3011.93	16.2	1,080,376
4-Jun-13	3445.26	10.1	3,252	15-Oct-13	3794.01	15.4	1,227,442
26-Jun-14	4379.05	0.9	3,281	21-Oct-14	4419.48	14.5	1,405,421
4-Jun-15	5059.12	−5.5	3,101	5-Oct-15	4781.26	1.4	1,425,097
13-Jun-16	4848.44	9.5	3,396	24-Oct-16	5309.83	18.8	1,693,015
2-Jun-17	6305.80	*As of 6/2/2017, MACD Sell Signal not triggered at press time*					
	46-Year Loss	**($6,604)**				**46-Year Gain**	**$1,683,015**

* MACD-generated entry and exit points (earlier or later) can lengthen or shorten eight-month periods.

Monday of Triple-Witching Week, Dow Down 12 of Last 20

MONDAY

D 33.3
S 42.9
N 42.9

11

Knowledge born from actual experience is the answer to why one profits; lack of it is the reason one loses.
— Gerald M. Loeb (E.F. Hutton, *The Battle for Investment Survival,* predicted 1929 Crash, 1900–1974)

FOMC Meeting (2 Days)

TUESDAY

D 42.9
S 38.1
N 38.1

12

Every successful enterprise requires three people—a dreamer, a businessman, and a son-of-a-bitch.
— Peter McArthur (1904)

Triple-Witching Week Often Up in Bull Markets and Down in Bears
(Page 78)

WEDNESDAY

D 52.4
S 52.4
N 47.6

13

The higher a people's intelligence and moral strength, the lower will be the prevailing rate of interest.
— Eugen von Bohm-Bawerk (Austrian economist, *Capital and Interest*, 1851–1914)

THURSDAY

D 61.9
S 61.9
N 52.4

14

Leadership is the ability to hide your panic from others.
— Lao Tzu (Chinese philosopher, Shaolin monk, founder of Taoism, 6th century BCE)

June Triple-Witching Day, Dow Up 9 of Last 14

FRIDAY

D 57.1
S 66.7
N 66.7

15

To find one man in a thousand who is your true friend from unselfish motives is to find one of the great wonders of the world.
— Leopold Mozart (Quoted by Maynard Solomon, *Mozart*, 1719–1787)

SATURDAY

16

Father's Day

SUNDAY

17

TRIPLE RETURNS, FEWER TRADES: BEST 6 + 4-YEAR CYCLE

We first introduced this strategy to *Almanac Investor* newsletter subscribers in October 2006. Recurring seasonal stock market patterns and the four-year Presidential Election/Stock Market Cycle (page 130) have been integral to our research since the first Almanac 49 years ago. Yale Hirsch discovered the Best Six Months in 1986 (page 60), and it has been a cornerstone of our seasonal investment analysis and strategies ever since.

Most of the market's gains have occurred during the Best Six Months, and the market generally hits a low point every four years in the first (post-election) or second (midterm) year and exhibits the greatest gains in the third (pre-election) year. This strategy combines the best of these two market phenomena, the Best Six Months and the four-year cycle, timing entries and exits with MACD (pages 52 and 58).

We've gone back to 1949 to include the full four-year cycle that began with post-election year 1949. Only four trades every four years are needed to nearly triple the results of the Best Six Months. Buy and sell during the post-election and midterm years and then hold from the mid-term MACD seasonal buy signal sometime after October 1 until the post-election MACD seasonal sell signal sometime after April 1, approximately 2.5 years: better returns, less effort, lower transaction fees, and fewer taxable events.

BEST SIX MONTHS+TIMING+4-YEAR CYCLE STRATEGY

	DJIA % Change May 1–Oct 31*	Investing $10,000	DJIA % Change Nov 1–Apr 30*	Investing $10,000
1949	3.0%	$10,300	17.5%	$11,750
1950	7.3	11,052	19.7	14,065
1951		11,052		14,065
1952		11,052		14,065
1953	0.2	11,074	17.1	16,470
1954	13.5	12,569	35.7	22,350
1955		12,569		22,350
1956		12,569		22,350
1957	−12.3	11,023	4.9	23,445
1958	17.3	12,930	27.8	29,963
1959		12,930		29,963
1960		12,930		29,963
1961	2.9	13,305	−1.5	29,514
1962	−15.3	11,269	58.5	46,780
1963		11,269		46,780
1964		11,269		46,780
1965	2.6	11,562	−2.5	45,611
1966	−16.4	9,666	22.2	55,737
1967		9,666		55,737
1968		9,666		55,737
1969	−11.9	8,516	−6.7	52,003
1970	−1.4	8,397	21.5	63,184
1971		8,397		63,184
1972		8,397		63,184
1973	−11.0	7,473	0.1	63,247
1974	−22.4	5,799	42.5	90,127
1975		5,799		90,127
1976		5,799		90,127
1977	−11.4	5,138	0.5	90,578
1978	−4.5	4,907	26.8	114,853
1979		4,907		114,853
1980		4,907		114,853
1981	−14.6	4,191	0.4	115,312
1982	15.5	4,841	25.9	145,178
1983		4,841		145,178
1984		4,841		145,178
1985	7.0	5,180	38.1	200,491
1986	−2.8	5,035	33.2	267,054
1987		5,035		267,054
1988		5,035		267,054
1989	9.8	5,528	3.3	275,867
1990	−6.7	5,158	35.1	372,696
1991		5,158		372,696
1992		5,158		372,696
1993	5.5	5,442	5.6	393,455
1994	3.7	5,643	88.2	740,482
1995		5,643		740,482
1996		5,643		740,482
1997	3.6	5,846	18.5	877,471
1998	−12.4	5,121	36.3	1,195,993
1999		5,121		1,195,993
2000		5,121		1,195,993
2001	−17.3	4,235	15.8	1,384,960
2002	−25.2	3,168	34.2	1,858,616
2003		3,168		1,858,616
2004		3,168		1,858,616
2005	−0.5	3,152	7.7	2,001,729
2006	4.7	3,300	−31.7	1,367,181
2007		3,300		1,367,181
2008		3,300		1,367,181
2009	23.8	4,085	10.8	1,514,738
2010	4.6	4,273	27.4	1,929,777
2011		4,273		1,929,777
2012		4,273		1,929,777
2013	4.1	4,448	7.1	2,066,791
2014	2.3	4,550	24.0	2,562,820
2015		4,550		2,562,820
2016		$4,550		$2,562,820
Average	−0.8%		9.8%	
# Up	18		30	
# Down	16		4	
68-Year Gain (Loss)		($5,450)		$2,552,820

* MACD and 2.5-year hold lengthen and shorten six-month periods

FOUR TRADES EVERY FOUR YEARS

Year	Worst Six Months May–Oct	Best Six Months Nov–April
Post-election	Sell	Buy
Midterm	Sell	Buy
Pre-election	Hold	Hold
Election	Hold	Hold

JUNE 2018

MONDAY
D 57.1
S 57.1
N 57.1
18

In nature there are no rewards or punishments; there are consequences.
— Horace Annesley Vachell (English writer, *The Face of Clay*, 1861–1955)

TUESDAY
D 57.1
S 57.1
N 61.9
19

The highest reward for a person's toil is not what they get for it, but what they become by it.
— John Ruskin (English writer, 1819–1900)

Week After June Triple Witching, Dow Down 24 of Last 27
Average Loss Since 1990, 1.1%

WEDNESDAY
D 57.1
S 52.4
N 47.6
20

Inflation is the one form of taxation that can be imposed without legislation.
— Milton Friedman (American economist, 1976 Nobel Prize, 1912–2006)

THURSDAY
D 38.1
S 47.6
N 33.3
21

The first human who hurled an insult instead of a stone was the founder of civilization.
— Sigmund Freud (Austrian neurologist, psychiatrist, "father of psychoanalysis," 1856–1939)

FRIDAY
D 42.9
S 42.9
N 42.9
22

The world hates change, but it is the only thing that has brought progress.
— Charles Kettering (Inventor of electric ignition, founded Delco in 1909, 1876–1958)

SATURDAY
23

SUNDAY
24

JULY ALMANAC

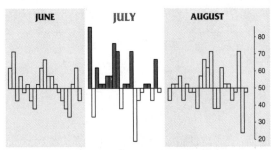

JUNE   JULY   AUGUST

JULY
S M T W T F S
1 2 3 4 5 6 7
8 9 10 11 12 13 14
15 16 17 18 19 20 21
22 23 24 25 26 27 28
29 30 31

AUGUST

S M T W T F S
1 2 3 4
5 6 7 8 9 10 11
12 13 14 15 16 17 18
19 20 21 22 23 24 25
26 27 28 29 30 31

Market Probability Chart above is a graphic representation of the S&P 500 Recent Market Probability Calendar on page 124.

◆ July is the best month of the third quarter (page 64) ◆ Start of 2nd half brings an inflow of retirement funds ◆ First trading day Dow up 23 of last 28 ◆ Graph above shows strength in the first half of July ◆ Huge gain in July usually provides better buying opportunity over next 4 months ◆ Start of NASDAQ's worst four months of the year (page 58) ◆ Midterm election year Julys are ranked #5 Dow (up 10, down 7) #6 S&P (up 9, down 8) and #12 NASDAQ (up 3, down 8).

July Vital Statistics

	DJIA		S&P 500		NASDAQ		Russell 1K		Russell 2K	
Rank	4		5		10		8		11	
Up	42		37		24		18		18	
Down	25		30		22		20		20	
Average % Change	1.2%		1.0%		0.4%		0.7%		−0.3%	
Midterm Year	1.1%		0.7%		−2.2%		−1.1%		−4.5%	
Best & Worst July										
	% Change		% Change		% Change		% Change		% Change	
Best	1989	9.0	1989	8.8	1997	10.5	1989	8.2	1980	11.0
Worst	1969	−6.6	2002	−7.9	2002	−9.2	2002	−7.5	2002	−15.2
Best & Worst July Weeks										
Best	07/17/09	7.3	07/17/09	7.0	07/17/09	7.4	07/17/09	7.0	07/17/09	8.0
Worst	07/19/02	−7.7	07/19/02	−8.0	07/28/00	−10.5	07/19/02	−7.4	07/02/10	−7.2
Best & Worst July Days										
Best	07/24/02	6.4	07/24/02	5.7	07/29/02	5.8	07/24/02	5.6	07/29/02	4.9
Worst	07/19/02	−4.6	07/19/02	−3.8	07/28/00	−4.7	07/19/02	−3.6	07/23/02	−4.1
First Trading Day of Expiration Week: 1980–2016										
Record (#Up − #Down)	23–14		24–13		25–12		23–14		21–16	
Current streak	U4		U4		U4		U4		U4	
Avg % Change	0.13		0.06		0.07		0.03		−0.02	
Options Expiration Day: 1980–2016										
Record (#Up − #Down)	17–18		19–18		16–21		19–18		15–22	
Current streak	U1		D1		D1		D1		U1	
Avg % Change	−0.24		−0.28		−0.41		−0.29		−0.44	
Options Expiration Week: 1980–2016										
Record (#Up − #Down)	24–13		21–16		20–17		21–16		20–17	
Current streak	U5		U5		U3		U5		U2	
Avg % Change	0.50		0.19		0.13		0.14		−0.05	
Week After Options Expiration: 1980–2016										
Record (#Up − #Down)	19–18		18–19		17–20		19–18		14–23	
Current streak	U1		U1		U1		U1		U1	
Avg % Change	−0.06		−0.17		−0.41		−0.18		−0.37	
First Trading Day Performance										
% of Time Up	65.7		71.6		63.0		73.7		65.8	
Avg % Change	0.27		0.26		0.13		0.31		0.10	
Last Trading Day Performance										
% of Time Up	49.3		61.2		50.0		57.9		65.8	
Avg % Change	0.02		0.07		−0.03		−0.03		−0.02	

Dow & S&P 1950–April 2017, NASDAQ 1971–April 2017, Russell 1K & 2K 1979–April 2017.

When Dow and S&P in July are inferior,
NASDAQ days tend to be even drearier.

JUNE/JULY 2018

MONDAY
D 33.3
S 38.1
N 38.1
25

We prefer to cut back exposure on what's going against us and add exposure where it's more favorable to our portfolio. This way, we're always attempting to tilt the odds in our favor. This is the exact opposite of a long investor that would average down. Averaging down is a very dangerous practice.
— John Del Vecchio & Brad Lamensdorf (Portfolio managers Active Bear ETF, 5/10/12 *Almanac Investor* Interview)

TUESDAY
D 42.9
S 33.3
N 42.9
26

The test of success is not what you do when you are on top. Success is how high you bounce when you hit bottom.
— General George S. Patton, Jr. (U.S. Army field commander WWII, 1885–1945)

WEDNESDAY
D 57.1
S 52.4
N 66.7
27

Change is the law of life. And those who look only to the past or present are certain to miss the future.
— John F. Kennedy (35th U.S. President, 1917–1963)

THURSDAY
D 57.1
S 61.9
N 66.7
28

Patriotism is when love of your own people comes first. Nationalism is when hate for people other that your own comes first.
— Charles de Gaulle (French president and WWII General, 1890–1970, May 1969)

Last Day of Q2 Bearish for Dow, Down 17 of Last 26
But Bullish for NASDAQ, Up 18 of 25

FRIDAY
D 38.1
S 42.9
N 66.7
29

Based on my own personal experience—both as an investor in recent years and an expert witness in years past—rarely do more than three or four variables really count. Everything else is noise.
— Martin J. Whitman (Founder Third Avenue Funds, b. 1924)

SATURDAY
30

July Almanac Investor Sector Seasonalities: See Pages 92, 94 and 96

SUNDAY
1

FIRST MONTH OF QUARTERS IS THE MOST BULLISH

We have observed over the years that the investment calendar reflects the annual, semiannual, and quarterly operations of institutions during January, April, and July. The opening month of the first three quarters produces the greatest gains in the Dow Jones Industrials and the S&P 500. NASDAQ's record differs slightly.

The fourth quarter had behaved quite differently, since it is affected by year-end portfolio adjustments and presidential and congressional elections in even-numbered years. Since 1991, major turnarounds have helped October join the ranks of bullish first months of quarters. October transformed into a bear-killing-turnaround month, posting some mighty gains in 13 of the last 18 years; 2008 was a significant exception. (See pages 152–160.)

After experiencing the most powerful bull market of all time during the 1990s, followed by two ferocious bear markets early in the millennium, we divided the monthly average percentage changes into two groups: before 1991 and after. Comparing the month-by-month quarterly behavior of the three major U.S. averages in the table, you'll see that first months of the first three quarters perform best overall. Nasty sell-offs in April 2000, 2002, 2004, and 2005, and July 2000–2002 and 2004 hit the NASDAQ hardest. The bear market of October 2007–March 2009, which more than cut the markets in half, took a toll on every first month except April. October 2008 was the worst month in a decade. January was also a difficult month in six of the last ten years, pulling its performance lower. (See pages 152–160.)

Between 1950 and 1990, the S&P 500 gained 1.3% (Dow, 1.4%) on average in first months of the first three quarters. Second months barely eked out any gain, while third months, thanks to March, moved up 0.23% (Dow, 0.07%) on average. NASDAQ's first month of the first three quarters averages 1.67% from 1971–1990, with July being a negative drag.

DOW JONES INDUSTRIALS, S&P 500, AND NASDAQ
AVERAGE MONTHLY % CHANGES BY QUARTER

	DJIA 1950–1990			S&P 500 1950–1990			NASDAQ 1971–1990		
	1st Mo	2nd Mo	3rd Mo	1st Mo	2nd Mo	3rd Mo	1st Mo	2nd Mo	3rd Mo
1Q	1.5%	−0.01%	1.0%	1.5%	−0.1%	1.1%	3.8%	1.2%	0.9%
2Q	1.6	−0.4	0.1	1.3	−0.1	0.3	1.7	0.8	1.1
3Q	1.1	0.3	−0.9	1.1	0.3	−0.7	−0.5	0.1	−1.6
Tot	4.2%	−0.1%	0.2%	3.9%	0.1%	0.7%	5.0%	2.1%	0.4%
Avg	1.40%	−0.04%	0.07%	1.30%	0.03%	0.23%	1.67%	0.70%	0.13%
4Q	−0.1%	1.4%	1.7%	0.4%	1.7%	1.6%	−1.4%	1.6%	1.4%

	DJIA 1991–May 2017			S&P 500 1991–May 2017			NASDAQ 1991–May 2017		
1Q	−0.1%	0.7%	1.3%	0.1%	0.4%	1.4%	1.6%	0.4%	0.9%
2Q	2.3	0.6	−0.9	1.7	0.7	−0.5	1.1	1.1	0.4
3Q	1.3	−0.9	−0.6	0.9	−0.7	−0.3	1.0	0.1	0.3
Tot	3.5%	0.4%	−0.2%	2.7%	0.4%	0.6%	3.7%	1.6%	1.6%
Avg	1.17%	0.14%	−0.07%	0.90%	0.13%	0.20%	1.23%	0.52%	0.53%
4Q	1.8%	1.8%	1.6%	1.7%	1.3%	1.7%	2.4%	1.7%	2.2%

	DJIA 1950–May 2017			S&P 500 1950–May 2017			NASDAQ 1971–May 2017		
1Q	0.9%	0.3%	1.1%	1.0%	0.1%	1.2%	2.6%	0.7%	0.9%
2Q	1.9	−0.02	−0.3	1.5	0.2	−0.03	1.4	1.0	0.7
3Q	1.2	−0.2	−0.8	1.0	−0.09	−0.5	0.4	0.1	−0.5
Tot	4.0%	0.1%	0.0%	3.5%	0.2%	0.7%	4.4%	1.8%	1.1%
Avg	1.33%	0.03%	0.00%	1.17%	0.07%	0.22%	1.45%	0.61%	0.37%
4Q	0.6%	1.6%	1.7%	0.9%	1.5%	1.6%	0.7%	1.6%	1.8%

Those who study market history are bound to profit from it!

Almanac Investor Ranked Top 5 Market Time[rs] by Hulbert 10 Years 2004-2014

What's even more gratifying is that the independent newsletter watchdog, the *Hulbert Financial Diges[t]* ranked my *Almanac Investor* among the Top 5 Market Timers in 2014 for the past decade.

Now you can find out which seasonal trends are on schedule and which are not, and how to tak[e] advantage of them. You will be kept abreast of upcoming market-moving events and what our indicato[rs] are saying about the next major market move. Every week you will receive timely dispatches about bullis[h] and bearish seasonal patterns.

Our digital subscription service, *Almanac Investor*, provides all this plus unusual investin[g] opportunities – exciting small-, mid- and large-cap stocks; seasoned, undervalued equities; time[ly] sector ETF trades and more. Our **Data-Rich and Data-Driven Market Cycle Analysis** is the on[ly] investment tool of its kind that helps traders and investors forecast market trends with accuracy and confidence.

YOU RECEIVE WEEKLY EMAIL ALERTS CONTAINING:

▶ Opportune ETF and Stock Trading Ideas with Specific Buy and Sell Price Limits

▶ Timely Data-Rich and Data-Driven Market Analysis

▶ Access to Webinars, Videos, Tools and Resources

▶ Market-Tested and Time-Proven Short- and Long-term Trading Strategies

▶ Best Six-Months Switching Strategy MACD Timing Signals.

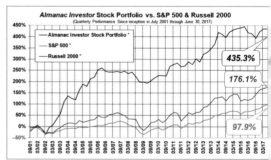

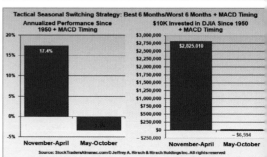

JULY 2018

First Trading Day in July, Dow Up 23 of Last 28, Average Gain 0.5%

MONDAY

D 81.0
S 85.7
N 76.2

2

The thing always happens that you really believe in. The belief in a thing makes it happen.
— Frank Lloyd Wright (American architect, 1867–1959)

(Shortened Trading Day)

TUESDAY

D 33.3
S 33.3
N 33.3

3

A committee is a cul de sac down which ideas are lured and then quietly strangled.
— Sir Barnett Cocks (Member of Parliament, 1907–1989)

Independence Day *(Market Closed)*

WEDNESDAY

4

A man will fight harder for his interests than his rights.
— Napoleon Bonaparte (Emperor of France 1804–1815, 1769–1821)

Market Subject to Elevated Volatility After July 4th

THURSDAY

D 52.4
S 61.9
N 57.1

5

You are your own Promised Land, your own new frontier.
— Julia Margaret Cameron (19th century English photographer, 1815–1879)

July Begins NASDAQ's "Worst Four Months" (Pages 56, 58 and 148)

FRIDAY

D 52.4
S 52.4
N 61.9

6

The usual bull market successfully weathers a number of tests until it is considered invulnerable, whereupon it is ripe for a bust.
— George Soros (Financier, philanthropist, political activist, author and philosopher, b. 1930)

SATURDAY

7

SUNDAY

8

2016 DAILY DOW POINT CHANGES
(DOW JONES INDUSTRIAL AVERAGE)

Week #		Monday**	Tuesday	Wednesday	Thursday	Friday**	Weekly Dow Close	Net Point Change
						2015 Close	**17425.03**	
1						Holiday		
2	J	−276.09	9.72	−252.15	−392.41	−167.65	16346.45	−1078.58
3	A	52.12	117.65	−364.81	227.64	−390.97	15988.08	−358.37
4	N	Holiday	27.94	−249.28	115.94	210.83	16093.51	105.43
5		−208.29	282.01	−222.77	125.18	396.66	16466.30	372.79
6		−17.12	−295.64	183.12	79.92	−211.61	16204.97	−261.33
7	F	−177.92	−12.67	−99.64	−254.56	313.66	15973.84	−231.13
8	E	Holiday	222.57	257.42	−40.40	−21.44	16391.99	418.15
9	B	228.67	−188.88	53.21	212.30	−57.32	16639.97	247.98
10		−123.47	348.58	34.24	44.58	62.87	17006.77	366.80
11		67.18	−109.85	36.26	−5.23	218.18	17213.31	206.54
12	M	15.82	22.40	74.23	155.73	120.81	17602.30	388.99
13	A	21.57	−41.30	−79.98	13.14	Holiday	17515.73	−86.57
14	R	19.66	97.72	83.55	−31.57	107.66	17792.75	277.02
15		−55.75	−133.68	112.73	−174.09	35.00	17576.96	−215.79
16	A	−20.55	164.84	187.03	18.15	−28.97	17897.46	320.50
17	P	106.70	49.44	42.67	−113.75	21.23	18003.75	106.29
18	R	−26.51	13.08	51.23	−210.79	−57.12	17773.64	−230.11
19		117.52	−140.25	−99.65	9.45	79.92	17740.63	−33.01
20	M	−34.72	222.44	−217.23	9.38	−185.18	17535.32	−205.31
21	A	175.39	−180.73	−3.36	−91.22	65.54	17500.94	−34.38
22	Y	−8.01	213.12	145.46	−23.22	44.93	17873.22	372.28
23		Holiday	−86.02	2.47	48.89	−31.50	17807.06	−66.16
24	J	113.27	17.95	66.77	−19.86	−119.85	17865.34	58.28
25	U	−132.86	−57.66	−34.65	92.93	−57.94	17675.16	−190.18
26	N	129.71	24.86	−48.90	230.24	−610.32	17400.75	−274.41
27		−260.51	269.48	284.96	235.31	19.38	17949.37	548.62
28	J	Holiday	−108.75	78.00	−22.74	250.86	18146.74	197.37
29	U	80.19	120.74	24.45	134.29	10.14	18516.55	369.81
30	L	16.50	25.96	36.02	−77.80	53.62	18570.85	54.30
31		−77.79	−19.31	−1.58	−15.82	−24.11	18432.24	−138.61
32		−27.73	−90.74	41.23	−2.95	191.48	18543.53	111.29
33	A	−14.24	3.76	−37.39	117.86	−37.05	18576.47	32.94
34	U	59.58	−84.03	21.92	23.76	−45.13	18552.57	−23.90
35	G	−23.15	17.88	−65.82	−33.07	−53.01	18395.40	−157.17
36		107.59	−48.69	−53.42	18.42	72.66	18491.96	96.56
37		Holiday	46.16	−11.98	−46.23	−394.46	18085.45	−406.51
38	S	239.62	−258.32	−31.98	177.71	−88.68	18123.80	38.35
39	E	−3.63	9.79	163.74	98.76	−131.01	18261.45	137.65
40	P	−166.62	133.47	110.94	−195.79	164.70	18308.15	46.70
41		−54.30	−85.40	112.58	−12.53	−28.01	18240.49	−67.66
42	O	88.55	−200.38	15.54	−45.26	39.44	18138.38	−102.11
43	C	−51.98	75.54	40.68	−40.27	−16.64	18145.71	7.33
44	T	77.32	−53.76	30.06	−29.65	−8.49	18161.19	15.48
45		−18.77	−105.32	−77.46	−28.97	−42.39	17888.28	−272.91
46		371.32	73.14	256.95	218.19	39.78	18847.66	959.38
47	N	21.03	54.37	−54.92	35.68	−35.89	18867.93	20.27
48	O	88.76	67.18	59.31	Holiday	68.96*	19152.14	284.21
49	V	−54.24	23.70	1.98	68.35	−21.51	19170.42	18.28
50		45.82	35.54	297.84	65.19	142.04	19756.85	586.43
51	D	39.58	114.78	−118.68	59.71	−8.83	19843.41	86.56
52	E	39.65	91.56	−32.66	−23.08	14.93	19933.81	90.40
53	C	Holiday	11.23	−111.36	−13.90	−57.18	**19762.60**	−171.21
TOTALS		**602.00**	**594.09**	**636.92**	**678.40**	**−173.84**		**2337.57**

Bold Color: Down Friday, Down Monday   * Shortened trading day: Nov 25

** Monday denotes first trading day of week, Friday denotes last trading day of week

MONDAY

D 61.9
S 52.4
N 57.1

9

There's nothing wrong with cash. It gives you time to think.
— Robert Prechter, Jr. (*Elliott Wave Theorist*)

TUESDAY

D 57.1
S 57.1
N 66.7

10

In the end, we will remember not the words of our enemies, but the silence of our friends.
— Martin Luther King Jr. (Civil rights leader, 1964 Nobel Peace Prize, 1929–1968)

July is the Best Performing Dow and S&P Month of the Third Quarter

WEDNESDAY

D 57.1
S 57.1
N 57.1

11

We always live in an uncertain world. What is certain is that the United States will go forward over time.
— Warren Buffett (CEO Berkshire Hathaway, investor & philanthropist, CNBC 9/22/2010, b. 1930)

THURSDAY

D 66.7
S 76.2
N 66.7

12

The soul is dyed the color of its thoughts. Think only on those things that are in line with your principles and can bear the light of day. The content of your character is your choice. Day by day, what you do is who you become.
— Heraclitus (Greek philosopher, 535–475 BC)

FRIDAY

D 66.7
S 71.4
N 71.4

13

When everybody thinks alike, everyone is likely to be wrong.
— Humphrey B. Neill (Investor, analyst, author, *Art of Contrary Thinking* 1954, 1895–1977)

SATURDAY

14

SUNDAY

15

DON'T SELL STOCKS ON MONDAY OR FRIDAY

Since 1989, Monday* and Tuesday have been the most consistently bullish days of the week for the Dow, Friday* the most bearish, as traders have become reluctant to stay long going into the weekend. Since 1989 Mondays and Tuesdays gained 14554.09 Dow points, while Fridays have lost 904.67 points. Also broken out are the last sixteen and a third years to illustrate Monday's and Friday's poor performance in bear market years 2001–2002 and 2008–2009. During uncertain market times traders often sell before the weekend and are reluctant to jump in on Monday. See pages 66, 74, and 141–144 for more.

ANNUAL DOW POINT CHANGES FOR DAYS OF THE WEEK SINCE 1953

Year	Monday*	Tuesday	Wednesday	Thursday	Friday*	Year's DJIA Closing	Year's Point Change
1953	−36.16	−7.93	19.63	5.76	7.70	280.90	−11.00
1954	15.68	3.27	24.31	33.96	46.27	404.39	123.49
1955	−48.36	26.38	46.03	−0.66	60.62	488.40	84.01
1956	−27.15	−9.36	−15.41	8.43	64.56	499.47	11.07
1957	−109.50	−7.71	64.12	3.32	−14.01	435.69	−63.78
1958	17.50	23.59	29.10	22.67	55.10	583.65	147.96
1959	−44.48	29.04	4.11	13.60	93.44	679.36	95.71
1960	−111.04	−3.75	−5.62	6.74	50.20	615.89	−63.47
1961	−23.65	10.18	87.51	−5.96	47.17	731.14	115.25
1962	−101.60	26.19	9.97	−7.70	−5.90	652.10	−79.04
1963	−8.88	47.12	16.23	22.39	33.99	762.95	110.85
1964	−0.29	−17.94	39.84	5.52	84.05	874.13	111.18
1965	−73.23	39.65	57.03	3.20	68.48	969.26	95.13
1966	−153.24	−27.73	56.13	−46.19	−12.54	785.69	−183.57
1967	−68.65	31.50	25.42	92.25	38.90	905.11	119.42
1968†	6.41	34.94	25.16	−72.06	44.19	943.75	38.64
1969	−164.17	−36.70	18.33	23.79	15.36	800.36	−143.39
1970	−100.05	−46.09	116.07	−3.48	72.11	838.92	38.56
1971	−2.99	9.56	13.66	8.04	23.01	890.20	51.28
1972	−87.40	−1.23	65.24	8.46	144.75	1020.02	129.82
1973	−174.11	10.52	−5.94	36.67	−36.30	850.86	−169.16
1974	−149.37	47.51	−20.31	−13.70	−98.75	616.24	−234.62
1975	39.46	−109.62	56.93	124.00	125.40	852.41	236.17
1976	70.72	71.76	50.88	−33.70	−7.42	1004.65	152.24
1977	−65.15	−44.89	−79.61	−5.62	21.79	831.17	−173.48
1978	−31.29	−70.84	71.33	−64.67	69.31	805.01	−26.16
1979	−32.52	9.52	−18.84	75.18	0.39	838.74	33.73
1980	−86.51	135.13	137.67	−122.00	60.96	963.99	125.25
1981	−45.68	−49.51	−13.95	−14.67	34.82	875.00	−88.99
1982	5.71	86.20	28.37	−1.47	52.73	1046.54	171.54
1983	30.51	−30.92	149.68	61.16	1.67	1258.64	212.10
1984	−73.80	78.02	−139.24	92.79	−4.84	1211.57	−47.07
1985	80.36	52.70	51.26	46.32	104.46	1546.67	335.10
1986	−39.94	97.63	178.65	29.31	83.63	1895.95	349.28
1987	−559.15	235.83	392.03	139.73	−165.56	1938.83	42.88
1988	268.12	166.44	−60.48	−230.84	86.50	2168.57	229.74
1989	−53.31	143.33	233.25	90.25	171.11	2753.20	584.63
Subtotal	*−1937.20*	*941.79*	*1708.54*	*330.82*	*1417.35*		*2461.30*
1990	219.90	−25.22	47.96	−352.55	−9.63	2633.66	−119.54
1991	191.13	47.97	174.53	254.79	−133.25	3168.83	535.17
1992	237.80	−49.67	3.12	108.74	−167.71	3301.11	132.28
1993	322.82	−37.03	243.87	4.97	−81.65	3754.09	452.98
1994	206.41	−95.33	29.98	−168.87	108.16	3834.44	80.35
1995	262.97	210.06	357.02	140.07	312.56	5117.12	1282.68
1996	626.41	155.55	−34.24	268.52	314.91	6448.27	1331.15
1997	1136.04	1989.17	−590.17	−949.80	−125.26	7908.25	1459.98
1998	649.10	679.95	591.63	−1579.43	931.93	9181.43	1273.18
1999	980.49	−1587.23	826.68	735.94	1359.81	11497.12	2315.69
2000	2265.45	306.47	−1978.34	238.21	−1542.06	10786.85	−710.27
Subtotal	*7098.52*	*1594.69*	*−327.96*	*−1299.41*	*967.81*		*8033.65*
2001	−389.33	336.86	−396.53	976.41	−1292.76	10021.50	−765.35
2002	−1404.94	−823.76	1443.69	−428.12	−466.74	8341.63	−1679.87
2003	978.87	482.11	−425.46	566.22	510.55	10453.92	2112.29
2004	201.12	523.28	358.76	−409.72	−344.35	10783.01	329.09
2005	316.23	−305.62	27.67	−128.75	24.96	10717.50	−65.51
2006	95.74	573.98	1283.87	193.34	−401.28	12463.15	1745.65
2007	278.23	−157.93	1316.74	−766.63	131.26	13264.82	801.67
2008	−1387.20	1704.51	−3073.72	−940.88	−791.14	8776.39	−4488.43
2009	−45.22	161.76	617.50	932.68	−15.12	10428.05	1651.66
2010	1236.88	−421.80	1019.66	−76.73	−608.55	11577.51	1149.46
2011	−571.02	1423.66	−776.05	246.27	317.19	12217.56	640.05
2012	254.59	−49.28	−456.37	847.34	299.30	13104.14	886.58
2013	−79.63	1091.75	170.93	653.64	1635.83	16576.66	3472.52
2014	−171.63	817.56	265.07	−337.48	672.89	17823.07	1246.41
2015	308.28	−879.14	926.70	982.16	−1736.04	17425.03	−398.04
2016	602.00	594.09	636.92	678.40	−173.84	19762.60	
2017 ‡	456.25	109.59	137.83	374.66	365.36		
Subtotal	*679.22*	*5181.62*	*3077.27*	*3362.81*	*−1872.48*		*6638.18*
Totals	**5840.54**	**7718.10**	**4457.85**	**2394.22**	**512.68**		**17133.13**

* Monday denotes first trading day of week, Friday denotes last trading day of week
† Most Wednesdays closed last 7 months of 1968   ‡ Partial year through June 2, 2017

JULY 2018

Monday Before July Expiration, Dow Up 11 of Last 14

🐻**MONDAY**

D 47.6
S 38.1
N 52.4

16

Of the S&P 500 companies in 1957, only 74 were still on the list in 1998 and only 12 outperformed the index itself over that period. By 2020, more than 375 companies in the S&P 500 will consist of companies we don't know today.
— Richard Foster and Sarah Kaplan (*Creative Destruction*)

TUESDAY

D 61.9
S 52.4
N 57.1

17

Most people can stay excited for two or three months. A few people can stay excited for two or three years. But a winner will stay excited for 20 to 30 years—or as long as it takes to win.
— A.L. Williams (Motivational speaker)

WEDNESDAY

D 57.1
S 52.4
N 61.9

18

I'm not better than the next trader, just quicker at admitting my mistakes and moving on to the next opportunity.
— George Soros (Financier, philanthropist, political activist, author and philosopher, b. 1930)

🐂**THURSDAY**

D 71.4
S 71.4
N 71.4

19

In every generation there has to be some fool who will speak the truth as he sees it.
— Boris Pasternak (Russian writer and poet, 1958 Nobel Laureate in Literature, *Doctor Zhivago*, 1890–1960)

July Expiration Day, Dow Down 10 of Last 17, –4.6% 2002, –2.5% 2010

🐻**FRIDAY**

D 19.0
S 19.0
N 14.3

20

The first rule is not to lose. The second rule is not to forget the first rule.
— Warren Buffett (CEO Berkshire Hathaway, investor and philanthropist, b. 1930)

SATURDAY

21

SUNDAY

22

A RALLY FOR ALL SEASONS

Most years, especially when the market sells off during the first half, prospects for the perennial summer rally become the buzz on the street. Parameters for this "rally" were defined by the late Ralph Rotnem as the lowest close in the Dow Jones Industrials in May or June to the highest close in July, August, or September. Such a big deal is made of the "summer rally" that one might get the impression the market puts on its best performance in the summertime. Nothing could be further from the truth! Not only does the market "rally" in every season of the year, but it does so with more gusto in the winter, spring, and fall than in the summer.

Winters in 54 years averaged a 12.8% gain as measured from the low in November or December to the first quarter closing high. Spring rose 11.3% followed by fall with 11.0%. Last and least was the average 9.0% "summer rally." Even 2009's impressive 19.7% "summer rally" was outmatched by spring. Nevertheless, no matter how thick the gloom or grim the outlook, don't despair! There's always a rally for all seasons, statistically.

SEASONAL GAINS IN DOW JONES INDUSTRIALS

	WINTER RALLY Nov/Dec Low to Q1 High	SPRING RALLY Feb/Mar Low to Q2 High	SUMMER RALLY May/Jun Low to Q3 High	FALL RALLY Aug/Sep Low to Q4 High
1964	15.3%	6.2%	9.4%	8.3%
1965	5.7	6.6	11.6	10.3
1966	5.9	4.8	3.5	7.0
1967	11.6	8.7	11.2	4.4
1968	7.0	11.5	5.2	13.3
1969	0.9	7.7	1.9	6.7
1970	5.4	6.2	22.5	19.0
1971	21.6	9.4	5.5	7.4
1972	19.1	7.7	5.2	11.4
1973	8.6	4.8	9.7	15.9
1974	13.1	8.2	1.4	11.0
1975	36.2	24.2	8.2	8.7
1976	23.3	6.4	5.9	4.6
1977	8.2	3.1	2.8	2.1
1978	2.1	16.8	11.8	5.2
1979	11.0	8.9	8.9	6.1
1980	13.5	16.8	21.0	8.5
1981	11.8	9.9	0.4	8.3
1982	4.6	9.3	18.5	37.8
1983	15.7	17.8	6.3	10.7
1984	5.9	4.6	14.1	9.7
1985	11.7	7.1	9.5	19.7
1986	31.1	18.8	9.2	11.4
1987	30.6	13.6	22.9	5.9
1988	18.1	13.5	11.2	9.8
1989	15.1	12.9	16.1	5.7
1990	8.8	14.5	12.4	8.6
1991	21.8	11.2	6.6	9.3
1992	14.9	6.4	3.7	3.3
1993	8.9	7.7	6.3	7.3
1994	9.7	5.2	9.1	5.0
1995	13.6	19.3	11.3	13.9
1996	19.2	7.5	8.7	17.3
1997	17.7	18.4	18.4	7.3
1998	20.3	13.6	8.2	24.3
1999	15.1	21.6	8.2	12.6
2000	10.8	15.2	9.8	3.5
2001	6.4	20.8	1.7	23.1
2002	14.8	7.9	2.8	17.6
2003	6.5	23.9	14.3	15.7
2004	11.6	5.2	4.4	10.6
2005	9.0	2.1	5.6	5.3
2006	8.8	8.3	9.5	13.0
2007	6.7	13.5	6.6	10.3
2008	2.5	11.2	3.8	4.5
2009	19.6	34.4	19.7	15.5
2010	11.6	13.1	11.1	16.0
2011	12.6	10.3	7.0	14.7
2012	18.0	4.5	12.4	5.7
2013	16.2	11.8	6.9	12.2
2014	6.0	10.2	5.5	10.3
2015	7.1	5.5	3.0	14.4
2016	3.4	15.6	8.7	10.8
2017	18.0	6.6*		
Totals	**692.7%**	**611.0%**	**479.6%**	**581.0%**
Average	**12.8%**	**11.3%**	**9.0%**	**11.0%**

* As of 6/2/2017

MONDAY

D 42.9
S 42.9
N 42.9

23

Major bottoms are usually made when analysts cut their earnings estimates and companies report earnings which are below expectations.
— Edward Babbitt, Jr. (Avatar Associates)

TUESDAY

D 42.9
S 47.6
N 42.9

24

There is nothing as invigorating as the ego boost that comes from having others sign on when your company is just a dream. What they are saying when they agree to service customers, suppliers, employers or distributors is that they believe in you.
— Joshua Hyatt (*Inc. Magazine, Mapping the Entrepreneurial Mind*, August 1991)

Week After July Expiration Prone to Wild Swings, Dow Up 10 of Last 15 1998 –4.3%, 2002 +3.1%, 2006 +3.2%, 2007 –4.2%, 2009 +4.0%, 2010 +3.2

WEDNESDAY

D 57.1
S 52.4
N 57.1

25

I want the whole of Europe to have one currency; it will make trading much easier.
— Napoleon Bonaparte (Emperor of France 1804–1815, 1769–1821)

THURSDAY

D 52.4
S 52.4
N 57.1

26

Statements by high officials are practically always misleading when they are designed to bolster a falling market.
— Gerald M. Loeb (E.F. Hutton, *The Battle for Investment Survival*, predicted 1929 Crash, 1900–1974)

Beware the "Summer Rally" Hype
Historically the Weakest Rally of All Seasons (Page 70)

FRIDAY

D 38.1
S 42.9
N 42.9

27

I would rather be positioned as a petrified bull rather than a penniless bear.
— John L. Person (Professional trader, author, speaker, *Commodity Trader's Almanac*, nationalfutures.com, 11/3/2010, b. 1961)

SATURDAY

28

August Almanac Investor Sector Seasonalities: See Pages 92, 94 and 96

SUNDAY

29

AUGUST ALMANAC

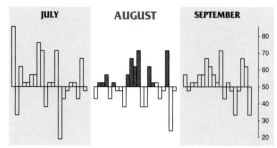

AUGUST							SEPTEMBER					
S	M	T	W	T	F	S	S	M	T	W	T	F	S
		1	2	3	4								1
5	6	7	8	9	10	11	30	2	3	4	5	6	7	8
12	13	14	15	16	17	18	9	10	11	12	13	14	15
19	20	21	22	23	24	25	16	17	18	19	20	21	22
26	27	28	29	30	31		23	24	25	26	27	28	29

Market Probability Chart above is a graphic representation of the S&P 500 Recent Market Probability Calendar on page 124.

◆ Harvesting made August the best stock market month 1901–1951 ◆ Now that about 2% farm, August is the worst Dow, S&P, and NASDAQ (2000 up 11.7%, 2001 down 10.9) month since 1987 ◆ Shortest bear in history (45 days) caused by turmoil in Russia, currency crisis and hedge fund debacle ended here in 1998, 1344.22-point drop in the Dow, second worst behind October 2008, off 15.1% ◆ Saddam Hussein triggered a 10.0% slide in 1990 ◆ Best Dow gains: 1982 (11.5%) and 1984 (9.8%) as bear markets ended ◆ Next-to-last day S&P up only five times last 20 years ◆ Midterm election year Augusts' rankings: #9 S&P, #8 Dow, and #11 NASDAQ.

August Vital Statistics

	DJIA	S&P 500	NASDAQ	Russell 1K	Russell 2K
Rank	10	11	11	10	9
Up	37	36	25	23	22
Down	30	31	21	15	16
Average % Change	−0.2%	−0.1%	0.1%	0.2%	0.2%
Midterm Year	−0.7%	−0.4%	−1.8%	−0.1%	−1.9%
Best & Worst August					
	% Change	% Change	% Change	% Change	% Change
Best	1982 11.5	1982 11.6	2000 11.7	1982 11.3	1984 11.5
Worst	1998 −15.1	1998 −14.6	1998 −19.9	1998 −15.1	1998 −19.5
Best & Worst August Weeks					
Best	08/20/82 10.3	08/20/82 8.8	08/03/84 7.4	08/20/82 8.5	08/03/84 7.0
Worst	08/23/74 −6.1	08/05/11 −7.2	08/28/98 −8.8	08/05/11 −7.7	08/05/11 −10.3
Best & Worst August Days					
Best	08/17/82 4.9	08/17/82 4.8	08/09/11 5.3	08/09/11 5.0	08/09/11 6.9
Worst	08/31/98 −6.4	08/31/98 −6.8	08/31/98 −8.6	08/08/11 −6.9	08/08/11 −8.9
First Trading Day of Expiration Week: 1980–2016					
Record (#Up – #Down)	24–13	27–10	28–9	27–10	24–13
Current streak	U3	U3	U7	U3	U4
Avg % Change	0.27	0.28	0.33	0.26	0.30
Options Expiration Day: 1980–2016					
Record (#Up – #Down)	18–19	19–18	20–17	20–17	21–16
Current streak	D4	D4	D2	D2	D4
Avg % Change	−0.15	−0.09	−0.16	−0.09	0.07
Options Expiration Week: 1980–2016					
Record (#Up – #Down)	18–19	21–16	21–16	21–16	23–14
Current streak	D2	D2	U1	D2	U1
Avg % Change	0.02	0.21	0.37	0.23	0.47
Week After Options Expiration: 1980–2016					
Record (#Up – #Down)	22–15	24–13	23–14	24–13	24–13
Current streak	D1	D1	D1	D1	U4
Avg % Change	0.28	0.32	0.53	0.32	0.10
First Trading Day Performance					
% of Time Up	46.3	49.3	52.2	44.7	47.4
Avg % Change	0.02	0.05	−0.06	0.10	−0.01
Last Trading Day Performance					
% of Time Up	59.7	62.7	65.2	57.9	68.4
Avg % Change	0.12	0.11	0.03	−0.05	0.04

Dow & S&P 1950–April 2017, NASDAQ 1971–April 2017, Russell 1K & 2K 1979–April 2017.

August's a good month to go on vacation;
Trading stocks will likely lead to frustration.

MONDAY

D 42.9
S 66.7
N 71.4

30

Every man is the architect of his own fortune.
— Appius Claudius

FOMC Meeting (2 Days)
Last Trading Day in July, NASDAQ Down 9 of Last 12

TUESDAY

D 33.3
S 47.6
N 42.9

31

The Stone Age didn't end for lack of stone, and the oil age will end long before the world runs out of oil.
— Sheik Ahmed Zaki Yamani (Saudi oil minister 1962–1986, b. 1930)

First Trading Day in August, Dow Down 14 of Last 20

WEDNESDAY

D 33.3
S 42.9
N 47.6

1

I don't believe in intuition. When you get sudden flashes of perception, it is just the brain working faster than usual.
— Katherine Anne Porter (American author, 1890–1980)

THURSDAY

D 57.1
S 52.4
N 42.9

2

Nothing is more uncertain than the favor of the crowd.
— Marcus Tullius Cicero (Great Roman Orator, Politician, 106–43 B.C.)

First Nine Trading Days of August Are Historically Weak (Pages 72 and 124)

FRIDAY

D 47.6
S 52.4
N 52.4

3

Every man with a new idea is a crank until the idea succeeds.
— Mark Twain (American novelist and satirist, pen name of Samuel Langhorne Clemens, 1835–1910)

SATURDAY

4

SUNDAY

5

TAKE ADVANTAGE OF DOWN FRIDAY/ DOWN MONDAY WARNING

Fridays and Mondays are the most important days of the week. Friday is the day for squaring positions—trimming longs or covering shorts before taking off for the weekend. Traders want to limit their exposure (particularly to stocks that are not acting well) since there could be unfavorable developments before trading resumes two or more days later.

Monday is important because the market then has the chance to reflect any weekend news, plus what traders think after digesting the previous week's action and the many Monday morning research and strategy comments.

For over 30 years, a down Friday followed by down Monday has frequently corresponded to important market inflection points that exhibit a clearly negative bias, often coinciding with market tops and, on a few climactic occasions, such as in October 2002 and March 2009, near major market bottoms.

One simple way to get a quick reading on which way the market may be heading is to keep track of the performance of the Dow Jones Industrial Average on Fridays and the following Mondays. Since 1995, there have been 227 occurrences of Down Friday/ Down Monday (DF/DM), with 69 falling in the bear market years of 2001, 2002, 2008, 2011, and 2015, producing an average decline of 12.1%.

To illustrate how Down Friday/Down Monday can telegraph market inflection points we created the chart below of the Dow Jones Industrials from November 2015 to June 2, 2017 with arrows pointing to occurrences of DF/DM. Use DF/DM as a warning to examine market conditions carefully. Unprecedented central bank liquidity has tempered subsequent pullbacks, but has not eliminated them.

DOWN FRIDAY/DOWN MONDAY

Year	Total Number Down Friday/ Down Monday	Subsequent Average % Dow Loss*	Average Number of Days it took
1995	8	−1.2%	18
1996	9	−3.0%	28
1997	6	−5.1%	45
1998	9	−6.4%	47
1999	9	−6.4%	39
2000	11	−6.6%	32
2001	13	−13.5%	53
2002	18	−11.9%	54
2003	9	−3.0%	17
2004	9	−3.7%	51
2005	10	−3.0%	37
2006	11	−2.0%	14
2007	8	−6.0%	33
2008	15	−17.0%	53
2009	10	−8.7%	15
2010	7	−3.1%	10
2011	11	−9.0%	53
2012	11	−4.0%	38
2013	7	−2.4%	15
2014	7	−2.5%	8
2015	12	−9.2%	44
2016	10	−2.7%	25
2017	7	−1.3%	14
Average	**10**	**−5.7%**	**32**

* Over next 3 months, ** Ending June 2, 2017

DOW JONES INDUSTRIALS (NOVEMBER 2015–JUNE 2, 2017)

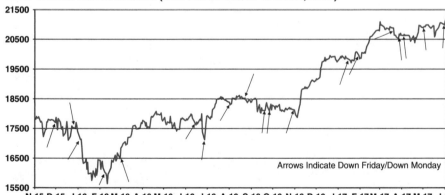

Arrows Indicate Down Friday/Down Monday

N-15 D-15 J-16 F-16 M-16 A-16 M-16 J-16 J-16 A-16 S-16 O-16 N-16 D-16 J-17 F-17 M-17 A-17 M-17 J-17

74

MONDAY

D 52.4
S 57.1
N 52.4

6

Learn from the mistakes of others; you can't live long enough to make them all yourself.
— Eleanor Roosevelt (First Lady, 1884–1962)

August Worst Dow and S&P Month 1988–2016
Harvesting Made August Best Dow Month 1901–1951

TUESDAY

D 52.4
S 42.9
N 38.1

7

Success is going from failure to failure without loss of enthusiasm.
— Winston Churchill (British statesman, 1874–1965)

WEDNESDAY

D 47.6
S 52.4
N 33.3

8

If you can buy all you want of a new issue, you do not want any; if you cannot obtain any, you want all you can buy.
— Rod Fadem (Stifel Nicolaus & Co., *Barron's* 1989)

Mid-August Stronger Than Beginning and End

THURSDAY

D 47.6
S 47.6
N 42.9

9

One determined person can make a significant difference; a small group of determined people can change the course of history.
— Sonia Johnson (Author, lecturer, b. 1936)

FRIDAY

D 42.9
S 47.6
N 47.6

10

In Wall Street, the man who does not change his mind will soon have no change to mind.
— William D. Gann (Trader, technical analyst, author, publisher, 1878–1955)

SATURDAY

11

SUNDAY

12

BEST INVESTMENT BOOK OF THE YEAR

Relationship Investing: Stock Market Therapy for Your Money
By Jeffrey S. Weiss

Our intention when selecting our list of the Year's Top Ten Investment Books (page 116) is to bring you new works that can immediately assist you in your investment and trading decisions and managing your portfolio. We seek out academic or industry books that explore new territory in behavioral finance, especially with respect to market seasonality, cycles, patterns and trends. We also have a soft spot for history pieces that reveal fresh analysis on the symbiotic relationship between the evolution of human behavior and financial markets. Finally, we hunt for groundbreaking insights from industry stalwarts.

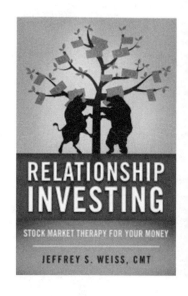

This year's list contains some very interesting and useful volumes we think you'll enjoy. But one book stood out, Jeffrey Weiss's *Relationship Investing: Stock Market Therapy for Your Money*. Our good friend and crack technical analyst Jeff Weiss shows you how to apply his key "relationship" rules to all your stock market investments. *Relationship Investing* is one of the most readable investment books we have come across in years. It's clear, concise, succinct and super manageable at 236 pages. For a seasoned veteran, Jeff really gets the need for brevity in this 24/7, information-overload, 140-character world we live in.

We've known Jeff for most of his thirty-five years in the business and his book is almost like being on the phone with him. It's fun, clever, witty; and it moves. Weiss studied under the tutelage of some top guys back in the day when he started, especially legendary technical analyst Newton Zinder at E. F. Hutton back in the 1980s. Technical analyst by trade, Weiss spares us the verbosity and jargon and instead presents, as he wrote in the message to us when he signed our review copy, his "*Investment rules for an investment lifetime.*"

Jeff's motivational brand of stock market analysis shines through in each and every chapter, which ends with a brief, crisp, summary that reinforces all the previous lessons along the way. It will pump you up like an energizing locker-room pep talk from your favorite coach. He really puts the driving forces of technical analysis into simple lay terms. As you move through the rules you develop a real feel for Jeff's discipline. It's a unique presentation of what breeds stock market mannerisms and movements—a nontechnical look at technical analysis, if you will.

Along the way you are taken on a joyride through Jeff's development and evolution into a top-notch technical analyst, with entertaining and compelling accounts of his mentors, real-world market experiences and lessons and, most importantly, how to implement these rules with examples. Jeff presents some of the most valuable investing rules and principles in an incredibly approachable plain-English style. Help yourself to a healthy helping of Jeff Weiss's homemade chicken soup for your portfolio!

Skyhorse Publishing, $21.99. **2018 Best Investment Book of the Year.**

Monday Before August Expiration, Dow Up 15 of Last 22, Average Gain 0.4%

MONDAY
D 42.9
S 38.1
N 47.6
13

History must repeat itself because we pay such little attention to it the first time.
— Blackie Sherrod (Sportswriter, 1919–2016)

TUESDAY
D 61.9
S 57.1
N 61.9
14

Small volume is usually accompanied by a fall in price; large volume by a rise in price.
— Charles C. Ying ("Stock Market Prices and Volumes of Sales," *Econometrica*, July 1966)

WEDNESDAY
D 52.4
S 66.7
N 71.4
15

A "tired businessman" is one whose business is usually not a successful one.
— Joseph R. Grundy (U.S. Senator Pennsylvania 1929–1930, businessman, 1863–1961)

THURSDAY
D 57.1
S 61.9
N 61.9
16

Among the simplest truths is that market risk tends to be unusually rewarding when market valuations are low and interest rates are falling.
— John P. Hussman, Ph.D. (Hussman Funds, 5/22/06)

August Expiration Day Less Bullish Lately, Dow Down 6 of Last 7 Down 531 Points (3.1%) in 2015

FRIDAY
D 71.4
S 71.4
N 61.9
17

No profession requires more hard work, intelligence, patience, and mental discipline than successful speculation.
— Robert Rhea (Economist, trader, *The Dow Theory*, 1887–1952)

SATURDAY
18

SUNDAY
19

AURA OF THE TRIPLE WITCH—4TH QUARTER MOST BULLISH: DOWN WEEKS TRIGGER MORE WEAKNESS WEEK AFTER

Standard options expire the third Friday of every month, but in March, June, September, and December, a powerful coven gathers. Since the S&P index futures began trading on April 21, 1982, stock options, index options, and index futures all expire at the same time four times each year—known as Triple Witching. Traders have long sought to understand and master the magic of this quarterly phenomenon.

The market for single-stock and ETF futures and weekly options continues to grow. However, their impact on the market has thus far been subdued. As their availability continues to expand, trading volumes and market influence are also likely to broaden. Until such time, we do not believe the term "quadruple witching" is applicable just yet.

We have analyzed what the market does prior to, during, and following Triple-Witching expirations in search of consistent trading patterns. Here are some of our findings of how the Dow Jones Industrials perform around Triple-Witching Week (TWW).

- TWWs have become more bullish since 1990, except in the second quarter.
- Following weeks have become more bearish. Since Q1 2000, only 24 of 68 were up, and 12 occurred in December, 7 in March, 4 in September, 1 in June.
- TWWs have tended to be down in flat periods and dramatically so during bear markets.
- DOWN WEEKS TEND TO FOLLOW DOWN TWWs is a most interesting pattern. Since 1991, of 34 down TWWs, 24 following weeks were also down. This is surprising, inasmuch as the previous decade had an exactly opposite pattern: There were 13 down TWWs then, but 12 up weeks followed them.
- TWWs in the second and third quarter (Worst Six Months May through October) are much weaker, and the weeks following, horrendous. But in the first and fourth quarter (Best Six Months period November through April), only the week after Q1 expiration is negative.

Throughout the *Almanac* you will also see notations on the performance of Mondays and Fridays of TWW, as we place considerable significance on the beginnings and ends of weeks (pages 68, 74, and 141–144).

TRIPLE-WITCHING WEEK AND WEEK AFTER DOW POINT CHANGES

	Expiration Week Q1	Week After	Expiration Week Q2	Week After	Expiration Week Q3	Week After	Expiration Week Q4	Week After
1991	−6.93	−89.36	−34.98	−58.81	33.54	−13.19	20.12	167.04
1992	40.48	−44.95	−69.01	−2.94	21.35	−76.73	9.19	12.97
1993	43.76	−31.60	−10.24	−3.88	−8.38	−70.14	10.90	6.15
1994	32.95	−120.92	3.33	−139.84	58.54	−101.60	116.08	26.24
1995	38.04	65.02	86.80	75.05	96.85	−33.42	19.87	−78.76
1996	114.52	51.67	55.78	−50.60	49.94	−15.54	179.53	76.51
1997	−130.67	−64.20	14.47	−108.79	174.30	4.91	−82.01	−76.98
1998	303.91	−110.35	−122.07	231.67	100.16	133.11	81.87	314.36
1999	27.20	−81.31	365.05	−303.00	−224.80	−524.30	32.73	148.33
2000	666.41	517.49	−164.76	−44.55	−293.65	−79.63	−277.95	200.60
2001	−821.21	−318.63	−353.36	−19.05	−1369.70	611.75	224.19	101.65
2002	34.74	−179.56	−220.42	−10.53	−326.67	−284.57	77.61	−207.54
2003	662.26	−376.20	83.63	−211.70	173.27	−331.74	236.06	46.45
2004	−53.48	26.37	6.31	−44.57	−28.61	−237.22	106.70	177.20
2005	−144.69	−186.80	110.44	−325.23	−36.62	−222.35	97.01	7.68
2006	203.31	0.32	122.63	−25.46	168.66	−52.67	138.03	−102.30
2007	−165.91	370.60	215.09	−279.22	377.67	75.44	110.80	−84.78
2008	410.23	−144.92	−464.66	−496.18	−33.55	−245.31	−50.57	−63.56
2009	54.40	497.80	−259.53	−101.34	214.79	−155.01	−142.61	191.21
2010	117.29	108.38	239.57	−306.83	145.08	252.41	81.59	81.58
2011	−185.88	362.07	52.45	−69.78	516.96	−737.61	−317.87	427.61
2012	310.60	−151.89	212.97	−126.39	−13.90	−142.34	55.83	−252.73
2013	117.04	−2.08	−270.78	110.20	75.03	−192.85	465.78	257.27
2014	237.10	20.29	171.34	−95.24	292.23	−166.59	523.97	248.91
2015	378.34	−414.99	117.11	−69.27	−48.51	−69.91	−136.66	423.62
2016	388.99	−86.57	−190.18	−274.41	38.35	137.65	86.56	90.40
2017	11.64	−317.90						
Up	**20**	**10**	**15**	**3**	**16**	**6**	**20**	**19**
Down	**7**	**17**	**11**	**23**	**10**	**20**	**6**	**7**

78

AUGUST 2018

Government is like fire—useful when used legitimately, but dangerous when not.
— David Brooks (*NY Times* columnist, 10/5/07)

TUESDAY
D 33.3
S 38.1
N 33.3
21

You have powers you never dreamed of. You can do things you never thought you could do. There are no limitations in what you can do except the limitations in your own mind.
— Darwin P. Kingsley (President New York Life, 1857–1932)

Week After August Expiration Mixed, Dow Down 7 of Last 12

WEDNESDAY
D 57.1
S 61.9
N 76.2
22

The years teach much which the days never know.
— Ralph Waldo Emerson (American author, poet and philosopher, *Self-Reliance*, 1803–1882)

THURSDAY
D 52.4
S 52.4
N 52.4
23

There is no great mystery to satisfying your customers. Build them a quality product and treat them with respect. It's that simple.
— Lee Iacocca (American industrialist, Former Chrysler CEO, b. 1924)

FRIDAY
D 52.4
S 52.4
N 47.6
24

Buy a stock the way you would buy a house. Understand and like it such that you'd be content to own it in the absence of any market.
— Warren Buffett (CEO Berkshire Hathaway, investor and philanthropist, b. 1930)

SATURDAY
25

September Almanac Investor Sector Seasonalities: See Pages 92, 94 and 96

SUNDAY
26

SEPTEMBER ALMANAC

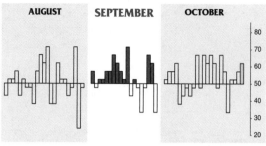

SEPTEMBER							OCTOBER						
S	M	T	W	T	F	S	S	M	T	W	T	F	S
30						1		1	2	3	4	5	6
2	3	4	5	6	7	8	7	8	9	10	11	12	13
9	10	11	12	13	14	15	14	15	16	17	18	19	20
16	17	18	19	20	21	22	21	22	23	24	25	26	27
23	24	25	26	27	28	29	28	29	30	31			

Market Probability Chart above is a graphic representation of the S&P 500 Recent Market Probability Calendar on page 124.

◆ Start of business year, end of vacations, and back to school made September a leading barometer month in first 60 years of 20th century; now portfolio managers back after Labor Day tend to clean house ◆ Biggest % loser on the S&P, Dow, and NASDAQ since 1950 (pages 48 & 56) ◆ Streak of four great Dow Septembers averaging 4.2% gains ended in 1999 with six losers in a row averaging –5.9% (see page 152), up three straight 2005–2007, down 6% in 2008 and 2011 ◆ Day after Labor Day Dow up 16 of last 23 ◆ S&P opened strong 13 of last 22 years but tends to close weak due to end-of-quarter mutual fund portfolio restructuring, last trading day: S&P down 16 of past 24 ◆ September Triple-Witching Week can be dangerous, week after is pitiful (see page 78).

September Vital Statistics

	DJIA	S&P 500	NASDAQ	Russell 1K	Russell 2K
Rank	12	12	12	12	12
Up	26	29	25	18	21
Down	41	37	21	20	17
Average % Change	–0.8%	–0.5%	–0.5%	–0.6%	–0.5%
Midterm Year	–1.0%	–0.4%	–0.8%	–1.1%	–0.6%
Best & Worst September					
	% Change	% Change	% Change	% Change	% Change
Best	2010　7.7	2010　8.8	1998　13.0	2010　9.0	2010　12.3
Worst	2002　–12.4	1974　–11.9	2001　–17.0	2002　–10.9	2001　–13.6
Best & Worst September Weeks					
Best	09/28/01　7.4	09/28/01　7.8	09/16/11　6.3	09/28/01　7.6	09/28/01　6.9
Worst	09/21/01　–14.3	09/21/01　–11.6	09/21/01　–16.1	09/21/01　–11.7	09/21/01　–14.0
Best & Worst September Days					
Best	09/08/98　5.0	09/30/08　5.4	09/08/98　6.0	09/30/08　5.3	09/18/08　7.0
Worst	09/17/01　–7.1	09/29/08　–8.8	09/29/08　–9.1	09/29/08　–8.7	09/29/08　–6.7
First Trading Day of Expiration Week: 1980–2016					
Record (#Up – #Down)	24–13	20–17	14–23	20–17	15–22
Current streak	U1	U1	U1	U1	U1
Avg % Change	–0.05	–0.09	–0.29	–0.11	–0.21
Options Expiration Day: 1980–2016					
Record (#Up – #Down)	18–19	19–18	23–14	20–17	23–14
Current streak	D2	D5	D4	D4	D4
Avg % Change	–0.05	0.08	0.11	0.06	0.11
Options Expiration Week: 1980–2016					
Record (#Up – #Down)	20–17	22–15	22–15	22–15	20–17
Current streak	U1	U1	U4	U1	U2
Avg % Change	–0.21	0.11	0.11	0.03	0.13
Week After Options Expiration: 1980–2016					
Record (#Up – #Down)	13–24	11–26	16–21	11–25	13–24
Current streak	U1	U1	U1	U1	U1
Avg % Change	–0.70	–0.75	–0.87	–0.76	–1.31
First Trading Day Performance					
% of Time Up	59.7	59.7	56.5	52.6	50.0
Avg % Change	–0.001	–0.02	–0.04	–0.08	–0.01
Last Trading Day Performance					
% of Time Up	38.8	41.8	47.8	47.4	60.5
Avg % Change	–0.11	–0.05	0.01	0.05	0.27

Dow & S&P 1950–April 2017, NASDAQ 1971–April 2017, Russell 1K & 2K 1979–April 2017

September is when leaves and stocks tend to fall;
On Wall Street it's the worst month of all.

AUGUST/SEPTEMBER 2018

A man isn't a man until he has to meet a payroll.
— Ivan Shaffer (*The Stock Promotion Game*)

TUESDAY

D 42.9
S 47.6
N 47.6

28

Some people are so boring they make you waste an entire day in five minutes.
— Jules Renard (French author, 1864–1910)

WEDNESDAY

D 71.4
S 71.4
N 76.2

29

I write an email about every week to ten days…and within about 24 hours everyone will have read it. The amazing thing is how I can change the direction of the entire company within 24 hours. Ten years ago I couldn't do that.
— Michael Marks (CEO Flextronics, *Forbes*, 7/7/03)

August's Next-to-Last Trading Day, S&P Down 16 of Last 21 Years

THURSDAY

D 23.8
S 23.8
N 47.6

30

Moses Shapiro (of General Instrument) told me, "Son, this is Talmudic wisdom. Always ask the question 'If not?' Few people have good strategies for when their assumptions are wrong." That's the best business advice I ever got.
— John Malone (CEO of cable giant TCI, *Fortune*, 2/16/98)

FRIDAY

D 47.6
S 47.6
N 52.4

31

Always grab the reader by the throat in the first paragraph, sink your thumbs into his windpipe in the second, and hold him against the wall until the tag line.
— Paul O'Neill (Marketer, quoted in *Writing Changes Everything*)

SATURDAY

1

SUNDAY

2

SUN MAY BE SETTING ON SUPER-8 DAYS OF THE MONTH VS. 13 REMAINING DAYS COMBINED

For many years, the last day plus the first four days were the best days of the month. The market currently exhibits greater bullish bias from the last three trading days of the previous month through the first two days of the current month, and now shows significant bullishness during the middle three trading days, 9 to 11, due to 401(k) cash inflows (see pages 145 and 146). This pattern was not as pronounced during the boom years of the 1990s, with market strength all month long. Since the 2009 market bottom, the Super-8 advantage appears to be fading. In times of weakness, such as from mid-May 2015 to January 2016, strength was evident, but the Super-8 are lagging again in 2017.

SUPER-8 DAYS* DOW % CHANGES VS. REST OF MONTH

	Super 8 Days	Rest of Month		Super 8 Days	Rest of Month		Super 8 Days	Rest of Month
	2009			**2010**			**2011**	
Jan	3.16%	−6.92%		0.66%	−3.92%		1.70%	1.80%
Feb	−6.05	−4.39		3.31	−2.38		0.45	0.57
Mar	−4.37	12.84		1.91	3.51		−1.40	2.21
Apr	1.52	−0.24		1.13	0.18		2.30	0.95
May	2.64	2.98		−3.08	−5.75		1.03	−2.61
Jun	1.71	−1.64		4.33	−3.26		−1.64	−1.19
Jul	2.30	5.03		−7.07	11.34		3.52	0.31
Aug	0.04	4.91		0.20	−5.49		2.04	−11.39
Sep	−0.81	2.21		3.83	4.22		3.24	−3.96
Oct	−0.05	2.40		−0.18	3.47		−4.47	10.71
Nov	0.00	5.57		−1.20	1.37		1.42	−6.66
Dec	0.62	0.46		1.98	1.45		5.74	3.58
Totals	**0.71%**	**23.21%**		**5.82%**	**4.74%**		**13.93%**	**−5.68%**
Average	**0.06%**	**1.93%**		**0.49%**	**0.40%**		**1.16%**	**−0.47%**
	2012			**2013**			**2014**	
Jan	1.90%	1.66%		2.28%	3.47%		0.92%	−4.26%
Feb	−0.39	2.33		−0.27	−0.41		−1.99	3.66
Mar	2.22	−0.55		2.93	1.82		0.77	−0.21
Apr	1.00	−1.80		0.11	1.65		2.44	−1.82
May	−0.38	−4.52		1.93	2.81		−0.56	2.50
Jun	−1.30	2.08		−0.27	−3.96		−0.09	1.24
Jul	5.11	−2.22		1.11	4.23		1.79	−1.10
Aug	−0.40	2.09		−1.35	−3.75		−1.81	2.61
Sep	−0.24	2.98		2.55	0.83		0.32	−1.26
Oct	0.77	−3.60		−0.64	2.60		−3.28	3.82
Nov	−2.01	0.55		1.79	1.41		2.42	2.28
Dec	0.49	1.35		−0.72	3.30		−1.66	3.14
Totals	**6.77%**	**0.35%**		**9.45%**	**14.00%**		**−0.73%**	**10.60%**
Average	**0.56%**	**0.03%**		**0.79%**	**1.17%**		**−0.06%**	**0.88%**
	2015			**2016**			**2017**	
Jan	−3.64%	−0.07%		−2.95%	−4.93%		−0.44%	1.24%
Feb	2.65	2.00		1.69	0.30		0.62	2.90
Mar	1.91	−4.78		4.02	2.21		1.16	−1.66
Apr	1.20	0.83		2.14	0.43		−0.39	1.83
May	1.31	−1.28		−1.33	0.57		−0.03	0.45
Jun	−1.32	0.49		−1.33	−2.68			
Jul	−0.11	−1.31		4.97	2.66			
Aug	0.37	−8.02		−0.11	−0.30			
Sep	2.27	−2.04		0.84	−1.72			
Oct	1.03	6.57		−0.65	0.49			
Nov	0.68	0.68		−0.71	5.93			
Dec	−0.74	−0.86		0.38	3.73			
Totals	**5.61%**	**−7.79%**		**6.96%**	**6.69%**		**0.92%**	**4.76%**
Average	**0.47%**	**−0.65%**		**0.58%**	**0.56%**		**0.18%**	**0.95%**

		Super-8 Days		Rest of Month (13 days)	
101	Net % Changes		49.44%	Net % Changes	50.88%
Month	Average Period		0.49%	Average Period	0.50%
Totals	Average Day		0.06%	Average Day	0.04%

* Super-8 Days = Last 3 + First 2 + Middle 3

SEPTEMBER 2018

Labor Day *(Market Closed)*

MONDAY

3

Choose a job you love, and you will never have to work a day in your life.
— Confucius (Chinese philosopher, 551–478 B.C.)

First Trading Day in September, S&P Up 13 of Last 22, But Down 7 of Last 9
Day After Labor Day, Dow Up 16 of Last 23, 1998 Up 5.0%, 2015 Up 2.4%

TUESDAY

D 57.1
S 57.1
N 66.7

4

The principles of successful stock speculation are based on the supposition that people will continue in the future to make the mistakes that they have made in the past.
— Thomas F. Woodlock (*Wall Street Journal* editor & columnist, quoted in *Reminiscences of a Stock Operator*, 1866–1945)

WEDNESDAY

D 71.4
S 47.6
N 52.4

5

The worse a situation becomes the less it takes to turn it around, the bigger the upside.
— George Soros (Financier, philanthropist, political activist, author and philosopher, b. 1930)

THURSDAY

D 52.4
S 52.4
N 47.6

6

Nothing will improve a person's hearing more than sincere praise.
— Harvey Mackay (*Pushing the Envelope*, 1999)

FRIDAY

D 42.9
S 52.4
N 57.1

7

We go to the movies to be entertained, not see rape, ransacking, pillage and looting. We can get all that in the stock market.
— Kennedy Gammage (*The Richland Report*)

SATURDAY

8

SUNDAY

9

A CORRECTION FOR ALL SEASONS

While there's a rally for every season (page 70), almost always there's a decline or correction, too. Fortunately, corrections tend to be smaller than rallies, and that's what gives the stock market its long-term upward bias. In each season the average bounce outdoes the average setback. On average, the net gain between the rally and the correction is smallest in summer and fall.

The summer setback tends to be slightly outdone by the average correction in the fall. Tax selling and portfolio cleaning are the usual explanations—individuals sell to register a tax loss, and institutions like to get rid of their losers before preparing year-end statements. The October jinx also plays a major part. Since 1964, there have been 18 fall declines of over 10%, and in 10 of them (1966, 1974, 1978, 1979, 1987, 1990, 1997, 2000, 2002, and 2008) much damage was done in October, where so many bear markets end. Recent October lows were also seen in 1998, 1999, 2004, 2005, and 2011. Most often, it has paid to buy after fourth quarter or late third quarter "waterfall declines" for a rally that may continue into January or even beyond. Anticipation of war in Iraq put the market down in 2003 Q1. Quick success rallied stocks through Q3. Financial crisis affected the pattern in 2008–2009, producing the worst winter decline since 1932. Easy monetary policy and strong corporate earnings spared Q1 2011 and 2012 from a seasonal slump.

SEASONAL CORRECTIONS IN DOW JONES INDUSTRIALS

	WINTER SLUMP Nov/Dec High to Q1 Low	SPRING SLUMP Feb/Mar High to Q2 Low	SUMMER SLUMP May/Jun High to Q3 Low	FALL SLUMP Aug/Sep High to Q4 Low
1964	−0.1%	−2.4%	−1.0%	−2.1%
1965	−2.5	−7.3	−8.3	−0.9
1966	−6.0	−13.2	−17.7	−12.7
1967	−4.2	−3.9	−5.5	−9.9
1968	−8.8	−0.3	−5.5	+0.4
1969	−8.7	−8.7	−17.2	−8.1
1970	−13.8	−20.2	−8.8	−2.5
1971	−1.4	−4.8	−10.7	−13.4
1972	−0.5	−2.6	−6.3	−5.3
1973	−11.0	−12.8	−10.9	−17.3
1974	−15.3	−10.8	−29.8	−27.6
1975	−6.3	−5.5	−9.9	−6.7
1976	−0.2	−5.1	−4.7	−8.9
1977	−8.5	−7.2	−11.5	−10.2
1978	−12.3	−4.0	−7.0	−13.5
1979	−2.5	−5.8	−3.7	−10.9
1980	−10.0	−16.0	−1.7	−6.8
1981	−6.9	−5.1	−18.6	−12.9
1982	−10.9	−7.5	−10.6	−3.3
1983	−4.1	−2.8	−6.8	−3.6
1984	−11.9	−10.5	−8.4	−6.2
1985	−4.8	−4.4	−2.8	−2.3
1986	−3.3	−4.7	−7.3	−7.6
1987	−1.4	−6.6	−1.7	−36.1
1988	−6.7	−7.0	−7.6	−4.5
1989	−1.7	−2.4	−3.1	−6.6
1990	−7.9	−4.0	−17.3	−18.4
1991	−6.3	−3.6	−4.5	−6.3
1992	+0.1	−3.3	−5.4	−7.6
1993	−2.7	−3.1	−3.0	−2.0
1994	−4.4	−9.6	−4.4	−7.1
1995	−0.8	−0.1	−0.2	−2.0
1996	−3.5	−4.6	−7.5	+0.2
1997	−1.8	−9.8	−2.2	−13.3
1998	−7.0	−3.1	−18.2	−13.1
1999	−2.7	−1.7	−8.0	−11.5
2000	−14.8	−7.4	−4.1	−11.8
2001	−14.5	−13.6	−27.4	−16.2
2002	−5.1	−14.2	−26.7	−19.5
2003	−15.8	−5.3	−3.1	−2.1
2004	−3.9	−7.7	−6.3	−5.7
2005	−4.5	−8.5	−3.3	−4.5
2006	−2.4	−5.4	−7.8	−0.4
2007	−3.7	−3.2	−6.1	−8.4
2008	−14.5	−11.0	−20.6	−35.9
2009	−32.0	−6.3	−7.4	−3.5
2010	−6.1	−10.4	−13.1	−1.0
2011	+0.2	−4.0	−16.3	−12.2
2012	+0.5	−8.7	−5.3	−7.8
2013	−0.2	−0.3	−4.1	−5.7
2014	−7.3	−2.6	−3.4	−6.7
2015	−4.9	−3.8	−14.4	−7.6
2016	−12.6	−3.3	−0.9	−4.0
2017	−1.2	−3.4*		
Totals	−343.6%	−343.6%	−468.1%	−473.5%
Average	−6.4%	−6.4%	−8.8%	−8.9%

* As of 6/2/2017

Rosh Hashanah

Monday Before September Triple Witching, Russell 2000 Down 11 of Last 18

MONDAY
10

D 61.9
S 57.1
N 61.9

Life is what happens, while you're busy making other plans.
— John Lennon (Beatle, 1940–1980)

2001 4-Day Closing, Longest Since 9-Day Banking
Moratorium in March 1933

TUESDAY
11

D 47.6
S 57.1
N 57.1

"In Memory"

In the business world, everyone is paid in two coins: cash and experience. Take the experience first;
the cash will come later.
—Harold S. Geneen (British-American businessman, CEO ITT Corp, 1910–1977)

Expiration Week 2001, Dow Lost 1370 Points (14.3%)
2nd Worst Weekly Point Loss Ever, 5th Worst Week Overall

WEDNESDAY
12

D 66.7
S 66.7
N 61.9

If the market prefers a system that looks inefficient that's a good sign that its more efficient than it looks.
— Matt Levine (Bloomberg View columnist, former investment banker, lawyer & high school Latin teacher)

THURSDAY
13

D 57.1
S 61.9
N 66.7

It is tact that is golden, not silence.
— Samuel Butler (English writer, 1600–1680)

September Triple Witching, Dow Up 10 of Last 15

FRIDAY
14

D 47.6
S 57.1
N 81.0

It has been said that politics is the second oldest profession. I have learned that it bears a striking resemblance to the first.
— Ronald Reagan (40th U.S. President, 1911–2004)

SATURDAY
15

SUNDAY
16

FIRST-TRADING-DAY-OF-THE-MONTH PHENOMENON

While the Dow Jones Industrial Average has gained 13583.87 points between September 2, 1997 (7622.42) and June 2, 2017 (21206.29), it is incredible that 6351.98 points were gained on the first trading days of these 238 months. The remaining 4733 trading days combined gained 7231.89 points during the period. This averages out to gains of 26.69 points on first days, in contrast to just 1.53 points on all others.

Note September 1997 through October 2000 racked up a total gain of 2632.39 Dow points on the first trading days of these 38 months (winners except for seven occasions). But between November 2000 and September 2002, when the 2000–2002 bear markets did the bulk of their damage, frightened investors switched from pouring money into the market on that day to pulling it out, fourteen months out of twenty-three, netting a 404.80 Dow point loss. The 2007–2009 bear market lopped off 964.14 Dow points on first days in 17 months November 2007–March 2009. First days had their worst year in 2014, declining eight times for a total loss of 820.86 Dow points.

First days of August have performed worst, declining 13 times in the last 19 years. May's first trading day is best. In rising market trends, first days tend to perform much better, as institutions are likely anticipating strong performance at each month's outset. S&P 500 first days differ slightly from Dow's pattern with June and October as losers. NASDAQ first days are not as strong, with weakness in April, August, and October.

DOW POINTS GAINED FIRST DAY OF MONTH
SEPTEMBER 1997–JUNE 2, 2017

	Jan	Feb	Mar	Apr	May	Jun	Jul	Aug	Sep	Oct	Nov	Dec	Totals
1997									257.36	70.24	232.31	189.98	749.89
1998	56.79	201.28	4.73	68.51	83.70	22.42	96.65	−96.55	288.36	−210.09	114.05	16.99	646.84
1999	2.84	−13.13	18.20	46.35	225.65	36.52	95.62	−9.19	108.60	−63.95	−81.35	120.58	486.74
2000	−139.61	100.52	9.62	300.01	77.87	129.87	112.78	84.97	23.68	49.21	−71.67	−40.95	636.30
2001	−140.70	96.27	−45.14	−100.85	163.37	78.47	91.32	−12.80	47.74	−10.73	188.76	−87.60	268.11
2002	51.90	−12.74	262.73	−41.24	113.41	−215.46	−133.47	−229.97	−355.45	346.86	120.61	−33.52	−126.34
2003	265.89	56.01	−53.22	77.73	−25.84	47.55	55.51	−79.83	107.45	194.14	57.34	116.59	819.22
2004	−44.07	11.11	94.22	15.63	88.43	14.20	−101.32	39.45	−5.46	112.38	26.92	162.20	413.69
2005	−53.58	62.00	63.77	−99.46	59.19	82.39	28.47	−17.76	−21.97	−33.22	−33.30	106.70	143.23
2006	129.91	89.09	60.12	35.62	−23.85	91.97	77.80	−59.95	83.00	−8.72	−49.71	−27.80	397.48
2007	11.37	51.99	−34.29	27.95	73.23	40.47	126.81	150.38	91.12	191.92	−362.14	−57.15	311.66
2008	−220.86	92.83	−7.49	391.47	189.87	−134.50	32.25	−51.70	−26.63	−19.59	−5.18	−679.95	−439.40
2009	258.30	−64.03	−299.64	152.68	44.29	221.11	57.06	114.95	−185.68	−203.00	76.71	126.74	299.49
2010	155.91	118.20	78.53	70.44	143.22	−112.61	−41.49	208.44	254.75	41.63	6.13	249.76	1172.91
2011	93.24	148.23	−168.32	56.99	−3.18	−279.65	168.43	−10.75	−119.96	−258.08	−297.05	−25.65	−695.75
2012	179.82	83.55	28.23	52.45	65.69	−274.88	−8.70	−37.62	−54.90	77.98	136.16	−59.98	187.80
2013	308.41	149.21	35.17	−5.69	−138.85	138.46	65.36	128.48	23.65	62.03	69.80	−77.64	758.39
2014	−135.31	−326.05	−153.68	74.95	−21.97	26.46	129.47	−69.93	−30.89	−238.19	−24.28	−51.44	−820.86
2015	9.92	196.09	155.93	−77.94	185.54	29.69	138.40	−91.66	−469.68	−11.99	165.22	168.43	395.95
2016	−276.09	−17.12	348.58	107.66	117.52	2.47	19.38	−27.73	18.42	−54.30	−105.32	68.35	201.82
2017	119.16	26.85	303.31	−13.01	−27.05	135.53							544.79
Totals	633.24	1050.16	701.36	1140.25	1388.24	80.48	1010.33	−68.77	33.51	34.53	164.01	184.64	6351.98

SUMMARY FIRST DAYS VS. OTHER DAYS OF MONTH

	# of Days	Total Points Gained	Average Daily Point Gain
First days	238	6351.98	26.69
Other days	4733	7231.89	1.53

SEPTEMBER 2018

D 57.1
S 52.4
N 38.1

17

The commodity futures game is a money game—not a game involving the supply-demand of the actual commodity as commonly depicted.
— R. Earl Hadady (*Bullish Consensus, Contrary Opinion*)

Week After Sepetmber Triple Witching Dow Down 21 of Last 27
Average Loss Since 1990, 1.1%

TUESDAY

D 71.4
S 71.4
N 76.2

18

If there's anything duller than being on a board in Corporate America, I haven't found it.
— H. Ross Perot (American businessman, *N Y Times*, 10/28/92, 2-time presidential candidate 1992 & 1996, b. 1930)

Yom Kippur

WEDNESDAY

D 38.1
S 42.9
N 52.4

19

Life is an illusion. You are what you think you are.
— Yale Hirsch (Creator of *Stock Trader's Almanac*, b. 1923)

THURSDAY

D 57.1
S 52.4
N 61.9

20

Excellent firms don't believe in excellence—only in constant improvement and constant change.
— Tom Peters (*In Search Of Excellence*, b. 1942)

End of September Prone to Weakness
From End-of-Q3 Institutional Portfolio Restructuring

FRIDAY

D 57.1
S 47.6
N 52.4

21

When new money is created on a grand scale, it must go somewhere and have some major consequences. One of these will be greatly increased volatility and instability in the economy and financial system.
— J. Anthony Boeckh, Ph.D (Chairman Bank Credit Analyst 1968–2002, *The Great Reflation, Boeckh Investment Letter*)

SATURDAY

22

SUNDAY

23

MARKET BEHAVIOR THREE DAYS BEFORE AND THREE DAYS AFTER HOLIDAYS

The *Stock Trader's Almanac* has tracked holiday seasonality annually since the first edition in 1968. Stocks used to rise on the day before holidays and sell off the day after, but nowadays, each holiday moves to its own rhythm. Eight holidays are separated into seven groups. Average percentage changes for the Dow, S&P 500, NASDAQ, and Russell 2000 are shown.

The Dow and S&P consist of blue chips and the largest cap stocks, whereas NASDAQ and the Russell 2000 would be more representative of smaller-cap stocks. This is evident on the last day of the year with NASDAQ and the Russell 2000 having a field day, while their larger brethren in the Dow and S&P are showing losses on average.

Thanks to the Santa Claus Rally, the three days before and after New Year's Day and Christmas are best. NASDAQ and the Russell 2000 average gains of 1.3% to 1.1% over the six-day spans. However, trading around the first day of the year has been mixed recently. Traders have been selling more the first trading day of the year, pushing gains and losses into the New Year.

Bullishness before Labor Day and after Memorial Day is affected by strength the first day of September and June. The second worst day after a holiday is the day after Easter. Surprisingly, the following day is one of the best second days after a holiday, right up there with the second day after New Year's Day.

Presidents' Day is the least bullish of all the holidays, bearish the day before and three days after. NASDAQ has dropped 19 of the last 28 days before Presidents' Day (Dow, 16 of 28; S&P, 18 of 28; Russell 2000, 14 of 28).

HOLIDAYS: 3 DAYS BEFORE, 3 DAYS AFTER (Average % change 1980–May 2017)

	−3	−2	−1	Mixed	+1	+2	+3
S&P 500	0.03	0.19	−0.13	**New Year's**	0.20	0.29	−0.01
DJIA	−0.002	0.15	−0.20	**Day**	0.30	0.28	0.09
NASDAQ	0.09	0.23	0.14	*1/1/18*	0.18	0.56	0.12
Russell 2K	0.07	0.35	0.39		0.02	0.23	0.02
S&P 500	0.33	0.02	−0.14	**Negative Before & After**	−0.14	−0.04	−0.13
DJIA	0.30	0.004	−0.07	**Presidents'**	−0.07	−0.07	−0.14
NASDAQ	0.53	0.28	−0.28	**Day**	−0.44	−0.02	−0.09
Russell 2K	0.40	0.17	−0.04	*2/19/18*	−0.29	−0.16	−0.07
S&P 500	0.17	−0.06	0.35	**Positive Before &**	−0.16	0.30	0.10
DJIA	0.14	−0.09	0.27	**Negative After**	−0.09	0.29	0.09
NASDAQ	0.38	0.19	0.45	**Good Friday**	−0.28	0.35	0.20
Russell 2K	0.21	0.02	0.48	*3/30/18*	−0.27	0.25	0.13
S&P 500	0.06	0.07	0.01	**Positive After**	0.30	0.11	0.26
DJIA	0.05	0.02	−0.05	**Memorial**	0.34	0.10	0.17
NASDAQ	0.11	0.25	0.05	**Day**	0.25	−0.01	0.48
Russell 2K	−0.03	0.30	0.11	*5/28/18*	0.25	0.05	0.45
S&P 500	0.19	0.13	0.07	**Negative After**	−0.16	0.06	0.03
DJIA	0.15	0.12	0.07	**Independence**	−0.09	0.09	0.01
NASDAQ	0.34	0.15	0.08	**Day**	−0.18	−0.09	0.18
Russell 2K	0.34	0.05	−0.02	*7/4/18*	−0.26	−0.02	0.01
S&P 500	0.20	−0.20	0.14	**Positive Before & After**	0.12	0.06	−0.07
DJIA	0.18	−0.25	0.13	**Labor**	0.14	0.11	−0.16
NASDAQ	0.41	−0.001	0.15	**Day**	0.06	−0.06	0.08
Russell 2K	0.51	0.03	0.12	*9/3/18*	0.12	0.12	0.04
S&P 500	0.15	0.01	0.25	**Thanksgiving**	0.19	−0.44	0.31
DJIA	0.14	0.03	0.26	*11/22/18*	0.16	−0.37	0.32
NASDAQ	0.11	−0.19	0.40		0.45	−0.44	0.14
Russell 2K	0.17	−0.05	0.39		0.30	−0.53	0.27
S&P 500	0.19	0.21	0.21	**Christmas**	0.14	0.00000	0.25
DJIA	0.27	0.24	0.26	*12/25/18*	0.18	0.01	0.22
NASDAQ	−0.05	0.41	0.40		0.12	0.05	0.30
Russell 2K	0.24	0.36	0.36		0.19	0.05	0.42

MONDAY

D 33.3
S 33.3
N 42.9

24

People's spending habits depend more on how wealthy they feel than with the actual amount of their current income.
— A.C. Pigou (English economist, *The Theory of Unemployment*, 1877–1959)

FOMC Meeting (2 Days)

TUESDAY

D 57.1
S 47.6
N 47.6

25

As for it being different this time, it is different every time. The question is in what way, and to what extent.
— Tom McClellan (*The McClellan Market Report*)

Start Looking for MACD BUY Signals on October 1 (Pages 52, 58 and 60)
Almanac Investor Subscribers Emailed When It Triggers (See Insert)

WEDNESDAY

D 61.9
S 66.7
N 47.6

26

All there is to investing is picking good stocks at good times and staying with them as long as they remain good companies.
— Warren Buffett (CEO Berkshire Hathaway, investor and philanthropist, b. 1930)

THURSDAY

D 57.1
S 61.9
N 42.9

27

Lack of money is the root of all evil.
— George Bernard Shaw (Irish dramatist, 1856–1950)

Last Day of Q3, Dow Down 14 of Last 20, Massive 4.7% Rally in 2008

FRIDAY

D 33.3
S 33.3
N 33.3

28

The task of leadership is not to put greatness into humanity, but to elicit it, for the greatness is already there.
— Sir John Buchan (Scottish author, Governor General of Canada 1935–1940, 1875–1940)

SATURDAY

29

October Almanac Investor Sector Seasonalities: See Pages 92, 94 and 96

SUNDAY

30

OCTOBER ALMANAC

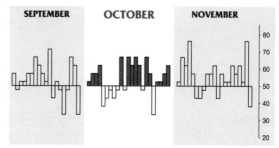

OCTOBER							NOVEMBER					
S	M	T	W	T	F	S	S	M	T	W	T	F	S
	1	2	3	4	5	6				1	2	3
7	8	9	10	11	12	13	4	5	6	7	8	9	10
14	15	16	17	18	19	20	11	12	13	14	15	16	17
21	22	23	24	25	26	27	18	19	20	21	22	23	24
28	29	30	31				25	26	27	28	29	30

Market Probability Chart above is a graphic representation of the S&P 500 Recent Market Probability Calendar on page 124.

◆ Known as the jinx month because of crashes in 1929 and 1987, the 554-point drop on October 27, 1997, back-to-back massacres in 1978 and 1979, Friday the 13th in 1989, and the meltdown in 2008 ◆ Yet October is a "bear killer" and turned the tide in 12 post–WWII bear markets: 1946, 1957, 1960, 1962, 1966, 1974, 1987, 1990, 1998, 2001, 2002, and 2011 ◆ First October Dow top in 2007, 20-year 1987 Crash anniversary –2.6% ◆ Worst six months of the year ends with October (page 50) ◆ No longer worst month (pages 48 & 56) ◆ Best Dow, S&P, and NASDAQ month from 1993 to 2007 ◆ Midterm election year Octobers since 1950: #1 Dow (3.1%), #1 S&P (3.3%) and #6 NASDAQ (4.2%) ◆ October is a great time to buy ◆ Big October gains five years 1999–2003 after atrocious Septembers ◆ Can get into Best Six Months earlier using MACD (page 52) ◆ October 2011, second month to gain 1000 Dow points, and again in 2015.

October Vital Statistics

	DJIA		S&P 500		NASDAQ		Russell 1K		Russell 2K	
Rank	7		7		8		5		10	
Up	40		40		25		24		21	
Down	27		27		21		14		17	
Average % Change	0.6%		0.9%		0.7%		1.0%		–0.3%	
Midterm Year	3.1%		3.3%		4.2%		4.7%		3.9%	
Best & Worst October										
	% Change		% Change		% Change		% Change		% Change	
Best	1982	10.7	1974	16.3	1974	17.2	1982	11.3	2011	15.0
Worst	1987	–23.2	1987	–21.8	1987	–27.2	1987	–21.9	1987	–30.8
Best & Worst October Weeks										
Best	10/11/74	12.6	10/11/74	14.1	10/31/08	10.9	10/31/08	10.8	10/31/08	14.1
Worst	10/10/08	–18.2	10/10/08	–18.2	10/23/87	–19.2	10/10/08	–18.2	10/23/87	–20.4
Best & Worst October Days										
Best	10/13/08	11.1	10/13/08	11.6	10/13/08	11.8	10/13/08	11.7	10/13/08	9.3
Worst	10/19/87	–22.6	10/19/87	–20.5	10/19/87	–11.4	10/19/87	–19.0	10/19/87	–12.5
First Trading Day of Expiration Week: 1980–2016										
Record (#Up – #Down)	29–8		27–10		25–12		28–9		26–11	
Current streak	D1		D1		D1		D1		D1	
Avg % Change	0.71		0.67		0.53		0.65		0.39	
Options Expiration Day: 1980–2016										
Record (#Up – #Down)	17–20		19–18		21–16		19–18		15–22	
Current streak	D1		D1		U4		D1		D3	
Avg % Change	–0.15		–0.21		–0.10		–0.20		–0.18	
Options Expiration Week: 1980–2016										
Record (#Up – #Down)	26–11		26–11		21–16		26–11		22–15	
Current streak	U2		U2		U2		U2		U1	
Avg % Change	0.59		0.65		0.71		0.65		0.41	
Week After Options Expiration: 1980–2016										
Record (#Up – #Down)	18–19		16–21		19–18		16–21		17–20	
Current streak	U4		D1		D1		D1		D1	
Avg % Change	–0.30		–0.32		–0.32		–0.35		–0.61	
First Trading Day Performance										
% of Time Up	47.8		49.3		47.8		52.6		47.4	
Avg % Change	0.05		0.04		–0.15		0.20		–0.26	
Last Trading Day Performance										
% of Time Up	52.2		53.7		63.0		63.2		71.1	
Avg % Change	0.06		0.14		0.48		0.33		0.59	

Dow & S&P 1950–April 2017, NASDAQ 1971–April 2017, Russell 1K & 2K 1979–April 2017.

October has killed many a bear,
Buy techs and small caps and soon wear a grin ear to ear.

OCTOBER 2018

First Trading Day in October, Dow Down 8 of Last 12, Off 2.4% in 2011

MONDAY

D 47.6
S 52.4
N 42.9

1

A fanatic is one who can't change his mind and won't change the subject.
— Winston Churchill (British statesman, 1874–1965)

TUESDAY

D 52.4
S 57.1
N 61.9

2

In Washington people tell the truth off the record and lie on the record. In the Middle East they lie off the record and tell the truth on the record.
— Thomas L. Friedman (*NY Times* Foreign Affairs columnist, "Meet the Press" 12/17/06)

October Ends Dow and S&P "Worst Six Months" (Pages 48, 50, 52, 60 and 147) And NASDAQ "Worst Four Months" (Pages 56, 58 and 148)

WEDNESDAY

D 57.1
S 57.1
N 66.7

3

It doesn't pay to anticipate the correction; there are already plenty who have been carried out on their shields trying to do that. Rather, we will wait for some confirmed sell signals before altering our still-bullish view.
— Lawrence G. McMillan (Professional trader, author, Registered Investment Advisor, speaker, educator, OptionStrategist.com, b. 1946)

THURSDAY

D 66.7
S 61.9
N 57.1

4

I cannot give you a formula for success but I can give you a formula for failure: Try to please everybody.
— Herbert Swope (American Journalist, 1882–1958)

Dow Lost 1874 Points (18.2%) on the Week Ending 10/10/08 Worst Dow Week in the History of Wall Street

FRIDAY

D 33.3
S 38.1
N 47.6

5

Those heroes of finance are like beads on a string, when one slips off, the rest follow.
— Henrik Ibsen (Norwegian playwright, 1828–1906)

SATURDAY

6

SUNDAY

7

SECTOR SEASONALITY: SELECTED PERCENTAGE PLAYS

Sector seasonality was featured in the first 1968 *Almanac*. A Merrill Lynch study showed that buying seven sectors around September or October and selling in the first few months of 1954–1964 tripled the gains of holding them for 10 years. Over the years we have honed this strategy significantly and now devote a large portion of our time and resources to investing and trading during positive and negative seasonal periods for different sectors with Exchange Traded Funds (ETFs).

Updated seasonalities appear in the table below. We specify whether the seasonality starts or finishes in the beginning third (B), middle third (M), or last third (E) of the month. These selected percentage plays are geared to take advantage of the bulk of seasonal sector strength or weakness.

By design, entry points are in advance of the major seasonal moves, providing traders ample opportunity to accumulate positions at favorable prices. Conversely, exit points have been selected to capture the majority of the move.

From the major seasonalities in the table below, we created the Sector Index Seasonality Strategy Calendar on pages 94 and 96. Note the concentration of bullish sector seasonalities during the Best Six Months, November to April, and bearish sector seasonalities during the Worst Six Months, May to October.

Almanac Investor eNewsletter subscribers receive specific entry and exit points for highly correlated ETFs and detailed analysis in ETF Trades Alerts. Visit *www.stocktradersalmanac.com,* or see the ad insert for additional details and a special offer for new subscribers.

SECTOR INDEX SEASONALITY TABLE

			Seasonality				Average % Return[†]		
Ticker	Sector Index	Type	Start		Finish		15-Year	10-Year	5-Year
XCI	Computer Tech	Short	January	B	March	B	−4.9	−2.9	0.8
XNG	Natural Gas	Long	February	E	June	B	14.5	16.6	14.9
MSH	High-Tech	Long	March	M	July	B	6.9	7.8	3.3
UTY	Utilities	Long	March	M	October	B	6.4	5.8	2.8
XCI	Computer Tech	Long	April	M	July	M	5.7	7.3	6.6
BKX	Banking	Short	May	B	July	B	−7.9	−10.5	−2.2
XAU	Gold & Silver	Short	May	M	June	E	−6.0	−6.6	−6.9
S5MATR	Materials	Short	May	M	October	M	−5.1	−5.3	−3.3
XNG	Natural Gas	Short	June	M	July	E	−6.8	−6.3	−5.0
XAU	Gold & Silver	Long	July	E	December	E	10.1	0.1	−8.8
DJT	Transports	Short	July	M	October	M	−3.8	−4.6	−2.9
BTK	Biotech	Long	August	B	March	B	14.7	14.0	18.3
MSH	High-Tech	Long	August	M	January	M	12.0	6.5	7.4
SOX	Semiconductor	Short	August	M	October	E	−5.4	−5.7	−1.8
XOI	Oil	Short	September	B	November	E	−3.9	−4.6	−3.9
BKX	Banking	Long	October	B	May	B	11.7	9.6	16.7
XBD	Broker/Dealer	Long	October	B	April	M	16.0	13.2	19.1
XCI	Computer Tech	Long	October	B	January	B	11.1	7.7	6.1
S5COND	Consumer Discretionary	Long	October	B	June	B	14.5	14.5	17.5
S5CONS	Consumer Staples	Long	October	B	June	B	9.5	9.7	12.8
S5HLTH	Healthcare	Long	October	B	May	B	9.4	11.0	15.8
S5MATR	Materials	Long	October	B	May	B	17.1	16.0	16.5
DRG	Pharmaceutical	Long	October	M	January	B	6.6	6.5	6.0
RMZ	Real Estate	Long	October	E	May	B	12.8	11.6	12.0
SOX	Semiconductor	Long	October	E	December	B	11.1	7.3	8.9
XTC	Telecom	Long	October	M	December	E	8.2	3.9	3.6
DJT	Transports	Long	October	B	May	B	18.3	16.8	18.5
XOI	Oil	Long	December	M	July	B	11.8	8.0	9.5

† *Average % Return based on full seasonality completion through April 28, 2017.*

OCTOBER 2018

Columbus Day *(Bond Market Closed)*

MONDAY
D 42.9
S 42.9
N 57.1
8

Doubt is the father of invention.
– Galileo Galilei (Italian physicist and astronomer, 1564–1642)

TUESDAY
D 47.6
S 47.6
N 52.4
9

If banking institutions are protected by the taxpayer and they are given free rein to speculate, I may not live long enough to see the crisis, but my soul is going to come back and haunt you.
– Paul A. Volcker (Fed Chairman 1979–1987, Chair Economic Recovery Advisory Board, 2/2/2010, b. 1927)

WEDNESDAY
D 42.9
S 42.9
N 47.6
10

Now a minority, Reaching majority, Seizing authority, Hates a minority.
– Leonard H. Robbins

THURSDAY
D 42.9
S 47.6
N 57.1
11

When a country lives on borrowed time, borrowed money and borrowed energy, it is just begging the markets to discipline it in their own way at their own time. Usually the markets do it in an orderly way—except when they don't.
– Thomas L. Friedman (*NY Times* Foreign Affairs columnist, 2/24/05)

FRIDAY
D 71.4
S 66.7
N 71.4
12

Don't put all your eggs in one basket.
– (Market maxim)

SATURDAY
13

SUNDAY
14

SECTOR INDEX SEASONALITY STRATEGY CALENDAR*

* Graphic representation of the Sector Index Seasonality Percentage Plays on page 92.
L = Long Trade, S = Short Trade, ➜ = Start of Trade

94

(continued on page 96)

OCTOBER 2018

MONDAY

D 47.6
S 47.6
N 47.6

15

Big money is made in the stock market by being on the right side of major moves. I don't believe in swimming against the tide.
— Martin Zweig (Fund manager, *Winning on Wall Street*, 1943–2013)

TUESDAY

D 57.1
S 66.7
N 57.1

16

The worst crime against working people is a company that fails to make a profit.
— Samuel Gompers (American labor union leader, 1850–1924)

October 2011, Second Dow Month to Gain 1000 Points

WEDNESDAY

D 52.4
S 61.9
N 47.6

17

That's the American way. If little kids don't aspire to make money like I did, what the hell good is this country?
— Lee Iacocca (American industrialist, Former Chrysler CEO, b. 1924)

Crash of October 19, 1987, Dow Down 22.6% in One Day

THURSDAY

D 61.9
S 66.7
N 66.7

18

In this age of instant information, investors can experience both fear and greed at the exact same moment.
— Sam Stovall (Chief Investment Strategist Standard & Poor's, October 2003)

October Expiration Day, Dow Down 6 Straight 2005–2010 and 9 of Last 14

FRIDAY

D 52.4
S 61.9
N 52.4

19

The job of central banks: To take away the punch bowl just as the party is getting going.
— William McChesney Martin (Federal Reserve Chairman 1951–1970, 1906–1998)

SATURDAY

20

SUNDAY

21

(continued from page 94)

SECTOR INDEX SEASONALITY STRATEGY CALENDAR*

* Graphic representation of the Sector Index Seasonality Percentage Plays on page 92.
L = Long Trade, S = Short Trade, ⟶ = Start of Trade

MONDAY

D 38.1
S 47.6
N 42.9

22

The biggest change we made was the move to a boundary-less company. We got rid of the corner offices, the bureaucracy, and the not-invented-here syndrome. Instead we got every mind in the game, got the best out of all our people.
— Jack Welch (retiring CEO of General Electric, *Business Week*, September 10, 2001, b. 1935)

TUESDAY

D 57.1
S 66.7
N 66.7

23

Anytime there is change there is opportunity. So it is paramount that an organization get energized rather than paralyzed.
— Jack Welch (GE CEO, *Fortune*, b. 1935)

*Late October is Time to Buy Depressed Stocks
Especially Techs and Small Caps*

WEDNESDAY

D 52.4
S 57.1
N 47.6

24

Unless you love EVERYBODY, you can't sell ANYBODY.
— (From *Jerry Maguire*, 1996)

THURSDAY

D 38.1
S 33.3
N 42.9

25

In a study of 3000 companies, researchers at the University of Pennsylvania found that spending 10% of revenue on capital improvements boosts productivity by 3.9%, but a similar investment in developing human capital increases productivity by 8.5%.
— John A. Byrne (Editor-in-Chief, *Fast Company Magazine*)

FRIDAY

D 61.9
S 52.4
N 47.6

26

I have seen it repeatedly throughout the world: politicians get a country in trouble but swear everything is okay in the face of overwhelming evidence to the contrary.
— Jim Rogers (Financier, *Adventure Capitalist*, b. 1942)

SATURDAY

27

November Almanac Investor Sector Seasonalities: See Pages 92, 94 and 96

SUNDAY

28

NOVEMBER ALMANAC

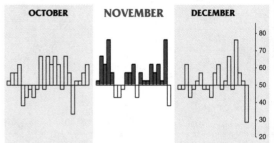

NOVEMBER

S	M	T	W	T	F	S
				1	2	3
4	5	6	7	8	9	10
11	12	13	14	15	16	17
18	19	20	21	22	23	24
25	26	27	28	29	30	

DECEMBER

S	M	T	W	T	F	S
						1
2	3	4	5	6	7	8
9	10	11	12	13	14	15
16	17	18	19	20	21	22
23	24	25	26	27	28	29
30	31					

Market Probability Chart above is a graphic representation of the S&P 500 Recent Market Probability Calendar on page 124.

◆ #2 S&P and #3 Dow month since 1950, #3 on NASDAQ since 1971 (pages 48 & 56) ◆ Start of the "Best Six Months" of the year (page 50), NASDAQ's Best Eight Months and Best Three (pages 147 & 148) ◆ Simple timing indicator almost triples "Best Six Months" strategy (page 52), doubles NASDAQ's Best Eight (page 58) ◆ Day before and after Thanksgiving Day combined, only 14 losses in 65 years (page 104) ◆ Week before Thanksgiving Dow up 19 of last 24 ◆ Midterm election year Novembers rank #2 Dow, S&P, and NASDAQ.

November Vital Statistics

	DJIA		S&P 500		NASDAQ		Russell 1K		Russell 2K	
Rank	3		2		3		1		2	
Up	45		45		31		28		25	
Down	22		22		15		10		13	
Average % Change	1.6%		1.5%		1.6%		1.7%		2.0%	
Midterm Year	2.5%		2.6%		3.7%		2.7%		3.5%	
Best & Worst November										
	% Change		% Change		% Change		% Change		% Change	
Best	1962	10.1	1980	10.2	2001	14.2	1980	10.1	2002	8.8
Worst	1973	−14.0	1973	−11.4	2000	−22.9	2000	−9.3	2008	−12.0
Best & Worst November Weeks										
Best	11/28/08	9.7	11/28/08	12.0	11/28/08	10.9	11/28/08	12.5	11/28/08	16.4
Worst	11/21/08	−5.3	11/21/08	−8.4	11/10/00	−12.2	11/21/08	−8.8	11/21/08	−11.0
Best & Worst November Days										
Best	11/13/08	6.7	11/13/08	6.9	11/13/08	6.5	11/13/08	7.0	11/13/08	8.5
Worst	11/20/08	−5.6	11/20/08	−6.7	11/19/08	−6.5	11/20/08	−6.9	11/19/08	−7.9
First Trading Day of Expiration Week: 1980–2016										
Record (#Up – #Down)	20–17		17–20		14–23		19–18		17–20	
Current streak	U4		D1		D1		U5		U2	
Avg % Change	0.001		−0.04		−0.13		−0.05		−0.06	
Options Expiration Day: 1980–2016										
Record (#Up – #Down)	24–13		22–15		20–17		22–15		20–16	
Current streak	D1		D1		D1		D1		U7	
Avg % Change	0.24		0.17		0.04		0.16		0.15	
Options Expiration Week: 1980–2016										
Record (#Up – #Down)	25–12		23–14		20–17		22–15		19–18	
Current streak	U4		U4		U4		U4		U2	
Avg % Change	0.35		0.13		0.10		0.11		−0.15	
Week After Options Expiration: 1980–2016										
Record (#Up – #Down)	22–15		24–13		25–12		24–13		23–14	
Current streak	U1		U5		U5		U5		U5	
Avg % Change	0.70		0.68		0.80		0.68		0.85	
First Trading Day Performance										
% of Time Up	62.7		62.7		65.2		71.1		60.5	
Avg % Change	0.27		0.29		0.29		0.37		0.19	
Last Trading Day Performance										
% of Time Up	55.2		52.2		63.0		44.7		65.8	
Avg % Change	0.10		0.12		−0.10		0.001		0.14	

Dow & S&P 1950–April 2017, NASDAQ 1971–April 2017, Russell 1K & 2K 1979–April 2017.

◆

Astute investors always smile and remember,
When stocks seasonally start soaring, and salute November.

OCTOBER/NOVEMBER 2018

88th Anniversary of 1929 Crash, Dow Down 23.0% in Two Days,
October 28 and 29

MONDAY
D 61.9
S 52.4
N 52.4
29

The greatest safety lies in putting all your eggs in one basket and watching the basket.
— Gerald M. Loeb (E.F. Hutton, *The Battle for Investment Survival*, predicted 1929 Crash, 1900–1974)

TUESDAY
D 57.1
S 57.1
N 57.1
30

With globalization, the big [countries] don't eat the small, the fast eat the slow.
— Thomas L. Friedman (*NY Times* Foreign Affairs columnist, referring to the Arab nations)

Halloween

WEDNESDAY
D 57.1
S 61.9
N 61.9
31

We will have to pay more and more attention to what the funds are doing. They are the ones who have been contributing to the activity, especially in the high-fliers.
— Humphrey B. Neill (Investor, analyst, author, *NY Times* 6/11/1966, 1895–1977)

First Trading Day in November, Dow Down 7 of Last 12

THURSDAY
D 52.4
S 52.4
N 66.7
1

The way a young man spends his evenings is a part of that thin area between success and failure.
— Robert R. Young (U.S. financier and railroad tycoon, 1897–1958)

November Begins Dow and S&P "Best Six Months" (Pages 50, 52, 54, 60
and 147) And NASDAQ "Best Eight Months" (Pages 56, 58 and 148)

FRIDAY
D 57.1
S 66.7
N 61.9
2

The difference between genius and stupidity is that genius has its limits.
— Anonymous

SATURDAY
3

Daylight Saving Time Ends

SUNDAY
4

MIDTERM ELECTION TIME UNUSUALLY BULLISH

Presidential election years tend to produce high drama and frenetic campaigns. Midterm years with only local or state candidates running are less stressful. Could this be the reason for the bullishness that seems to occur in the five days before and three days after midterm congressional elections? We don't think so. So many bear markets seem to occur in midterm years, very often bottoming in October. Also, major military involvements began or were in their early stages in midterm years, such as World War II, Korea, Vietnam, Kuwait and Iraq. Solidly bullish midterm years as 1954, 1958, 1986, 2006, 2010 and 2014 were exceptions. With so many negative occurrences in midterm years, perhaps the opportunity for investors to make a change for the better by casting their votes translates into an inner bullish feeling before and after midterm elections.

An impressive 2.7% has been the average gain during the eight trading days surrounding midterm election days since 1934. This is equivalent to roughly 567 Dow points per day at present levels. There was only one losing period: in 1994 when the Republicans took control of both the House and the Senate for the first time in 40 years. Four other midterm switches occurred in 1946, when control of Congress passed to the Republicans for just two years; in 1954, when Democrats took back control; in 2006 when Democrats regained control; and in 2010, when Republicans reclaimed the House.

There were eleven occasions when the percentage of House seats lost by the president's party was in double digits. The average market gain during the eight-day trading period was 2.1%. In contrast, the average gain in the eight occasions when there were no losses, or losses were in single digits, gains averaged 3.4%.

BULLS WIN BATTLE BETWEEN ELEPHANTS AND DONKEYS

| | Dow Jones Industrials | | | President's | President |
Midterm Year	5 Trading Days Before E. Day	3 Trading Days After E. Day	% Change	Party % Seats Lost	in Power
1934	93.36	99.02	6.1%	2.9%	Dem
1938	152.21	158.41	4.1	−21.3	Dem
1942	113.11	116.12	2.7	−16.9	Dem
1946	164.20	170.79	4.0	−22.6	Dem*
1950	225.69	229.29	1.6	−11.0	Dem
1954	356.32	366.00	2.7	−8.1	Rep*
1958	536.88	554.26	3.2	−23.9	Rep
1962	588.98	616.13	4.6	−1.5	Dem
1966	809.63	819.09	1.2	−15.9	Dem
1970	754.45	771.97	2.3	−6.3	Rep
1974	659.34	667.16	1.2	−25.0	Rep
1978	792.45	807.09	1.8	−5.1	Dem
1982	1006.07	1051.78	4.5	−13.5	Rep
1986	1845.47	1886.53	2.2	−2.7	Rep
1990	2448.02	2488.61	1.7	−4.6	Rep
1994	3863.37	3801.47	−1.6	−20.9	Dem*
1998	8366.04	8975.46	7.3	2.4	Dem
2002	8368.94	8537.13	2.0	3.6	Rep
2006	12080.73	12108.43	0.2	−12.9	Rep*
2010	11169.46	11444.08	2.5	−24.6	Dem*
2014	17005.75	17573.93	3.3	−6.5	Dem*
		Total	57.6%		
		Average	2.7%	−11.2	

Control switches to other Party

MONDAY

D 61.9
S 61.9
N 66.7

5

The fewer analysts who follow a situation, the more pregnant its possibilities…if Wall Street hates a stock, buy it.
— Martin Sosnoff (Atalanta Sosnoff Capital, *Silent Investor, Silent Loser*)

Election Day

TUESDAY

D 76.2
S 76.2
N 66.7

6

I know nothing grander, better exercise…more positive proof of the past, the triumphant result of faith in humankind, than a well-contested national election.
— Walt Whitman (American poet, 1819–1892)

FOMC Meeting (2 Days)

WEDNESDAY

D 61.9
S 57.1
N 61.9

7

In the twenty-two presidential elections from 1900 through 1984, Americans chose the most optimistic-sounding candidate eighteen times.
— Martin E. Seligman, Ph.D (Professor of Psychology, University of Pennsylvania, *Learned Optimism*, 1990)

THURSDAY

D 47.6
S 42.9
N 52.4

8

Politics ought to be the part-time profession of every citizen who would protect the rights and privileges of free people and who would preserve what is good and fruitful in our national heritage.
— Dwight D. Eisenhower (34th U.S. President, 1890–1969)

FRIDAY

D 47.6
S 42.9
N 42.9

9

If investing is entertaining, if you're having fun, you're probably not making any money. Good investing is boring.
— George Soros (Financier, philanthropist, political activist, author and philosopher, b. 1930)

SATURDAY

10

Veterans' Day

SUNDAY

11

FOURTH-QUARTER MARKET MAGIC

Examining market performance on a quarterly basis reveals several intriguing and helpful patterns. Fourth-quarter market gains have been magical, providing the greatest and most consistent gains over the years. First-quarter performance runs a respectable second. This should not be surprising, as cash inflows, trading volume, and buying bias are generally elevated during these two quarters.

Positive market psychology hits a fever pitch as the holiday season approaches, and does not begin to wane until spring. Professionals drive the market higher, as they make portfolio adjustments to maximize year-end numbers. Bonuses are paid and invested around the turn of the year.

The market's sweet spot of the four-year cycle begins in the fourth quarter of the midterm year. The best two-quarter span runs from the fourth quarter of the midterm year through the first quarter of the pre-election year, averaging 14.6% for the Dow, 15.4% for the S&P 500, and an amazing 22.0% for NASDAQ. Pre-election Q2 is smoking, too, the third best quarter of the cycle, creating a three-quarter sweet spot from midterm Q4 to pre-election Q2.

Quarterly strength fades in the latter half of the pre-election year, but stays impressively positive through the election year. Losses dominate the first quarter of post-election years and the second and third quarters of midterm years.

QUARTERLY % CHANGES

	Q1	Q2	Q3	Q4	Year	Q2–Q3	Q4–Q1
Dow Jones Industrials (1949-March 2017)							
Average	2.3%	1.5%	0.4%	4.0%	8.4%	2.0%	6.5%
Post-election	−0.1%	1.6%	0.3%	3.8%	5.7%	2.0%	5.4%
Midterm	1.4%	−1.5%	−0.4%	7.1%	6.7%	−1.8%	14.6%
Pre-election	7.1%	4.9%	1.0%	2.6%	15.8%	5.9%	3.5%
Election	1.0%	1.0%	0.7%	2.3%	5.3%	1.8%	2.4%
S&P 500 (1949-March 2017)							
Average	2.3%	1.6%	0.6%	4.1%	8.9%	2.3%	6.7%
Post-election	−0.2%	2.2%	0.7%	3.5%	6.2%	3.0%	4.7%
Midterm	1.0%	−2.4%	0.1%	7.8%	6.7%	−2.2%	15.4%
Pre-election	7.1%	4.9%	0.6%	3.2%	16.1%	5.5%	4.7%
Election	1.6%	1.8%	1.1%	2.0%	6.7%	2.9%	2.0%
NASDAQ Composite (1971-March 2017)							
Average	4.3%	3.1%	0.1%	4.5%	12.4%	3.4%	8.9%
Post-election	−1.2%	6.6%	2.2%	4.8%	11.1%	8.7%	6.7%
Midterm	2.0%	−2.7%	−4.5%	8.6%	2.8%	−6.7%	22.0%
Pre-election	12.9%	7.5%	0.9%	5.4%	28.8%	8.5%	9.3%
Election	4.4%	0.7%	1.8%	−0.6%	6.0%	2.8%	−1.3%

NOVEMBER 2018

Monday Before November Expiration, Dow Up 9 of Last 13

MONDAY
D 42.9
S 47.6
N 52.4
12

There are one-story intellects, two-story intellects, and three-story intellects with skylights. All fact collectors with no aim beyond their facts are one-story men. Two-story men compare, reason and generalize, using labors of the fact collectors as well as their own. Three-story men idealize, imagine and predict. Their best illuminations come from above through the skylight.
— Oliver Wendell Holmes (American author, poet and physician, 1809–1894)

TUESDAY
D 66.7
S 57.1
N 66.7
13

...those inquirers who desire an exact knowledge of the past as an aid to the interpretation of the future...
— Thucydides (Greek aristocrat and historian, *The Peloponnesian War*, 460–400 BC)

Week Before Thanksgiving, Dow Up 19 of Last 24,
2003 –1.4%, 2004 –0.8%, 2008 –5.3%, 2011 –2.9%, 2012 –1.8%

WEDNESDAY
D 61.9
S 57.1
N 52.4
14

All great truths begin as blasphemies.
— George Bernard Shaw (Irish dramatist, 1856–1950)

THURSDAY
D 71.4
S 61.9
N 47.6
15

There has never been a commercial technology like this (Internet) in the history of the world, whereby the minute you adopt it, it forces you to think and act globally.
— Robert D. Hormats (Under Secretary of State for Economic, Business, and Agricultural Affairs, 2009–2013, Goldman Sachs 1982–2009, b.1943)

November Expiration Day, Dow Up 12 of Last 15
Dow Surged in 2008, Up 494 Points (6.5%)

FRIDAY
D 42.9
S 42.9
N 52.4
16

Tell me and I'll forget; show me and I may remember; involve me and I'll understand.
— Confucius (Chinese philosopher, 551–478 B.C.)

SATURDAY
17

SUNDAY
18

TRADING THE THANKSGIVING MARKET

For 35 years, the "holiday spirit" gave the Wednesday before Thanksgiving and the Friday after a great track record, except for two occasions. Publishing it in the 1987 *Almanac* was the kiss of death. Since 1988, Wednesday–Friday gained 18 of 29 times, with a total Dow point gain of 813.85 versus Monday's total Dow point loss of 923.27, down 14 of 19 since 1998. The best strategy appears to be coming into the week long and exiting into strength Friday.

DOW JONES INDUSTRIALS BEFORE AND AFTER THANKSGIVING

	Tuesday Before	Wednesday Before		Friday After	Total Gain Dow Points	Dow Close	Next Monday
1952	-0.18	1.54		1.22	2.76	283.66	0.04
1953	1.71	0.65		2.45	3.10	280.23	1.14
1954	3.27	1.89		3.16	5.05	387.79	0.72
1955	4.61	0.71		0.26	0.97	482.88	-1.92
1956	-4.49	-2.16		4.65	2.49	472.56	-2.27
1957	-9.04	10.69		3.84	14.53	449.87	-2.96
1958	-4.37	8.63		8.31	16.94	557.46	2.61
1959	2.94	1.41		1.42	2.83	652.52	6.66
1960	-3.44	1.37		4.00	5.37	606.47	-1.04
1961	-0.77	1.10		2.18	3.28	732.60	-0.61
1962	6.73	4.31		7.62	11.93	644.87	-2.81
1963	32.03	-2.52	T	9.52	7.00	750.52	1.39
1964	-1.68	-5.21		-0.28	-5.49	882.12	-6.69
1965	2.56	N/C	H	-0.78	-0.78	948.16	-1.23
1966	-3.18	1.84		6.52	8.36	803.34	-2.18
1967	13.17	3.07	A	3.58	6.65	877.60	4.51
1968	8.14	-3.17		8.76	5.59	985.08	-1.74
1969	-5.61	3.23	N	1.78	5.01	812.30	-7.26
1970	5.21	1.98		6.64	8.62	781.35	12.74
1971	-5.18	0.66	K	17.96	18.62	816.59	13.14
1972	8.21	7.29		4.67	11.96	1025.21	-7.45
1973	-17.76	10.08	S	-0.98	9.10	854.00	-29.05
1974	5.32	2.03		-0.63	1.40	618.66	-15.64
1975	9.76	3.15	G	2.12	5.27	860.67	-4.33
1976	-6.57	1.66		5.66	7.32	956.62	-6.57
1977	6.41	0.78	I	1.12	1.90	844.42	-4.85
1978	-1.56	2.95		3.12	6.07	810.12	3.72
1979	-6.05	-1.80	V	4.35	2.55	811.77	16.98
1980	3.93	7.00		3.66	10.66	993.34	-23.89
1981	18.45	7.90	I	7.80	15.70	885.94	3.04
1982	-9.01	9.01		7.36	16.37	1007.36	-4.51
1983	7.01	-0.20	N	1.83	1.63	1277.44	-7.62
1984	9.83	6.40		18.78	25.18	1220.30	-7.95
1985	0.12	18.92	G	-3.56	15.36	1472.13	-14.22
1986	6.05	4.64		-2.53	2.11	1914.23	-1.55
1987	40.45	-16.58		-36.47	-53.05	1910.48	-76.93
1988	11.73	14.58	D	-17.60	-3.02	2074.68	6.76
1989	7.25	17.49		18.77	36.26	2675.55	19.42
1990	-35.15	9.16	A	-12.13	-2.97	2527.23	5.94
1991	14.08	-16.10		-5.36	-21.46	2894.68	40.70
1992	25.66	17.56	Y	15.94	33.50	3282.20	22.96
1993	3.92	13.41		-3.63	9.78	3683.95	-6.15
1994	-91.52	-3.36		33.64	30.28	3708.27	31.29
1995	40.46	18.06		7.23*	25.29	5048.84	22.04
1996	-19.38	-29.07		22.36*	-6.71	6521.70	N/C
1997	41.03	-14.17		28.35*	14.18	7823.13	189.98
1998	-73.12	13.13		18.80*	31.93	9333.08	-216.53
1999	-93.89	12.54		-19.26*	-6.72	10988.91	-40.99
2000	31.85	-95.18		70.91*	-24.27	10470.23	75.84
2001	-75.08	-66.70		125.03*	58.33	9959.71	23.04
2002	-172.98	255.26		-35.59*	219.67	8896.09	-33.52
2003	16.15	15.63		2.89*	18.52	9782.46	116.59
2004	3.18	27.71		1.92*	29.63	10522.23	-46.33
2005	51.15	44.66		15.53*	60.19	10931.62	-40.90
2006	5.05	5.36		-46.78*	-41.42	12280.17	-158.46
2007	51.70	-211.10		181.84*	-29.26	12980.88	-237.44
2008	36.08	247.14		102.43*	349.57	8829.04	-679.95
2009	-17.24	30.69		-154.48*	-123.79	10309.92	34.92
2010	-142.21	150.91		-95.28*	55.63	11092.00	-39.51
2011	-53.59	-236.17		-25.77*	-261.94	11231.78	291.23
2012	-7.45	48.38		172.79*	221.17	13009.68	-42.31
2013	0.26	24.53		-10.92*	13.61	16086.41	-77.64
2014	-2.96	-2.69		15.99*	13.30	17828.24	-51.44
2015	19.51	1.20		-14.90*	-13.70	17798.49	-78.57
2016	67.18	59.31		68.96*	128.27	19152.14	-54.24

*Shortened trading day

NOVEMBER 2018

Stocks are super-attractive when the Fed is loosening and interest rates are falling. In sum: Don't fight the Fed!
— Martin Zweig (Fund manager, *Winning on Wall Street*, 1943–2013)

What people in the Middle East tell you in private is irrelevant. All that matters is what they will defend in public in their language.
— Thomas L. Friedman (*NY Times* Foreign Affairs columnist, "Meet the Press" 12/17/06)

Trading Thanksgiving Market: Long into Weakness Prior,
Exit into Strength After (Page 104)

Those who are of the opinion that money will do everything may very well be suspected to do everything for money.
— Sir George Savile (British statesman and author, 1633–1695)

Thanksgiving *(Market Closed)*

Let me end my talk by abusing slightly my status as an official representative of the Federal Reserve. I would like to say to Milton [Friedman]: regarding the Great Depression, you're right; we did it. We're very sorry. But thanks to you, we won't do it again.
— Ben Bernanke (Fed Chairman 2006–2014, 11/8/02 speech as Fed Governor, b. 1953)

(Shortened Trading Day)

I was absolutely unemotional about numbers. Losses did not have an effect on me because I viewed them as purely probability-driven, which meant sometimes you came up with a loss. Bad days, bad weeks, bad months never impacted the way I approached markets the next day.
— James Leitner (Trader, hedge fund manager, Falcon Management Corp, b. 1953)

DECEMBER ALMANAC

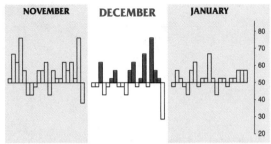

DECEMBER							JANUARY					
S	M	T	W	T	F	S	S	M	T	W	T	F	S
30	31					1		1	2	3	4	5
2	3	4	5	6	7	8	6	7	8	9	10	11	12
9	10	11	12	13	14	15	13	14	15	16	17	18	19
16	17	18	19	20	21	22	20	21	22	23	24	25	26
23	24	25	26	27	28	29	27	28	29	30	31

Market Probability Chart above is a graphic representation of the S&P 500 Recent Market Probability Calendar on page 124.

◆ #1 S&P (+1.6%) and #2 Dow (+1.7%) month since 1950 (page 48), #2 NASDAQ 1.8% since 1971 ◆ 2002 worst December since 1931, down over 6% Dow and S&P, –9.7% on NASDAQ (pages 152, 155, & 157) ◆ "Free lunch" served on Wall Street before Christmas (page 112) ◆ Small caps start to outperform larger caps near middle of month (pages 108 & 110) ◆ "Santa Claus Rally" visible in graph above and on page 114 ◆ In 1998 was part of best fourth quarter since 1928 (page 167) ◆ Fourth quarter expiration week most bullish triple-witching week, Dow up 20 of last 26 (page 78) ◆ Midterm election year Decembers rankings: #3 Dow and S&P, #5 NASDAQ.

December Vital Statistics

	DJIA	S&P 500	NASDAQ	Russell 1K	Russell 2K
Rank	2	1	2	3	1
Up	47	50	27	29	30
Down	20	17	19	9	8
Average % Change	1.7%	1.6%	1.8%	1.5%	2.6%
Midterm Year	1.5%	1.6%	0.6%	1.1%	1.7%

		Best & Worst December							
	% Change		% Change		% Change		% Change		% Change	
Best	1991	9.5	1991	11.2	1999	22.0	1991	11.2	1999	11.2
Worst	2002	–6.2	2002	–6.0	2002	–9.7	2002	–5.8	2002	–5.7

		Best & Worst December Weeks							
Best	12/02/11	7.0	12/02/11	7.4	12/08/00	10.3	12/02/11	7.4	12/02/11	10.3
Worst	12/04/87	–7.5	12/06/74	–7.1	12/15/00	–9.1	12/04/87	–7.0	12/12/80	–6.5

		Best & Worst December Days							
Best	12/16/08	4.2	12/16/08	5.1	12/05/00	10.5	12/16/08	5.2	12/16/08	6.7
Worst	12/01/08	–7.7	12/01/08	–8.9	12/01/08	–9.0	12/01/08	–9.1	12/01/08	–11.9

	First Trading Day of Expiration Week: 1980–2016				
Record (#Up – #Down)	22–15	22–15	16–21	22–15	16–21
Current streak	U2	D1	D1	D1	D3
Avg % Change	0.18	0.13	–0.06	0.10	–0.19

	Options Expiration Day: 1980–2016				
Record (#Up – #Down)	23–14	26–11	25–12	26–11	23–14
Current streak	D2	D2	D2	D2	D2
Avg % Change	0.25	0.32	0.30	0.31	0.39

	Options Expiration Week: 1980–2016				
Record (#Up – #Down)	28–9	26–11	21–16	25–12	19–18
Current streak	U1	D2	D2	D2	D2
Avg % Change	0.73	0.75	0.27	0.70	0.61

	Week After Options Expiration: 1980–2016				
Record (#Up – #Down)	26–10	23–14	24–13	23–14	26–11
Current streak	U4	U4	U4	U4	U4
Avg % Change	0.79	0.53	0.70	0.56	0.87

	First Trading Day Performance				
% of Time Up	47.8	49.3	58.7	50.0	50.0
Avg % Change	–0.04	–0.03	0.10	–0.05	–0.15

	Last Trading Day Performance				
% of Time Up	52.2	59.7	69.6	50.0	65.8
Avg % Change	0.05	0.08	0.29	–0.09	0.39

Dow & S&P 1950–April 2017, NASDAQ 1971–April 2017, Russell 1K & 2K 1979–April 2017.

If Santa Claus should fail to call,
Bears may come to Broad and Wall.

NOVEMBER/DECEMBER 2018

There have been three great inventions since the beginning of time: Fire, the wheel, and central banking.
— Will Rogers (American humorist and showman, 1879–1935)

TUESDAY

D 66.7
S 61.9
N 61.9

27

Mankind is divided into three classes: Those that are immovable, those that are movable, and those that move.
— Arabian proverb (also attributed to Benjamin Franklin)

WEDNESDAY

D 57.1
S 52.4
N 57.1

28

The worst bankrupt in the world is the person who has lost his enthusiasm.
— H.W. Arnold (American Lieutenant General, 1901–1976)

THURSDAY

D 57.1
S 76.2
N 71.4

29

The more feted by the media, the worse a pundit's accuracy.
— Sharon Begley (Senior editor *Newsweek*, 2/23/2009, referencing Philip E. Tetlock's 2005 *Expert Political Judgment*)

Last Trading Day of November, S&P Down 13 of Last 19

FRIDAY

D 52.4
S 38.1
N 42.9

30

Individualism, private property, the law of accumulation of wealth and the law of competition…are the highest result of human experience, the soil in which, so far, has produced the best fruit.
— Andrew Carnegie (Scottish-born U.S. industrialist, philanthropist, *The Gospel Of Wealth*, 1835–1919)

SATURDAY

1

December Almanac Investor Sector Seasonalities: See Pages 92, 94 and 96

SUNDAY

2

MOST OF THE SO-CALLED "JANUARY EFFECT" TAKES PLACE IN THE LAST HALF OF DECEMBER

Over the years we have reported annually on the fascinating January Effect, showing that small-cap stocks handily outperformed large-cap stocks during January 40 out of 43 years between 1953 and 1995. Readers saw that "Cats and Dogs" on average quadrupled the returns of blue chips in this period. Then, the January Effect disappeared over the next four years.

Looking at the graph on page 110, comparing the Russell 1000 index of large-capitalization stocks to the Russell 2000 smaller-capitalization stocks, shows small-cap stocks beginning to outperform the blue chips in mid-December. Narrowing the comparison down to half-month segments was an inspiration and proved to be quite revealing, as you can see in the table below.

30-YEAR AVERAGE RATES OF RETURN (DEC 1987 – FEB 2017)

From mid-Dec*	Russell 1000 Change	Annualized	Russell 2000 Change	Annualized
12/15–12/31	1.7%	47.1%	3.3%	110.4%
12/15–01/15	1.9	24.1	3.3	45.0
12/15–01/31	2.1	18.4	3.6	33.3
12/15–02/15	3.1	20.1	5.2	35.5
12/15–02/28	2.6	13.8	5.0	27.9
end-Dec*				
12/31–01/15	0.1	2.1	0.1	2.1
12/31–01/31	0.3	3.7	0.3	3.7
12/31–02/15	1.4	11.6	1.8	15.1
12/31–02/28	0.9	5.8	1.7	11.2

38-YEAR AVERAGE RATES OF RETURN (DEC 1979 – FEB 2017)

From mid-Dec*	Russell 1000 Change	Annualized	Russell 2000 Change	Annualized
12/15–12/31	1.6%	43.9%	2.9%	92.5%
12/15–01/15	2.1	26.9	3.8	53.3
12/15–01/31	2.4	21.3	4.1	38.6
12/15–02/15	3.3	21.5	5.7	39.5
12/15–02/28	3.0	15.7	5.6	30.9
end-Dec*				
12/31–01/15	0.5	11.0	0.9	20.7
12/31–01/31	0.8	10.0	1.2	15.4
12/31–02/15	1.7	14.2	2.7	23.3
12/31–02/28	1.4	9.2	2.6	17.6

Mid-month dates are the 11th trading day of the month; month end dates are monthly closes.

Small-cap strength in the last half of December became even more magnified after the 1987 market crash. Note the dramatic shift in gains in the last half of December during the 30-year period starting in 1987, versus the 38 years from 1979 to 2017. With all the beaten-down small stocks being dumped for tax-loss purposes, it generally pays to get a head start on the January Effect in mid-December. You don't have to wait until December either; the small-cap sector often begins to turn around toward the beginning of November.

First Trading Day in December, NASDAQ Up 20 of 30, But Down 7 of Last 11

Chanukah

MONDAY

D 47.6
S 47.6
N 61.9

3

The fireworks begin today. Each diploma is a lighted match. Each one of you is a fuse.
— Edward Koch (NYC Mayor, Commencement Address, 1983, 1924–2013)

TUESDAY

D 38.1
S 47.6
N 57.1

4

When Paris sneezes, Europe catches cold.
— Prince Klemens Metternich (Austrian statesman, 1773–1859)

WEDNESDAY

D 66.7
S 61.9
N 61.9

5

Another factor contributing to productivity is technology, particularly the rapid introduction of new microcomputers based on single-chip circuits....The results over the next decade will be a second industrial revolution.
— Yale Hirsch (Creator of *Stock Trader's Almanac, Smart Money Newsletter 9/22/1976, b. 1923*)

THURSDAY

D 52.4
S 42.9
N 61.9

6

Every truth passes through three stages before it is recognized. In the first it is ridiculed; in the second it is opposed; in the third it is regarded as self evident.
— Arthur Schopenhauer (German philosopher, 1788–1860)

FRIDAY

D 52.4
S 47.6
N 42.9

7

The only way to even begin to manage this new world is by focusing on...nation building—helping others restructure their economies and put in place decent non-corrupt government.
— Thomas L. Friedman (*NY Times* Foreign Affairs columnist)

SATURDAY

8

SUNDAY

9

JANUARY EFFECT NOW STARTS IN MID-DECEMBER

Small-cap stocks tend to outperform big caps in January. Known as the "January Effect," the tendency is clearly revealed by the graph below. Thirty-seven years of daily data for the Russell 2000 index of smaller companies are divided by the Russell 1000 index of largest companies, and then compressed into a single year to show an idealized yearly pattern. When the graph is descending, big blue chips are outperforming smaller companies; when the graph is rising, smaller companies are moving up faster than their larger brethren.

In a typical year, the smaller fry stay on the sidelines while the big boys are on the field. Then, around early November, small stocks begin to wake up, and in mid-December they take off. Anticipated year-end dividends, payouts, and bonuses could be a factor. Other major moves are quite evident just before Labor Day—possibly because individual investors are back from vacations. Small caps hold the lead through the beginning of June, though the bulk of the move is complete by early March.

RUSSELL 2000/RUSSELL 1000 ONE-YEAR SEASONAL PATTERN

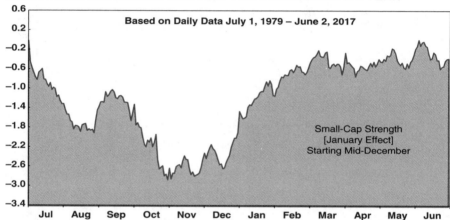

The bottom graph shows the actual ratio of the Russell 2000 divided by the Russell 1000 from 1979. Smaller companies had the upper hand for five years into 1983, as the last major bear trend wound to a close and the nascent bull market logged its first year. After falling behind for about eight years, they came back after the Persian Gulf War bottom in 1990, moving up until 1994, when big caps ruled the latter stages of the millennial bull. For six years, the picture was bleak for small fry, as the blue chips and tech stocks moved to stratospheric PE ratios. Small caps spiked in late 1999 and early 2000 and reached a peak in early 2006, as the four-year-old bull entered its final year. Note how the small-cap advantage has waned during major bull moves and intensified during weak market times.

RUSSELL 2000/RUSSELL 1000 (1979–MAY 2017)

MONDAY

D 52.4
S 52.4
N 57.1

10

One machine can do the work of fifty ordinary men. No machine can do the work of one extraordinary man.
— Elbert Hubbard (American author, *A Message to Garcia*, 1856–1915)

TUESDAY

D 52.4
S 57.1
N 66.7

11

The symbol of all relationships among such men, the moral symbol of respect for human beings, is the trader.
— Ayn Rand (Russian-born American novelist and philosopher, from Galt's Speech, *Atlas Shrugged*, 1957, 1905–1982)

Small Cap Strength Starts in Mid-December (Page 108)

WEDNESDAY

D 47.6
S 47.6
N 42.9

12

You get stepped on, passed over, knocked down, but you have to come back.
— 90-year old Walter Watson (MD, *Fortune*, 11/13/2000)

THURSDAY

D 47.6
S 47.6
N 42.9

13

You know a country is falling apart when even the government will not accept its own currency.
— Jim Rogers (Financier, *Adventure Capitalist*, b. 1942)

FRIDAY

D 52.4
S 42.9
N 42.9

14

Setting a goal is not the main thing. It is deciding how you will go about achieving it and staying with that plan.
— Tom Landry (Head Coach Dallas Cowboys, 1960–1988)

SATURDAY

15

SUNDAY

16

WALL STREET'S ONLY "FREE LUNCH" SERVED BEFORE CHRISTMAS

Investors tend to get rid of their losers near year-end for tax purposes, often hammering these stocks down to bargain levels. Over the years, the *Almanac* has shown that NYSE stocks selling at their lows on December 15 will usually outperform the market by February 15 in the following year. Preferred stocks, closed-end funds, splits, and new issues are eliminated.

BARGAIN STOCKS VS. THE MARKET*

Short Span* Late Dec–Jan/Feb	New Lows Late Dec	% Change Jan/Feb	% Change NYSE Composite	Bargain Stocks Advantage
1974–75	112	48.9%	22.1%	26.8%
1975–76	21	34.9	14.9	20.0
1976–77	2	1.3	−3.3	4.6
1977–78	15	2.8	−4.5	7.3
1978–79	43	11.8	3.9	7.9
1979–80	5	9.3	6.1	3.2
1980–81	14	7.1	−2.0	9.1
1981–82	21	−2.6	−7.4	4.8
1982–83	4	33.0	9.7	23.3
1983–84	13	−3.2	−3.8	0.6
1984–85	32	19.0	12.1	6.9
1985–86	4	−22.5	3.9	−26.4
1986–87	22	9.3	12.5	−3.2
1987–88	23	13.2	6.8	6.4
1988–89	14	30.0	6.4	23.6
1989–90	25	−3.1	−4.8	1.7
1990–91	18	18.8	12.6	6.2
1991–92	23	51.1	7.7	43.4
1992–93	9	8.7	0.6	8.1
1993–94	10	−1.4	2.0	−3.4
1994–95	25	14.6	5.7	8.9
1995–96	5	−11.3	4.5	−15.8
1996–97	16	13.9	11.2	2.7
1997–98	29	9.9	5.7	4.2
1998–99	40	−2.8	4.3	−7.1
1999–00	26	8.9	−5.4	14.3
2000–01	51	44.4	0.1	44.3
2001–02	12	31.4	−2.3	33.7
2002–03	33	28.7	3.9	24.8
2003–04	15	16.7	2.3	14.4
2004–05	36	6.8	−2.8	9.6
2005–06	71	12.0	2.6	9.4
2006–07	43	5.1	−0.5	5.6
2007–08	71	−3.2	−9.4	6.2
2008–09	88	11.4	−2.4	13.8
2009–10	25	1.8	−3.0	4.8
2010–11	20	8.3	3.4	4.9
2011–12	65	18.1	6.1	12.0
2012–13	17	20.9	3.4	17.5
2013–14	18	25.7	1.7	24.0
2014–15	17	0.2	−0.4	0.6
2015–16	38	−9.2%	5.6%	−14.8%
2016–17	19	2.8%	0.6%	2.2%
43-Year Totals		**521.5%**	**130.4%**	**391.1%**
Average		**12.1%**	**3.0%**	**9.1%**

Dec 15–Feb 15 (1974–1999), Dec 1999–2017 based on actual newsletter portfolio.

In response to changing market conditions, we tweaked the strategy the last 18 years, adding selections from NASDAQ and AMEX, and selling in mid-January some years. We e-mail the list of stocks to our *Almanac Investor eNewsletter* subscribers. Visit *www.stocktradersalmanac.com,* or see the ad insert for additional details and a special offer for new subscribers.

We have come to the conclusion that the most prudent course of action is to compile our list from the stocks making new lows on Triple-Witching Friday before Christmas, capitalizing on the Santa Claus Rally (page 114). This also gives us the weekend to evaluate the issues in greater depth and weed out any glaringly problematic stocks. Subscribers will receive the list of stocks selected from the new lows made on December 15, 2017 and December 21, 2018, via e-mail.

This "Free Lunch" strategy is an extremely short-term strategy reserved for the nimblest traders. It has performed better after market corrections and when there are more new lows to choose from. The object is to buy bargain stocks near their 52-week lows and sell any quick, generous gains, as these issues can be real dogs.

Monday Before December Triple Witching S&P Up 11 of Last 17

MONDAY
D 57.1
S 57.1
N 52.4
17

It isn't the incompetent who destroy an organization. It is those who have achieved something and want to rest upon their achievements who are forever clogging things up.
— Charles E. Sorenson (Danish-American engineer, officer, director of Ford Motor Co. 1907–1950, helped develop 1st auto assembly line, 1881–1968)

FOMC Meeting (2 Days)

TUESDAY
D 57.1
S 61.9
N 57.1
18

I sold enough papers last year of high school to pay cash for a BMW.
— Michael Dell (Founder Dell Computer, *Forbes*, b. 1965)

December Triple-Witching Week, S&P Up 25 of Last 33

WEDNESDAY
D 42.9
S 47.6
N 38.1
19

We can guarantee cash benefits as far out and at whatever size you like, but we cannot guarantee their purchasing power.
— Alan Greenspan (Fed Chairman 1987–2006, on funding Social Security to Senate Banking Committee 2/15/05)

THURSDAY
D 52.4
S 52.4
N 52.4
20

What's the difference between when you pray in church or at your screen? When you pray at your screen you really mean it!
— Vince Stanzione (British entrepreneur, trader, author, b.1968)

December Triple Witching, S&P Up 24 of 35, Average Gain 0.3%

FRIDAY
D 71.4
S 66.7
N 61.9
21

I don't know where speculation got such a bad name, since I know of no forward leap which was not fathered by speculation.
— John Steinbeck (American author, 1902–1968)

The Only FREE LUNCH on Wall Street is Served (Page 112)
Almanac Investors Emailed Alert Before the Open, Monday (See Insert)

SATURDAY
22

SUNDAY
23

IF SANTA CLAUS SHOULD FAIL TO CALL, BEARS MAY COME TO BROAD AND WALL

Santa Claus tends to come to Wall Street nearly every year, bringing a short, sweet, respectable rally within the last five days of the year and the first two in January. This has been good for an average 1.3% gain since 1969 (1.3% since 1950 as well). Santa's failure to show tends to precede bear markets, or times stocks could be purchased later in the year at much lower prices. We discovered this phenomenon in 1972.

DAILY % CHANGE IN S&P 500 AT YEAR END

	Trading Days Before Year End						First Days in January			Rally %
	6	5	4	3	2	1	1	2	3	Change
1969	−0.4	1.1	0.8	−0.7	0.4	0.5	1.0	0.5	−0.7	3.6
1970	0.1	0.6	0.5	1.1	0.2	−0.1	−1.1	0.7	0.6	1.9
1971	−0.4	0.2	1.0	0.3	−0.4	0.3	−0.4	0.4	1.0	1.3
1972	−0.3	−0.7	0.6	0.4	0.5	1.0	0.9	0.4	−0.1	3.1
1973	−1.1	−0.7	3.1	2.1	−0.2	0.01	0.1	2.2	−0.9	6.7
1974	−1.4	1.4	0.8	−0.4	0.03	2.1	2.4	0.7	0.5	7.2
1975	0.7	0.8	0.9	−0.1	−0.4	0.5	0.8	1.8	1.0	4.3
1976	0.1	1.2	0.7	−0.4	0.5	0.5	−0.4	−1.2	−0.9	0.8
1977	0.8	0.9	N/C	0.1	0.2	0.2	−1.3	−0.3	−0.8	−0.3
1978	0.03	1.7	1.3	−0.9	−0.4	−0.2	0.6	1.1	0.8	3.3
1979	−0.6	0.1	0.1	0.2	−0.1	0.1	−2.0	−0.5	1.2	−2.2
1980	−0.4	0.4	0.5	−1.1	0.2	0.3	0.4	1.2	0.1	2.0
1981	−0.5	0.2	−0.2	−0.5	0.5	0.2	0.2	−2.2	−0.7	−1.8
1982	0.6	1.8	−1.0	0.3	−0.7	0.2	−1.6	2.2	0.4	1.2
1983	−0.2	−0.03	0.9	0.3	−0.2	0.05	−0.5	1.7	1.2	2.1
1984	−0.5	0.8	−0.2	−0.4	0.3	0.6	−1.1	−0.5	−0.5	−0.6
1985	−1.1	−0.7	0.2	0.9	0.5	0.3	−0.8	0.6	−0.1	1.1
1986	−1.0	0.2	0.1	−0.9	−0.5	−0.5	1.8	2.3	0.2	2.4
1987	1.3	−0.5	−2.6	−0.4	1.3	−0.3	3.6	1.1	0.1	2.2
1988	−0.2	0.3	−0.4	0.1	0.8	−0.6	−0.9	1.5	0.2	0.9
1989	0.6	0.8	−0.2	0.6	0.5	0.8	1.8	−0.3	−0.9	4.1
1990	0.5	−0.6	0.3	−0.8	0.1	0.5	−1.1	−1.4	−0.3	−3.0
1991	2.5	0.6	1.4	0.4	2.1	0.5	0.04	0.5	−0.3	5.7
1992	−0.3	0.2	−0.1	−0.3	0.2	−0.7	−0.1	−0.2	0.04	−1.1
1993	0.01	0.7	0.1	−0.1	−0.4	−0.5	−0.2	0.3	0.1	−0.1
1994	0.01	0.2	0.4	−0.3	0.1	−0.4	−0.03	0.3	−0.1	0.2
1995	0.8	0.2	0.4	0.04	−0.1	0.3	0.8	0.1	−0.6	1.8
1996	−0.3	0.5	0.6	0.1	−0.4	−1.7	−0.5	1.5	−0.1	0.1
1997	−1.5	−0.7	0.4	1.8	1.8	−0.04	0.5	0.2	−1.1	4.0
1998	2.1	−0.2	−0.1	1.3	−0.8	−0.2	−0.1	1.4	2.2	1.3
1999	1.6	−0.1	0.04	0.4	0.1	0.3	−1.0	−3.8	0.2	−4.0
2000	0.8	2.4	0.7	1.0	0.4	−1.0	−2.8	5.0	−1.1	5.7
2001	0.4	−0.02	0.4	0.7	0.3	−1.1	0.6	0.9	0.6	1.8
2002	0.2	−0.5	−0.3	−1.6	0.5	0.05	3.3	−0.05	2.2	1.2
2003	0.3	−0.2	0.2	1.2	0.01	0.2	−0.3	1.2	0.1	2.4
2004	0.1	−0.4	0.7	−0.01	0.01	−0.1	−0.8	−1.2	−0.4	−1.8
2005	0.4	0.04	−1.0	0.1	−0.3	−0.5	1.6	0.4	0.002	0.4
2006	−0.4	−0.5	0.4	0.7	−0.1	−0.5	−0.1	0.1	−0.6	0.003
2007	1.7	0.8	0.1	−1.4	0.1	−0.7	−1.4	N/C	−2.5	−2.5
2008	−1.0	0.6	0.5	−0.4	2.4	1.4	3.2	−0.5	0.8	7.4
2009	0.2	0.5	0.1	−0.1	0.02	−1.0	1.6	0.3	0.05	1.4
2010	−0.2	0.1	0.1	0.1	−0.2	−0.02	1.1	−0.1	0.5	1.1
2011	0.8	0.9	0.01	−1.3	1.1	−0.4	1.6	0.02	0.3	1.9
2012	−0.9	−0.2	−0.5	−0.1	−1.1	1.7	2.5	−0.2	0.5	2.0
2013	0.5	0.3	0.5	−0.03	−0.02	0.4	−0.9	−0.03	−0.3	0.2
2014	0.2	−0.01	0.3	0.1	−0.5	−1.0	−0.03	−1.8	−0.9	−3.0
2015	1.2	−0.2	−0.2	1.1	−0.7	−0.9	−1.5	0.2	−1.3	−2.3
2016	−0.2	0.1	0.2	−0.8	−0.03	−0.5	0.9	0.6	−0.1	0.4
Avg	0.12	0.30	0.26	0.05	0.16	−0.0004	0.22	0.36	−0.01	1.3

The couplet above was certainly on the mark in 1999, as the period suffered a horrendous 4.0% loss. On January 14, 2000, the Dow started its 33-month 37.8% slide to the October 2002 midterm election year bottom. NASDAQ cracked eight weeks later, falling 37.3% in 10 weeks, eventually dropping 77.9% by October 2002. Energy prices and Middle East terror woes may have grounded Santa in 2004. In 2007, the third worst reading since 1950 was recorded, as a full-blown financial crisis led to the second worst bear market in history. In 2016, the period was hit again as global growth concerns escalated and the market digested the first interest rate hike in nearly a decade.

DECEMBER 2018

Last Trading Day Before Christmas, Dow Up 8 of Last 10 Years
(Shortened Trading Day)

MONDAY
D 47.6
S 47.6
N 61.9
24

A weak currency is the sign of a weak economy, and a weak economy leads to a weak nation.
— H. Ross Perot (American businessman, _The Dollar Crisis_, 2-time 3rd-party presidential candidate 1992 & 1996, b. 1930)

Christmas Day _(Market Closed)_

TUESDAY
25

Don't fritter away your time. Create, act, take a place wherever you are and be somebody.
— Theodore Roosevelt (26th U.S. President, 1858–1919)

WEDNESDAY
D 76.2
S 76.2
N 66.7
26

Make sure you have a jester because people in high places are seldom told the truth.
— Radio caller to President Ronald Reagan

THURSDAY
D 52.4
S 57.1
N 52.4
27

Intellect and Emotion are partners who do not speak the same language. The intellect finds logic to justify what the emotions have decided. WIN THE HEARTS OF PEOPLE, THEIR MINDS WILL FOLLOW.
— Roy H. Williams (_The Wizard of Ads_)

FRIDAY
D 42.9
S 52.4
N 38.1
28

New indicator: CFO Magazine gave Excellence awards to WorldCom's Scott Sullivan (1998), Enron's Andrew Fastow (1999), and to Tyco's Mark Swartz (2000). All were subsequently indicted.
— Roger Lowenstein (Financial journalist and author, _Origins of the Crash_, b. 1954)

SATURDAY
29

January Almanac Investor Sector Seasonalities: See Pages 92, 94 and 96

SUNDAY
30

YEAR'S TOP INVESTMENT BOOKS

Relationship Investing: Stock Market Therapy for Your Money, Jeffrey Weiss CMT, Skyhorse Publishing, $21.99. **2018 Best Investment Book of the Year**. See page 76.

Money Changes Everything: How Finance Made Civilization Possible, William N. Goetzmann, Princeton University Press, $35.00. Pulitzer-prize winning, veteran historian and distinguished Professor of Finance and Management Studies at Yale takes us on an amazing journey through human history tracing the inextricable link between the development of finance and the growth of civilization. Best book on economic history ever written.

Finance for Normal People: How Investors and Markets Behave, Meir Statman, Oxford University Press, $34.95. Renowned professor and a founder of behavioral finance is a man after our own hearts. Prof. Statman unlocks the behavioral finance crypt and reveals the simple moving parts of behavioral finance in lay terms.

Adaptive Markets: Financial Evolution at the Speed of Thought, Andrew W. Lo, Princeton University Press, $37.50. Heavy-hitting behavioral finance academic at MIT and industry pro who founded RIA AlphaSimplex Group cleanly tackles one of the biggest debates in finance and economics: Are investors and markets rational and efficient or irrational and inefficient?

Modern Investing: Gambling in Disguise, David Schneider, CreateSpace (self-published), $12.98. David Schneider, former international investment banker and asset manager gone independent who co-hosts *The 80/20 Investing Show* financial podcast, provides strategies to help you make the right investment decisions and protect your capital from Wall Street chicanery.

Your Complete Guide to Factor-Based Investing: The Way Smart Money Invests Today, Andrew L Berkin & Larry E. Swedroe, Buckingham, $12.99. Navigate your way through the investment "factor zoo" with two seasoned game wardens of factor investing. Learn how to select the finest factor specimens with a quantitative, evidence-based approach that helps you outperform the market.

A Man for All Markets: From Las Vegas to Wall Street, How I Beat the Dealer and the Market, Edward O. Thorp, Random House, $30.00. Card-counting mathematician, hedge fund manager, father of the wearable computer and pioneer of market probability theory who averaged 20% per year for 30 years tells all.

Rule of 72: How to Compound Your Money and Uncover Hidden Stock Profits, Tom Jacobs & John Del Vecchio, Dent Research, $14.95. The latest installment from the duo that brought us our Best Investment Book of 2013: *What's Behind the Numbers?* (McGraw-Hill, 2012). The power of compounding is no secret to us, just take a gander at our table on page 190 that we've had in the *Almanac* for decades. Six tests for finding top stocks from forensic accounting short-seller and value investment advisor/manager.

Narrative and Numbers: The Value of Stories in Business, Aswath Damodaran, Columbia Business School Publishing, $29.95. Valuation guru and Professor of Finance at NYU's Stern School of Business helps us navigate the often murky waters of company valuations and corporate narratives through case studies on Tesla, Uber, Facebook, Twitter, Apple, Amazon and others with a series of tests for discerning the veracity these stories.

Principles: Life and Work, Ray Dalio, Simon & Schuster, $30.00. Bigtime hedge fund manager shares the unique and unconventional principles he developed that have driven his success and his firm's most effective culture. According to *Fortune* Bridgewater is the fifth most important private company in the U.S. Dalio has been named to *Time's* 100 most influential people in the world. Dalio's *Principles* will help you better achieve your goals.

DECEMBER 2018/JANUARY 2019

Last Trading Day of the Year, NASDAQ Down 15 of last 17
NASDAQ Was Up 29 Years in a Row 1971–1999

MONDAY

D 33.3
S 28.6
N 33.3

31

...the most successful positions I've taken have been those about which I've been most nervous (and ignored that emotion anyway). Courage is not about being fearless; courage is about acting appropriately even when you are fearful.
— Daniel Turov (*Turov on Timing*)

New Year's Day *(Market Closed)*

TUESDAY

1

If you torture the data long enough, it will confess to anything.
— Darrell Huff (*How to Lie With Statistics*, 1954)

Small Caps Punished First Trading Day of Year
Russell 2000 Down 16 of Last 28, But Up 6 of Last 9

WEDNESDAY

D 61.9
S 47.6
N 66.7

2

A good new chairman of the Federal Reserve Bank is worth a $10 billion tax cut.
— Paul H. Douglas (U.S. Senator Illinois 1949–1967, 1892–1976)

Second Trading Day of the Year, Dow Up 18 of Last 26
Santa Claus Rally Ends (Page 114)

THURSDAY

D 66.7
S 57.1
N 47.6

3

I am young, powerful and successful, and I produce at least $10,000 a month.
—Mantra of Suze Orman, *The 9 Steps to Financial Freedom*, as a young Merrill Lynch broker

FRIDAY

D 47.6
S 52.4
N 47.6

4

The secret to business is to know something that nobody else knows.
— Aristotle Onassis (Greek shipping billionaire, 1906–1975)

SATURDAY

5

SUNDAY

6

2019 STRATEGY CALENDAR

(Option expiration dates circled)

	MONDAY	TUESDAY	WEDNESDAY	THURSDAY	FRIDAY	SATURDAY	SUNDAY
JANUARY	31	1 JANUARY New Year's Day	2	3	4	5	6
	7	8	9	10	11	12	13
	14	15	16	17	(18)	19	20
	21 Martin Luther King Day	22	23	24	25	26	27
	28	29	30	31	1 FEBRUARY	2	3
FEBRUARY	4	5	6	7	8	9	10
	11	12	13	14 ♥	(15)	16	17
	18 President's Day	19	20	21	22	23	24
	25	26	27	28	1 MARCH	2	3
MARCH	4	5	6 Ash Wednesday	7	8	9	10 Daylight Saving Time Begins
	11	12	13	14	(15)	16	17 ♣ St. Patrick's Day
	18	19	20	21	22	23	24
	25	26	27	28	29	30	31
APRIL	1 APRIL	2	3	4	5	6	7
	8	9	10	11	12	13	14
	15 Tax Deadline	16	17	18	(19) Good Friday	20 Passover	21 Easter
	22	23	24	25	26	27	28
	29	30	1 MAY	2	3	4	5
MAY	6	7	8	9	10	11	12 Mother's Day
	13	14	15	16	(17)	18	19
	20	21	22	23	24	25	26
	27 Memorial Day	28	29	30	31	1 JUNE	2
JUNE	3	4	5	6	7	8	9
	10	11	12	13	14	15	16 Father's Day
	17	18	19	20	(21)	22	23
	24	25	26	27	28	29	30

Market closed on shaded weekdays; closes early when half-shaded.

2019 STRATEGY CALENDAR

(Option expiration dates circled)

MONDAY	TUESDAY	WEDNESDAY	THURSDAY	FRIDAY	SATURDAY	SUNDAY	
1 JULY	2	3	4 Independence Day	5	6	7	JULY
8	9	10	11	12	13	14	
15	16	17	18	(19)	20	21	
22	23	24	25	26	27	28	
29	30	31	1 AUGUST	2	3	4	
5	6	7	8	9	10	11	AUGUST
12	13	14	15	(16)	17	18	
19	20	21	22	23	24	25	
26	27	28	29	30	31	1 SEPTEMBER	
2 Labor Day	3	4	5	6	7	8	SEPTEMBER
9	10	11	12	13	14	15	
16	17	18	19	(20)	21	22	
23	24	25	26	27	28	29	
30 Rosh Hashanah	1 OCTOBER	2	3	4	5	6	OCTOBER
7	8	9 Yom Kippur	10	11	12	13	
14 Columbus Day	15	16	17	(18)	19	20	
21	22	23	24	25	26	27	
28	29	30	31	1 NOVEMBER	2	3 Daylight Saving Time Ends	NOVEMBER
4	5 Election Day	6	7	8	9	10	
11 Veterans' Day	12	13	14	(15)	16	17	
18	19	20	21	22	23	24	
25	26	27	28 Thanksgiving Day	29	30	1 DECEMBER	DECEMBER
2	3	4	5	6	7	8	
9	10	11	12	13	14	15	
16	17	18	19	(20)	21	22	
23 Chanukah	24	25 Christmas	26	27	28	29	
30	31	1 JANUARY New Year's Day	2	3	4	5	

DIRECTORY OF TRADING PATTERNS AND DATABANK

CONTENTS

DOW JONES INDUSTRIALS MARKET PROBABILITY CALENDAR 2018

THE % CHANCE OF THE MARKET RISING ON ANY TRADING DAY OF THE YEAR*
(Based on the number of times the DJIA rose on a particular trading day during January 1954–December 2016)

Date	Jan	Feb	Mar	Apr	May	Jun	Jul	Aug	Sep	Oct	Nov	Dec
1	H	58.7	65.1	S	57.1	58.7	S	42.9	S	46.0	60.3	S
2	57.1	54.0	63.5	60.3	63.5	S	65.1	46.0	S	55.6	52.4	S
3	71.4	S	S	60.3	49.2	S	57.1	49.2	H	54.0	S	46.0
4	47.6	S	S	52.4	47.6	50.8	H	S	57.1	61.9	S	50.8
5	55.6	41.3	58.7	57.1	S	52.4	60.3	S	60.3	44.4	65.1	63.5
6	S	57.1	50.8	50.8	S	58.7	55.6	49.2	60.3	S	58.7	58.7
7	S	47.6	47.6	S	47.6	52.4	S	54.0	44.4	S	49.2	49.2
8	46.0	42.9	54.0	S	52.4	46.0	S	47.6	S	52.4	60.3	S
9	49.2	47.6	58.7	60.3	49.2	S	61.9	47.6	S	42.9	54.0	S
10	47.6	S	S	63.5	52.4	S	57.1	46.0	47.6	41.3	S	46.0
11	47.6	S	S	63.5	46.0	36.5	50.8	S	42.9	50.8	S	54.0
12	57.1	58.7	52.4	55.6	S	55.6	44.4	S	60.3	58.7	57.1	57.1
13	S	46.0	57.1	71.4	S	58.7	66.7	47.6	58.7	S	49.2	44.4
14	S	50.8	52.4	S	52.4	57.1	S	63.5	46.0	S	49.2	52.4
15	H	55.6	60.3	S	55.6	50.8	S	57.1	S	50.8	58.7	S
16	55.6	41.3	60.3	63.5	44.4	S	50.8	50.8	S	52.4	50.8	S
17	60.3	S	S	57.1	54.0	S	47.6	49.2	55.6	44.4	S	47.6
18	41.3	S	S	55.6	41.3	50.8	50.8	S	55.6	60.3	S	55.6
19	38.1	H	60.3	55.6	S	50.8	54.0	S	39.7	50.8	50.8	49.2
20	S	47.6	54.0	52.4	S	46.0	39.7	54.0	50.8	S	49.2	55.6
21	S	49.2	49.2	S	49.2	46.0	S	41.3	47.6	S	57.1	52.4
22	42.9	36.5	36.5	S	41.3	42.9	S	57.1	S	46.0	H	S
23	58.7	44.4	50.8	54.0	34.9	S	46.0	49.2	S	42.9	68.3	S
24	47.6	S	S	50.8	52.4	S	46.0	52.4	49.2	50.8	S	60.3
25	57.1	S	S	57.1	46.0	34.9	58.7	S	54.0	28.6	S	H
26	57.1	60.3	44.4	57.1	S	47.6	52.4	S	52.4	54.0	58.7	71.4
27	S	47.6	55.6	49.2	S	47.6	44.4	47.6	49.2	S	65.1	47.6
28	S	50.8	46.0	S	H	55.6	S	46.0	39.7	S	58.7	54.0
29	49.2		42.9	S	46.0	52.4	S	61.9	S	54.0	52.4	S
30	58.7		H	50.8	57.1	S	57.1	39.7	S	58.7	52.4	S
31	57.1		S		57.1		47.6	60.3		52.4		52.4

* See new trends developing on pages 70, 92, 141–146.

RECENT DOW JONES INDUSTRIALS MARKET PROBABILITY CALENDAR 2018

THE % CHANCE OF THE MARKET RISING ON ANY TRADING DAY OF THE YEAR*

(Based on the number of times the DJIA rose on a particular trading day during January 1996–December 2016**)

Date	Jan	Feb	Mar	Apr	May	Jun	Jul	Aug	Sep	Oct	Nov	Dec
1	H	71.4	66.7	S	71.4	66.7	S	33.3	S	47.6	52.4	S
2	61.9	42.9	47.6	76.2	61.9	S	81.0	57.1	S	52.4	57.1	S
3	66.7	S	S	66.7	28.6	S	33.3	47.6	H	57.1	S	47.6
4	47.6	S	S	42.9	38.1	52.4	H	S	57.1	66.7	S	38.1
5	47.6	47.6	57.1	61.9	S	47.6	52.4	S	71.4	33.3	61.9	66.7
6	S	57.1	47.6	42.9	S	57.1	52.4	52.4	52.4	S	76.2	52.4
7	S	52.4	66.7	S	52.4	66.7	S	52.4	42.9	S	61.9	52.4
8	38.1	47.6	47.6	S	66.7	57.1	S	47.6	S	42.9	47.6	S
9	47.6	57.1	57.1	52.4	52.4	S	61.9	47.6	S	47.6	47.6	S
10	52.4	S	S	57.1	66.7	S	57.1	42.9	61.9	42.9	S	52.4
11	57.1	S	S	61.9	42.9	33.3	57.1	S	47.6	42.9	S	52.4
12	52.4	52.4	57.1	52.4	S	42.9	66.7	S	66.7	71.4	42.9	47.6
13	S	61.9	57.1	76.2	S	52.4	66.7	42.9	57.1	S	66.7	47.6
14	S	47.6	61.9	S	52.4	61.9	S	61.9	47.6	S	61.9	52.4
15	H	66.7	71.4	S	57.1	57.1	S	52.4	S	47.6	71.4	S
16	52.4	42.9	52.4	66.7	47.6	S	47.6	57.1	S	57.1	42.9	S
17	57.1	S	S	61.9	57.1	S	61.9	71.4	57.1	52.4	S	57.1
18	42.9	S	S	57.1	38.1	57.1	57.1	S	71.4	61.9	S	57.1
19	38.1	H	66.7	66.7	S	57.1	71.4	S	38.1	52.4	52.4	42.9
20	S	38.1	57.1	66.7	S	57.1	19.0	47.6	57.1	S	52.4	52.4
21	S	47.6	38.1	S	47.6	38.1	S	33.3	57.1	S	52.4	71.4
22	38.1	47.6	38.1	S	28.6	42.9	S	57.1	S	38.1	H	S
23	47.6	38.1	61.9	57.1	38.1	S	42.9	52.4	S	57.1	66.7	S
24	38.1	S	S	42.9	47.6	S	42.9	52.4	33.3	52.4	S	47.6
25	57.1	S	S	57.1	52.4	33.3	57.1	S	57.1	38.1	S	H
26	61.9	47.6	28.6	71.4	S	42.9	52.4	S	61.9	61.9	61.9	76.2
27	S	47.6	52.4	66.7	S	57.1	38.1	42.9	57.1	S	66.7	52.4
28	S	38.1	57.1	S	H	57.1	S	42.9	33.3	S	57.1	42.9
29	57.1		38.1	S	47.6	38.1	S	71.4	S	61.9	57.1	S
30	52.4		H	33.3	61.9	S	42.9	23.8	S	57.1	52.4	S
31	52.4		S		42.9		33.3	47.6		57.1		33.3

*See new trends developing on pages 70, 92, 141–146.   ** Based on most recent 21-year period.*

S&P 500 MARKET PROBABILITY CALENDAR 2018

THE % CHANCE OF THE MARKET RISING ON ANY TRADING DAY OF THE YEAR*
(Based on the number of times the S&P 500 rose on a particular trading day during January 1954–December 2016)

Date	Jan	Feb	Mar	Apr	May	Jun	Jul	Aug	Sep	Oct	Nov	Dec
1	H	60.3	61.9	S	57.1	57.1	S	46.0	S	47.6	60.3	S
2	47.6	57.1	58.7	65.1	66.7	S	71.4	44.4	S	65.1	57.1	S
3	68.3	S	S	60.3	54.0	S	54.0	50.8	H	55.6	S	46.0
4	52.4	S	S	54.0	42.9	60.3	H	S	58.7	61.9	S	52.4
5	50.8	47.6	61.9	54.0	S	52.4	55.6	S	54.0	46.0	66.7	61.9
6	S	52.4	49.2	52.4	S	57.1	58.7	50.8	60.3	S	55.6	57.1
7	S	50.8	49.2	S	46.0	46.0	S	54.0	46.0	S	47.6	44.4
8	44.4	44.4	57.1	S	52.4	44.4	S	47.6	S	50.8	58.7	S
9	52.4	41.3	58.7	61.9	49.2	S	60.3	54.0	S	41.3	60.3	S
10	54.0	S	S	63.5	52.4	S	57.1	46.0	49.2	46.0	S	50.8
11	52.4	S	S	55.6	44.4	41.3	52.4	S	50.8	50.8	S	55.6
12	58.7	60.3	50.8	50.8	S	55.6	52.4	S	60.3	54.0	57.1	49.2
13	S	54.0	63.5	61.9	S	61.9	71.4	47.6	63.5	S	47.6	49.2
14	S	47.6	44.4	S	49.2	57.1	S	63.5	50.8	S	49.2	44.4
15	H	55.6	60.3	S	55.6	57.1	S	63.5	S	50.8	50.8	S
16	61.9	38.1	61.9	61.9	49.2	S	52.4	54.0	S	57.1	49.2	S
17	57.1	S	S	60.3	55.6	S	44.4	55.6	54.0	44.4	S	47.6
18	50.8	S	S	54.0	38.1	49.2	46.0	S	55.6	65.1	S	57.1
19	47.6	H	58.7	55.6	S	55.6	54.0	S	46.0	52.4	54.0	46.0
20	S	50.8	50.8	55.6	S	42.9	39.7	52.4	52.4	S	52.4	47.6
21	S	42.9	42.9	S	46.0	50.8	S	44.4	49.2	S	55.6	49.2
22	49.2	41.3	50.8	S	49.2	44.4	S	60.3	S	47.6	H	S
23	60.3	39.7	44.4	47.6	44.4	S	46.0	47.6	S	42.9	65.1	S
24	60.3	S	S	47.6	52.4	S	46.0	50.8	47.6	46.0	S	60.3
25	54.0	S	S	57.1	50.8	34.9	55.6	S	49.2	31.7	S	H
26	52.4	57.1	46.0	50.8	S	41.3	54.0	S	58.7	58.7	58.7	73.0
27	S	50.8	55.6	46.0	S	50.8	47.6	46.0	49.2	S	66.7	52.4
28	S	57.1	39.7	S	H	58.7	S	46.0	42.9	S	58.7	60.3
29	46.0		41.3	S	47.6	50.8	S	61.9	S	57.1	60.3	S
30	61.9		H	57.1	57.1	S	65.1	44.4	S	58.7	49.2	S
31	61.9		S		58.7		60.3	63.5		54.0		60.3

* See new trends developing on pages 70, 92, 141–146.

RECENT S&P 500 MARKET PROBABILITY CALENDAR 2018

THE % CHANCE OF THE MARKET RISING ON ANY TRADING DAY OF THE YEAR*

(Based on the number of times the S&P 500 rose on a particular trading day during January 1996–December 2016**)

Date	Jan	Feb	Mar	Apr	May	Jun	Jul	Aug	Sep	Oct	Nov	Dec
1	H	76.2	66.7	S	71.4	61.9	S	42.9	S	52.4	52.4	S
2	47.6	47.6	42.9	76.2	52.4	S	85.7	52.4	S	57.1	66.7	S
3	57.1	S	S	66.7	33.3	S	33.3	52.4	H	57.1	S	47.6
4	52.4	S	S	52.4	33.3	71.4	H	S	57.1	61.9	S	47.6
5	47.6	42.9	66.7	57.1	S	42.9	61.9	S	47.6	38.1	61.9	61.9
6	S	57.1	52.4	42.9	S	57.1	52.4	57.1	52.4	S	76.2	42.9
7	S	52.4	66.7	S	47.6	47.6	S	42.9	52.4	S	57.1	47.6
8	42.9	57.1	52.4	S	57.1	52.4	S	52.4	S	42.9	42.9	S
9	57.1	47.6	52.4	57.1	47.6	S	52.4	47.6	S	47.6	42.9	S
10	61.9	S	S	52.4	57.1	S	57.1	47.6	57.1	42.9	S	52.4
11	47.6	S	S	52.4	42.9	42.9	57.1	S	57.1	47.6	S	57.1
12	52.4	61.9	52.4	47.6	S	38.1	76.2	S	66.7	66.7	47.6	47.6
13	S	66.7	66.7	61.9	S	52.4	71.4	38.1	61.9	S	57.1	47.6
14	S	47.6	42.9	S	42.9	61.9	S	57.1	57.1	S	57.1	42.9
15	H	71.4	66.7	S	57.1	66.7	S	66.7	S	47.6	61.9	S
16	52.4	38.1	57.1	61.9	47.6	S	38.1	61.9	S	66.7	42.9	S
17	66.7	S	S	71.4	57.1	S	52.4	71.4	52.4	61.9	S	57.1
18	52.4	S	S	61.9	38.1	57.1	52.4	S	71.4	66.7	S	61.9
19	42.9	H	71.4	61.9	S	57.1	71.4	S	42.9	61.9	57.1	47.6
20	S	42.9	42.9	71.4	S	52.4	19.0	38.1	52.4	S	52.4	52.4
21	S	42.9	33.3	S	47.6	47.6	S	38.1	47.6	S	52.4	66.7
22	52.4	52.4	61.9	S	38.1	42.9	S	61.9	S	47.6	H	S
23	52.4	42.9	57.1	52.4	42.9	S	42.9	52.4	S	66.7	61.9	S
24	47.6	S	S	38.1	52.4	S	47.6	52.4	33.3	57.1	S	47.6
25	52.4	S	S	52.4	57.1	38.1	52.4	S	47.6	33.3	S	H
26	52.4	47.6	28.6	57.1	S	33.3	52.4	S	66.7	52.4	57.1	76.2
27	S	52.4	52.4	61.9	S	52.4	42.9	42.9	61.9	S	61.9	57.1
28	S	38.1	47.6	S	H	61.9	S	47.6	33.3	S	52.4	52.4
29	57.1		42.9	S	47.6	42.9	S	71.4	S	52.4	76.2	S
30	57.1		H	42.9	61.9	S	66.7	23.8	S	57.1	38.1	S
31	57.1		S		52.4		47.6	47.6		61.9		28.6

* See new trends developing on pages 70, 92, 141–146.   ** Based on most recent 21-year period.

NASDAQ COMPOSITE MARKET PROBABILITY CALENDAR 2018

THE % CHANCE OF THE MARKET RISING ON ANY TRADING DAY OF THE YEAR*
(Based on the number of times the NASDAQ rose on a particular trading day during January 1972–December 2016)

Date	Jan	Feb	Mar	Apr	May	Jun	Jul	Aug	Sep	Oct	Nov	Dec
1	H	71.1	62.2	S	64.4	57.8	S	51.1	S	46.7	66.7	S
2	53.3	66.7	55.6	46.7	68.9	S	62.2	42.2	S	60.0	55.6	S
3	64.4	S	S	62.2	57.8	S	44.4	53.3	H	57.8	S	57.8
4	55.6	S	S	62.2	51.1	71.1	H	S	55.6	60.0	S	62.2
5	62.2	53.3	66.7	53.3	S	55.6	46.7	S	60.0	55.6	66.7	64.4
6	S	64.4	51.1	44.4	S	60.0	53.3	57.8	57.8	S	55.6	60.0
7	S	55.6	48.9	S	55.6	48.9	S	53.3	57.8	S	51.1	42.2
8	53.3	51.1	55.6	S	64.4	46.7	S	42.2	S	62.2	55.6	S
9	57.8	48.9	55.6	62.2	53.3	S	60.0	53.3	S	48.9	57.8	S
10	57.8	S	S	62.2	40.0	S	64.4	48.9	55.6	48.9	S	53.3
11	57.8	S	S	62.2	55.6	42.2	60.0	S	48.9	71.1	S	48.9
12	62.2	64.4	48.9	51.1	S	51.1	71.1	S	55.6	64.4	62.2	42.2
13	S	60.0	71.1	57.8	S	60.0	75.6	55.6	62.2	S	55.6	42.2
14	S	64.4	51.1	S	53.3	64.4	S	60.0	62.2	S	51.1	42.2
15	H	60.0	51.1	S	55.6	57.8	S	60.0	S	51.1	44.4	S
16	62.2	51.1	62.2	51.1	55.6	S	62.2	48.9	S	55.6	48.9	S
17	68.9	S	S	60.0	53.3	S	51.1	60.0	37.8	44.4	S	46.7
18	60.0	S	S	55.6	40.0	48.9	55.6	S	53.3	68.9	S	55.6
19	42.2	H	60.0	57.8	S	53.3	60.0	S	53.3	48.9	53.3	48.9
20	S	55.6	64.4	57.8	S	48.9	37.8	51.1	64.4	S	53.3	53.3
21	S	40.0	57.8	S	48.9	46.7	S	35.6	53.3	S	51.1	64.4
22	48.9	51.1	53.3	S	48.9	48.9	S	68.9	S	55.6	H	S
23	51.1	53.3	51.1	53.3	48.9	S	48.9	53.3	S	48.9	71.1	S
24	57.8	S	S	51.1	53.3	S	51.1	51.1	51.1	46.7	S	71.1
25	46.7	S	S	44.4	55.6	40.0	55.6	S	44.4	35.6	S	H
26	66.7	62.2	40.0	64.4	S	46.7	51.1	S	48.9	44.4	57.8	71.1
27	S	57.8	53.3	62.2	S	60.0	46.7	51.1	44.4	S	60.0	48.9
28	S	48.9	55.6	S	H	66.7	S	55.6	46.7	S	66.7	60.0
29	60.0		64.4	S	60.0	68.9	S	64.4	S	57.8	66.7	S
30	55.6		H	66.7	57.8	S	60.0	60.0	S	57.8	62.2	S
31	62.2		S		66.7		51.1	66.7		62.2		68.9

* See new trends developing on pages 70, 92, 141–146.
Based on NASDAQ composite, prior to Feb. 5, 1971; based on National Quotation Bureau indices.

RECENT NASDAQ COMPOSITE MARKET PROBABILITY CALENDAR 2018

THE % CHANCE OF THE MARKET RISING ON ANY TRADING DAY OF THE YEAR*

(Based on the number of times the NASDAQ rose on a particular trading day during January 1996–December 2016**)

Date	Jan	Feb	Mar	Apr	May	Jun	Jul	Aug	Sep	Oct	Nov	Dec
1	H	81.0	61.9	S	76.2	52.4	S	47.6	S	42.9	66.7	S
2	66.7	52.4	38.1	66.7	57.1	S	76.2	42.9	S	61.9	61.9	S
3	47.6	S	S	61.9	42.9	S	33.3	52.4	H	66.7	S	61.9
4	47.6	S	S	66.7	42.9	66.7	H	S	66.7	57.1	S	57.1
5	52.4	38.1	66.7	57.1	S	47.6	57.1	S	52.4	47.6	66.7	61.9
6	S	57.1	42.9	33.3	S	57.1	61.9	52.4	47.6	S	66.7	61.9
7	S	52.4	42.9	S	42.9	42.9	S	38.1	57.1	S	61.9	42.9
8	52.4	57.1	47.6	S	76.2	42.9	S	33.3	S	57.1	52.4	S
9	57.1	42.9	42.9	66.7	47.6	S	57.1	42.9	S	52.4	42.9	S
10	66.7	S	S	47.6	47.6	S	66.7	47.6	61.9	47.6	S	57.1
11	47.6	S	S	61.9	52.4	42.9	57.1	S	57.1	57.1	S	66.7
12	47.6	57.1	42.9	42.9	S	38.1	66.7	S	61.9	71.4	52.4	42.9
13	S	66.7	66.7	52.4	S	47.6	71.4	47.6	66.7	S	66.7	42.9
14	S	66.7	47.6	S	42.9	52.4	S	61.9	81.0	S	52.4	42.9
15	H	57.1	47.6	S	52.4	66.7	S	71.4	S	47.6	47.6	S
16	38.1	47.6	57.1	47.6	52.4	S	52.4	61.9	S	57.1	52.4	S
17	71.4	S	S	61.9	61.9	S	57.1	61.9	38.1	47.6	S	52.4
18	61.9	S	S	52.4	33.3	57.1	61.9	S	76.2	66.7	S	57.1
19	38.1	H	66.7	61.9	S	61.9	71.4	S	52.4	52.4	52.4	38.1
20	S	47.6	61.9	66.7	S	47.6	14.3	38.1	61.9	S	57.1	52.4
21	S	42.9	52.4	S	57.1	33.3	S	33.3	52.4	S	52.4	61.9
22	42.9	61.9	57.1	S	42.9	42.9	S	76.2	S	42.9	H	S
23	47.6	57.1	66.7	52.4	47.6	S	42.9	52.4	S	66.7	71.4	S
24	57.1	S	S	52.4	42.9	S	42.9	47.6	42.9	47.6	S	61.9
25	47.6	S	S	38.1	52.4	38.1	57.1	S	47.6	42.9	S	H
26	76.2	57.1	28.6	52.4	S	42.9	57.1	S	47.6	47.6	57.1	66.7
27	S	57.1	52.4	71.4	S	66.7	42.9	52.4	42.9	S	61.9	52.4
28	S	23.8	57.1	S	28	66.7	S	47.6	33.3	S	57.1	38.1
29	61.9		57.1	S	61.9	66.7	S	76.2	S	52.4	71.4	S
30	52.4		H	57.1	71.4	S	71.4	47.6	S	57.1	42.9	S
31	52.4		S		52.4		42.9	52.4		61.9		33.3

* See new trends developing on pages 70, 92, 141–146.   ** Based on most recent 21-year period.

RUSSELL 1000 INDEX MARKET PROBABILITY CALENDAR 2018

THE % CHANCE OF THE MARKET RISING ON ANY TRADING DAY OF THE YEAR*

(Based on the number of times the RUSSELL 1000 rose on a particular trading day during January 1980–December 2016)

Date	Jan	Feb	Mar	Apr	May	Jun	Jul	Aug	Sep	Oct	Nov	Dec
1	H	64.9	59.5	S	59.5	59.5	S	43.2	S	54.1	70.3	S
2	40.5	59.5	48.6	62.2	62.2	S	75.7	40.5	S	56.8	56.8	S
3	56.8	S	S	62.2	51.4	S	37.8	51.4	H	54.1	S	51.4
4	56.8	S	S	51.4	37.8	56.8	H	S	54.1	56.8	S	54.1
5	51.4	56.8	59.5	54.1	S	48.6	45.9	S	51.4	40.5	59.5	62.2
6	S	54.1	45.9	45.9	S	56.8	56.8	45.9	54.1	S	59.5	43.2
7	S	59.5	45.9	S	45.9	35.1	S	51.4	43.2	S	48.6	45.9
8	51.4	48.6	56.8	S	56.8	43.2	S	56.8	S	56.8	54.1	S
9	62.2	40.5	54.1	67.6	56.8	S	56.8	48.6	S	37.8	51.4	S
10	56.8	S	S	56.8	51.4	S	54.1	45.9	48.6	43.2	S	48.6
11	54.1	S	S	54.1	51.4	40.5	59.5	S	54.1	62.2	S	54.1
12	56.8	70.3	43.2	48.6	S	48.6	67.6	S	64.9	64.9	56.8	43.2
13	S	64.9	62.2	56.8	S	56.8	81.1	43.2	64.9	S	56.8	45.9
14	S	48.6	43.2	S	51.4	59.5	S	59.5	56.8	S	54.1	43.2
15	H	64.9	56.8	S	56.8	59.5	S	64.9	S	56.8	51.4	S
16	67.6	40.5	59.5	64.9	54.1	S	45.9	59.5	S	56.8	45.9	S
17	64.9	S	S	59.5	54.1	S	54.1	64.9	54.1	45.9	S	54.1
18	43.2	S	S	51.4	43.2	54.1	48.6	S	51.4	70.3	S	59.5
19	37.8	H	59.5	54.1	S	62.2	64.9	S	45.9	56.8	62.2	51.4
20	S	43.2	51.4	54.1	S	40.5	35.1	62.2	45.9	S	48.6	45.9
21	S	40.5	43.2	S	48.6	51.4	S	45.9	43.2	S	51.4	59.5
22	51.4	45.9	45.9	S	48.6	43.2	S	67.6	S	51.4	H	S
23	56.8	45.9	54.1	56.8	43.2	S	45.9	51.4	S	48.6	64.9	S
24	51.4	S	S	45.9	59.5	S	40.5	54.1	40.5	43.2	S	62.2
25	51.4	S	S	54.1	62.2	32.4	70.3	S	45.9	32.4	S	H
26	62.2	59.5	35.1	59.5	S	40.5	54.1	S	64.9	54.1	59.5	70.3
27	S	56.8	51.4	54.1	S	51.4	43.2	40.5	54.1	S	67.6	56.8
28	S	54.1	45.9	S	H	59.5	S	54.1	48.6	S	70.3	62.2
29	56.8		48.6	S	56.8	51.4	S	59.5	S	54.1	67.6	S
30	59.5		H	56.8	56.8	S	67.6	45.9	S	62.2	45.9	S
31	59.5		S		54.1		56.8	56.8		64.9		48.6

* See new trends developing on pages 70, 92, 141–146.

RUSSELL 2000 INDEX MARKET PROBABILITY CALENDAR 2018

THE % CHANCE OF THE MARKET RISING ON ANY TRADING DAY OF THE YEAR*

(Based on the number of times the RUSSELL 2000 rose on a particular trading day during January 1980–December 2016)

Date	Jan	Feb	Mar	Apr	May	Jun	Jul	Aug	Sep	Oct	Nov	Dec
1	H	67.6	64.9	S	59.5	62.2	S	45.9	S	48.6	59.5	S
2	43.2	62.2	59.5	51.4	64.9	S	67.6	43.2	S	48.6	67.6	S
3	62.2	S	S	59.5	56.8	S	45.9	51.4	H	51.4	S	51.4
4	56.8	S	S	45.9	56.8	67.6	H	S	51.4	64.9	S	62.2
5	59.5	54.1	64.9	51.4	S	51.4	43.2	S	62.2	40.5	64.9	64.9
6	S	70.3	56.8	40.5	S	56.8	54.1	48.6	54.1	S	62.2	62.2
7	S	62.2	59.5	S	56.8	56.8	S	45.9	64.9	S	56.8	45.9
8	56.8	59.5	51.4	S	56.8	37.8	S	45.9	S	51.4	54.1	S
9	62.2	43.2	54.1	59.5	62.2	S	51.4	56.8	S	45.9	54.1	S
10	56.8	S	S	59.5	48.6	S	62.2	45.9	54.1	51.4	S	54.1
11	64.9	S	S	64.9	51.4	43.2	54.1	S	56.8	64.9	S	48.6
12	62.2	67.6	40.5	48.6	S	51.4	62.2	S	62.2	59.5	67.6	45.9
13	S	62.2	62.2	56.8	S	56.8	67.6	45.9	64.9	S	51.4	40.5
14	S	67.6	51.4	S	48.6	64.9	S	73.0	54.1	S	48.6	40.5
15	H	56.8	48.6	S	45.9	59.5	S	62.2	S	59.5	48.6	S
16	64.9	54.1	59.5	62.2	54.1	S	54.1	59.5	S	45.9	24.3	S
17	70.3	S	S	56.8	54.1	S	51.4	56.8	37.8	48.6	S	40.5
18	70.3	S	S	51.4	51.4	51.4	48.6	S	51.4	67.6	S	56.8
19	32.4	H	67.6	59.5	S	40.5	51.4	S	45.9	56.8	59.5	62.2
20	S	40.5	59.5	64.9	S	43.2	35.1	48.6	40.5	S	48.6	59.5
21	S	40.5	56.8	S	51.4	43.2	S	45.9	45.9	S	35.1	67.6
22	51.4	54.1	45.9	S	48.6	48.6	S	64.9	S	51.4	H	S
23	48.6	56.8	54.1	54.1	51.4	S	40.5	48.6	S	48.6	64.9	S
24	56.8	S	S	48.6	56.8	S	45.9	59.5	45.9	45.9	S	78.4
25	45.9	S	S	59.5	54.1	37.8	59.5	S	32.4	32.4	S	H
26	67.6	62.2	40.5	64.9	S	48.6	62.2	S	54.1	37.8	62.2	67.6
27	S	67.6	54.1	59.5	S	56.8	48.6	56.8	54.1	S	62.2	54.1
28	S	56.8	54.1	S	H	70.3	S	59.5	62.2	S	62.2	59.5
29	59.5		81.1	S	67.6	67.6	S	64.9	S	54.1	67.6	S
30	56.8		H	67.6	67.6	S	56.8	62.2	S	54.1	64.9	S
31	75.7		S		67.6		64.9	67.6		73.0		64.9

* See new trends developing on pages 70, 92, 141–146.

DECENNIAL CYCLE: A MARKET PHENOMENON

By arranging each year's market gain or loss so that the first and succeeding years of each decade fall into the same column, certain interesting patterns emerge—strong fifth and eighth years; weak first, seventh, and zero years.

This fascinating phenomenon was first presented by Edgar Lawrence Smith in *Common Stocks and Business Cycles* (William-Frederick Press, 1959). Anthony Gaubis co-pioneered the decennial pattern with Smith.

When Smith first cut graphs of market prices into 10-year segments and placed them above one another, he observed that each decade tended to have three bull market cycles and that the longest and strongest bull markets seem to favor the middle years of a decade.

Don't place too much emphasis on the decennial cycle nowadays, other than the extraordinary fifth and zero years, as the stock market is more influenced by the quadrennial presidential election cycle, shown on page 130. Also, the last half-century, which has been the most prosperous in U.S. history, has distributed the returns among most years of the decade. Interestingly, NASDAQ suffered its worst bear market ever in a zero year.

Eighth years of decades have the second best record next to fifth years. But 2018 is also a midterm year that has suffered numerous declines over the years. Plus past big eighth years were often preceded by rough seventh years. As of late-May, 2017 was on track for solid gains, potentially further hindering the prospects of a robust 2018.

THE 10-YEAR STOCK MARKET CYCLE
Annual % Change in Dow Jones Industrial Average
Year of Decade

DECADES	1st	2nd	3rd	4th	5th	6th	7th	8th	9th	10th
1881–1890	3.0%	−2.9%	−8.5%	−18.8%	20.1%	12.4%	−8.4%	4.8%	5.5%	−14.1%
1891–1900	17.6	−6.6	−24.6	−0.6	2.3	−1.7	21.3	22.5	9.2	7.0
1901–1910	−8.7	−0.4	−23.6	41.7	38.2	−1.9	−37.7	46.6	15.0	−17.9
1911–1920	0.4	7.6	−10.3	−5.4	81.7	−4.2	−21.7	10.5	30.5	−32.9
1921–1930	12.7	21.7	−3.3	26.2	30.0	0.3	28.8	48.2	−17.2	−33.8
1931–1940	−52.7	−23.1	66.7	4.1	38.5	24.8	−32.8	28.1	−2.9	−12.7
1941–1950	−15.4	7.6	13.8	12.1	26.6	−8.1	2.2	−2.1	12.9	17.6
1951–1960	14.4	8.4	−3.8	44.0	20.8	2.3	−12.8	34.0	16.4	−9.3
1961–1970	18.7	−10.8	17.0	14.6	10.9	−18.9	15.2	4.3	−15.2	4.8
1971–1980	6.1	14.6	−16.6	−27.6	38.3	17.9	−17.3	−3.1	4.2	14.9
1981–1990	−9.2	19.6	20.3	−3.7	27.7	22.6	2.3	11.8	27.0	−4.3
1991–2000	20.3	4.2	13.7	2.1	33.5	26.0	22.6	16.1	25.2	−6.2
2001–2010	−7.1	−16.8	25.3	3.1	−0.6	16.3	6.4	−33.8	18.8	11.0
2011–2020	5.5	7.3	26.5	7.5	−2.2	13.4				
Total % Change	**5.6%**	**30.4%**	**92.6%**	**99.3%**	**365.8%**	**101.2%**	**−31.9%**	**187.9%**	**129.4%**	**−75.9%**
Avg % Change	**0.4%**	**2.2%**	**6.6%**	**7.1%**	**26.1%**	**7.2%**	**−2.5%**	**14.5%**	**10.0%**	**−5.8%**
Up Years	9	8	7	9	12	9	7	10	10	5
Down Years	5	6	7	5	2	5	6	3	3	8

Based on annual close; Cowles indices 1881–1885; 12 Mixed Stocks, 10 Rails, 2 Inds 1886–1889;
20 Mixed Stocks, 18 Rails, 2 Inds 1890–1896; Railroad average 1897 (First industrial average published May 26, 1896).

PRESIDENTIAL ELECTION/STOCK MARKET CYCLE: THE 184-YEAR SAGA CONTINUES

It is no mere coincidence that the last two years (pre-election year and election year) of the 45 administrations since 1833 produced a total net market gain of 742.5%, dwarfing the 307.1% gain of the first two years of these administrations.

Presidential elections every four years have a profound impact on the economy and the stock market. Wars, recessions, and bear markets tend to start or occur in the first half of the term; prosperous times and bull markets, in the latter half. After nine straight annual Dow gains during the millennial bull, the four-year election cycle reasserted its overarching domination of market behavior until 2008. Recovery from the worst recession since the Great Depression produced six straight annual gains, until 2015, when the Dow suffered its first pre-election year loss since 1939.

STOCK MARKET ACTION SINCE 1833
Annual % Change in Dow Jones Industrial Average[1]

4-Year Cycle Beginning	Elected President	Post-Election Year	Mid-Term Year	Pre-Election Year	Election Year
1833	Jackson (D)	−0.9	13.0	3.1	−11.7
1837	Van Buren (D)	−11.5	1.6	−12.3	5.5
1841*	W. H. Harrison (W)**	−13.3	−18.1	45.0	15.5
1845*	Polk (D)	8.1	−14.5	1.2	−3.6
1849*	Taylor (W)	N/C	18.7	−3.2	19.6
1853*	Pierce (D)	−12.7	−30.2	1.5	4.4
1857	Buchanan (D)	−31.0	14.3	−10.7	14.0
1861*	Lincoln (R)	−1.8	55.4	38.0	6.4
1865	Lincoln (R)**	−8.5	3.6	1.6	10.8
1869	Grant (R)	1.7	5.6	7.3	6.8
1873	Grant (R)	−12.7	2.8	−4.1	−17.9
1877	Hayes (R)	−9.4	6.1	43.0	18.7
1881	Garfield (R)**	3.0	−2.9	−8.5	−18.8
1885*	Cleveland (D)	20.1	12.4	−8.4	4.8
1889*	B. Harrison (R)	5.5	−14.1	17.6	−6.6
1893*	Cleveland (D)	−24.6	−0.6	2.3	−1.7
1897*	McKinley (R)	21.3	22.5	9.2	7.0
1901	McKinley (R)**	−8.7	−0.4	−23.6	41.7
1905	T. Roosevelt (R)	38.2	−1.9	−37.7	46.6
1909	Taft (R)	15.0	−17.9	0.4	7.6
1913*	Wilson (D)	−10.3	−5.4	81.7	−4.2
1917	Wilson (D)	−21.7	10.5	30.5	−32.9
1921*	Harding (R)**	12.7	21.7	−3.3	26.2
1925	Coolidge (R)	30.0	0.3	28.8	48.2
1929	Hoover (R)	−17.2	−33.8	−52.7	−23.1
1933*	F. Roosevelt (D)	66.7	4.1	38.5	24.8
1937	F. Roosevelt (D)	−32.8	28.1	−2.9	−12.7
1941	F. Roosevelt (D)	−15.4	7.6	13.8	12.1
1945	F. Roosevelt (D)**	26.6	−8.1	2.2	−2.1
1949	Truman (D)	12.9	17.6	14.4	8.4
1953*	Eisenhower (R)	−3.8	44.0	20.8	2.3
1957	Eisenhower (R)	−12.8	34.0	16.4	−9.3
1961*	Kennedy (D)**	18.7	−10.8	17.0	14.6
1965	Johnson (D)	10.9	−18.9	15.2	4.3
1969*	Nixon (R)	−15.2	4.8	6.1	14.6
1973	Nixon (R)***	−16.6	−27.6	38.3	17.9
1977*	Carter (D)	−17.3	−3.1	4.2	14.9
1981*	Reagan (R)	−9.2	19.6	20.3	−3.7
1985	Reagan (R)	27.7	22.6	2.3	11.8
1989	G. H. W. Bush (R)	27.0	−4.3	20.3	4.2
1993*	Clinton (D)	13.7	2.1	33.5	26.0
1997	Clinton (D)	22.6	16.1	25.2	−6.2
2001*	G. W. Bush (R)	−7.1	−16.8	25.3	3.1
2005	G. W. Bush (R)	−0.6	16.3	6.4	−33.8
2009*	Obama (D)	18.8	11.0	5.5	7.3
2013	Obama (D)	26.5	7.5	−2.2	13.4
Total % Gain		**112.6%**	**194.5%**	**467.3%**	**275.2%**
Average % Gain		**2.5%**	**4.2%**	**10.2%**	**6.0%**
# Up		21	28	34	31
# Down		24	18	12	15

*Party in power ousted   **Death in office   ***Resigned   D–Democrat, W–Whig, R–Republican

[1] Based on annual close; prior to 1886 based on Cowles and other indices; 12 Mixed Stocks, 10 Rails, 2 Inds 1886–1889; 20 Mixed Stocks, 18 Rails, 2 Inds 1890–1896; Railroad average 1897 (First industrial average published May 26, 1896).

DOW JONES INDUSTRIALS BULL AND BEAR MARKETS SINCE 1900

Bear markets begin at the end of one bull market and end at the start of the next bull market (7/17/90 to 10/11/90 as an example). The longest bull market on record ended on 7/17/98, and the shortest bear market on record ended on 8/31/98, when the new bull market began. The greatest bull super cycle in history that began 8/12/82 ended in 2000 after the Dow gained 1409% and NASDAQ climbed 3072%. The Dow gained only 497% in the eight-year super bull from 1921 to the top in 1929. NASDAQ suffered its worst loss ever from the 2000 top to the 2002 bottom, down 77.9%, nearly as much as the 89.2% drop in the Dow from the 1929 top to the 1932 bottom. The third-longest Dow bull since 1900 that began 10/9/02 ended on its fifth anniversary. The ensuing bear market was the second worst bear market since 1900, slashing the Dow 53.8%. At press time, the Dow has left the mild bear market ending 2/11/2016 in its dust and is currently trading above 21,000. (See page 132 for S&P 500 and NASDAQ bulls and bears.)

DOW JONES INDUSTRIALS BULL AND BEAR MARKETS SINCE 1900

— Beginning —		— Ending —		Bull		Bear	
Date	DJIA	Date	DJIA	% Gain	Days	% Change	Days
9/24/00	38.80	6/17/01	57.33	47.8%	266	−46.1%	875
11/9/03	30.88	1/19/06	75.45	144.3	802	−48.5	665
11/15/07	38.83	11/19/09	73.64	89.6	735	−27.4	675
9/25/11	53.43	9/30/12	68.97	29.1	371	−24.1	668
7/30/14	52.32	11/21/16	110.15	110.5	845	−40.1	393
12/19/17	65.95	11/3/19	119.62	81.4	684	−46.6	660
8/24/21	63.90	3/20/23	105.38	64.9	573	−18.6	221
10/27/23	85.76	9/3/29	381.17	344.5	2138	−47.9	71
11/13/29	198.69	4/17/30	294.07	48.0	155	−86.0	813
7/8/32	41.22	9/7/32	79.93	93.9	61	−37.2	173
2/27/33	50.16	2/5/34	110.74	120.8	343	−22.8	171
7/26/34	85.51	3/10/37	194.40	127.3	958	−49.1	386
3/31/38	98.95	11/12/38	158.41	60.1	226	−23.3	147
4/8/39	121.44	9/12/39	155.92	28.4	157	−40.4	959
4/28/42	92.92	5/29/46	212.50	128.7	1492	−23.2	353
5/17/47	163.21	6/15/48	193.16	18.4	395	−16.3	363
6/13/49	161.60	1/5/53	293.79	81.8	1302	−13.0	252
9/14/53	255.49	4/6/56	521.05	103.9	935	−19.4	564
10/22/57	419.79	1/5/60	685.47	63.3	805	−17.4	294
10/25/60	566.05	12/13/61	734.91	29.8	414	−27.1	195
6/26/62	535.76	2/9/66	995.15	85.7	1324	−25.2	240
10/7/66	744.32	12/3/68	985.21	32.4	788	−35.9	539
5/26/70	631.16	4/28/71	950.82	50.6	337	−16.1	209
11/23/71	797.97	1/11/73	1051.70	31.8	415	−45.1	694
12/6/74	577.60	9/21/76	1014.79	75.7	655	−26.9	525
2/28/78	742.12	9/8/78	907.74	22.3	192	−16.4	591
4/21/80	759.13	4/27/81	1024.05	34.9	371	−24.1	472
8/12/82	776.92	11/29/83	1287.20	65.7	474	−15.6	238
7/24/84	1086.57	8/25/87	2722.42	150.6	1127	−36.1	55
10/19/87	1738.74	7/17/90	2999.75	72.5	1002	−21.2	86
10/11/90	2365.10	7/17/98	9337.97	294.8	2836	−19.3	45
8/31/98	7539.07	1/14/00	11722.98	55.5	501	−29.7	616
9/21/01	8235.81	3/19/02	10635.25	29.1	179	−31.5	204
10/9/02	7286.27	10/9/07	14164.53	94.4	1826	−53.8	517
3/9/09	6547.05	4/29/11	12810.54	95.7	781	−16.8	157
10/3/11	10655.30	5/19/15	18312.39	71.9	1324*	−14.5	351
2/11/16	15660.18	3/1/17	21115.55	34.8*	384*		
							* As of May 12, 2017—not in averages
		Average		**85.6%**	**772**	**−30.6%**	**401**

Based on Dow Jones Industrial Average.
The NYSE was closed from 7/31/1914 to 12/11/1914 due to World War I.
DJIA figures were then adjusted back to reflect the composition change from 12 to 20 stocks in September 1916.

1900–2000 Data: Ned Davis Research

STANDARD & POOR'S 500 BULL AND BEAR MARKETS SINCE 1929 NASDAQ COMPOSITE SINCE 1971

A constant debate of the definition and timing of bull and bear markets permeates Wall Street like the bell that signals the open and close of every trading day. We have relied on the Ned Davis Research parameters for years to track bulls and bears on the Dow (see page 131). Standard & Poor's 500 index has been a stalwart indicator for decades and at times marched to a different beat than the Dow. The moves of the S&P 500 and NASDAQ have been correlated to the bull and bear dates on page 131. Many dates line up for the three indices, but you will notice quite a lag or lead on several occasions, including NASDAQ's independent cadence from 1975 to 1980.

STANDARD & POOR'S 500 BULL AND BEAR MARKETS

— Beginning —		— Ending —		Bull		Bear	
Date	S&P 500	Date	S&P 500	% Gain	Days	% Change	Days
11/13/29	17.66	4/10/30	25.92	46.8%	148	−83.0%	783
6/1/32	4.40	9/7/32	9.31	111.6	98	−40.6	173
2/27/33	5.53	2/6/34	11.82	113.7	344	−31.8	401
3/14/35	8.06	3/6/37	18.68	131.8	723	−49.0	390
3/31/38	8.50	11/9/38	13.79	62.2	223	−26.2	150
4/8/39	10.18	10/25/39	13.21	29.8	200	−43.5	916
4/28/42	7.47	5/29/46	19.25	157.7	1492	−28.8	353
5/17/47	13.71	6/15/48	17.06	24.4	395	−20.6	363
6/13/49	13.55	1/5/53	26.66	96.8	1302	−14.8	252
9/14/53	22.71	8/2/56	49.74	119.0	1053	−21.6	446
10/22/57	38.98	8/3/59	60.71	55.7	650	−13.9	449
10/25/60	52.30	12/12/61	72.64	38.9	413	−28.0	196
6/26/62	52.32	2/9/66	94.06	79.8	1324	−22.2	240
10/7/66	73.20	11/29/68	108.37	48.0	784	−36.1	543
5/26/70	69.29	4/28/71	104.77	51.2	337	−13.9	209
11/23/71	90.16	1/11/73	120.24	33.4	415	−48.2	630
10/3/74	62.28	9/21/76	107.83	73.1	719	−19.4	531
3/6/78	86.90	9/12/78	106.99	23.1	190	−8.2	562
3/27/80	98.22	11/28/80	140.52	43.1	246	−27.1	622
8/12/82	102.42	10/10/83	172.65	68.6	424	−14.4	288
7/24/84	147.82	8/25/87	336.77	127.8	1127	−33.5	101
12/4/87	223.92	7/16/90	368.95	64.8	955	−19.9	87
10/11/90	295.46	7/17/98	1186.75	301.7	2836	−19.3	45
8/31/98	957.28	3/24/00	1527.46	59.6	571	−36.8	546
9/21/01	965.80	1/4/02	1172.51	21.4	105	−33.8	278
10/9/02	776.76	10/9/07	1565.15	101.5	1826	−56.8	517
3/9/09	676.53	4/29/11	1363.61	101.6	781	−19.4	157
10/3/11	1099.23	5/21/15	2130.82	93.8	1326	−14.2*	349*
2/11/16	1829.08	5/10/17	2399.63	31.2*	454*	*As of May 12, 2017 — not in averages	
		Average		**81.5%**	**750**	**−30.2%**	**379**

NASDAQ COMPOSITE BULL AND BEAR MARKETS

— Beginning —		— Ending —		Bull		Bear	
Date	NASDAQ	Date	NASDAQ	% Gain	Days	% Change	Days
11/23/71	100.31	1/11/73	136.84	36.4%	415	−59.9%	630
10/3/74	54.87	7/15/75	88.00	60.4	285	−16.2	63
9/16/75	73.78	9/13/78	139.25	88.7	1093	−20.4	62
11/14/78	110.88	2/8/80	165.25	49.0	451	−24.9	48
3/27/80	124.09	5/29/81	223.47	80.1	428	−28.8	441
8/13/82	159.14	6/24/83	328.91	106.7	315	−31.5	397
7/25/84	225.30	8/26/87	455.26	102.1	1127	−35.9	63
10/28/87	291.88	10/9/89	485.73	66.4	712	−33.0	372
10/16/90	325.44	7/20/98	2014.25	518.9	2834	−29.5	80
10/8/98	1419.12	3/10/00	5048.62	255.8	519	−71.8	560
9/21/01	1423.19	1/4/02	2059.38	44.7	105	−45.9	278
10/9/02	1114.11	10/31/07	2859.12	156.6	1848	−55.6	495
3/9/09	1268.64	4/29/11	2873.54	126.5	781	−18.7	157
10/3/11	2335.83	7/20/15	5218.86	123.4	1386	−18.2*	289*
2/11/16	4266.84	5/10/17	6129.14	43.6*	454*	*As of May 12, 2017 — not in averages	
		Average		**129.7%**	**878**	**−36.3%**	**280**

JANUARY DAILY POINT CHANGES DOW JONES INDUSTRIALS

Previous Month Close	2008	2009	2010	2011	2012	2013	2014	2015	2016	2017
	13264.82	8776.39	10428.05	11577.51	12217.56	13104.14	16576.66	17823.07	17425.03	19762.60
1	H	H	H	S	S	H	H	H	H	S
2	-220.86	258.30	S	S	H	308.41	-135.31	9.92	S	H
3	12.76	S	S	93.24	179.82	-21.19	28.64	S	S	119.16
4	-256.54	S	155.91	20.43	21.04	43.85	S	S	-276.09	60.40
5	S	-81.80	-11.94	31.71	-2.72	S	S	-331.34	9.72	-42.87
6	S	62.21	1.66	-25.58	-55.78	S	-44.89	-130.01	-252.15	64.51
7	27.31	-245.40	33.18	-22.55	S	-50.92	105.84	212.88	-392.41	S
8	-238.42	-27.24	11.33	S	S	-55.44	-68.20	323.35	-167.65	S
9	146.24	-143.28	S	S	32.77	61.66	-17.98	-170.50	S	-76.42
10	117.78	S	S	-37.31	69.78	80.71	-7.71	S	S	-31.85
11	-246.79	S	45.80	34.43	-13.02	17.21	S	S	52.12	98.75
12	S	-125.21	-36.73	83.56	21.57	S	S	-96.53	117.65	-63.28
13	S	-25.41	53.51	-23.54	-48.96	S	-179.11	-27.16	-364.81	-5.27
14	171.85	-248.42	29.78	55.48	S	S	18.89	115.92	227.64	S
15	-277.04	12.35	-100.90	S	S	27.57	108.08	-106.38	-390.97	S
16	-34.95	68.73	S	S	H	-23.66	-64.93	190.86	S	H
17	-306.95	S	S	H	60.01	84.79	41.55	S	S	-58.96
18	-59.91	S	H	50.55	96.88	53.68	S	S	H	-22.05
19	S	H	115.78	-12.64	45.03	S	S	H	27.94	-72.32
20	S	-332.13	-122.28	-2.49	96.50	S	H	3.66	-249.28	94.85
21	H	279.01	-213.27	49.04	S	H	-44.12	39.05	115.94	S
22	-128.11	-105.30	-216.90	S	S	62.51	-41.10	259.70	210.83	S
23	298.98	-45.24	S	S	-11.66	67.12	-175.99	-141.38	S	-27.40
24	108.44	S	S	108.68	-33.07	46.00	-318.24	S	S	112.86
25	-171.44	S	23.88	-3.33	81.21	70.65	S	S	-208.29	155.80
26	S	38.47	-2.57	8.25	-22.33	S	S	6.10	282.01	32.40
27	S	58.70	41.87	4.39	-74.17	S	-41.23	-291.49	-222.77	-7.13
28	176.72	200.72	-115.70	-166.13	S	-14.05	90.68	-195.84	125.18	S
29	96.41	-226.44	-53.13	S	S	72.49	-189.77	225.48	396.66	S
30	-37.47	-148.15	S	S	-6.74	-44.00	109.82	-251.90	S	-122.65
31	207.53	S	S	68.23	-20.81	-49.84	-149.76	S	S	-107.04
Close	12650.36	8000.86	10067.33	11891.93	12632.91	13860.58	15698.85	17164.95	16466.30	19864.09
Change	-614.46	-775.53	-360.72	314.42	415.35	756.44	-877.81	-658.12	-958.73	101.49

FEBRUARY DAILY POINT CHANGES DOW JONES INDUSTRIALS

Previous Month Close	2008	2009	2010	2011	2012	2013	2014	2015	2016	2017
	12650.36	8000.86	10067.33	11891.93	12632.91	13860.58	15698.85	17164.95	16466.30	19864.09
1	92.83	S	118.20	148.23	83.55	149.21	S	S	-17.12	26.85
2	S	-64.03	111.32	1.81	-11.05	S	S	196.09	-295.64	-6.03
3	S	141.53	-26.30	20.29	156.82	S	-326.05	305.36	183.12	186.55
4	-108.03	-121.70	-268.37	29.89	S	-129.71	72.44	6.62	79.92	S
5	-370.03	106.41	10.05	S	S	99.22	-5.01	211.86	-211.61	S
6	-65.03	217.52	S	S	-17.10	7.22	188.30	-60.59	S	-19.04
7	46.90	S	S	69.48	33.07	-42.47	165.55	S	S	37.87
8	-64.87	S	-103.84	71.52	5.75	48.92	S	S	-177.92	-35.95
9	S	-9.72	150.25	6.74	6.51	S	S	-95.08	-12.67	118.06
10	S	-381.99	-20.26	-10.60	-89.23	S	7.71	139.55	-99.64	96.97
11	57.88	50.65	105.81	43.97	S	-21.73	192.98	-6.62	-254.56	S
12	133.40	-6.77	-45.05	S	S	47.46	-30.83	110.24	313.66	S
13	178.83	-82.35	S	S	72.81	-35.79	63.65	46.97	S	142.79
14	-175.26	S	S	-5.07	4.24	-9.52	126.80	S	S	92.25
15	-28.77	S	H	-41.55	-97.33	8.37	S	S	H	107.45
16	S	H	169.67	61.53	123.13	S	S	H	222.57	7.91
17	S	-297.81	40.43	29.97	45.79	S	H	28.23	257.42	4.28
18	H	3.03	83.66	73.11	S	H	-23.99	-17.73	-40.40	S
19	-10.99	-89.68	9.45	S	S	53.91	-89.84	-44.08	-21.44	S
20	90.04	-100.28	S	S	H	-108.13	92.67	154.67	S	H
21	-142.96	S	S	H	15.82	-46.92	-29.93	S	S	118.95
22	96.72	S	-18.97	-178.46	-27.02	119.95	S	S	228.67	32.60
23	S	-250.89	-100.97	-107.01	46.02	S	S	-23.60	-188.88	34.72
24	S	236.16	91.75	-37.28	-1.74	S	103.84	92.35	53.21	11.44
25	189.20	-80.05	-53.13	61.95	S	-216.40	-27.48	15.38	212.30	S
26	114.70	-88.81	4.23	S	S	15.96	18.75	-10.15	-57.32	S
27	9.36	-119.15	S	S	-1.44	175.24	74.24	-81.72	S	15.68
28	-112.10	S	S	95.89	23.61	-20.88	49.06	S	S	-25.20
29	-315.79	S	—	—	-53.05	—	—	—	-123.47	—
Close	12266.39	7062.93	10325.26	12226.34	12952.07	14054.49	16321.71	18132.70	16516.50	20812.24
Change	-383.97	-937.93	257.93	334.41	319.16	193.91	622.86	967.75	50.20	948.15

MARCH DAILY POINT CHANGES DOW JONES INDUSTRIALS

Previous Month Close	2008	2009	2010	2011	2012	2013	2014	2015	2016	2017
	12266.39	7062.93	10325.26	12226.34	12952.07	14054.49	16321.71	18132.70	16516.50	20812.24
1	S	S	78.53	−168.32	28.23	35.17	S	S	348.58	303.31
2	S	−299.64	2.19	8.78	−2.73	S	S	155.93	34.24	−112.58
3	−7.49	−37.27	−9.22	191.40	S	S	−153.68	−85.26	44.58	2.74
4	−45.10	149.82	47.38	−88.32	S	38.16	227.85	−106.47	62.87	S
5	41.19	−281.40	122.06	S	−14.76	125.95	−35.70	38.82	S	S
6	−214.60	32.50	S	S	−203.66	42.47	61.71	−278.94	S	−51.37
7	−146.70	S	S	−79.85	78.18	33.25	30.83	S	67.18	−29.58
8	S	S	−13.68	124.35	70.61	67.58	S	S	−109.85	−69.03
9	S	−79.89	11.86	−1.29	14.08	S	S	138.94	36.26	2.46
10	−153.54	379.44	2.95	−228.48	S	S	−34.04	−332.78	−5.23	44.79
11	416.66	3.91	44.51	59.79	S	50.22	−67.43	−27.55	218.18	S
12	−46.57	239.66	12.85	S	37.69	2.77	−11.17	259.83	S	S
13	35.50	53.92	S	S	217.97	5.22	−231.19	−145.91	S	−21.50
14	−194.65	S	S	−51.24	16.42	83.86	−43.22	S	15.82	−44.11
15	S	S	17.46	−137.74	58.66	−25.03	S	S	22.40	112.73
16	S	−7.01	43.83	−242.12	−20.14	S	S	228.11	74.23	−15.55
17	21.16	178.73	47.69	161.29	S	S	181.55	−128.34	155.73	−19.93
18	420.41	90.88	45.50	83.93	S	−62.05	88.97	227.11	120.81	S
19	−293.00	−85.78	−37.19	S	6.51	3.76	−114.02	−117.16	S	S
20	261.66	−122.42	S	S	−68.94	55.91	108.88	168.62	S	−8.76
21	H	S	S	178.01	−45.57	−90.24	−28.28	S	21.57	−237.85
22	S	S	43.91	−17.90	−78.48	90.54	S	S	−41.30	−6.71
23	S	497.48	102.94	67.39	34.59	S	S	−11.61	−79.98	−4.72
24	187.32	−115.89	−52.68	84.54	S	S	−26.08	−104.90	13.14	−59.86
25	−16.04	89.84	5.06	50.03	S	−64.28	91.19	−292.60	H	S
26	−109.74	174.75	9.15	S	160.90	111.90	−98.89	−40.31	S	S
27	−120.40	−148.38	S	S	−43.90	−33.49	−4.76	34.43	S	−45.74
28	−86.06	S	S	−22.71	−71.52	52.38	58.83	S	19.66	150.52
29	S	S	45.50	81.13	19.61	H	S	S	97.72	−42.18
30	S	−254.16	11.56	71.60	66.22	S	S	263.65	83.55	69.17
31	46.49	86.90	−50.79	−30.88	S	S	134.60	−200.19	−31.57	−65.27
Close	12262.89	7608.92	10856.63	12319.73	13212.04	14578.54	16457.66	17776.12	17685.09	20663.22
Change	−3.50	545.99	531.37	93.39	259.97	524.05	135.95	−356.58	1168.59	−149.02

APRIL DAILY POINT CHANGES DOW JONES INDUSTRIALS

Previous Month Close	2008	2009	2010	2011	2012	2013	2014	2015	2016	2017
	12262.89	7608.92	10856.63	12319.73	13212.04	14578.54	16457.66	17776.12	17685.09	20663.22
1	391.47	152.68	70.44	56.99	S	−5.69	74.95	−77.94	107.66	S
2	−48.53	216.48	H	S	52.45	89.16	40.39	65.06	S	S
3	20.20	39.51	S	S	−64.94	−111.66	−0.45	H	S	−13.01
4	−16.61	S	S	23.31	−124.80	55.76	−159.84	S	−55.75	39.03
5	S	S	46.48	−6.13	−14.61	−40.86	S	S	−133.68	−41.09
6	S	−41.74	−3.56	32.85	H	S	S	117.61	112.73	14.80
7	3.01	−186.29	−72.47	−17.26	S	S	−166.84	−5.43	−174.09	−6.85
8	−35.99	47.55	29.55	−29.44	S	48.23	10.27	27.09	35.00	S
9	−49.18	246.27	70.28	S	−130.55	59.98	181.04	56.22	S	S
10	54.72	H	S	S	−213.66	128.78	−266.96	98.92	S	1.92
11	−256.56	S	S	1.06	89.46	62.90	−143.47	S	−20.55	−6.72
12	S	S	8.62	−117.53	181.19	−0.08	S	S	164.84	−59.44
13	S	−25.57	13.45	7.41	−136.99	S	S	−80.61	187.03	−138.61
14	−23.36	−137.63	103.69	14.16	S	S	146.49	59.66	18.15	H
15	60.41	109.44	21.46	56.68	S	−265.86	89.32	75.91	−28.97	S
16	256.80	95.81	−125.91	S	71.82	157.58	162.29	−6.84	S	S
17	1.22	5.90	S	S	194.13	−138.19	−16.31	−279.47	S	183.67
18	228.87	S	S	−140.24	−82.79	−81.45	H	S	106.70	−113.64
19	S	S	73.39	65.16	−68.65	10.37	S	S	49.44	−118.79
20	S	−289.60	25.01	186.79	65.16	S	S	208.63	42.67	174.22
21	−24.34	127.83	7.86	52.45	S	S	40.71	−85.34	−113.75	−30.95
22	−104.79	−82.99	9.37	H	S	19.66	65.12	88.68	21.23	S
23	42.99	70.49	69.99	S	−102.09	152.29	−12.72	20.42	S	S
24	85.73	119.23	S	S	74.39	−43.16	0.00	21.45	S	216.13
25	42.91	S	S	−26.11	89.16	24.50	−140.19	S	−26.51	232.23
26	S	S	0.75	115.49	113.90	11.75	S	S	13.08	−21.03
27	S	−51.29	−213.04	95.59	23.69	S	S	−42.17	51.23	6.24
28	−20.11	168.78	53.28	72.35	S	S	87.28	72.17	−210.79	−40.82
29	−39.81	−17.61	122.05	47.23	S	106.20	86.63	−74.61	−57.12	S
30	−11.81	−8.05	−158.71	S	−14.68	21.05	45.47	−195.01	S	S
Close	12820.13	8168.12	11008.61	12810.54	13213.63	14839.80	16580.84	17840.52	17773.64	20940.51
Change	557.24	559.20	151.98	490.81	1.59	261.26	123.18	64.40	88.55	277.29

134

MAY DAILY POINT CHANGES DOW JONES INDUSTRIALS

Previous Month Close	2007	2008	2009	2010	2011	2012	2013	2014	2015	2016
	13062.91	12820.13	8168.12	11008.61	12810.54	13213.63	14839.80	16580.84	17840.52	17773.64
1	73.23	189.87	44.29	S	S	65.69	-138.85	-21.97	183.54	S
2	75.74	48.20	S	S	-3.18	-10.75	130.63	-45.98	S	117.52
3	29.50	S	S	143.22	0.15	-61.98	142.38	S	S	-140.25
4	23.24	S	214.33	-225.06	-83.93	-168.32	S	S	46.34	-99.65
5	S	-88.66	-16.09	-58.65	-139.41	S	S	17.66	-142.20	9.45
6	S	51.29	101.63	-347.80	54.57	S	-5.07	-129.53	-86.22	79.92
7	48.35	-206.48	-102.43	-139.89	S	-29.74	87.31	117.52	82.08	S
8	-3.90	52.43	164.80	S	S	-76.44	48.92	32.43	267.05	S
9	53.80	-120.90	S	S	45.94	-97.03	-22.50	32.37	S	-34.72
10	-147.74	S	S	404.71	75.68	19.98	35.87	S	S	222.44
11	111.09	S	-155.88	-36.88	-130.33	-34.44	S	S	-85.94	-217.23
12	S	130.43	50.34	148.65	65.89	S	S	112.13	-36.94	9.38
13	S	-44.13	-184.22	-113.96	-100.17	S	-26.81	19.97	-7.74	-185.18
14	20.56	66.20	46.43	-162.79	S	-125.25	123.57	-101.47	191.75	S
15	37.06	94.28	-62.68	S	S	-63.35	60.44	-167.16	20.32	S
16	103.69	-5.86	S	S	-47.38	-33.45	-42.47	44.50	S	175.39
17	-10.81	S	S	5.67	-68.79	-156.06	121.18	S	S	-180.73
18	79.81	S	235.44	-114.88	80.60	-73.11	S	S	26.32	-3.36
19	S	41.36	-29.23	-66.58	45.14	S	S	20.55	13.51	-91.22
20	-13.65	-199.48	-52.81	-376.36	-93.28	S	-19.12	-137.55	-26.99	65.54
21	-13.65	-227.49	-129.91	125.38	S	135.10	52.30	158.75	0.34	S
22	-2.93	24.43	-14.81	S	S	-1.67	-80.41	10.02	-53.72	S
23	-14.30	-145.99	S	S	-130.78	-6.66	-12.67	63.19	S	-8.01
24	-84.52	S	S	-126.82	-25.05	33.60	8.60	S	S	213.12
25	66.15	S	H	-22.82	38.45	-74.92	S	S	H	145.46
26	S	H	196.17	-69.30	8.10	S	S	H	-190.48	-23.22
27	S	68.72	-173.47	284.54	38.82	S	H	69.23	121.45	44.93
28	H	45.68	103.78	-122.36	S	S	106.29	-42.32	-36.87	S
29	14.06	52.19	96.53	S	S	125.86	-106.59	65.56	-115.44	S
30	111.74	-7.90	S	S	H	-160.83	21.73	18.43	S	H
31	-5.44	S	S	H	128.21	-26.41	-208.96	S	S	-86.02
Close	13627.64	12638.32	8500.33	10136.63	12569.79	12393.45	15115.57	16717.17	18010.68	17787.20
Change	564.73	-181.81	332.21	-871.98	-240.75	-820.18	275.77	136.33	170.16	13.56

JUNE DAILY POINT CHANGES DOW JONES INDUSTRIALS

Previous Month Close	2007	2008	2009	2010	2011	2012	2013	2014	2015	2016
	13627.64	12638.32	8500.33	10136.63	12569.79	12393.45	15115.57	16717.17	18010.68	17787.20
1	40.47	S	221.11	-112.61	-279.65	-274.88	S	S	29.69	2.47
2	S	-134.50	19.43	225.52	-41.59	S	S	26.46	-28.43	48.89
3	S	-100.97	-65.59	5.74	-97.29	S	138.46	-21.29	64.33	-31.50
4	8.21	-12.37	74.96	-323.31	S	-17.11	-76.49	15.19	-170.69	S
5	-80.86	213.97	12.89	S	S	26.49	-216.95	98.58	-56.12	S
6	-129.79	-394.64	S	S	-61.30	286.84	80.03	88.17	S	113.27
7	-198.94	S	S	-115.48	-19.15	46.17	207.50	S	S	17.95
8	157.66	S	1.36	123.49	-21.87	93.24	S	S	-82.91	66.77
9	S	70.51	-1.43	-40.73	75.42	S	S	18.82	-2.51	-19.86
10	S	9.44	-24.04	273.28	-172.45	S	-9.53	2.82	236.36	-119.85
11	0.57	-205.99	31.90	38.54	S	-142.97	-116.57	-102.04	38.97	S
12	-129.95	57.81	28.34	S	S	162.57	-126.79	-109.69	-140.53	S
13	187.34	165.77	S	S	1.06	-77.42	180.85	41.55	S	-132.86
14	71.37	S	S	-20.18	123.14	155.53	-105.90	S	S	-57.66
15	85.76	S	-187.13	213.88	-178.84	115.26	S	S	-107.67	-34.65
16	S	-38.27	-107.46	4.69	64.25	S	S	5.27	113.31	92.93
17	S	-108.78	-7.49	24.71	42.84	S	109.67	27.48	31.26	-57.94
18	-26.50	-131.24	58.42	16.47	S	-25.35	138.38	98.13	180.10	S
19	22.44	34.03	-15.87	S	S	95.51	-206.04	14.84	-99.89	S
20	-146.00	-220.40	S	S	76.02	-12.94	-353.87	25.62	S	129.71
21	56.42	S	S	-8.23	109.63	-250.82	41.08	S	S	24.86
22	-185.58	S	-200.72	-148.89	-80.34	67.21	S	S	103.83	-48.90
23	S	-0.33	-16.10	4.92	-59.67	S	S	-9.82	24.29	230.24
24	S	-34.93	-23.05	-145.64	-115.42	S	-139.84	-119.13	-178.00	-610.32
25	-8.21	4.40	172.54	-8.99	S	-138.12	100.75	49.38	-75.71	S
26	-14.39	-358.41	-34.01	S	S	32.01	149.83	-21.38	56.32	S
27	90.07	-106.91	S	S	108.98	92.34	114.35	5.71	S	-260.51
28	-5.45	S	S	-5.29	145.13	-24.75	-114.89	S	S	269.48
29	-13.66	S	90.99	-268.22	72.73	277.83	S	S	-350.33	284.96
30	S	3.50	-82.38	-96.28	152.92	S	S	-25.24	23.16	235.31
Close	13408.62	11350.01	8447.00	9774.02	12414.34	12880.09	14909.60	16826.60	17619.51	17929.99
Change	-219.02	-1288.31	-53.33	-362.61	-155.45	486.64	-205.97	109.43	-391.17	142.79

Previous Month Close	2007	2008	2009	2010	2011	2012	2013	2014	2015	2016
	13408.62	11350.01	8447.00	9774.02	12414.34	12880.09	14909.60	16826.60	17619.51	17929.99
1	S	32.25	57.06	-41.49	168.43	S	65.36	129.47	138.40	19.38
2	126.81	-166.75	-223.32	-46.05	S	-8.70	-42.55	20.17	-27.80	S
3	41.87*	73.03*	H	S	S	72.43*	56.14*	92.02	H	S
4	H	H	S	S	H	H	H	H	S	H
5	-11.46	S	H	H	-12.90	-47.15	147.29	S	S	-108.75
6	45.84	S	44.13	57.14	56.15	-124.20	S	S	-46.53	78.00
7	S	-56.58	-161.27	274.66	93.47	S	S	-44.05	93.33	-22.74
8	S	152.25	14.81	120.71	-62.29	S	88.85	-117.59	-261.49	250.86
9	38.29	-236.77	4.76	59.04	S	S	75.65	78.99	33.20	S
10	-148.27	81.58	-36.65	S	S	-83.17	-8.68	-70.54	211.79	S
11	76.17	-128.48	S	S	-151.44	-48.59	169.26	28.74	S	80.19
12	283.86	S	S	18.24	-58.88	-31.26	3.38	S	S	120.74
13	45.52	S	185.16	146.75	44.73	203.82	S	S	217.27	24.45
14	S	-45.35	27.81	3.70	-54.49	S	S	111.61	75.90	134.29
15	S	-92.65	256.72	-7.41	42.61	S	19.96	5.26	-3.41	10.14
16	43.73	276.74	95.61	-261.41	S	-49.88	-32.41	77.52	70.08	S
17	20.57	207.38	32.12	S		78.33	18.67	-161.39	-33.80	S
18	-53.33	49.91	S	S	-94.57	103.16	78.02	123.37	S	16.50
19	82.19	S	S	56.53	202.26	34.66	-4.80	S	S	25.96
20	-149.33	S	104.21	75.53	-15.51	-120.79	S	S	13.96	36.02
21	S	-29.23	67.79	-109.43	152.50	S	S	-48.45	-181.12	-77.80
22	S	135.16	-34.68	201.77	-43.25	S	1.81	61.81	-68.25	53.62
23	92.34	29.88	188.03	102.32	S	-101.11	22.19	-26.91	-119.12	S
24	-226.47	-283.10	23.95	S	S	-104.14	-25.50	-2.83	-163.39	S
25	68.12	21.41	S	S	-88.36	58.73	13.37	-123.23	S	-77.79
26	-311.50	S	S	100.81	-91.50	211.88	3.22	S	S	-19.31
27	-208.10	S	15.27	12.26	-198.75	187.73	S	S	-127.94	-1.58
28	S	-239.61	-11.79	-39.81	-62.44	S	S	22.02	189.68	-15.82
29	S	266.48	-26.00	-30.72	-96.87	S	-36.86	-70.48	121.12	-24.11
30	92.84	186.13	83.74	-1.22	S	-2.65	-1.38	-31.75	-5.41	S
31	-146.32	-205.67	17.15	S	S	-64.33	-21.05	-317.06	-56.12	S
Close	13211.99	11378.02	9171.61	10465.94	12143.24	13008.68	15499.54	16563.30	17689.86	18432.24
Change	-196.63	28.01	724.61	691.92	-271.10	128.59	589.94	-263.30	70.35	502.25

* Shortened trading day

Previous Month Close	2007	2008	2009	2010	2011	2012	2013	2014	2015	2016
	13211.99	11378.02	9171.61	10465.94	12143.24	13008.68	15499.54	16563.30	17689.86	18432.24
1	150.38	-51.70	S	S	-10.75	-37.62	128.48	-69.93	S	-27.73
2	100.96	S	S	208.44	-265.87	-92.18	30.34	S	S	-90.74
3	-281.42	S	114.95	-38.00	29.82	217.29	S	S	-91.66	41.23
4	S	-42.17	33.63	44.05	-512.76	S	S	75.91	-47.51	-2.95
5	S	331.62	-39.22	-5.45	60.93	S	-46.23	-139.81	-10.22	191.48
6	286.87	40.30	-24.71	-21.42	S	21.34	-93.39	13.87	-120.72	S
7	35.52	-224.64	113.81	S	S	51.09	-48.07	-75.07	-46.37	S
8	153.56	302.89	S	S	-634.76	7.04	27.65	185.66	S	-14.24
9	-387.18	S	S	45.19	429.92	-10.45	-72.81	S	S	3.76
10	-31.14	S	-32.12	-54.50	-519.83	42.76	S	S	241.79	-37.39
11	S	48.03	-96.50	-265.42	423.37	S		16.05	-212.33	117.86
12	S	-139.88	120.16	-58.88	125.71	S	-5.83	-9.44	-0.33	-37.05
13	-3.01	-109.51	36.58	-16.80	S	-38.52	31.33	91.26	5.74	
14	-207.61	82.97	-76.79	S	S	2.71	-113.35	61.78	69.15	S
15	-167.45	43.97	S	S	213.88	-7.36	-225.47	-50.67	S	59.58
16	-15.69	S	S	-1.14	-76.97	85.33	-30.72	S	S	-84.03
17	233.30	S	-186.06	103.84	4.28	25.09	S	S	67.78	21.92
18	S	-180.51	82.60	9.69	-419.63	S		175.83	-33.84	23.76
19	S	-130.84	61.22	-144.33	-172.93	S	-70.73	80.85	-162.61	-45.13
20	42.27	68.88	70.89	-57.59	S	-3.56	-7.75	59.54	-358.04	S
21	-30.49	12.78	155.91	S	S	-68.06	-105.44	60.36	-530.94	S
22	145.27	197.85	S	S	37.00	-30.82	66.19	-38.27	S	-23.15
23	-0.25	S	S	-39.21	322.11	-115.30	46.77	S	S	17.88
24	142.99	S	3.32	-133.96	143.95	100.51	S	S	-588.40	-65.82
25	S	-241.81	30.01	19.61	-170.89	S		75.65	-204.91	-33.07
26	S	26.62	4.23	-74.25	134.72	S	-64.05	29.83	619.07	-53.01
27	-56.74	89.64	37.11	164.84	S	-33.30	-170.33	15.31	369.26	S
28	-280.28	212.67	-36.43	S	S	-21.68	48.38	-42.44	-11.76	S
29	247.44	-171.63	S	S	254.71	4.49	16.44	18.88	S	107.59
30	-50.56	S	S	-140.92	20.70	-106.77	-30.64	S	S	-48.69
31	119.01	S	-47.92	9.99	S	90.13	S	S	-114.98	-53.42
Close	13357.74	11543.55	9496.28	10014.72	11613.53	13090.84	14810.31	17098.45	16528.03	18400.88
Change	145.75	165.53	324.67	-451.22	-529.71	82.16	-689.23	535.15	-1161.83	-31.36

SEPTEMBER DAILY POINT CHANGES DOW JONES INDUSTRIALS

Previous Month Close	2007	2008	2009	2010	2011	2012	2013	2014	2015	2016
	13357.74	11543.55	9496.28	10014.72	11613.53	13090.84	14810.31	17098.45	16528.03	18400.88
1	S	H	-185.68	254.75	-119.96	S	S	H	-469.68	18.42
2	S	-26.63	-29.93	50.63	-253.31	S	H	-30.89	293.03	72.66
3	H	15.96	63.94	157.83	S	H	23.65	10.72	23.38	S
4	91.12	-344.65	96.66	S	S	-54.90	96.91	-8.70	-272.38	S
5	-143.39	32.73	S	S	H	11.54	6.61	67.78	S	H
6	57.88	S	S	H	-100.96	244.52	-14.98	S	S	46.16
7	-249.97	S	H	-137.24	275.56	14.64	S	S	H	-11.98
8	S	289.78	56.07	46.32	-119.05	S	S	-25.94	390.30	-46.23
9	S	-280.01	49.88	28.23	-303.68	S	140.62	-97.55	-239.11	-394.46
10	14.47	38.19	80.26	47.53	S	-52.35	127.94	54.84	76.83	S
11	180.54	164.79	-22.07	S	S	69.07	135.54	-19.71	102.69	S
12	-16.74	-11.72	S	S	68.99	9.99	-25.96	-61.49	S	239.62
13	133.23	S	S	81.36	44.73	206.51	75.42	S	S	-285.32
14	17.64	S	21.39	-17.64	140.88	53.51	S	S	-62.13	-31.98
15	S	-504.48	56.61	46.24	186.45	S	S	43.63	228.89	177.71
16	S	141.51	108.30	22.10	75.91	S	118.72	100.83	140.10	-88.68
17	-39.10	-449.36	-7.79	13.02	S	-40.27	34.95	24.88	-65.21	S
18	335.97	410.03	36.28	S	S	11.54	147.21	109.14	-290.16	S
19	76.17	368.75	S	S	-108.08	13.32	-40.39	13.75	S	-3.63
20	-48.86	S	S	145.77	7.65	18.97	-185.46	S	S	9.79
21	53.49	S	-41.34	7.41	-283.82	-17.46	S	S	125.61	163.74
22	S	-372.75	51.01	-21.72	-391.01	S	S	-107.06	-179.72	98.76
23	S	-161.52	-81.32	-76.89	37.65	S	-49.71	-116.81	-50.58	-131.01
24	-61.13	-29.00	-41.11	197.84	S	-20.55	-66.79	154.19	-78.57	S
25	19.59	196.89	-42.25	S	S	-101.37	-61.33	-264.26	113.35	S
26	99.50	121.07	S	S	272.38	-44.04	55.04	167.35	S	-166.62
27	34.79	S	S	-48.22	146.83	72.46	-70.06	S	S	133.47
28	-17.31	S	124.17	46.10	-179.79	-48.84	S	S	-312.78	110.94
29	S	-777.68	-47.16	-22.86	143.08	S	S	-41.93	47.24	-195.79
30	S	485.21	-29.92	-47.23	-240.60	S	-128.57	-28.32	234.87	164.70
Close	13895.63	10850.66	9712.28	10788.05	10913.38	13437.13	15129.67	17042.90	16284.00	18308.15
Change	537.89	-692.89	216.00	773.33	-700.15	346.29	319.36	-55.55	-244.03	-92.73

OCTOBER DAILY POINT CHANGES DOW JONES INDUSTRIALS

Previous Month Close	2007	2008	2009	2010	2011	2012	2013	2014	2015	2016
	13895.63	10850.66	9712.28	10788.05	10913.38	13437.13	15129.67	17042.90	16284.00	18308.15
1	191.92	-19.59	-203.00	41.63	S	77.98	62.03	-238.19	-11.99	S
2	-40.24	-348.22	-21.61	S	S	-32.75	-58.56	-3.66	200.36	S
3	-79.26	-157.47	S	S	-258.08	12.25	-136.66	208.64	S	-54.30
4	6.26	S	S	-78.41	153.41	80.75	76.10	S	S	-85.40
5	91.70	S	112.08	193.45	131.24	34.79	S	S	304.06	112.58
6	S	-369.88	131.50	22.93	183.38	S	S	-17.78	13.76	-12.53
7	S	-508.39	-5.67	-19.07	-20.21	S	-136.34	-272.52	122.10	-28.01
8	-22.28	-189.01	61.29	57.90	S	-26.50	-159.71	274.83	138.46	S
9	120.80	-678.91	78.07	S	S	-110.12	26.45	-334.97	33.74	S
10	-85.84	-128.00	S	S	330.06	-128.56	323.09	-115.15	S	88.55
11	-63.57	S	S	3.86	-16.88	-18.58	111.04	S	S	-200.38
12	77.96	936.42	20.86	10.06	102.55	2.46	S	S	47.37	15.54
13	S	-76.62	-14.74	75.68	-40.72	S	S	-223.03	-49.97	-45.26
14	S	-733.08	144.80	-1.51	166.36	S	64.15	-5.88	-157.14	39.44
15	-108.28	401.35	47.08	-31.79	S	95.38	-133.25	-173.45	217.00	S
16	-71.86	-127.04	-67.03	S	S	127.55	205.82	-24.50	74.22	S
17	-20.40	S	S	80.91	-247.49	5.22	-2.18	263.17	S	-51.98
18	-3.58	S	96.28	-165.07	180.05	-8.06	28.00	S	S	75.54
19	-366.94	413.21	-50.71	129.35	-72.43	-205.43	S	S	14.57	40.68
20	S	-231.77	-92.12	38.60	37.16	S	S	19.26	-13.43	-40.27
21	S	-231.77	-92.12	38.60	267.01	S	-7.45	215.14	-48.50	-16.64
22	44.95	-514.45	131.95	-14.01	S	2.38	75.46	-153.49	320.55	S
23	109.26	172.04	-109.13	S	S	-243.36	-54.33	216.58	157.54	S
24	-0.98	-312.30	S	S	104.83	-25.19	95.88	127.51	S	77.32
25	-3.33	S	S	31.49	-207.00	26.34	61.07	S	S	-53.76
26	134.78	S	-104.22	5.41	162.42	3.53	S	S	-23.65	30.06
27	S	-203.18	14.21	-43.18	339.51	S	S	12.53	-41.62	-29.65
28	S	889.35	-119.48	-12.33	22.56	H*	-1.35	187.81	198.09	-8.49
29	63.56	-74.16	199.89	4.54	S	H*	111.42	-31.44	-23.72	S
30	-77.79	189.73	-249.85	S	S	H*	-61.59	221.11	-92.26	S
31	137.54	144.32	S	S	-276.10	-10.75	-73.01	195.10	S	-18.77
Close	13930.01	9325.01	9712.73	11118.49	11955.01	13096.46	15545.75	17390.52	17663.54	18142.42
Change	34.38	-1525.65	0.45	330.44	1041.63	-340.67	416.08	347.62	1379.54	-165.73

* Hurricane Sandy

NOVEMBER DAILY POINT CHANGES DOW JONES INDUSTRIALS

Previous Month Close	2007	2008	2009	2010	2011	2012	2013	2014	2015	2016
	13930.01	9325.01	9712.73	11118.49	11955.01	13096.46	15545.75	17390.52	17663.54	18142.42
1	-362.14	S	S	6.13	-297.05	136.16	69.80	S	S	-105.32
2	27.23	S	76.71	64.10	178.08	-139.46	S	S	165.22	-77.46
3	S	-5.18	-17.53	26.41	208.43	S	S	-24.28	89.39	-28.97
4	S	305.45	30.23	219.71	-61.23	S	23.57	17.60	-50.57	-42.39
5	-51.70	-486.01	203.82	9.24	S	19.28	-20.90	100.69	-4.15	S
6	117.54	-443.48	17.46	S	S	133.24	128.66	69.94	46.90	S
7	-360.92	248.02	S	S	85.15	-312.95	-152.90	19.46	S	371.32
8	-33.73	S	S	-37.24	101.79	-121.41	167.80	S	S	73.14
9	-223.55	S	203.52	-60.09	-389.24	4.07	S	S	-179.85	256.95
10	S	-73.27	20.03	10.29	112.85	S	S	39.81	27.73	218.19
11	S	-176.58	44.29	-73.94	259.89	S	21.32	1.16	-55.99	39.78
12	-55.19	-411.30	-93.79	-90.52	S	-0.31	-32.43	-2.70	-254.15	S
13	319.54	552.59	73.00	S	S	-58.90	70.96	40.59	-202.83	S
14	-76.08	-337.94	S	S	-74.70	-185.23	54.59	-18.05	S	21.03
15	-120.96	S	S	9.39	17.18	-28.57	85.48	S	S	54.37
16	66.74	S	136.49	-178.47	-190.57	45.93	S	S	237.77	-54.92
17	S	-223.73	30.46	-15.62	-134.86	S	S	13.01	6.49	35.68
18	S	151.17	-11.11	173.35	25.43	S	14.32	40.07	247.66	-35.89
19	-218.35	-427.47	-93.87	22.32	S	207.65	-8.99	-2.09	-4.41	S
20	51.70	-444.99	-14.28	S	S	-7.45	-66.21	33.27	91.06	S
21	-211.10	494.13	S	S	-248.85	48.38	109.17	91.06	S	88.76
22	H	S	S	-24.97	-53.59	H	54.78	S	S	67.18
23	181.84*	S	132.79	-142.21	-236.17	172.79*	S	S	-31.13	59.31
24	S	396.97	-17.24	150.91	H	S	H	7.84	19.51	H
25	S	36.08	30.69	H	-25.77*	S	7.77	-2.96	1.20	68.96*
26	-237.44	247.14	H	-95.28*	S	-42.31	0.26	-2.69	H	S
27	215.00	H	-154.48*	S	S	-89.24	24.53	H	-14.9*	S
28	331.01	102.43*	S	S	291.23	106.98	H	15.99*	S	-54.24
29	22.28	S	S	-39.51	32.62	36.71	-10.92*	S	S	23.70
30	59.99	S	34.92	-46.47	490.05	3.76	S	S	-78.57	1.98
Close	13371.72	8829.04	10344.84	11006.02	12045.68	13025.58	16086.41	17828.24	17719.92	19123.58
Change	-558.29	-495.97	632.11	-112.47	90.67	-70.88	540.66	437.72	56.38	981.16

* Shortened trading day

DECEMBER DAILY POINT CHANGES DOW JONES INDUSTRIALS

Previous Month Close	2007	2008	2009	2010	2011	2012	2013	2014	2015	2016
	13371.72	8829.04	10344.84	11006.02	12045.68	13025.58	16086.41	17828.24	17719.92	19123.58
1	S	-679.95	126.74	249.76	-25.65	S	S	-51.44	168.43	68.35
2	S	270.00	-18.90	106.63	-0.61	S	-77.64	102.75	-158.67	-21.51
3	-57.15	172.60	-86.53	19.68	S	-59.98	-94.15	33.07	-252.01	S
4	-65.84	-215.45	22.75	S	S	-13.82	-24.85	-12.52	369.96	S
5	196.23	259.18	S	S	78.41	82.71	-68.26	58.69	S	45.82
6	174.93	S	S	-19.90	52.30	39.55	198.69	S	S	35.54
7	5.69	S	1.21	-3.03	46.24	81.09	S	S	-117.12	297.84
8	S	298.76	-104.14	13.32	-198.67	S	S	-106.31	-162.51	65.19
9	S	-242.85	51.08	-2.42	186.56	S	5.33	-51.28	-75.70	142.04
10	101.45	70.09	68.78	40.26	S	14.75	-52.40	-268.05	82.45	S
11	-294.26	-196.33	65.67	S	S	78.56	-129.60	63.19	-309.54	S
12	41.13	64.59	S	S	-162.87	-2.99	-104.10	-315.51	S	39.58
13	44.06	S	S	18.24	-66.45	-74.73	15.93	S	S	114.78
14	-178.11	S	29.55	47.98	-131.46	-35.71	S	S	103.29	-118.68
15	S	-65.15	-49.05	-19.07	45.33	S	S	-99.99	156.41	59.71
16	S	359.61	-10.88	41.78	-2.42	S	129.21	-111.97	224.18	-8.83
17	-172.65	-99.80	-132.86	-7.34	S	100.38	-9.31	288.00	-253.25	S
18	65.27	-219.35	20.63	S	S	115.57	292.71	421.28	-367.29	S
19	-25.20	-25.88	S	S	-100.13	-98.99	11.11	26.65	S	39.65
20	38.37	S	S	-13.78	337.32	59.75	42.06	S	S	91.56
21	205.01	S	85.25	55.03	4.16	-120.88	S	S	123.07	-32.66
22	S	-59.34	50.79	26.33	61.91	S	S	154.64	165.65	-23.08
23	S	-100.28	1.51	14.00	124.35	S	73.47	64.73	185.34	14.93
24	98.68*	48.99*	53.66*	H	S	-51.76*	62.94*	6.04*	-50.44*	S
25	H	H	H	S	S	H	H	H	H	S
26	2.36	47.07	H	S	H	-24.49	122.33	23.50	S	H
27	-192.08	S	S	-18.46	-2.65	-18.28	-1.47	S	S	11.23
28	6.26	S	26.98	20.51	-139.94	-158.20	S	S	-23.90	-111.36
29	S	-31.62	-1.67	9.84	135.63	S	S	-15.48	192.71	-13.90
30	S	184.46	3.10	-15.67	-69.48	S	25.88	-55.16	-117.11	-57.18
31	-101.05	108.00	-120.46	7.80	S	166.03	72.37	-160.00	-178.84	S
Close	13264.82	8776.39	10428.05	11577.51	12217.56	13104.14	16576.66	17823.07	17425.03	19762.60
Change	-106.90	-52.65	83.21	571.49	171.88	78.56	490.25	-5.17	-294.89	639.02

* Shortened trading day

A TYPICAL DAY IN THE MARKET

Half-hourly data became available for the Dow Jones Industrial Average starting in January 1987. The NYSE switched 10:00 a.m. openings to 9:30 a.m. in October 1985. Below is the comparison between half-hourly performance from January 1987 to May 12, 2017 and hourly performance from November 1963 to June 1985. Stronger openings and closings in a more bullish climate are evident. Morning and afternoon weaknesses appear an hour earlier.

MARKET % PERFORMANCE EACH HALF-HOUR OF THE DAY
(January 1987–May 12, 2017)

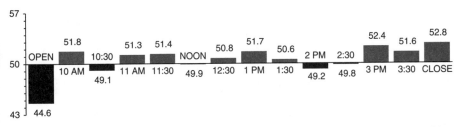

Based on the number of times the Dow Jones Industrial Average increased over previous half-hour.

MARKET % PERFORMANCE EACH HOUR OF THE DAY
(November 1963–June 1985)

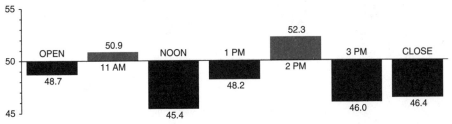

Based on the number of times the Dow Jones Industrial Average increased over the previous hour.

On the next page, half-hourly movements since January 1987 are separated by day of the week. From 1953 to 1989, Monday was the worst day of the week, especially during long bear markets, but times changed. Monday reversed positions and became the best day of the week and on the plus side eleven years in a row from 1990 to 2000.

During the last 16 years (2001–May 12, 2017) Friday is a net loser. Tuesday through Thursday are solid gainers, Tuesday the best (page 70). On all days, stocks do tend to firm up near the close with weakness in the early morning and from 1:30 to 2:30 frequently.

THROUGH THE WEEK ON A HALF-HOURLY BASIS

From the chart showing the percentage of times the Dow Jones Industrial Average rose over the preceding half-hour (January 1987 to May 12, 2017*), the typical week unfolds.

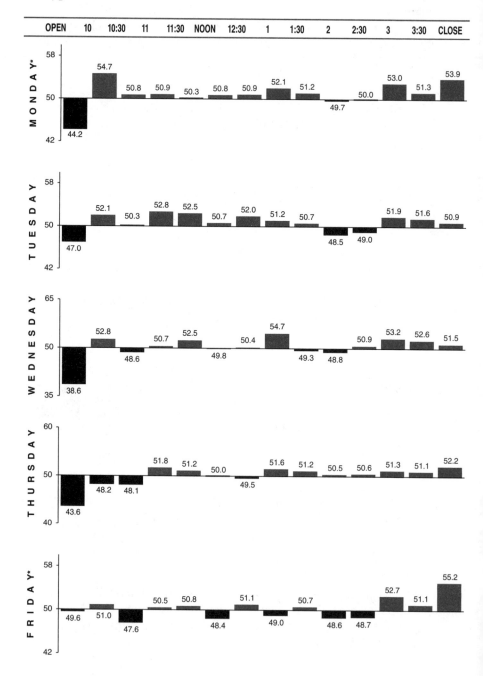

*Monday denotes first trading day of the week, Friday denotes last trading day of the week.

TUESDAY MOST PROFITABLE DAY OF WEEK

Between 1952 and 1989, Monday was the worst trading day of the week. The first trading day of the week (including Tuesday, when Monday is a holiday) rose only 44.3% of the time, while the other trading days closed higher 54.8% of the time. (NYSE Saturday trading was discontinued June 1952.)

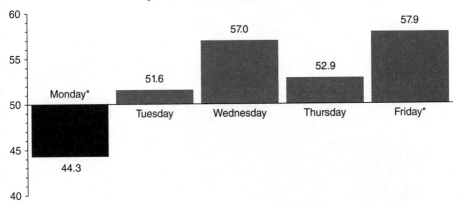

MARKET % PERFORMANCE EACH DAY OF THE WEEK
(June 1952–December 1989)

A dramatic reversal occurred in 1990—Monday became the most powerful day of the week. However, during the last 16 and a third years, Tuesday has produced the most gains. Since the top in 2000, traders have not been inclined to stay long over the weekend nor buy up equities at the outset of the week. This is not uncommon during uncertain market times. Monday was the worst day during the 2007–2009 bear, and only Tuesday was a net gainer. Since the March 2009 bottom, Tuesday and Thursday are best. See pages 68 and 143.

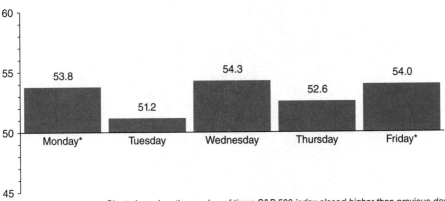

MARKET % PERFORMANCE EACH DAY OF THE WEEK
(January 1990–May 12, 2017)

Charts based on the number of times S&P 500 index closed higher than previous day.
*Monday denotes first trading day of the week, Friday denotes last trading day of the week.

NASDAQ STRONGEST LAST 3 DAYS OF WEEK

Despite 20 years less data, daily trading patterns on NASDAQ through 1989 appear to be fairly similar to the S&P on page 141, except for more bullishness on Thursdays. During the mostly flat markets of the 1970s and early 1980s, it would appear that apprehensive investors decided to throw in the towel over weekends and sell on Mondays and Tuesdays.

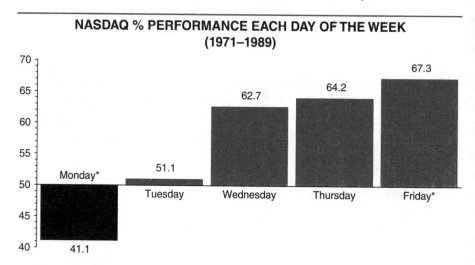

NASDAQ % PERFORMANCE EACH DAY OF THE WEEK (1971–1989)

Notice the vast difference in the daily trading pattern between NASDAQ and S&P from January 1, 1990, to recent times. The reason for so much more bullishness is that NASDAQ moved up 1010%, over three times as much during the 1990 to 2000 period. The gain for the S&P was 332% and for the Dow Jones industrials, 326%. NASDAQ's weekly patterns are beginning to move in step with the rest of the market. Notice the similarities to the S&P since 2001 on pages 143 and 144—Monday and Friday weakness, midweek strength.

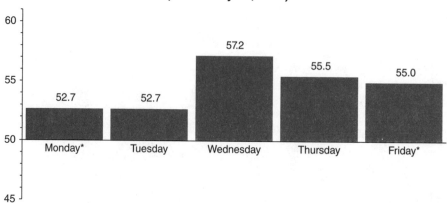

NASDAQ % PERFORMANCE EACH DAY OF THE WEEK (1990– May 12, 2017)

Based on NASDAQ composite, prior to February 5, 1971, based on National Quotation Bureau indices.
*Monday denotes first trading day of the week, Friday denotes last trading day of the week.

S&P DAILY PERFORMANCE EACH YEAR SINCE 1952

To determine if market trend alters performance of different days of the week, we separated 23 bear years—1953, '56, '57, '60, '62, '66, '69, '70, '73, '74, '77, '78, '81, '84, '87, '90, '94, 2000, 2001, 2002, 2008, 2011, and 2015—from 42 bull market years. While Tuesday and Thursday did not vary much between bull and bear years, Mondays and Fridays were sharply affected. There was a swing of 10.1 percentage points in Monday's performance and 9.5 in Friday's. Tuesday is the best day of the week based upon total points gained. See page 68.

PERCENTAGE OF TIMES MARKET CLOSED HIGHER THAN PREVIOUS DAY
(JUNE 1952–MAY 12, 2017)

	Monday*	Tuesday	Wednesday	Thursday	Friday*
1952	48.4%	55.6%	58.1%	51.9%	66.7%
1953	32.7	50.0	54.9	57.5	56.6
1954	50.0	57.5	63.5	59.2	73.1
1955	50.0	45.7	63.5	60.0	78.9
1956	36.5	39.6	46.9	50.0	59.6
1957	25.0	54.0	66.7	48.9	44.2
1958	59.6	52.0	59.6	68.1	72.6
1959	42.3	53.1	55.8	48.9	69.8
1960	34.6	50.0	44.2	54.0	59.6
1961	52.9	54.4	64.7	56.0	67.3
1962	28.3	52.1	54.0	51.0	50.0
1963	46.2	63.3	51.0	57.5	69.2
1964	40.4	48.0	61.5	58.7	77.4
1965	44.2	57.5	55.8	51.0	71.2
1966	36.5	47.8	53.9	42.0	57.7
1967	38.5	50.0	60.8	64.0	69.2
1968†	49.1	57.5	64.3	42.6	54.9
1969	30.8	45.8	50.0	67.4	50.0
1970	38.5	46.0	63.5	48.9	52.8
1971	44.2	64.6	57.7	55.1	51.9
1972	38.5	60.9	57.7	51.0	67.3
1973	32.1	51.1	52.9	44.9	44.2
1974	32.7	57.1	51.0	36.7	30.8
1975	53.9	38.8	61.5	56.3	55.8
1976	55.8	55.3	55.8	40.8	58.5
1977	40.4	40.4	46.2	53.1	53.9
1978	51.9	43.5	59.6	54.0	48.1
1979	54.7	53.2	58.8	66.0	44.2
1980	55.8	54.2	71.7	35.4	59.6
1981	44.2	38.8	55.8	53.2	47.2
1982	46.2	39.6	44.2	44.9	50.0
1983	55.8	46.8	61.5	52.0	55.8
1984	39.6	63.8	31.4	46.0	44.2
1985	44.2	61.2	54.9	56.3	53.9
1986	51.9	44.9	67.3	58.3	55.8
1987	51.9	57.1	63.5	61.7	49.1
1988	51.9	61.7	51.9	48.0	59.6
1989	51.9	47.8	69.2	58.0	69.2
1990	67.9	53.2	52.9	40.0	51.9
1991	44.2	46.9	52.9	49.0	51.9
1992	51.9	49.0	53.9	56.3	45.3
1993	65.4	41.7	55.8	44.9	48.1
1994	55.8	46.8	52.9	48.0	59.6
1995	63.5	56.5	63.5	62.0	63.5
1996	54.7	44.9	51.0	57.1	63.5
1997	67.3	67.4	42.3	41.7	57.7
1998	57.7	62.5	57.7	38.3	60.4
1999	46.2	29.8	67.3	53.1	57.7
2000	51.9	43.5	40.4	56.0	46.2
2001	45.3	51.1	44.0	59.2	43.1
2002	40.4	37.5	56.9	38.8	48.1
2003	59.6	62.5	42.3	58.3	50.0
2004	51.9	61.7	59.6	52.1	52.8
2005	59.6	47.8	59.6	56.0	55.8
2006	55.8	55.6	67.3	52.0	48.1
2007	47.2	50.0	64.0	50.0	61.5
2008	42.3	50.0	41.5	60.4	55.8
2009	53.9	50.0	57.7	63.8	52.8
2010	61.5	57.5	55.8	53.1	57.7
2011	48.1	56.5	55.8	56.0	57.7
2012	52.8	48.9	50.0	58.0	53.9
2013	51.9	60.4	54.9	59.2	65.4
2014	53.9	56.3	57.7	56.3	61.5
2015	51.9	43.8	44.2	53.2	43.4
2016	50.0	58.7	55.8	50.0	46.2
2017‡	52.6	43.8	63.2	50.0	52.6
Average	**48.2%**	**51.6%**	**55.7%**	**52.8%**	**56.3%**
42 Bull Years	**51.8%**	**53.1%**	**58.1%**	**53.6%**	**59.7%**
23 Bear Years	**41.7%**	**48.7%**	**51.4%**	**51.3%**	**50.2%**

Based on S&P 500

† Most Wednesdays closed last 7 months of 1968.   ‡ Through 5/12/2017 only, not included in averages.
*Monday denotes first trading day of the week, Friday denotes last trading day of the week.

NASDAQ DAILY PERFORMANCE EACH YEAR SINCE 1971

After dropping a hefty 77.9% from its 2000 high (versus −37.8% on the Dow and −49.1% on the S&P 500), NASDAQ tech stocks still outpace the blue chips and big caps—but not by nearly as much as they did. From January 1, 1971 through May 12, 2017, NASDAQ, moved up an impressive 6731%. The Dow (up 2391%) and the S&P (up 2169%) gained less than half as much.

Monday's performance on NASDAQ was lackluster during the three-year bear market of 2000–2002. As NASDAQ rebounded (up 50% in 2003), strength returned to Monday during 2003–2006. During the bear market from late 2007 to early 2009, weakness was most consistent on Monday and Friday. At press time, Mondays and Tuesdays have been treacherous.

PERCENTAGE OF TIMES NASDAQ CLOSED HIGHER THAN PREVIOUS DAY
(1971–MAY 12, 2017)

	Monday*	Tuesday	Wednesday	Thursday	Friday*
1971	51.9%	52.1%	59.6%	65.3%	71.2%
1972	30.8	60.9	63.5	57.1	78.9
1973	34.0	48.9	52.9	53.1	48.1
1974	30.8	44.9	52.9	51.0	42.3
1975	44.2	42.9	63.5	64.6	63.5
1976	50.0	63.8	67.3	59.2	58.5
1977	51.9	40.4	53.9	63.3	73.1
1978	48.1	47.8	73.1	72.0	84.6
1979	45.3	53.2	64.7	86.0	82.7
1980	46.2	64.6	84.9	52.1	73.1
1981	42.3	32.7	67.3	76.6	69.8
1982	34.6	47.9	59.6	51.0	63.5
1983	42.3	44.7	67.3	68.0	73.1
1984	22.6	53.2	35.3	52.0	51.9
1985	36.5	59.2	62.8	68.8	66.0
1986	38.5	55.1	65.4	72.9	75.0
1987	42.3	49.0	65.4	68.1	66.0
1988	50.0	55.3	61.5	66.0	63.5
1989	38.5	54.4	71.2	72.0	75.0
1990	54.7	42.6	60.8	46.0	55.8
1991	51.9	59.2	66.7	65.3	51.9
1992	44.2	53.1	59.6	60.4	45.3
1993	55.8	56.3	69.2	57.1	67.3
1994	51.9	46.8	54.9	52.0	55.8
1995	50.0	52.2	63.5	64.0	63.5
1996	50.9	57.1	64.7	61.2	63.5
1997	65.4	59.2	53.9	52.1	55.8
1998	59.6	58.3	65.4	44.7	58.5
1999	61.5	40.4	63.5	57.1	65.4
2000	40.4	41.3	42.3	60.0	57.7
2001	41.5	57.8	52.0	55.1	47.1
2002	44.2	37.5	56.9	46.9	46.2
2003	57.7	60.4	40.4	60.4	46.2
2004	57.7	59.6	53.9	50.0	50.9
2005	61.5	47.8	51.9	48.0	59.6
2006	55.8	51.1	65.4	50.0	44.2
2007	47.2	63.0	66.0	56.0	57.7
2008	34.6	52.1	49.1	54.2	42.3
2009	51.9	54.2	63.5	63.8	50.9
2010	61.5	53.2	61.5	55.1	61.5
2011	50.0	56.5	50.0	64.0	53.9
2012	49.1	53.3	50.0	54.0	51.9
2013	57.7	60.4	52.9	59.2	67.3
2014	57.7	58.3	57.7	52.1	59.6
2015	55.8	39.6	53.9	59.6	49.1
2016	51.9	52.2	55.8	50.0	57.7
2017†	35.3	40.0	58.8	50.0	64.7
Average	**47.8%**	**52.0%**	**59.6%**	**59.3%**	**60.2%**
33 Bull Years	**50.2%**	**50.2%**	**50.2%**	**50.2%**	**50.2%**
13 Bear Years	**41.9%**	**46.4%**	**53.4%**	**56.8%**	**52.8%**

Based on NASDAQ composite; prior to February 5, 1971, based on National Quotation Bureau indices.
† Through 5/12/2017 only, not included in averages.
*Monday denotes first trading day of the week, Friday denotes last trading day of the week.

MONTHLY CASH INFLOWS INTO S&P STOCKS

For many years, the last trading day of the month, plus the first four of the following month, were the best market days of the month. This pattern is quite clear in the first chart, showing these five consecutive trading days towering above the other 16 trading days of the average month in the 1953–1981 period. The rationale was that individuals and institutions tended to operate similarly, causing a massive flow of cash into stocks near beginnings of months.

MARKET % PERFORMANCE EACH DAY OF THE MONTH
(January 1953 to December 1981)
Based on the number of times the S&P 500
closed higher than previous day.

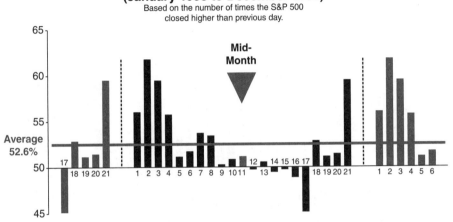

Clearly, "front-running" traders took advantage of this phenomenon, drastically altering the previous pattern. The second chart from 1982 onward shows the trading shift caused by these "anticipators" to the last three trading days of the month, plus the first two. Another astonishing development shows the ninth, tenth, and eleventh trading days rising strongly as well. Growth of 401(k) retirement plans, IRAs, and similar plans (participants' salaries are usually paid twice monthly) is responsible for this mid-month bulge. First trading days of the month have produced the greatest gains in recent years (see page 86).

MARKET % PERFORMANCE EACH DAY OF THE MONTH
(January 1982 to December 2016)

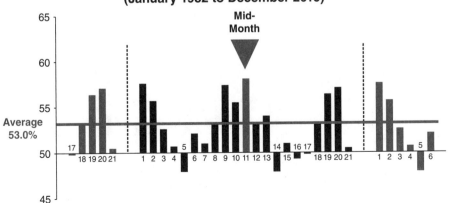

Trading Days (excluding Saturdays, Sundays, and holidays).

MONTHLY CASH INFLOWS INTO NASDAQ STOCKS

NASDAQ stocks moved up 58.1% of the time through 1981 compared to 52.6% for the S&P on page 145. Ends and beginnings of the month are fairly similar, specifically the last plus the first four trading days. But notice how investors piled into NASDAQ stocks until mid-month. NASDAQ rose 118.6% from January 1, 1971, to December 31, 1981, compared to 33.0% for the S&P.

NASDAQ % PERFORMANCE EACH DAY OF THE MONTH
(January 1971 to December 1981)
Based on the number of times the NASDAQ composite
closed higher than previous day.

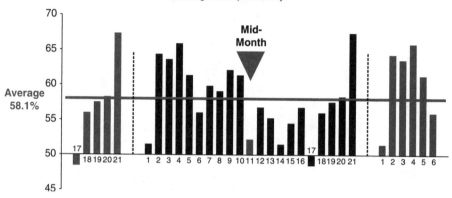

After the air was let out of the tech market 2000–2002, S&P's 1727% gain over the last 35 years is more evenly matched with NASDAQ's 2649% gain. Last three, first four, and middle eighth and tenth days rose the most. Where the S&P has three days of the month that go down more often than up, NASDAQ has one. NASDAQ exhibits the most strength on the first trading day of the month. Over the past 18 years, last days have weakened considerably, down more often than not.

NASDAQ % PERFORMANCE EACH DAY OF THE MONTH
(January 1982 to December 2016)

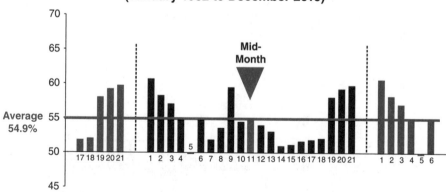

Trading Days (excluding Saturdays, Sundays, and holidays).
Based on NASDAQ composite, prior to February 5, 1971, based on National Quotation Bureau indices.

NOVEMBER, DECEMBER, AND JANUARY: YEAR'S BEST THREE-MONTH SPAN

The most important observation to be made from a chart showing the average monthly percent change in market prices since 1950 is that institutions (mutual funds, pension funds, banks, etc.) determine the trading patterns in today's market.

The "investment calendar" reflects the annual, semi-annual, and quarterly operations of institutions during January, April, and July. October, besides being the last campaign month before elections, is also the time when most bear markets seem to end, as in 1946, 1957, 1960, 1966, 1974, 1987, 1990, 1998, and 2002. (August and September tend to combine to make the worst consecutive two-month period.)

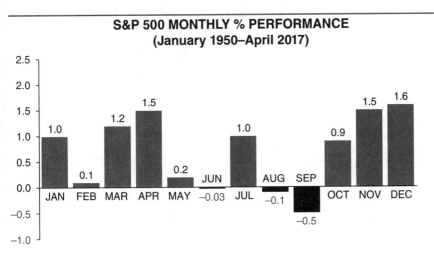

S&P 500 MONTHLY % PERFORMANCE
(January 1950–April 2017)

Average month-to-month % change in S&P 500.
(Based on monthly closing prices.)

Unusual year-end strength comes from corporate and private pension funds, producing a 4.1% gain on average between November 1 and January 31. In 2007–2008, these three months were all down for the fourth time since 1930; previously in 1931–1932, 1940–1941, and 1969–1970, also bear markets. September's dismal performance makes it the worst month of the year. However, in the last 13 years, it has been up 8 times after being down five in a row 1999–2003.

In midterm years since 1950, October is the best month, +3.3% (13–4). November is second best with a 2.6% average gain. February, March, April, July and December are also positive. June is worst, –1.9% (6–11), while January, May, August and September are net losers.

See page 50 for monthly performance tables for the S&P 500 and the Dow Jones industrials. See pages 52, 54, and 62 for unique switching strategies.

On page 64, you can see how the first month of the first three quarters far outperforms the second and the third months since 1950, and note the improvement in May's and October's performance since 1991.

NOVEMBER THROUGH JUNE: NASDAQ'S EIGHT-MONTH RUN

The two-and-a-half-year plunge of 77.9% in NASDAQ stocks, between March 10, 2000, and October 9, 2002, brought several horrendous monthly losses (the two greatest were November 2000, −22.9%, and February 2001, −22.4%), which trimmed average monthly performance over the $46^1/_3$-year period. Ample Octobers in 13 of the last 19 years, including three huge turnarounds in 2001 (+12.8%), 2002 (+13.5%), and 2011 (+11.1%) have put bear-killing October in the number one spot since 1998. January's 2.6% average gain is still awesome, and more than twice S&P's 1.1% January average since 1971.

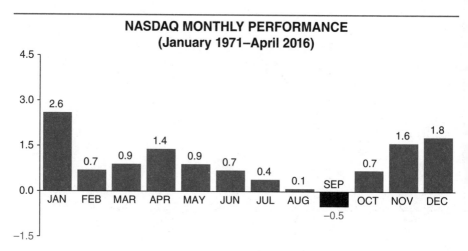

NASDAQ MONTHLY PERFORMANCE
(January 1971–April 2016)

Average month-to-month % change in NASDAQ composite, prior to Feb. 5, 1971, based on National Quotation Bureau indices. (Based on monthly closing prices.)

Bear in mind, when comparing NASDAQ to the S&P on page 147, that there are 22 fewer years of data here. During this $46^1/_3$-year (1971–April 2016) period, NASDAQ gained 6649%, while the S&P and the Dow rose only 2487% and 2396%, respectively. On page 56, you can see a statistical monthly comparison between NASDAQ and the Dow.

Year-end strength is even more pronounced in NASDAQ, producing a 6.0% gain on average between November 1 and January 31—nearly 1.5 times greater than that of the S&P 500 on page 147. September is the worst month of the year for the over-the-counter index as well, posting an average loss of −0.5%. These extremes underscore NASDAQ's higher volatility—and moves of greater magnitude.

In midterm years since 1974, October is best with an average gain of 4.2% (9–2). February, March, November and December also produced average gains. July is the worst month, off 2.2% (3–8). January, April, May, June, August and September were net losers as well.

DOW JONES INDUSTRIALS ANNUAL HIGHS, LOWS, & CLOSES SINCE 1901

YEAR	HIGH DATE	HIGH CLOSE	LOW DATE	LOW CLOSE	YEAR CLOSE	YEAR	HIGH DATE	HIGH CLOSE	LOW DATE	LOW CLOSE	YEAR CLOSE
1901	6/17	57.33	12/24	45.07	47.29	1960	1/5	685.47	10/25	566.05	615.89
1902	4/24	50.14	12/15	43.64	47.10	1961	12/13	734.91	1/3	610.25	731.14
1903	2/16	49.59	11/9	30.88	35.98	1962	1/3	726.01	6/26	535.76	652.10
1904	12/5	53.65	3/12	34.00	50.99	1963	12/18	767.21	1/2	646.79	762.95
1905	12/29	70.74	1/25	50.37	70.47	1964	11/18	891.71	1/2	766.08	874.13
1906	1/19	75.45	7/13	62.40	69.12	1965	12/31	969.26	6/28	840.59	969.26
1907	1/7	70.60	11/15	38.83	43.04	1966	2/9	995.15	10/7	744.32	785.69
1908	11/13	64.74	2/13	42.94	63.11	1967	9/25	943.08	1/3	786.41	905.11
1909	11/19	73.64	2/23	58.54	72.56	1968	12/3	985.21	3/21	825.13	943.75
1910	1/3	72.04	7/26	53.93	59.60	1969	5/14	968.85	12/17	769.93	800.36
1911	6/19	63.78	9/25	53.43	59.84	1970	12/29	842.00	5/26	631.16	838.92
1912	9/30	68.97	2/10	58.72	64.37	1971	4/28	950.82	11/23	797.97	890.20
1913	1/9	64.88	6/11	52.83	57.71	1972	12/11	1036.27	1/26	889.15	1020.02
1914	3/20	61.12	7/30	52.32	54.58	1973	1/11	1051.70	12/5	788.31	850.86
1915	12/27	99.21	2/24	54.22	99.15	1974	3/13	891.66	12/6	577.60	616.24
1916	11/21	110.15	4/22	84.96	95.00	1975	7/15	881.81	1/2	632.04	852.41
1917	1/3	99.18	12/19	65.95	74.38	1976	9/21	1014.79	1/2	858.71	1004.65
1918	10/18	89.07	1/15	73.38	82.20	1977	1/3	999.75	11/2	800.85	831.17
1919	11/3	119.62	2/8	79.15	107.23	1978	9/8	907.74	2/28	742.12	805.01
1920	1/3	109.88	12/21	66.75	71.95	1979	10/5	897.61	11/7	796.67	838.74
1921	12/15	81.50	8/24	63.90	81.10	1980	11/20	1000.17	4/21	759.13	963.99
1922	10/14	103.43	1/10	78.59	98.73	1981	4/27	1024.05	9/25	824.01	875.00
1923	3/20	105.38	10/27	85.76	95.52	1982	12/27	1070.55	8/12	776.92	1046.54
1924	12/31	120.51	5/20	88.33	120.51	1983	11/29	1287.20	1/3	1027.04	1258.64
1925	11/6	159.39	3/30	115.00	156.66	1984	1/6	1286.64	7/24	1086.57	1211.57
1926	8/14	166.64	3/30	135.20	157.20	1985	12/16	1553.10	1/4	1184.96	1546.67
1927	12/31	202.40	1/25	152.73	202.40	1986	12/2	1955.57	1/22	1502.29	1895.95
1928	12/31	300.00	2/20	191.33	300.00	1987	8/25	2722.42	10/19	1738.74	1938.83
1929	9/3	381.17	11/13	198.69	248.48	1988	10/21	2183.50	1/20	1879.14	2168.57
1930	4/17	294.07	12/16	157.51	164.58	1989	10/9	2791.41	1/3	2144.64	2753.20
1931	2/24	194.36	12/17	73.79	77.90	1990	7/17	2999.75	10/11	2365.10	2633.66
1932	3/8	88.78	7/8	41.22	59.93	1991	12/31	3168.83	1/9	2470.30	3168.83
1933	7/18	108.67	2/27	50.16	99.90	1992	6/1	3413.21	10/9	3136.58	3301.11
1934	2/5	110.74	7/26	85.51	104.04	1993	12/29	3794.33	1/20	3241.95	3754.09
1935	11/19	148.44	3/14	96.71	144.13	1994	1/31	3978.36	4/4	3593.35	3834.44
1936	11/17	184.90	1/6	143.11	179.90	1995	12/13	5216.47	1/30	3832.08	5117.12
1937	3/10	194.40	11/24	113.64	120.85	1996	12/27	6560.91	1/10	5032.94	6448.27
1938	11/12	158.41	3/31	98.95	154.76	1997	8/6	8259.31	4/11	6391.69	7908.25
1939	9/12	155.92	4/8	121.44	150.24	1998	11/23	9374.27	8/31	7539.07	9181.43
1940	1/3	152.80	6/10	111.84	131.13	1999	12/31	11497.12	1/22	9120.67	11497.12
1941	1/10	133.59	12/23	106.34	110.96	2000	1/14	11722.98	3/7	9796.03	10786.85
1942	12/26	119.71	4/28	92.92	119.40	2001	5/21	11337.92	9/21	8235.81	10021.50
1943	7/14	145.82	1/8	119.26	135.89	2002	3/19	10635.25	10/9	7286.27	8341.63
1944	12/16	152.53	2/7	134.22	152.32	2003	12/31	10453.92	3/11	7524.06	10453.92
1945	12/11	195.82	1/24	151.35	192.91	2004	12/28	10854.54	10/25	9749.99	10783.01
1946	5/29	212.50	10/9	163.12	177.20	2005	3/4	10940.55	4/20	10012.36	10717.50
1947	7/24	186.85	5/17	163.21	181.16	2006	12/27	12510.57	1/20	10667.39	12463.15
1948	6/15	193.16	3/16	165.39	177.30	2007	10/9	14164.53	3/5	12050.41	13264.82
1949	12/30	200.52	6/13	161.60	200.13	2008	5/2	13058.20	11/20	7552.29	8776.39
1950	11/24	235.47	1/13	196.81	235.41	2009	12/30	10548.51	3/9	6547.05	10428.05
1951	9/13	276.37	1/3	238.99	269.23	2010	12/29	11585.38	7/2	9686.48	11577.51
1952	12/30	292.00	5/1	256.35	291.90	2011	4/29	12810.54	10/3	10655.30	12217.56
1953	1/5	293.79	9/14	255.49	280.90	2012	10/5	13610.15	6/4	12101.46	13104.14
1954	12/31	404.39	1/11	279.87	404.39	2013	12/31	16576.66	1/8	13328.85	16576.66
1955	12/30	488.40	1/17	388.20	488.40	2014	12/26	18053.71	2/3	15372.80	17823.07
1956	4/6	521.05	1/23	462.35	499.47	2015	5/19	18312.39	8/25	15666.44	17425.03
1957	7/12	520.77	10/22	419.79	435.69	2016	12/20	19974.62	2/11	15660.18	19762.60
1958	12/31	583.65	2/25	436.89	583.65	2017*	3/1	21115.55	1/19	19732.40	*At Press-time*
1959	12/31	679.36	2/9	574.46	679.36						

*Through May 12, 2017

S&P 500 ANNUAL HIGHS, LOWS, & CLOSES SINCE 1930

YEAR	HIGH DATE	HIGH CLOSE	LOW DATE	LOW CLOSE	YEAR CLOSE	YEAR	HIGH DATE	HIGH CLOSE	LOW DATE	LOW CLOSE	YEAR CLOSE
1930	4/10	25.92	12/16	14.44	15.34	1974	1/3	99.80	10/3	62.28	68.56
1931	2/24	18.17	12/17	7.72	8.12	1975	7/15	95.61	1/8	70.04	90.19
1932	9/7	9.31	6/1	4.40	6.89	1976	9/21	107.83	1/2	90.90	107.46
1933	7/18	12.20	2/27	5.53	10.10	1977	1/3	107.00	11/2	90.71	95.10
1934	2/6	11.82	7/26	8.36	9.50	1978	9/12	106.99	3/6	86.90	96.11
1935	11/19	13.46	3/14	8.06	13.43	1979	10/5	111.27	2/27	96.13	107.94
1936	11/9	17.69	1/2	13.40	17.18	1980	11/28	140.52	3/27	98.22	135.76
1937	3/6	18.68	11/24	10.17	10.55	1981	1/6	138.12	9/25	112.77	122.55
1938	11/9	13.79	3/31	8.50	13.21	1982	11/9	143.02	8/12	102.42	140.64
1939	1/4	13.23	4/8	10.18	12.49	1983	10/10	172.65	1/3	138.34	164.93
1940	1/3	12.77	6/10	8.99	10.58	1984	11/6	170.41	7/24	147.82	167.24
1941	1/10	10.86	12/29	8.37	8.69	1985	12/16	212.02	1/4	163.68	211.28
1942	12/31	9.77	4/28	7.47	9.77	1986	12/2	254.00	1/22	203.49	242.17
1943	7/14	12.64	1/2	9.84	11.67	1987	8/25	336.77	12/4	223.92	247.08
1944	12/16	13.29	2/7	11.56	13.28	1988	10/21	283.66	1/20	242.63	277.72
1945	12/10	17.68	1/23	13.21	17.36	1989	10/9	359.80	1/3	275.31	353.40
1946	5/29	19.25	10/9	14.12	15.30	1990	7/16	368.95	10/11	295.46	330.22
1947	2/8	16.20	5/17	13.71	15.30	1991	12/31	417.09	1/9	311.49	417.09
1948	6/15	17.06	2/14	13.84	15.20	1992	12/18	441.28	4/8	394.50	435.71
1949	12/30	16.79	6/13	13.55	16.76	1993	12/28	470.94	1/8	429.05	466.45
1950	12/29	20.43	1/14	16.65	20.41	1994	2/2	482.00	4/4	438.92	459.27
1951	10/15	23.85	1/3	20.69	23.77	1995	12/13	621.69	1/3	459.11	615.93
1952	12/30	26.59	2/20	23.09	26.57	1996	11/25	757.03	1/10	598.48	740.74
1953	1/5	26.66	9/14	22.71	24.81	1997	12/5	983.79	1/2	737.01	970.43
1954	12/31	35.98	1/11	24.80	35.98	1998	12/29	1241.81	1/9	927.69	1229.23
1955	11/14	46.41	1/17	34.58	45.48	1999	12/31	1469.25	1/14	1212.19	1469.25
1956	8/2	49.74	1/23	43.11	46.67	2000	3/24	1527.46	12/20	1264.74	1320.28
1957	7/15	49.13	10/22	38.98	39.99	2001	2/1	1373.47	9/21	965.80	1148.08
1958	12/31	55.21	1/2	40.33	55.21	2002	1/4	1172.51	10/9	776.76	879.82
1959	8/3	60.71	2/9	53.58	59.89	2003	12/31	1111.92	3/11	800.73	1111.92
1960	1/5	60.39	10/25	52.30	58.11	2004	12/30	1213.55	8/12	1063.23	1211.92
1961	12/12	72.64	1/3	57.57	71.55	2005	12/14	1272.74	4/20	1137.50	1248.29
1962	1/3	71.13	6/26	52.32	63.10	2006	12/15	1427.09	6/13	1223.69	1418.30
1963	12/31	75.02	1/2	62.69	75.02	2007	10/9	1565.15	3/5	1374.12	1468.36
1964	11/20	86.28	1/2	75.43	84.75	2008	1/2	1447.16	11/20	752.44	903.25
1965	11/15	92.63	6/28	81.60	92.43	2009	12/28	1127.78	3/9	676.53	1115.10
1966	2/9	94.06	10/7	73.20	80.33	2010	12/29	1259.78	7/2	1022.58	1257.64
1967	9/25	97.59	1/3	80.38	96.47	2011	4/29	1363.61	10/3	1099.23	1257.60
1968	11/29	108.37	3/5	87.72	103.86	2012	9/14	1465.77	1/3	1277.06	1426.19
1969	5/14	106.16	12/17	89.20	92.06	2013	12/31	1848.36	1/8	1457.15	1848.36
1970	1/5	93.46	5/26	69.29	92.15	2014	12/29	2090.57	2/3	1741.89	2058.90
1971	4/28	104.77	11/23	90.16	102.09	2015	5/21	2130.82	8/25	1867.61	2043.94
1972	12/11	119.12	1/3	101.67	118.05	2016	12/13	2271.72	2/11	1829.08	2238.83
1973	1/11	120.24	12/5	92.16	97.55	2017*	5/10	2399.63	1/3	2257.83	At Press-time

*Through May 12, 2017

150

NASDAQ ANNUAL HIGHS, LOWS, & CLOSES SINCE 1971

YEAR	HIGH DATE	HIGH CLOSE	LOW DATE	LOW CLOSE	YEAR CLOSE	YEAR	HIGH DATE	HIGH CLOSE	LOW DATE	LOW CLOSE	YEAR CLOSE
1971	12/31	114.12	1/5	89.06	114.12	1995	12/4	1069.79	1/3	743.58	1052.13
1972	12/8	135.15	1/3	113.65	133.73	1996	12/9	1316.27	1/15	988.57	1291.03
1973	1/11	136.84	12/24	88.67	92.19	1997	10/9	1745.85	4/2	1201.00	1570.35
1974	3/15	96.53	10/3	54.87	59.82	1998	12/31	2192.69	10/8	1419.12	2192.69
1975	7/15	88.00	1/2	60.70	77.62	1999	12/31	4069.31	1/4	2208.05	4069.31
1976	12/31	97.88	1/2	78.06	97.88	2000	3/10	5048.62	12/20	2332.78	2470.52
1977	12/30	105.05	4/5	93.66	105.05	2001	1/24	2859.15	9/21	1423.19	1950.40
1978	9/13	139.25	1/11	99.09	117.98	2002	1/4	2059.38	10/9	1114.11	1335.51
1979	10/5	152.29	1/2	117.84	151.14	2003	12/30	2009.88	3/11	1271.47	2003.37
1980	11/28	208.15	3/27	124.09	202.34	2004	12/30	2178.34	8/12	1752.49	2175.44
1981	5/29	223.47	9/28	175.03	195.84	2005	12/2	2273.37	4/28	1904.18	2205.32
1982	12/8	240.70	8/13	159.14	232.41	2006	11/22	2465.98	7/21	2020.39	2415.29
1983	6/24	328.91	1/3	230.59	278.60	2007	10/31	2859.12	3/5	2340.68	2652.28
1984	1/6	287.90	7/25	225.30	247.35	2008	1/2	2609.63	11/20	1316.12	1577.03
1985	12/16	325.16	1/2	245.91	324.93	2009	12/30	2291.28	3/9	1268.64	2269.15
1986	7/3	411.16	1/9	323.01	349.33	2010	12/22	2671.48	7/2	2091.79	2652.87
1987	8/26	455.26	10/28	291.88	330.47	2011	4/29	2873.54	10/3	2335.83	2605.15
1988	7/5	396.11	1/12	331.97	381.38	2012	9/14	3183.95	1/4	2648.36	3019.51
1989	10/9	485.73	1/3	378.56	454.82	2013	12/31	4176.59	1/8	3091.81	4176.59
1990	7/16	469.60	10/16	325.44	373.84	2014	12/29	4806.91	2/3	3996.96	4736.05
1991	12/31	586.34	1/14	355.75	586.34	2015	7/20	5218.86	8/25	4506.49	5007.41
1992	12/31	676.95	6/26	547.84	676.95	2016	12/27	5487.44	2/11	4266.84	5383.12
1993	10/15	787.42	4/26	645.87	776.80	2017*	5/10	6129.14	1/3	5429.08	At Press-time
1994	3/18	803.93	6/24	693.79	751.96						

RUSSELL 1000 ANNUAL HIGHS, LOWS, & CLOSES SINCE 1979

YEAR	HIGH DATE	HIGH CLOSE	LOW DATE	LOW CLOSE	YEAR CLOSE	YEAR	HIGH DATE	HIGH CLOSE	LOW DATE	LOW CLOSE	YEAR CLOSE
1979	10/5	61.18	2/27	51.83	59.87	1999	12/31	767.97	2/9	632.53	767.97
1980	11/28	78.26	3/27	53.68	75.20	2000	9/1	813.71	12/20	668.75	700.09
1981	1/6	76.34	9/25	62.03	67.93	2001	1/30	727.35	9/21	507.98	604.94
1982	11/9	78.47	8/12	55.98	77.24	2002	3/19	618.74	10/9	410.52	466.18
1983	10/10	95.07	1/3	76.04	90.38	2003	12/31	594.56	3/11	425.31	594.56
1984	1/6	92.80	7/24	79.49	90.31	2004	12/30	651.76	8/13	566.06	650.99
1985	12/16	114.97	1/4	88.61	114.39	2005	12/14	692.09	4/20	613.37	679.42
1986	7/2	137.87	1/22	111.14	130.00	2006	12/15	775.08	6/13	665.81	770.08
1987	8/25	176.22	12/4	117.65	130.02	2007	10/9	852.32	3/5	749.85	799.82
1988	10/21	149.94	1/20	128.35	146.99	2008	1/2	788.62	11/20	402.91	487.77
1989	10/9	189.93	1/3	145.78	185.11	2009	12/28	619.22	3/9	367.55	612.01
1990	7/16	191.56	10/11	152.36	171.22	2010	12/29	698.11	7/2	562.58	696.90
1991	12/31	220.61	1/9	161.94	220.61	2011	4/29	758.45	10/3	604.42	693.36
1992	12/18	235.06	4/8	208.87	233.59	2012	9/14	809.01	1/4	703.72	789.90
1993	10/15	252.77	1/8	229.91	250.71	2013	12/31	1030.36	1/8	807.95	1030.36
1994	2/1	258.31	4/4	235.38	244.65	2014	12/29	1161.45	2/3	972.95	1144.37
1995	12/13	331.18	1/3	244.41	328.89	2015	5/21	1189.55	8/25	1042.77	1131.88
1996	12/2	401.21	1/10	318.24	393.75	2016	12/13	1260.06	2/11	1005.89	1241.66
1997	12/5	519.72	4/11	389.03	513.79	2017*	5/5	1330.23	1/3	1252.11	At Press-time
1998	12/29	645.36	1/9	490.26	642.87						

RUSSELL 2000 ANNUAL HIGHS, LOWS, & CLOSES SINCE 1979

YEAR	HIGH DATE	HIGH CLOSE	LOW DATE	LOW CLOSE	YEAR CLOSE	YEAR	HIGH DATE	HIGH CLOSE	LOW DATE	LOW CLOSE	YEAR CLOSE
1979	12/31	55.91	1/2	40.81	55.91	1999	12/31	504.75	3/23	383.37	504.75
1980	11/28	77.70	3/27	45.36	74.80	2000	3/9	606.05	12/20	443.80	483.53
1981	6/15	85.16	9/25	65.37	73.67	2001	5/22	517.23	9/21	378.89	488.50
1982	12/8	91.01	8/12	60.33	88.90	2002	4/16	522.95	10/9	327.04	383.09
1983	6/24	126.99	1/3	88.29	112.27	2003	12/30	565.47	3/12	345.94	556.91
1984	1/12	116.69	7/25	93.95	101.49	2004	12/28	654.57	8/12	517.10	651.57
1985	12/31	129.87	1/2	101.21	129.87	2005	12/2	690.57	4/28	575.02	673.22
1986	7/3	155.30	1/9	128.23	135.00	2006	12/27	797.73	7/21	671.94	787.66
1987	8/25	174.44	10/28	106.08	120.42	2007	7/13	855.77	11/26	735.07	766.03
1988	7/15	151.42	1/12	121.23	147.37	2008	6/5	763.27	11/20	385.31	499.45
1989	10/9	180.78	1/3	146.79	168.30	2009	12/24	634.07	3/9	343.26	625.39
1990	6/15	170.90	10/30	118.82	132.16	2010	12/27	792.35	2/8	586.49	783.65
1991	12/31	189.94	1/15	125.25	189.94	2011	4/29	865.29	10/3	609.49	740.92
1992	12/31	221.01	7/8	185.81	221.01	2012	9/14	864.70	6/4	737.24	849.35
1993	11/2	260.17	2/23	217.55	258.59	2013	12/31	1163.64	1/3	872.60	1163.64
1994	3/18	271.08	12/9	235.16	250.36	2014	12/29	1219.11	10/13	1049.30	1204.70
1995	9/14	316.12	1/30	246.56	315.97	2015	6/23	1295.80	9/29	1083.91	1135.89
1996	5/22	364.61	1/16	301.75	362.61	2016	12/9	1388.07	2/11	953.72	1357.13
1997	10/13	465.21	4/25	335.85	437.02	2017*	4/26	1419.43	4/13	1345.24	At Press-time
1998	4/21	491.41	10/8	310.28	421.96						

*Through May 12, 2017

DOW JONES INDUSTRIALS MONTHLY PERCENT CHANGES SINCE 1950

	Jan	Feb	Mar	Apr	May	Jun	Jul	Aug	Sep	Oct	Nov	Dec	Year's Change
1950	0.8	0.8	1.3	4.0	4.2	-6.4	0.1	3.6	4.4	-0.6	1.2	3.4	17.6
1951	5.7	1.3	-1.6	4.5	-3.7	-2.8	6.3	4.8	0.3	-3.2	-0.4	3.0	14.4
1952	0.5	-3.9	3.6	-4.4	2.1	4.3	1.9	-1.6	-1.6	-0.5	5.4	2.9	8.4
1953	-0.7	-1.9	-1.5	-1.8	-0.9	-1.5	2.7	-5.1	1.1	4.5	2.0	-0.2	-3.8
1954	4.1	0.7	3.0	5.2	2.6	1.8	4.3	-3.5	7.3	-2.3	9.8	4.6	44.0
1955	1.1	0.7	-0.5	3.9	-0.2	6.2	3.2	0.5	-0.3	-2.5	6.2	1.1	20.8
1956	-3.6	2.7	5.8	0.8	-7.4	3.1	5.1	-3.0	-5.3	1.0	-1.5	5.6	2.3
1957	-4.1	-3.0	2.2	4.1	2.1	-0.3	1.0	-4.8	-5.8	-3.3	2.0	-3.2	-12.8
1958	3.3	-2.2	1.6	2.0	1.5	3.3	5.2	1.1	4.6	2.1	2.6	4.7	34.0
1959	1.8	1.6	-0.3	3.7	3.2	-0.03	4.9	-1.6	-4.9	2.4	1.9	3.1	16.4
1960	-8.4	1.2	-2.1	-2.4	4.0	2.4	-3.7	1.5	-7.3	0.04	2.9	3.1	-9.3
1961	5.2	2.1	2.2	0.3	2.7	-1.8	3.1	2.1	-2.6	0.4	2.5	1.3	18.7
1962	-4.3	1.1	-0.2	-5.9	-7.8	-8.5	6.5	1.9	-5.0	1.9	10.1	0.4	-10.8
1963	4.7	-2.9	3.0	5.2	1.3	-2.8	-1.6	4.9	0.5	3.1	-0.6	1.7	17.0
1964	2.9	1.9	1.6	-0.3	1.2	1.3	1.2	-0.3	4.4	-0.3	0.3	-0.1	14.6
1965	3.3	0.1	-1.6	3.7	-0.5	-5.4	1.6	1.3	4.2	3.2	-1.5	2.4	10.9
1966	1.5	-3.2	-2.8	1.0	-5.3	-1.6	-2.6	-7.0	-1.8	4.2	-1.9	-0.7	-18.9
1967	8.2	-1.2	3.2	3.6	-5.0	0.9	5.1	-0.3	2.8	-5.1	-0.4	3.3	15.2
1968	-5.5	-1.7	0.02	8.5	-1.4	-0.1	-1.6	1.5	4.4	1.8	3.4	-4.2	4.3
1969	0.2	-4.3	3.3	1.6	-1.3	-6.9	-6.6	2.6	-2.8	5.3	-5.1	-1.5	-15.2
1970	-7.0	4.5	1.0	-6.3	-4.8	-2.4	7.4	4.1	-0.5	-0.7	5.1	5.6	4.8
1971	3.5	1.2	2.9	4.1	-3.6	-1.8	-3.7	4.6	-1.2	-5.4	-0.9	7.1	6.1
1972	1.3	2.9	1.4	1.4	0.7	-3.3	-0.5	4.2	-1.1	0.2	6.6	0.2	14.6
1973	-2.1	-4.4	-0.4	-3.1	-2.2	-1.1	3.9	-4.2	6.7	1.0	-14.0	3.5	-16.6
1974	0.6	0.6	-1.6	-1.2	-4.1	0.03	-5.6	-10.4	-10.4	9.5	-7.0	-0.4	-27.6
1975	14.2	5.0	3.9	6.9	1.3	5.6	-5.4	0.5	-5.0	5.3	2.9	-1.0	38.3
1976	14.4	-0.3	2.8	-0.3	-2.2	2.8	-1.8	-1.1	1.7	-2.6	-1.8	6.1	17.9
1977	-5.0	-1.9	-1.8	0.8	-3.0	2.0	-2.9	-3.2	-1.7	-3.4	1.4	0.2	-17.3
1978	-7.4	-3.6	2.1	10.6	0.4	-2.6	5.3	1.7	-1.3	-8.5	0.8	0.7	-3.1
1979	4.2	-3.6	6.6	-0.8	-3.8	2.4	0.5	4.9	-1.0	-7.2	0.8	2.0	4.2
1980	4.4	-1.5	-9.0	4.0	4.1	2.0	7.8	-0.3	-0.02	-0.9	7.4	-3.0	14.9
1981	-1.7	2.9	3.0	-0.6	-0.6	-1.5	-2.5	-7.4	-3.6	0.3	4.3	-1.6	-9.2
1982	-0.4	-5.4	-0.2	3.1	-3.4	-0.9	-0.4	11.5	-0.6	10.7	4.8	0.7	19.6
1983	2.8	3.4	1.6	8.5	-2.1	1.8	-1.9	1.4	1.4	-0.6	4.1	-1.4	20.3
1984	-3.0	-5.4	0.9	0.5	-5.6	2.5	-1.5	9.8	-1.4	0.1	-1.5	1.9	-3.7
1985	6.2	-0.2	-1.3	-0.7	4.6	1.5	0.9	-1.0	-0.4	3.4	7.1	5.1	27.7
1986	1.6	8.8	6.4	-1.9	5.2	0.9	-6.2	6.9	-6.9	6.2	1.9	-1.0	22.6
1987	13.8	3.1	3.6	-0.8	0.2	5.5	6.3	3.5	-2.5	-23.2	-8.0	5.7	2.3
1988	1.0	5.8	-4.0	2.2	-0.1	5.4	-0.6	-4.6	4.0	1.7	-1.6	2.6	11.8
1989	8.0	-3.6	1.6	5.5	2.5	-1.6	9.0	2.9	-1.6	-1.8	2.3	1.7	27.0
1990	-5.9	1.4	3.0	-1.9	8.3	0.1	0.9	-10.0	-6.2	-0.4	4.8	2.9	-4.3
1991	3.9	5.3	1.1	-0.9	4.8	-4.0	4.1	0.6	-0.9	1.7	-5.7	9.5	20.3
1992	1.7	1.4	-1.0	3.8	1.1	-2.3	2.3	-4.0	0.4	-1.4	2.4	-0.1	4.2
1993	0.3	1.8	1.9	-0.2	2.9	-0.3	0.7	3.2	-2.6	3.5	0.1	1.9	13.7
1994	6.0	-3.7	-5.1	1.3	2.1	-3.5	3.8	4.0	-1.8	1.7	-4.3	2.5	2.1
1995	0.2	4.3	3.7	3.9	3.3	2.0	3.3	-2.1	3.9	-0.7	6.7	0.8	33.5
1996	5.4	1.7	1.9	-0.3	1.3	0.2	-2.2	1.6	4.7	2.5	8.2	-1.1	26.0
1997	5.7	0.9	-4.3	6.5	4.6	4.7	7.2	-7.3	4.2	-6.3	5.1	1.1	22.6
1998	-0.02	8.1	3.0	3.0	-1.8	0.6	-0.8	-15.1	4.0	9.6	6.1	0.7	16.1
1999	1.9	-0.6	5.2	10.2	-2.1	3.9	-2.9	1.6	-4.5	3.8	1.4	5.7	25.2
2000	-4.8	-7.4	7.8	-1.7	-2.0	-0.7	0.7	6.6	-5.0	3.0	-5.1	3.6	-6.2
2001	0.9	-3.6	-5.9	8.7	1.6	-3.8	0.2	-5.4	-11.1	2.6	8.6	1.7	-7.1
2002	-1.0	1.9	2.9	-4.4	-0.2	-6.9	-5.5	-0.8	-12.4	10.6	5.9	-6.2	-16.8
2003	-3.5	-2.0	1.3	6.1	4.4	1.5	2.8	2.0	-1.5	5.7	-0.2	6.9	25.3
2004	0.3	0.9	-2.1	-1.3	-0.4	2.4	-2.8	0.3	-0.9	-0.5	4.0	3.4	3.1
2005	-2.7	2.6	-2.4	-3.0	2.7	-1.8	3.6	-1.5	0.8	-1.2	3.5	-0.8	-0.6
2006	1.4	1.2	1.1	2.3	-1.7	-0.2	0.3	1.7	2.6	3.4	1.2	2.0	16.3
2007	1.3	-2.8	0.7	5.7	4.3	-1.6	-1.5	1.1	4.0	0.2	-4.0	-0.8	6.4
2008	-4.6	-3.0	-0.03	4.5	-1.4	-10.2	0.2	1.5	-6.0	-14.1	-5.3	-0.6	-33.8
2009	-8.8	-11.7	7.7	7.3	4.1	-0.6	8.6	3.5	2.3	0.005	6.5	0.8	18.8
2010	-3.5	2.6	5.1	1.4	-7.9	-3.6	7.1	-4.3	7.7	3.1	-1.0	5.2	11.0
2011	2.7	2.8	0.8	4.0	-1.9	-1.2	-2.2	-4.4	-6.0	9.5	0.8	1.4	5.5
2012	3.4	2.5	2.0	0.01	-6.2	3.9	1.0	0.6	2.6	-2.5	-0.5	0.6	7.3
2013	5.8	1.4	3.7	1.8	1.9	-1.4	4.0	-4.4	2.2	2.8	3.5	3.0	26.5
2014	-5.3	4.0	0.8	0.7	0.8	0.7	-1.6	3.2	-0.3	2.0	2.5	-0.03	7.5
2015	-3.7	5.6	-2.0	0.4	1.0	-2.2	0.4	-6.6	-1.5	8.5	0.3	-1.7	-2.2
2016	-5.5	0.3	7.1	0.5	0.1	0.8	2.8	-0.2	-0.5	-0.9	5.4	3.3	13.4
2017	0.5	4.8	-0.7	1.3									
TOTALS	58.2	18.9	77.0	128.9	-1.4	-21.1	78.7	-12.2	-50.6	42.4	104.5	111.1	
AVG.	0.9	0.3	1.1	1.9	-0.02	-0.3	1.2	-0.2	-0.8	0.6	1.6	1.7	
# Up	43	41	44	46	35	31	42	37	26	40	45	47	
# Down	25	27	24	22	32	36	25	30	41	27	22	20	

152

DOW JONES INDUSTRIALS MONTHLY POINT CHANGES SINCE 1950

	Jan	Feb	Mar	Apr	May	Jun	Jul	Aug	Sep	Oct	Nov	Dec	Year's Close
1950	1.66	1.65	2.61	8.28	9.09	−14.31	0.29	7.47	9.49	−1.35	2.59	7.81	235.41
1951	13.42	3.22	−4.11	11.19	−9.48	−7.01	15.22	12.39	0.91	−8.81	−1.08	7.96	269.23
1952	1.46	−10.61	9.38	−11.83	5.31	11.32	5.30	−4.52	−4.43	−1.38	14.43	8.24	291.90
1953	−2.13	−5.50	−4.40	−5.12	−2.47	−4.02	7.12	−14.16	2.82	11.77	5.56	−0.47	280.90
1954	11.49	2.15	8.97	15.82	8.16	6.04	14.39	−12.12	24.66	−8.32	34.63	17.62	404.39
1955	4.44	3.04	−2.17	15.95	−0.79	26.52	14.47	2.33	−1.56	−11.75	28.39	5.14	488.40
1956	−17.66	12.91	28.14	4.33	−38.07	14.73	25.03	−15.77	−26.79	4.60	−7.07	26.69	499.47
1957	−20.31	−14.54	10.19	19.55	10.57	−1.64	5.23	−24.17	−28.05	−15.26	8.83	−14.18	435.69
1958	14.33	−10.10	6.84	9.10	6.84	15.48	24.81	5.64	23.46	11.13	14.24	26.19	583.65
1959	10.31	9.54	−1.79	22.04	20.04	−0.19	31.28	−10.47	−32.73	14.92	12.58	20.18	679.36
1960	−56.74	7.50	−13.53	−14.89	23.80	15.12	−23.89	9.26	−45.85	0.22	16.86	18.67	615.89
1961	32.31	13.88	14.55	2.08	18.01	−12.76	21.41	14.57	−18.73	2.71	17.68	9.54	731.14
1962	−31.14	8.05	−1.10	−41.62	−51.97	−52.08	36.65	11.25	−30.20	10.79	59.53	2.80	652.10
1963	30.75	−19.91	19.58	35.18	9.26	−20.08	−11.45	33.89	3.47	22.44	−4.71	12.43	762.95
1964	22.39	14.80	13.15	−2.52	9.79	10.94	9.60	−2.62	36.89	−2.29	2.35	−1.30	874.13
1965	28.73	0.62	−14.43	33.26	−4.27	−50.01	13.71	11.36	37.48	30.24	−14.11	22.55	969.26
1966	14.25	−31.62	−27.12	8.91	−49.61	−13.97	−22.72	−58.97	−14.19	32.85	−15.48	−5.90	785.69
1967	64.20	−10.52	26.61	31.07	−44.49	7.70	43.98	−2.95	25.37	−46.92	−3.93	29.30	905.11
1968	−49.64	−14.97	0.17	71.55	−13.22	−1.20	−14.80	13.01	39.78	16.60	32.69	−41.33	943.75
1969	2.30	−40.84	30.27	14.70	−12.62	−64.37	−57.72	21.25	−23.63	42.90	−43.69	−11.94	800.36
1970	−56.30	33.53	7.98	−49.50	−35.63	−16.91	50.59	30.46	−3.90	−5.07	38.48	44.83	838.92
1971	29.58	10.33	25.54	37.38	−33.94	−16.67	−32.71	39.64	−10.88	−48.19	−7.66	58.86	890.20
1972	11.97	25.96	12.57	13.47	6.55	−31.69	−4.29	38.99	−10.46	2.25	62.69	1.81	1020.02
1973	−21.00	−43.95	−4.06	−29.58	−20.02	−9.70	34.69	−38.83	59.53	9.48	−134.33	28.61	850.86
1974	4.69	4.98	−13.85	−9.93	−34.58	0.24	−44.98	−78.85	−70.71	57.65	−46.86	−2.42	616.24
1975	87.45	35.36	29.10	53.19	10.95	46.70	−47.48	3.83	−41.46	42.16	24.63	−8.26	852.41
1976	122.87	−2.67	26.84	−2.60	−21.62	27.55	−18.14	−10.90	16.45	−25.26	−17.71	57.43	1004.65
1977	−50.28	−17.95	−17.29	7.77	−28.24	17.64	−26.23	−28.58	−14.38	−28.76	11.35	1.47	831.17
1978	−61.25	−27.80	15.24	79.96	3.29	−21.66	43.32	14.55	−11.00	−73.37	6.58	5.98	805.01
1979	34.21	−30.40	53.36	−7.28	−32.57	19.65	4.44	41.21	−9.05	−62.88	6.65	16.39	838.74
1980	37.11	−12.71	−77.39	31.31	33.79	17.07	67.40	−2.73	−0.17	−7.93	68.85	−29.35	963.99
1981	−16.72	27.31	29.29	−6.12	−6.00	−14.87	−24.54	−70.87	−31.49	2.57	36.43	−13.98	875.00
1982	−3.90	−46.71	−1.62	25.59	−28.82	−7.61	−3.33	92.71	−5.06	95.47	47.56	7.26	1046.54
1983	29.16	36.92	17.41	96.17	−26.22	21.98	−22.74	16.94	16.97	−7.93	50.82	−17.38	1258.64
1984	−38.06	−65.95	10.26	5.86	−65.90	27.55	−17.12	109.10	−17.67	0.67	−18.44	22.63	1211.57
1985	75.20	−2.76	−17.23	−8.72	57.35	20.05	11.99	−13.44	−5.38	45.68	97.82	74.54	1546.67
1986	24.32	138.07	109.55	−34.63	92.73	16.01	−117.41	123.03	−130.76	110.23	36.42	−18.28	1895.95
1987	262.09	65.95	80.70	−18.33	5.21	126.96	153.54	90.88	−66.67	−602.75	−159.98	105.28	1938.83
1988	19.39	113.40	−83.56	44.27	−1.21	110.59	−12.98	−97.08	81.26	35.74	−34.14	54.06	2168.57
1989	173.75	−83.93	35.23	125.18	61.35	−40.09	220.60	76.61	−44.45	−47.74	61.19	46.93	2753.20
1990	−162.66	36.71	79.96	−50.45	219.90	4.03	24.51	−290.84	−161.88	−10.15	117.32	74.01	2633.66
1991	102.73	145.79	31.68	−25.99	139.63	−120.75	118.07	18.78	−26.83	52.33	−174.42	274.15	3168.83
1992	54.56	44.28	−32.20	123.65	37.76	−78.36	75.26	−136.43	14.31	−45.38	78.88	−4.05	3301.11
1993	8.92	60.78	64.30	−7.56	99.88	−11.35	23.39	111.78	−96.13	125.47	3.36	70.14	3754.09
1994	224.27	−146.34	−196.06	45.73	76.68	−133.41	139.54	148.92	−70.23	64.93	−168.89	95.21	3834.44
1995	9.42	167.19	146.64	163.58	143.87	90.96	152.37	−97.91	178.52	−33.60	319.01	42.63	5117.12
1996	278.18	90.32	101.52	−18.06	74.10	11.45	−125.72	87.30	265.96	147.21	492.32	−73.43	6448.27
1997	364.82	64.65	−294.26	425.51	322.05	341.75	549.82	−600.19	322.84	−503.18	381.05	85.12	7908.25
1998	−1.75	639.22	254.09	263.56	−163.42	52.07	−68.73	−1344.22	303.55	749.48	524.45	64.88	9181.43
1999	177.40	−52.25	479.58	1002.88	−229.30	411.06	−315.65	174.13	−492.33	392.91	147.95	619.31	11497.12
2000	−556.59	−812.22	793.61	−188.01	−211.58	−74.44	74.09	693.12	−564.18	320.22	−556.65	372.36	10786.85
2001	100.51	−392.08	−616.50	856.19	176.97	−409.54	20.41	−573.06	−1102.19	227.58	776.42	169.94	10021.50
2002	−101.50	186.13	297.81	−457.72	−20.97	−681.99	−506.67	−73.09	−1071.57	805.10	499.06	−554.46	8341.63
2003	−287.82	−162.73	101.05	487.96	370.17	135.18	248.36	182.02	−140.76	526.06	−18.66	671.46	10453.92
2004	34.15	95.85	−226.22	−132.13	−37.12	247.03	−295.77	34.21	−93.65	−52.80	400.55	354.99	10783.01
2005	−293.07	276.29	−262.47	−311.25	274.97	−192.51	365.94	−159.31	87.10	−128.63	365.80	−88.37	10717.50
2006	147.36	128.55	115.91	257.82	−198.83	−18.09	35.46	195.47	297.92	401.66	141.20	241.22	12463.15
2007	158.54	−353.06	85.72	708.56	564.73	−219.02	−196.63	145.75	537.89	34.38	−558.29	−106.90	13264.82
2008	−614.46	−383.97	−3.50	557.24	−181.81	−1288.31	28.01	165.53	−692.89	−1525.65	−495.97	−52.65	8776.39
2009	−775.53	−937.93	545.99	559.20	332.21	−53.33	724.61	324.67	216.00	0.45	632.11	83.21	10428.05
2010	−360.72	257.93	531.37	151.98	−871.98	−362.61	691.92	−451.22	773.33	330.44	−112.47	571.49	11577.51
2011	314.42	334.41	93.39	490.81	−240.75	−155.45	−271.10	−529.71	−700.15	1041.63	90.67	171.88	12217.56
2012	415.35	319.16	259.97	1.59	−820.18	486.64	128.59	82.16	346.29	−340.67	−70.88	78.56	13104.14
2013	756.44	193.91	524.05	261.26	275.77	−205.97	589.94	−689.23	319.36	416.08	540.66	490.25	16576.66
2014	−877.81	622.86	135.95	123.18	136.33	109.43	−263.30	535.15	−55.55	347.62	437.72	−5.17	17823.07
2015	−658.12	967.75	−356.58	64.40	170.16	−391.17	70.35	−1161.83	−244.03	1379.54	56.38	−294.89	17425.03
2016	−958.73	50.20	1168.59	88.55	13.56	142.79	502.25	−31.36	−92.73	−165.73	981.16	639.02	19762.60
2017	101.49	948.15	−149.02	277.29									
TOTALS	−1661.50	2465.28	4014.25	6300.26	283.15	−2204.91	2871.85	−2906.07	−2263.14	4154.41	5120.48	4566.32	
# Up	43	41	44	46	35	31	42	37	26	40	45	47	
# Down	25	27	24	22	32	36	25	30	41	27	22	20	

153

DOW JONES INDUSTRIALS MONTHLY CLOSING PRICES SINCE 1950

	Jan	Feb	Mar	Apr	May	Jun	Jul	Aug	Sep	Oct	Nov	Dec
1950	201.79	203.44	206.05	214.33	223.42	209.11	209.40	216.87	226.36	225.01	227.60	235.41
1951	248.83	252.05	247.94	259.13	249.65	242.64	257.86	270.25	271.16	262.35	261.27	269.23
1952	270.69	260.08	269.46	257.63	262.94	274.26	279.56	275.04	270.61	269.23	283.66	291.90
1953	289.77	284.27	279.87	274.75	272.28	268.26	275.38	261.22	264.04	275.81	281.37	280.90
1954	292.39	294.54	303.51	319.33	327.49	333.53	347.92	335.80	360.46	352.14	386.77	404.39
1955	408.83	411.87	409.70	425.65	424.86	451.38	465.85	468.18	466.62	454.87	483.26	488.40
1956	470.74	483.65	511.79	516.12	478.05	492.78	517.81	502.04	475.25	479.85	472.78	499.47
1957	479.16	464.62	474.81	494.36	504.93	503.29	508.52	484.35	456.30	441.04	449.87	435.69
1958	450.02	439.92	446.76	455.86	462.70	478.18	502.99	508.63	532.09	543.22	557.46	583.65
1959	593.96	603.50	601.71	623.75	643.79	643.60	674.88	664.41	631.68	646.60	659.18	679.36
1960	622.62	630.12	616.59	601.70	625.50	640.62	616.73	625.99	580.14	580.36	597.22	615.89
1961	648.20	662.08	676.63	678.71	696.72	683.96	705.37	719.94	701.21	703.92	721.60	731.14
1962	700.00	708.05	706.95	665.33	613.36	561.28	597.93	609.18	578.98	589.77	649.30	652.10
1963	682.85	662.94	682.52	717.70	726.96	706.88	695.43	729.32	732.79	755.23	750.52	762.95
1964	785.34	800.14	813.29	810.77	820.56	831.50	841.10	838.48	875.37	873.08	875.43	874.13
1965	902.86	903.48	889.05	922.31	918.04	868.03	881.74	893.10	930.58	960.82	946.71	969.26
1966	983.51	951.89	924.77	933.68	884.07	870.10	847.38	788.41	774.22	807.07	791.59	785.69
1967	849.89	839.37	865.98	897.05	852.56	860.26	904.24	901.29	926.66	879.74	875.81	905.11
1968	855.47	840.50	840.67	912.22	899.00	897.80	883.00	896.01	935.79	952.39	985.08	943.75
1969	946.05	905.21	935.48	950.18	937.56	873.19	815.47	836.72	813.09	855.99	812.30	800.36
1970	744.06	777.59	785.57	736.07	700.44	683.53	734.12	764.58	760.68	755.61	794.09	838.92
1971	868.50	878.83	904.37	941.75	907.81	891.14	858.43	898.07	887.19	839.00	831.34	890.20
1972	902.17	928.13	940.70	954.17	960.72	929.03	924.74	963.73	953.27	955.52	1018.21	1020.02
1973	999.02	955.07	951.01	921.43	901.41	891.71	926.40	887.57	947.10	956.58	822.25	850.86
1974	855.55	860.53	846.68	836.75	802.17	802.41	757.43	678.58	607.87	665.52	618.66	616.24
1975	703.69	739.05	768.15	821.34	832.29	878.99	831.51	835.34	793.88	836.04	860.67	852.41
1976	975.28	972.61	999.45	996.85	975.23	1002.78	984.64	973.74	990.19	964.93	947.22	1004.65
1977	954.37	936.42	919.13	926.90	898.66	916.30	890.07	861.49	847.11	818.35	829.70	831.17
1978	769.92	742.12	757.36	837.32	840.61	818.95	862.27	876.82	865.82	792.45	799.03	805.01
1979	839.22	808.82	862.18	854.90	822.33	841.98	846.42	887.63	878.58	815.70	822.35	838.74
1980	875.85	863.14	785.75	817.06	850.85	867.92	935.32	932.59	932.42	924.49	993.34	963.99
1981	947.27	974.58	1003.87	997.75	991.75	976.88	952.34	881.47	849.98	852.55	888.98	875.00
1982	871.10	824.39	822.77	848.36	819.54	811.93	808.60	901.31	896.25	991.72	1039.28	1046.54
1983	1075.70	1112.62	1130.03	1226.20	1199.98	1221.96	1199.22	1216.16	1233.13	1225.20	1276.02	1258.64
1984	1220.58	1154.63	1164.89	1170.75	1104.85	1132.40	1115.28	1224.38	1206.71	1207.38	1188.94	1211.57
1985	1286.77	1284.01	1266.78	1258.06	1315.41	1335.46	1347.45	1334.01	1328.63	1374.31	1472.13	1546.67
1986	1570.99	1709.06	1818.61	1783.98	1876.71	1892.72	1775.31	1898.34	1767.58	1877.81	1914.23	1895.95
1987	2158.04	2223.99	2304.69	2286.36	2291.57	2418.53	2572.07	2662.95	2596.28	1993.53	1833.55	1938.83
1988	1958.22	2071.62	1988.06	2032.33	2031.12	2141.71	2128.73	2031.65	2112.91	2148.65	2114.51	2168.57
1989	2342.32	2258.39	2293.62	2418.80	2480.15	2440.06	2660.66	2737.27	2692.82	2645.08	2706.27	2753.20
1990	2590.54	2627.25	2707.21	2656.76	2876.66	2880.69	2905.20	2614.36	2452.48	2442.33	2559.65	2633.66
1991	2736.39	2882.18	2913.86	2887.87	3027.50	2906.75	3024.82	3043.60	3016.77	3069.10	2894.68	3168.83
1992	3223.39	3267.67	3235.47	3359.12	3396.88	3318.52	3393.78	3257.35	3271.66	3226.28	3305.16	3301.11
1993	3310.03	3370.81	3435.11	3427.55	3527.43	3516.08	3539.47	3651.25	3555.12	3680.59	3683.95	3754.09
1994	3978.36	3832.02	3635.96	3681.69	3758.37	3624.96	3764.50	3913.42	3843.19	3908.12	3739.23	3834.44
1995	3843.86	4011.05	4157.69	4321.27	4465.14	4556.10	4708.47	4610.56	4789.08	4755.48	5074.49	5117.12
1996	5395.30	5485.62	5587.14	5569.08	5643.18	5654.63	5528.91	5616.21	5882.17	6029.38	6521.70	6448.27
1997	6813.09	6877.74	6583.48	7008.99	7331.04	7672.79	8222.61	7622.42	7945.26	7442.08	7823.13	7908.25
1998	7906.50	8545.72	8799.81	9063.37	8899.95	8952.02	8883.29	7539.07	7842.62	8592.10	9116.55	9181.43
1999	9358.83	9306.58	9786.16	10789.04	10559.74	10970.80	10655.15	10829.28	10336.95	10729.86	10877.81	11497.12
2000	10940.53	10128.31	10921.92	10733.91	10522.33	10447.89	10521.98	11215.10	10650.92	10971.14	10414.49	10786.85
2001	10887.36	10495.28	9878.78	10734.97	10911.94	10502.40	10522.81	9949.75	8847.56	9075.14	9851.56	10021.50
2002	9920.00	10106.13	10403.94	9946.22	9925.25	9243.26	8736.59	8663.50	7591.93	8397.03	8896.09	8341.63
2003	8053.81	7891.08	7992.13	8480.09	8850.26	8985.44	9233.80	9415.82	9275.06	9801.12	9782.46	10453.92
2004	10488.07	10583.92	10357.70	10225.57	10188.45	10435.48	10139.71	10173.92	10080.27	10027.47	10428.02	10783.01
2005	10489.94	10766.23	10503.76	10192.51	10467.48	10274.97	10640.91	10481.60	10568.70	10440.07	10805.87	10717.50
2006	10864.86	10993.41	11109.32	11367.14	11168.31	11150.22	11185.68	11381.15	11679.07	12080.73	12221.93	12463.15
2007	12621.69	12268.63	12354.35	13062.91	13627.64	13408.62	13211.99	13357.74	13895.63	13930.01	13371.72	13264.82
2008	12650.36	12266.39	12262.89	12820.13	12638.32	11350.01	11378.02	11543.55	10850.66	9325.01	8829.04	8776.39
2009	8000.86	7062.93	7608.92	8168.12	8500.33	8447.00	9171.61	9496.28	9712.28	9712.73	10344.84	10428.05
2010	10067.33	10325.26	10856.63	11008.61	10136.63	9774.02	10465.94	10014.72	10788.05	11118.49	11006.02	11577.51
2011	11891.93	12226.34	12319.73	12810.54	12569.79	12414.34	12143.24	11613.53	10913.38	11955.01	12045.68	12217.56
2012	12632.91	12952.07	13212.04	13213.63	12393.45	12880.09	13008.68	13090.84	13437.13	13096.46	13025.58	13104.14
2013	13860.58	14054.49	14578.54	14839.80	15115.57	14909.60	15499.54	14810.31	15129.67	15545.75	16086.41	16576.66
2014	15698.85	16321.71	16457.66	16580.84	16717.17	16826.60	16563.30	17098.45	17042.90	17390.52	17828.24	17823.07
2015	17164.95	18132.70	17776.12	17840.52	18010.68	17619.51	17689.86	16528.03	16284.00	17663.54	17719.92	17425.03
2016	16466.30	16516.50	17685.09	17773.64	17787.20	17929.99	18432.24	18400.88	18308.15	18142.42	19123.58	19762.60
2017	19864.09	20812.24	20663.22	20940.51								

154

STANDARD & POOR'S 500 MONTHLY PERCENT CHANGES SINCE 1950

	Jan	Feb	Mar	Apr	May	Jun	Jul	Aug	Sep	Oct	Nov	Dec	Year's Change
1950	1.7	1.0	0.4	4.5	3.9	-5.8	0.8	3.3	5.6	0.4	-0.1	4.6	21.8
1951	6.1	0.6	-1.8	4.8	-4.1	-2.6	6.9	3.9	-0.1	-1.4	-0.3	3.9	16.5
1952	1.6	-3.6	4.8	-4.3	2.3	4.6	1.8	-1.5	-2.0	-0.1	4.6	3.5	11.8
1953	-0.7	-1.8	-2.4	-2.6	-0.3	-1.6	2.5	-5.8	0.1	5.1	0.9	0.2	-6.6
1954	5.1	0.3	3.0	4.9	3.3	0.1	5.7	-3.4	8.3	-1.9	8.1	5.1	45.0
1955	1.8	0.4	-0.5	3.8	-0.1	8.2	6.1	-0.8	1.1	-3.0	7.5	-0.1	26.4
1956	-3.6	3.5	6.9	-0.2	-6.6	3.9	5.2	-3.8	-4.5	0.5	-1.1	3.5	2.6
1957	-4.2	-3.3	2.0	3.7	3.7	-0.1	1.1	-5.6	-6.2	-3.2	1.6	-4.1	-14.3
1958	4.3	-2.1	3.1	3.2	1.5	2.6	4.3	1.2	4.8	2.5	2.2	5.2	38.1
1959	0.4	-0.02	0.1	3.9	1.9	-0.4	3.5	-1.5	-4.6	1.1	1.3	2.8	8.5
1960	-7.1	0.9	-1.4	-1.8	2.7	2.0	-2.5	2.6	-6.0	-0.2	4.0	4.6	-3.0
1961	6.3	2.7	2.6	0.4	1.9	-2.9	3.3	2.0	-2.0	2.8	3.9	0.3	23.1
1962	-3.8	1.6	-0.6	-6.2	-8.6	-8.2	6.4	1.5	-4.8	0.4	10.2	1.3	-11.8
1963	4.9	-2.9	3.5	4.9	1.4	-2.0	-0.3	4.9	-1.1	3.2	-1.1	2.4	18.9
1964	2.7	1.0	1.5	0.6	1.1	1.6	1.8	-1.6	2.9	0.8	-0.5	0.4	13.0
1965	3.3	-0.1	-1.5	3.4	-0.8	-4.9	1.3	2.3	3.2	2.7	-0.9	0.9	9.1
1966	0.5	-1.8	-2.2	2.1	-5.4	-1.6	-1.3	-7.8	-0.7	4.8	0.3	-0.1	-13.1
1967	7.8	0.2	3.9	4.2	-5.2	1.8	4.5	-1.2	3.3	-2.9	0.1	2.6	20.1
1968	-4.4	-3.1	0.9	8.2	1.1	0.9	-1.8	1.1	3.9	0.7	4.8	-4.2	7.7
1969	-0.8	-4.7	3.4	2.1	-0.2	-5.6	-6.0	4.0	-2.5	4.4	-3.5	-1.9	-11.4
1970	-7.6	5.3	0.1	-9.0	-6.1	-5.0	7.3	4.4	3.3	-1.1	4.7	5.7	0.1
1971	4.0	0.9	3.7	3.6	-4.2	0.1	-4.1	3.6	-0.7	-4.2	-0.3	8.6	10.8
1972	1.8	2.5	0.6	0.4	1.7	-2.2	0.2	3.4	-0.5	0.9	4.6	1.2	15.6
1973	-1.7	-3.7	-0.1	-4.1	-1.9	-0.7	3.8	-3.7	4.0	-0.1	-11.4	1.7	-17.4
1974	-1.0	-0.4	-2.3	-3.9	-3.4	-1.5	-7.8	-9.0	-11.9	16.3	-5.3	-2.0	-29.7
1975	12.3	6.0	2.2	4.7	4.4	4.4	-6.8	-2.1	-3.5	6.2	2.5	-1.2	31.5
1976	11.8	-1.1	3.1	-1.1	-1.4	4.1	-0.8	-0.5	2.3	-2.2	-0.8	5.2	19.1
1977	-5.1	-2.2	-1.4	0.02	-2.4	4.5	-1.6	-2.1	-0.2	-4.3	2.7	0.3	-11.5
1978	-6.2	-2.5	2.5	8.5	0.4	-1.8	5.4	2.6	-0.7	-9.2	1.7	1.5	1.1
1979	4.0	-3.7	5.5	0.2	-2.6	3.9	0.9	5.3	N/C	-6.9	4.3	1.7	12.3
1980	5.8	-0.4	-10.2	4.1	4.7	2.7	6.5	0.6	2.5	1.6	10.2	-3.4	25.8
1981	-4.6	1.3	3.6	-2.3	-0.2	-1.0	-0.2	-6.2	-5.4	4.9	3.7	-3.0	-9.7
1982	-1.8	-6.1	-1.0	4.0	-3.9	-2.0	-2.3	11.6	0.8	11.0	3.6	1.5	14.8
1983	3.3	1.9	3.3	7.5	-1.2	3.5	-3.3	1.1	1.0	-1.5	1.7	-0.9	17.3
1984	-0.9	-3.9	1.3	0.5	-5.9	1.7	-1.6	10.6	-0.3	-0.01	-1.5	2.2	1.4
1985	7.4	0.9	-0.3	-0.5	5.4	1.2	-0.5	-1.2	-3.5	4.3	6.5	4.5	26.3
1986	0.2	7.1	5.3	-1.4	5.0	1.4	-5.9	7.1	-8.5	5.5	2.1	-2.8	14.6
1987	13.2	3.7	2.6	-1.1	0.6	4.8	4.8	3.5	-2.4	-21.8	-8.5	7.3	2.0
1988	4.0	4.2	-3.3	0.9	0.3	4.3	-0.5	-3.9	4.0	2.6	-1.9	1.5	12.4
1989	7.1	-2.9	2.1	5.0	3.5	-0.8	8.8	1.6	-0.7	-2.5	1.7	2.1	27.3
1990	-6.9	0.9	2.4	-2.7	9.2	-0.9	-0.5	-9.4	-5.1	-0.7	6.0	2.5	-6.6
1991	4.2	6.7	2.2	0.03	3.9	-4.8	4.5	2.0	-1.9	1.2	-4.4	11.2	26.3
1992	-2.0	1.0	-2.2	2.8	0.1	-1.7	3.9	-2.4	0.9	0.2	3.0	1.0	4.5
1993	0.7	1.0	1.9	-2.5	2.3	0.1	-0.5	3.4	-1.0	1.9	-1.3	1.0	7.1
1994	3.3	-3.0	-4.6	1.2	1.2	-2.7	3.1	3.8	-2.7	2.1	-4.0	1.2	-1.5
1995	2.4	3.6	2.7	2.8	3.6	2.1	3.2	-0.03	4.0	-0.5	4.1	1.7	34.1
1996	3.3	0.7	0.8	1.3	2.3	0.2	-4.6	1.9	5.4	2.6	7.3	-2.2	20.3
1997	6.1	0.6	-4.3	5.8	5.9	4.3	7.8	-5.7	5.3	-3.4	4.5	1.6	31.0
1998	1.0	7.0	5.0	0.9	-1.9	3.9	-1.2	-14.6	6.2	8.0	5.9	5.6	26.7
1999	4.1	-3.2	3.9	3.8	-2.5	5.4	-3.2	-0.6	-2.9	6.3	1.9	5.8	19.5
2000	-5.1	-2.0	9.7	-3.1	-2.2	2.4	-1.6	6.1	-5.3	-0.5	-8.0	0.4	-10.1
2001	3.5	-9.2	-6.4	7.7	0.5	-2.5	-1.1	-6.4	-8.2	1.8	7.5	0.8	-13.0
2002	-1.6	-2.1	3.7	-6.1	-0.9	-7.2	-7.9	0.5	-11.0	8.6	5.7	-6.0	-23.4
2003	-2.7	-1.7	1.0	8.0	5.1	1.1	1.6	1.8	-1.2	5.5	0.7	5.1	26.4
2004	1.7	1.2	-1.6	-1.7	1.2	1.8	-3.4	0.2	0.9	1.4	3.9	3.2	9.0
2005	-2.5	1.9	-1.9	-2.0	3.0	-0.01	3.6	-1.1	0.7	-1.8	3.5	-0.1	3.0
2006	2.5	0.05	1.1	1.2	-3.1	0.01	0.5	2.1	2.5	3.2	1.6	1.3	13.6
2007	1.4	-2.2	1.0	4.3	3.3	-1.8	-3.2	1.3	3.6	1.5	-4.4	-0.9	3.5
2008	-6.1	-3.5	-0.6	4.8	1.1	-8.6	-1.0	1.2	-9.1	-16.9	-7.5	0.8	-38.5
2009	-8.6	-11.0	8.5	9.4	5.3	0.02	7.4	3.4	3.6	-2.0	5.7	1.8	23.5
2010	-3.7	2.9	5.9	1.5	-8.2	-5.4	6.9	-4.7	8.8	3.7	-0.2	6.5	12.8
2011	2.3	3.2	-0.1	2.8	-1.4	-1.8	-2.1	-5.7	-7.2	10.8	-0.5	0.9	-0.003
2012	4.4	4.1	3.1	-0.7	-6.3	4.0	1.3	2.0	2.4	-2.0	0.3	0.7	13.4
2013	5.0	1.1	3.6	1.8	2.1	-1.5	4.9	-3.1	3.0	4.5	2.8	2.4	29.6
2014	-3.6	4.3	0.7	0.6	2.1	1.9	-1.5	3.8	-1.6	2.3	2.5	-0.4	11.4
2015	-3.1	5.5	-1.7	0.9	1.0	-2.1	2.0	-6.3	-2.6	8.3	0.1	-1.8	-0.7
2016	-5.1	-0.4	6.6	0.3	1.5	0.1	3.6	-0.1	-0.1	-1.9	3.4	1.8	9.5
2017	1.8	3.7	-0.04	0.9									
TOTALS	64.6	6.8	83.4	99.7	14.5	-2.1	68.1	-6.1	-34.3	60.4	102.4	108.5	
AVG.	1.0	0.1	1.2	1.5	0.2	-0.03	1.0	-0.1	-0.5	0.9	1.5	1.6	
# Up	41	38	44	48	39	35	37	36	29	40	45	50	
# Down	27	30	24	20	28	32	30	31	37	27	22	17	

155

STANDARD & POOR'S 500 MONTHLY CLOSING PRICES SINCE 1950

	Jan	Feb	Mar	Apr	May	Jun	Jul	Aug	Sep	Oct	Nov	Dec
1950	17.05	17.22	17.29	18.07	18.78	17.69	17.84	18.42	19.45	19.53	19.51	20.41
1951	21.66	21.80	21.40	22.43	21.52	20.96	22.40	23.28	23.26	22.94	22.88	23.77
1952	24.14	23.26	24.37	23.32	23.86	24.96	25.40	25.03	24.54	24.52	25.66	26.57
1953	26.38	25.90	25.29	24.62	24.54	24.14	24.75	23.32	23.35	24.54	24.76	24.81
1954	26.08	26.15	26.94	28.26	29.19	29.21	30.88	29.83	32.31	31.68	34.24	35.98
1955	36.63	36.76	36.58	37.96	37.91	41.03	43.52	43.18	43.67	42.34	45.51	45.48
1956	43.82	45.34	48.48	48.38	45.20	46.97	49.39	47.51	45.35	45.58	45.08	46.67
1957	44.72	43.26	44.11	45.74	47.43	47.37	47.91	45.22	42.42	41.06	41.72	39.99
1958	41.70	40.84	42.10	43.44	44.09	45.24	47.19	47.75	50.06	51.33	52.48	55.21
1959	55.42	55.41	55.44	57.59	58.68	58.47	60.51	59.60	56.88	57.52	58.28	59.89
1960	55.61	56.12	55.34	54.37	55.83	56.92	55.51	56.96	53.52	53.39	55.54	58.11
1961	61.78	63.44	65.06	65.31	66.56	64.64	66.76	68.07	66.73	68.62	71.32	71.55
1962	68.84	69.96	69.55	65.24	59.63	54.75	58.23	59.12	56.27	56.52	62.26	63.10
1963	66.20	64.29	66.57	69.80	70.80	69.37	69.13	72.50	71.70	74.01	73.23	75.02
1964	77.04	77.80	78.98	79.46	80.37	81.69	83.18	81.83	84.18	84.86	84.42	84.75
1965	87.56	87.43	86.16	89.11	88.42	84.12	85.25	87.17	89.96	92.42	91.61	92.43
1966	92.88	91.22	89.23	91.06	86.13	84.74	83.60	77.10	76.56	80.20	80.45	80.33
1967	86.61	86.78	90.20	94.01	89.08	90.64	94.75	93.64	96.71	93.90	94.00	96.47
1968	92.24	89.36	90.20	97.59	98.68	99.58	97.74	98.86	102.67	103.41	108.37	103.86
1969	103.01	98.13	101.51	103.69	103.46	97.71	91.83	95.51	93.12	97.24	93.81	92.06
1970	85.02	89.50	89.63	81.52	76.55	72.72	78.05	81.52	84.21	83.25	87.20	92.15
1971	95.88	96.75	100.31	103.95	99.63	99.70	95.58	99.03	98.34	94.23	93.99	102.09
1972	103.94	106.57	107.20	107.67	109.53	107.14	107.39	111.09	110.55	111.58	116.67	118.05
1973	116.03	111.68	111.52	106.97	104.95	104.26	108.22	104.25	108.43	108.29	95.96	97.55
1974	96.57	96.22	93.98	90.31	87.28	86.00	79.31	72.15	63.54	73.90	69.97	68.56
1975	76.98	81.59	83.36	87.30	91.15	95.19	88.75	86.88	83.87	89.04	91.24	90.19
1976	100.86	99.71	102.77	101.64	100.18	104.28	103.44	102.91	105.24	102.90	102.10	107.46
1977	102.03	99.82	98.42	98.44	96.12	100.48	98.85	96.77	96.53	92.34	94.83	95.10
1978	89.25	87.04	89.21	96.83	97.24	95.53	100.68	103.29	102.54	93.15	94.70	96.11
1979	99.93	96.28	101.59	101.76	99.08	102.91	103.81	109.32	109.32	101.82	106.16	107.94
1980	114.16	113.66	102.09	106.29	111.24	114.24	121.67	122.38	125.46	127.47	140.52	135.76
1981	129.55	131.27	136.00	132.81	132.59	131.21	130.92	122.79	116.18	121.89	126.35	122.55
1982	120.40	113.11	111.96	116.44	111.88	109.61	107.09	119.51	120.42	133.71	138.54	140.64
1983	145.30	148.06	152.96	164.42	162.39	168.11	162.56	164.40	166.07	163.55	166.40	164.93
1984	163.41	157.06	159.18	160.05	150.55	153.18	150.66	166.68	166.10	166.09	163.58	167.24
1985	179.63	181.18	180.66	179.83	189.55	191.85	190.92	188.63	182.08	189.82	202.17	211.28
1986	211.78	226.92	238.90	235.52	247.35	250.84	236.12	252.93	231.32	243.98	249.22	242.17
1987	274.08	284.20	291.70	288.36	290.10	304.00	318.66	329.80	321.83	251.79	230.30	247.08
1988	257.07	267.82	258.89	261.33	262.16	273.50	272.02	261.52	271.91	278.97	273.70	277.72
1989	297.47	288.86	294.87	309.64	320.52	317.98	346.08	351.45	349.15	340.36	345.99	353.40
1990	329.08	331.89	339.94	330.80	361.23	358.02	356.15	322.56	306.05	304.00	322.22	330.22
1991	343.93	367.07	375.22	375.35	389.83	371.16	387.81	395.43	387.86	392.46	375.22	417.09
1992	408.79	412.70	403.69	414.95	415.35	408.14	424.21	414.03	417.80	418.68	431.35	435.71
1993	438.78	443.38	451.67	440.19	450.19	450.53	448.13	463.56	458.93	467.83	461.79	466.45
1994	481.61	467.14	445.77	450.91	456.50	444.27	458.26	475.49	462.69	472.35	453.69	459.27
1995	470.42	487.39	500.71	514.71	533.40	544.75	562.06	561.88	584.41	581.50	605.37	615.93
1996	636.02	640.43	645.50	654.17	669.12	670.63	639.95	651.99	687.31	705.27	757.02	740.74
1997	786.16	790.82	757.12	801.34	848.28	885.14	954.29	899.47	947.28	914.62	955.40	970.43
1998	980.28	1049.34	1101.75	1111.75	1090.82	1133.84	1120.67	957.28	1017.01	1098.67	1163.63	1229.23
1999	1279.64	1238.33	1286.37	1335.18	1301.84	1372.71	1328.72	1320.41	1282.71	1362.93	1388.91	1469.25
2000	1394.46	1366.42	1498.58	1452.43	1420.60	1454.60	1430.83	1517.68	1436.51	1429.40	1314.95	1320.28
2001	1366.01	1239.94	1160.33	1249.46	1255.82	1224.42	1211.23	1133.58	1040.94	1059.78	1139.45	1148.08
2002	1130.20	1106.73	1147.39	1076.92	1067.14	989.82	911.62	916.07	815.28	885.76	936.31	879.82
2003	855.70	841.15	849.18	916.92	963.59	974.50	990.31	1008.01	995.97	1050.71	1058.20	1111.92
2004	1131.13	1144.94	1126.21	1107.30	1120.68	1140.84	1101.72	1104.24	1114.58	1130.20	1173.82	1211.92
2005	1181.27	1203.60	1180.59	1156.85	1191.50	1191.33	1234.18	1220.33	1228.81	1207.01	1249.48	1248.29
2006	1280.08	1280.66	1294.83	1310.61	1270.09	1270.20	1276.66	1303.82	1335.85	1377.94	1400.63	1418.30
2007	1438.24	1406.82	1420.86	1482.37	1530.62	1503.35	1455.27	1473.99	1526.75	1549.38	1481.14	1468.36
2008	1378.55	1330.63	1322.70	1385.59	1400.38	1280.00	1267.38	1282.83	1166.36	968.75	896.24	903.25
2009	825.88	735.09	797.87	872.81	919.14	919.32	987.48	1020.62	1057.08	1036.19	1095.63	1115.10
2010	1073.87	1104.49	1169.43	1186.69	1089.41	1030.71	1101.60	1049.33	1141.20	1183.26	1180.55	1257.64
2011	1286.12	1327.22	1325.83	1363.61	1345.20	1320.64	1292.28	1218.89	1131.42	1253.30	1246.96	1257.60
2012	1312.41	1365.68	1408.47	1397.91	1310.33	1362.16	1379.32	1406.58	1440.67	1412.16	1416.18	1426.19
2013	1498.11	1514.68	1569.19	1597.57	1630.74	1606.28	1685.73	1632.97	1681.55	1756.54	1805.81	1848.36
2014	1782.59	1859.45	1872.34	1883.95	1923.57	1960.23	1930.67	2003.37	1972.29	2018.05	2067.56	2058.90
2015	1994.99	2104.50	2067.89	2085.51	2107.39	2063.11	2103.84	1972.18	1920.03	2079.36	2080.41	2043.94
2016	1940.24	1932.23	2059.74	2065.30	2096.96	2098.86	2173.60	2170.95	2168.27	2126.15	2198.81	2238.83
2017	2278.87	2363.64	2362.72	2384.20								

	Jan	Feb	Mar	Apr	May	Jun	Jul	Aug	Sep	Oct	Nov	Dec	Year's Change
1971	10.2	2.6	4.6	6.0	-3.6	-0.4	-2.3	3.0	0.6	-3.6	-1.1	9.8	27.4
1972	4.2	5.5	2.2	2.5	0.9	-1.8	-1.8	1.7	-0.3	0.5	2.1	0.6	17.2
1973	-4.0	-6.2	-2.4	-8.2	-4.8	-1.6	7.6	-3.5	6.0	-0.9	-15.1	-1.4	-31.1
1974	3.0	-0.6	-2.2	-5.9	-7.7	-5.3	-7.9	-10.9	-10.7	17.2	-3.5	-5.0	-35.1
1975	16.6	4.6	3.6	3.8	5.8	4.7	-4.4	-5.0	-5.9	3.6	2.4	-1.5	29.8
1976	12.1	3.7	0.4	-0.6	-2.3	2.6	1.1	-1.7	1.7	-1.0	0.9	7.4	26.1
1977	-2.4	-1.0	-0.5	1.4	0.1	4.3	0.9	-0.5	0.7	-3.3	5.8	1.8	7.3
1978	-4.0	0.6	4.7	8.5	4.4	0.05	5.0	6.9	-1.6	-16.4	3.2	2.9	12.3
1979	6.6	-2.6	7.5	1.6	-1.8	5.1	2.3	6.4	-0.3	-9.6	6.4	4.8	28.1
1980	7.0	-2.3	-17.1	6.9	7.5	4.9	8.9	5.7	3.4	2.7	8.0	-2.8	33.9
1981	-2.2	0.1	6.1	3.1	3.1	-3.5	-1.9	-7.5	-8.0	8.4	3.1	-2.7	-3.2
1982	-3.8	-4.8	-2.1	5.2	-3.3	-4.1	-2.3	6.2	5.6	13.3	9.3	0.04	18.7
1983	6.9	5.0	3.9	8.2	5.3	3.2	-4.6	-3.8	1.4	-7.4	4.1	-2.5	19.9
1984	-3.7	-5.9	-0.7	-1.3	-5.9	2.9	-4.2	10.9	-1.8	-1.2	-1.8	2.0	-11.2
1985	12.7	2.0	-1.7	0.5	3.6	1.9	1.7	-1.2	-5.8	4.4	7.3	3.5	31.4
1986	3.3	7.1	4.2	2.3	4.4	1.3	-8.4	3.1	-8.4	2.9	-0.3	-2.8	7.5
1987	12.2	8.4	1.2	-2.8	-0.3	2.0	2.4	4.6	-2.3	-27.2	-5.6	8.3	-5.4
1988	4.3	6.5	2.1	1.2	-2.3	6.6	-1.9	-2.8	3.0	-1.4	-2.9	2.7	15.4
1989	5.2	-0.4	1.8	5.1	4.4	-2.4	4.3	3.4	0.8	-3.7	0.1	-0.3	19.3
1990	-8.6	2.4	2.3	-3.6	9.3	0.7	-5.2	-13.0	-9.6	-4.3	8.9	4.1	-17.8
1991	10.8	9.4	6.5	0.5	4.4	-6.0	5.5	4.7	0.2	3.1	-3.5	11.9	56.8
1992	5.8	2.1	-4.7	-4.2	1.1	-3.7	3.1	-3.0	3.6	3.8	7.9	3.7	15.5
1993	2.9	-3.7	2.9	-4.2	5.9	0.5	0.1	5.4	2.7	2.2	-3.2	3.0	14.7
1994	3.0	-1.0	-6.2	-1.3	0.2	-4.0	2.3	6.0	-0.2	1.7	-3.5	0.2	-3.2
1995	0.4	5.1	3.0	3.3	2.4	8.0	7.3	1.9	2.3	-0.7	2.2	-0.7	39.9
1996	0.7	3.8	0.1	8.1	4.4	-4.7	-8.8	5.6	7.5	-0.4	5.8	-0.1	22.7
1997	6.9	-5.1	-6.7	3.2	11.1	3.0	10.5	-0.4	6.2	-5.5	0.4	-1.9	21.6
1998	3.1	9.3	3.7	1.8	-4.8	6.5	-1.2	-19.9	13.0	4.6	10.1	12.5	39.6
1999	14.3	-8.7	7.6	3.3	-2.8	8.7	-1.8	3.8	0.2	8.0	12.5	22.0	85.6
2000	-3.2	19.2	-2.6	-15.6	-11.9	16.6	-5.0	11.7	-12.7	-8.3	-22.9	-4.9	-39.3
2001	12.2	-22.4	-14.5	15.0	-0.3	2.4	-6.2	-10.9	-17.0	12.8	14.2	1.0	-21.1
2002	-0.8	-10.5	6.6	-8.5	-4.3	-9.4	-9.2	-1.0	-10.9	13.5	11.2	-9.7	-31.5
2003	-1.1	1.3	0.3	9.2	9.0	1.7	6.9	4.3	-1.3	8.1	1.5	2.2	50.0
2004	3.1	-1.8	-1.8	-3.7	3.5	3.1	-7.8	-2.6	3.2	4.1	6.2	3.7	8.6
2005	-5.2	-0.5	-2.6	-3.9	7.6	-0.5	6.2	-1.5	-0.02	-1.5	5.3	-1.2	1.4
2006	4.6	-1.1	2.6	-0.7	-6.2	-0.3	-3.7	4.4	3.4	4.8	2.7	-0.7	9.5
2007	2.0	-1.9	0.2	4.3	3.1	-0.05	-2.2	2.0	4.0	5.8	-6.9	-0.3	9.8
2008	-9.9	-5.0	0.3	5.9	4.6	-9.1	1.4	1.8	-11.6	-17.7	-10.8	2.7	-40.5
2009	-6.4	-6.7	10.9	12.3	3.3	3.4	7.8	1.5	5.6	-3.6	4.9	5.8	43.9
2010	-5.4	4.2	7.1	2.6	-8.3	-6.5	6.9	-6.2	12.0	5.9	-0.4	6.2	16.9
2011	1.8	3.0	-0.04	3.3	-1.3	-2.2	-0.6	-6.4	-6.4	11.1	-2.4	-0.6	-1.8
2012	8.0	5.4	4.2	-1.5	-7.2	3.8	0.2	4.3	1.6	-4.5	1.1	0.3	15.9
2013	4.1	0.6	3.4	1.9	3.8	-1.5	6.6	-1.0	5.1	3.9	3.6	2.9	38.3
2014	-1.7	5.0	-2.5	-2.0	3.1	3.9	-0.9	4.8	-1.9	3.1	3.5	-1.2	13.4
2015	-2.1	7.1	-1.3	0.8	2.6	-1.6	2.8	-6.9	-3.3	9.4	1.1	-2.0	5.7
2016	-7.9	-1.2	6.8	-1.9	3.6	-2.1	6.6	1.0	1.9	-2.3	2.6	1.1	7.5
2017	4.3	3.8	1.5	2.3									
TOTALS	119.9	34.4	42.7	64.2	43.4	31.1	16.1	5.4	-24.3	34.4	74.5	84.8	
AVG.	2.6	0.7	0.9	1.4	0.9	0.7	0.4	0.1	-0.5	0.7	1.6	1.8	
# Up	30	26	30	30	28	25	24	25	25	25	31	27	
# Down	17	21	17	17	18	21	22	21	21	21	15	19	

Based on NASDAQ composite; prior to February 5, 1971, based on National Quotation Bureau indices.

NASDAQ COMPOSITE MONTHLY CLOSING PRICES SINCE 1971

	Jan	Feb	Mar	Apr	May	Jun	Jul	Aug	Sep	Oct	Nov	Dec
1971	98.77	101.34	105.97	112.30	108.25	107.80	105.27	108.42	109.03	105.10	103.97	114.12
1972	118.87	125.38	128.14	131.33	132.53	130.08	127.75	129.95	129.61	130.24	132.96	133.73
1973	128.40	120.41	117.46	107.85	102.64	100.98	108.64	104.87	111.20	110.17	93.51	92.19
1974	94.93	94.35	92.27	86.86	80.20	75.96	69.99	62.37	55.67	65.23	62.95	59.82
1975	69.78	73.00	75.66	78.54	83.10	87.02	83.19	79.01	74.33	76.99	78.80	77.62
1976	87.05	90.26	90.62	90.08	88.04	90.32	91.29	89.70	91.26	90.35	91.12	97.88
1977	95.54	94.57	94.13	95.48	95.59	99.73	100.65	100.10	100.85	97.52	103.15	105.05
1978	100.84	101.47	106.20	115.18	120.24	120.30	126.32	135.01	132.89	111.12	114.69	117.98
1979	125.82	122.56	131.76	133.82	131.42	138.13	141.33	150.44	149.98	135.53	144.26	151.14
1980	161.75	158.03	131.00	139.99	150.45	157.78	171.81	181.52	187.76	192.78	208.15	202.34
1981	197.81	198.01	210.18	216.74	223.47	215.75	211.63	195.75	180.03	195.24	201.37	195.84
1982	188.39	179.43	175.65	184.70	178.54	171.30	167.35	177.71	187.65	212.63	232.31	232.41
1983	248.35	260.67	270.80	293.06	308.73	318.70	303.96	292.42	296.65	274.55	285.67	278.60
1984	268.43	252.57	250.78	247.44	232.82	239.65	229.70	254.64	249.94	247.03	242.53	247.35
1985	278.70	284.17	279.20	280.56	290.80	296.20	301.29	297.71	280.33	292.54	313.95	324.93
1986	335.77	359.53	374.72	383.24	400.16	405.51	371.37	382.86	350.67	360.77	359.57	349.33
1987	392.06	424.97	430.05	417.81	416.54	424.67	434.93	454.97	444.29	323.30	305.16	330.47
1988	344.66	366.95	374.64	379.23	370.34	394.66	387.33	376.55	387.71	382.46	371.45	381.38
1989	401.30	399.71	406.73	427.55	446.17	435.29	453.84	469.33	472.92	455.63	456.09	454.82
1990	415.81	425.83	435.54	420.07	458.97	462.29	438.24	381.21	344.51	329.84	359.06	373.84
1991	414.20	453.05	482.30	484.72	506.11	475.92	502.04	525.68	526.88	542.98	523.90	586.34
1992	620.21	633.47	603.77	578.68	585.31	563.60	580.83	563.12	583.27	605.17	652.73	676.95
1993	696.34	670.77	690.13	661.42	700.53	703.95	704.70	742.84	762.78	779.26	754.39	776.80
1994	800.47	792.50	743.46	733.84	735.19	705.96	722.16	765.62	764.29	777.49	750.32	751.96
1995	755.20	793.73	817.21	843.98	864.58	933.45	1001.21	1020.11	1043.54	1036.06	1059.20	1052.13
1996	1059.79	1100.05	1101.40	1190.52	1243.43	1185.02	1080.59	1141.50	1226.92	1221.51	1292.61	1291.03
1997	1379.85	1309.00	1221.70	1260.76	1400.32	1442.07	1593.81	1587.32	1685.69	1593.61	1600.55	1570.35
1998	1619.36	1770.51	1835.68	1868.41	1778.87	1894.74	1872.39	1499.25	1693.84	1771.39	1949.54	2192.69
1999	2505.89	2288.03	2461.40	2542.85	2470.52	2686.12	2638.49	2739.35	2746.16	2966.43	3336.16	4069.31
2000	3940.35	4696.69	4572.83	3860.66	3400.91	3966.11	3766.99	4206.35	3672.82	3369.63	2597.93	2470.52
2001	2772.73	2151.83	1840.26	2116.24	2110.49	2160.54	2027.13	1805.43	1498.80	1690.20	1930.58	1950.40
2002	1934.03	1731.49	1845.35	1688.23	1615.73	1463.21	1328.26	1314.85	1172.06	1329.75	1478.78	1335.51
2003	1320.91	1337.52	1341.17	1464.31	1595.91	1622.80	1735.02	1810.45	1786.94	1932.21	1960.26	2003.37
2004	2066.15	2029.82	1994.22	1920.15	1986.74	2047.79	1887.36	1838.10	1896.84	1974.99	2096.81	2175.44
2005	2062.41	2051.72	1999.23	1921.65	2068.22	2056.96	2184.83	2152.09	2151.69	2120.30	2232.82	2205.32
2006	2305.82	2281.39	2339.79	2322.57	2178.88	2172.09	2091.47	2183.75	2258.43	2366.71	2431.77	2415.29
2007	2463.93	2416.15	2421.64	2525.09	2604.52	2603.23	2545.57	2596.36	2701.50	2859.12	2660.96	2652.28
2008	2389.86	2271.48	2279.10	2412.80	2522.66	2292.98	2325.55	2367.52	2091.88	1720.95	1535.57	1577.03
2009	1476.42	1377.84	1528.59	1717.30	1774.33	1835.04	1978.50	2009.06	2122.42	2045.11	2144.60	2269.15
2010	2147.35	2238.26	2397.96	2461.19	2257.04	2109.24	2254.70	2114.03	2368.62	2507.41	2498.23	2652.87
2011	2700.08	2782.27	2781.07	2873.54	2835.30	2773.52	2756.38	2579.46	2415.40	2684.41	2620.34	2605.15
2012	2813.84	2966.89	3091.57	3046.36	2827.34	2935.05	2939.52	3066.96	3116.23	2977.23	3010.24	3019.51
2013	3142.13	3160.19	3267.52	3328.79	3455.91	3403.25	3626.37	3589.87	3771.48	3919.71	4059.89	4176.59
2014	4103.88	4308.12	4198.99	4114.56	4242.62	4408.18	4369.77	4580.27	4493.39	4630.74	4791.63	4736.05
2015	4635.24	4963.53	4900.88	4941.42	5070.03	4986.87	5128.28	4776.51	4620.16	5053.75	5108.67	5007.41
2016	4613.95	4557.95	4869.85	4775.36	4948.05	4842.67	5162.13	5213.22	5312.00	5189.13	5323.68	5383.12
2017	5614.79	5825.44	5911.74	6047.61								

Based on NASDAQ composite; prior to February 5, 1971, based on National Quotation Bureau indices.

158

RUSSELL 1000 INDEX MONTHLY PERCENT CHANGES SINCE 1979

	Jan	Feb	Mar	Apr	May	Jun	Jul	Aug	Sep	Oct	Nov	Dec	Year's Change
1979	4.2	-3.5	6.0	0.3	-2.2	4.3	1.1	5.6	0.02	-7.1	5.1	2.1	16.1
1980	5.9	-0.5	-11.5	4.6	5.0	3.2	6.4	1.1	2.6	1.8	10.1	-3.9	25.6
1981	-4.6	1.0	3.8	-1.9	0.2	-1.2	-0.1	-6.2	-6.4	5.4	4.0	-3.3	-9.7
1982	-2.7	-5.9	-1.3	3.9	-3.6	-2.6	-2.3	11.3	1.2	11.3	4.0	1.3	13.7
1983	3.2	2.1	3.2	7.1	-0.2	3.7	-3.2	0.5	1.3	-2.4	2.0	-1.2	17.0
1984	-1.9	-4.4	1.1	0.3	-5.9	2.1	-1.8	10.8	-0.2	-0.1	-1.4	2.2	-0.1
1985	7.8	1.1	-0.4	-0.3	5.4	1.6	-0.8	-1.0	-3.9	4.5	6.5	4.1	26.7
1986	0.9	7.2	5.1	-1.3	5.0	1.4	-5.9	6.8	-8.5	5.1	1.4	-3.0	13.6
1987	12.7	4.0	1.9	-1.8	0.4	4.5	4.2	3.8	-2.4	-21.9	-8.0	7.2	0.02
1988	4.3	4.4	-2.9	0.7	0.2	4.8	-0.9	-3.3	3.9	2.0	-2.0	1.7	13.1
1989	6.8	-2.5	2.0	4.9	3.8	-0.8	8.2	1.7	-0.5	-2.8	1.5	1.8	25.9
1990	-7.4	1.2	2.2	-2.8	8.9	-0.7	-1.1	-9.6	-5.3	-0.8	6.4	2.7	-7.5
1991	4.5	6.9	2.5	-0.1	3.8	-4.7	4.6	2.2	-1.5	1.4	-4.1	11.2	28.8
1992	-1.4	0.9	-2.4	2.3	0.3	-1.9	4.1	-2.5	1.0	0.7	3.5	1.4	5.9
1993	0.7	0.6	2.2	-2.8	2.4	0.4	-0.4	3.5	-0.5	1.2	-1.7	1.6	7.3
1994	2.9	-2.9	-4.5	1.1	1.0	-2.9	3.1	3.9	-2.6	1.7	-3.9	1.2	-2.4
1995	2.4	3.8	2.3	2.5	3.5	2.4	3.7	0.5	3.9	-0.6	4.2	1.4	34.4
1996	3.1	1.1	0.7	1.4	2.1	-0.1	-4.9	2.5	5.5	2.1	7.1	-1.8	19.7
1997	5.8	0.2	-4.6	5.3	6.2	4.0	8.0	-4.9	5.4	-3.4	4.2	1.9	30.5
1998	0.6	7.0	4.9	0.9	-2.3	3.6	-1.3	-15.1	6.5	7.8	6.1	6.2	25.1
1999	3.5	-3.3	3.7	4.2	-2.3	5.1	-3.2	-1.0	-2.8	6.5	2.5	6.0	19.5
2000	-4.2	-0.4	8.9	-3.3	-2.7	2.5	-1.8	7.4	-4.8	-1.2	-9.3	1.1	-8.8
2001	3.2	-9.5	-6.7	8.0	0.5	-2.4	-1.4	-6.2	-8.6	2.0	7.5	0.9	-13.6
2002	-1.4	-2.1	4.0	-5.8	-1.0	-7.5	-7.5	0.3	-10.9	8.1	5.7	-5.8	-22.9
2003	-2.5	-1.7	0.9	7.9	5.5	1.2	1.8	1.9	-1.2	5.7	1.0	4.6	27.5
2004	1.8	1.2	-1.5	-1.9	1.3	1.7	-3.6	0.3	1.1	1.5	4.1	3.5	9.5
2005	-2.6	2.0	-1.7	-2.0	3.4	0.3	3.8	-1.1	0.8	-1.9	3.5	0.01	4.4
2006	2.7	0.01	1.3	1.1	-3.2	0.003	0.1	2.2	2.3	3.3	1.9	1.1	13.3
2007	1.8	-1.9	0.9	4.1	3.4	-2.0	-3.2	1.2	3.7	1.6	-4.5	-0.8	3.9
2008	-6.1	-3.3	-0.8	5.0	1.6	-8.5	-1.3	1.2	-9.7	-17.6	-7.9	1.3	-39.0
2009	-8.3	-10.7	8.5	10.0	5.3	0.1	7.5	3.4	3.9	-2.3	5.6	2.3	25.5
2010	-3.7	3.1	6.0	1.8	-8.1	-5.7	6.8	-4.7	9.0	3.8	0.1	6.5	13.9
2011	2.3	3.3	0.1	2.9	-1.3	-1.9	-2.3	-6.0	-7.6	11.1	-0.5	0.7	-0.5
2012	4.8	4.1	3.0	-0.7	-6.4	3.7	1.1	2.2	2.4	-1.8	0.5	0.8	13.9
2013	5.3	1.1	3.7	1.7	2.0	-1.5	5.2	-3.0	3.3	4.3	2.6	2.5	30.4
2014	-3.3	4.5	0.5	0.4	2.1	2.1	-1.7	3.9	-1.9	2.3	2.4	-0.4	11.1
2015	-2.8	5.5	-1.4	0.6	1.1	-2.0	1.8	-6.2	-2.9	8.0	0.1	-2.0	-1.1
2016	-5.5	-0.3	6.8	0.4	1.5	0.1	3.7	-0.1	-0.1	-2.1	3.7	1.7	9.7
2017	1.9	3.6	-0.1	0.9									
TOTALS	34.7	17.0	46.4	59.6	36.7	6.4	26.5	7.3	-24.5	37.2	64.0	58.8	
AVG.	0.9	0.4	1.2	1.5	1.0	0.2	0.7	0.2	-0.6	1.0	1.7	1.5	
# Up	24	24	26	27	26	22	18	23	18	24	28	29	
# Down	15	15	13	12	12	16	20	15	20	14	10	9	

RUSSELL 1000 INDEX MONTHLY CLOSING PRICES SINCE 1979

	Jan	Feb	Mar	Apr	May	Jun	Jul	Aug	Sep	Oct	Nov	Dec
1979	53.76	51.88	54.97	55.15	53.92	56.25	56.86	60.04	60.05	55.78	58.65	59.87
1980	63.40	63.07	55.79	58.38	61.31	63.27	67.30	68.05	69.84	71.08	78.26	75.20
1981	71.75	72.49	75.21	73.77	73.90	73.01	72.92	68.42	64.06	67.54	70.23	67.93
1982	66.12	62.21	61.43	63.85	61.53	59.92	58.54	65.14	65.89	73.34	76.28	77.24
1983	79.75	81.45	84.06	90.04	89.89	93.18	90.18	90.65	91.85	89.69	91.50	90.38
1984	88.69	84.76	85.73	86.00	80.94	82.61	81.13	89.87	89.67	89.62	88.36	90.31
1985	97.31	98.38	98.03	97.72	103.02	104.65	103.78	102.76	98.75	103.16	109.91	114.39
1986	115.39	123.71	130.07	128.44	134.82	136.75	128.74	137.43	125.70	132.11	133.97	130.00
1987	146.48	152.29	155.20	152.39	152.94	159.84	166.57	172.95	168.83	131.89	121.28	130.02
1988	135.55	141.54	137.45	138.37	138.66	145.31	143.99	139.26	144.68	147.55	144.56	146.99
1989	156.93	152.98	155.99	163.63	169.85	168.49	182.27	185.33	184.40	179.17	181.85	185.11
1990	171.44	173.43	177.28	172.32	187.66	186.29	184.32	166.69	157.83	156.62	166.69	171.22
1991	179.00	191.34	196.15	195.94	203.32	193.78	202.67	207.18	204.02	206.96	198.46	220.61
1992	217.52	219.50	214.29	219.13	219.71	215.60	224.37	218.86	221.15	222.65	230.44	233.59
1993	235.25	236.67	241.80	235.13	240.80	241.78	240.78	249.20	247.95	250.97	246.70	250.71
1994	258.08	250.52	239.19	241.71	244.13	237.11	244.44	254.04	247.49	251.62	241.82	244.65
1995	250.52	260.08	266.11	272.81	282.48	289.29	299.98	301.40	313.28	311.37	324.36	328.89
1996	338.97	342.56	345.00	349.84	357.35	357.10	339.44	347.79	366.77	374.38	401.05	393.75
1997	416.77	417.46	398.19	419.15	445.06	462.95	499.89	475.33	500.78	483.86	504.25	513.79
1998	517.02	553.14	580.31	585.46	572.16	592.57	584.97	496.66	529.11	570.63	605.31	642.87
1999	665.64	643.67	667.49	695.25	679.10	713.61	690.51	683.27	663.83	707.19	724.66	767.97
2000	736.08	733.04	797.99	771.58	750.98	769.68	755.57	811.17	772.60	763.06	692.40	700.09
2001	722.55	654.25	610.36	658.90	662.39	646.64	637.43	597.67	546.46	557.29	599.32	604.94
2002	596.66	583.88	607.35	572.04	566.18	523.72	484.39	486.08	433.22	468.51	495.00	466.18
2003	454.30	446.37	450.35	486.09	512.92	518.94	528.53	538.40	532.15	562.51	568.32	594.56
2004	605.21	612.58	603.42	591.83	599.40	609.31	587.21	589.09	595.66	604.51	629.26	650.99
2005	633.99	646.93	635.78	623.32	644.28	645.92	670.26	663.13	668.53	656.09	679.35	679.42
2006	697.79	697.83	706.74	714.37	691.78	691.80	692.59	707.55	723.48	747.30	761.43	770.08
2007	784.11	768.92	775.97	807.82	835.14	818.17	792.11	801.22	830.59	844.20	806.44	799.82
2008	750.97	726.42	720.32	756.03	768.28	703.22	694.07	702.17	634.08	522.47	481.43	487.77
2009	447.32	399.61	433.67	476.84	501.95	502.27	539.88	558.21	579.97	566.50	598.41	612.01
2010	589.41	607.45	643.79	655.06	601.79	567.37	606.09	577.68	629.78	653.57	654.24	696.90
2011	712.97	736.24	737.07	758.45	748.75	734.48	717.77	674.79	623.45	692.41	688.77	693.36
2012	726.33	756.42	778.92	773.50	724.12	750.61	758.60	775.07	793.74	779.35	783.37	789.90
2013	831.74	840.97	872.11	886.89	904.44	890.67	937.16	909.28	939.50	979.68	1004.91	1030.36
2014	996.48	1041.36	1046.42	1050.20	1071.96	1094.59	1075.60	1117.71	1096.43	1121.98	1148.90	1144.37
2015	1111.85	1173.46	1156.95	1164.03	1176.67	1152.64	1173.55	1100.51	1068.46	1153.55	1154.66	1131.88
2016	1069.78	1066.58	1138.84	1143.76	1160.95	1161.57	1204.43	1203.05	1202.25	1177.22	1220.68	1241.66
2017	1265.35	1311.34	1310.06	1322.44								

RUSSELL 2000 INDEX MONTHLY PERCENT CHANGES SINCE 1979

	Jan	Feb	Mar	Apr	May	Jun	Jul	Aug	Sep	Oct	Nov	Dec	Year's Change
1979	9.0	-3.2	9.7	2.3	-1.8	5.3	2.9	7.8	-0.7	-11.3	8.1	6.6	38.0
1980	8.2	-2.1	-18.5	6.0	8.0	4.0	11.0	6.5	2.9	3.9	7.0	-3.7	33.8
1981	-0.6	0.3	7.7	2.5	3.0	-2.5	-2.6	-8.0	-8.6	8.2	2.8	-2.0	-1.5
1982	-3.7	-5.3	-1.5	5.1	-3.2	-4.0	-1.7	7.5	3.6	14.1	8.8	1.1	20.7
1983	7.5	6.0	2.5	7.2	7.0	4.4	-3.0	-4.0	1.6	-7.0	5.0	-2.1	26.3
1984	-1.8	-5.9	0.4	-0.7	-5.4	2.6	-5.0	11.5	-1.0	-2.0	-2.9	1.4	-9.6
1985	13.1	2.4	-2.2	-1.4	3.4	1.0	2.7	-1.2	-6.2	3.6	6.8	4.2	28.0
1986	1.5	7.0	4.7	1.4	3.3	-0.2	-9.5	3.0	-6.3	3.9	-0.5	-3.1	4.0
1987	11.5	8.2	2.4	-3.0	-0.5	2.3	2.8	2.9	-2.0	-30.8	-5.5	7.8	-10.8
1988	4.0	8.7	4.4	2.0	-2.5	7.0	-0.9	-2.8	2.3	-1.2	-3.6	3.8	22.4
1989	4.4	0.5	2.2	4.3	4.2	-2.4	4.2	2.1	0.01	-6.0	0.4	0.1	14.2
1990	-8.9	2.9	3.7	-3.4	6.8	0.1	-4.5	-13.6	-9.2	-6.2	7.3	3.7	-21.5
1991	9.1	11.0	6.9	-0.2	4.5	-6.0	3.1	3.7	0.6	2.7	-4.7	7.7	43.7
1992	8.0	2.9	-3.5	-3.7	1.2	-5.0	3.2	-3.1	2.2	3.1	7.5	3.4	16.4
1993	3.2	-2.5	3.1	-2.8	4.3	0.5	1.3	4.1	2.7	2.5	-3.4	3.3	17.0
1994	3.1	-0.4	-5.4	0.6	-1.3	-3.6	1.6	5.4	-0.5	-0.4	-4.2	2.5	-3.2
1995	-1.4	3.9	1.6	2.1	1.5	5.0	5.7	1.9	1.7	-4.6	4.2	2.4	26.2
1996	-0.2	3.0	1.8	5.3	3.9	-4.2	-8.8	5.7	3.7	-1.7	4.0	2.4	14.8
1997	1.9	-2.5	-4.9	0.1	11.0	4.1	4.6	2.2	7.2	-4.5	-0.8	1.7	20.5
1998	-1.6	7.4	4.1	0.5	-5.4	0.2	-8.2	-19.5	7.6	4.0	5.2	6.1	-3.4
1999	1.2	-8.2	1.4	8.8	1.4	4.3	-2.8	-3.8	-0.1	0.3	5.9	11.2	19.6
2000	-1.7	16.4	-6.7	-6.1	-5.9	8.6	-3.2	7.4	-3.1	-4.5	-10.4	8.4	-4.2
2001	5.1	-6.7	-5.0	7.7	2.3	3.3	-5.4	-3.3	-13.6	5.8	7.6	6.0	1.0
2002	-1.1	-2.8	7.9	0.8	-4.5	-5.1	-15.2	-0.4	-7.3	3.1	8.8	-5.7	-21.6
2003	-2.9	-3.1	1.1	9.4	10.6	1.7	6.2	4.5	-2.0	8.3	3.5	1.9	45.4
2004	4.3	0.8	0.8	-5.2	1.5	4.1	-6.8	-0.6	4.6	1.9	8.6	2.8	17.0
2005	-4.2	1.6	-3.0	-5.8	6.4	3.7	6.3	-1.9	0.2	-3.2	4.7	-0.6	3.3
2006	8.9	-0.3	4.7	-0.1	-5.7	0.5	-3.3	2.9	0.7	5.7	2.5	0.2	17.0
2007	1.6	-0.9	0.9	1.7	4.0	-1.6	-6.9	2.2	1.6	2.8	-7.3	-0.2	-2.7
2008	-6.9	-3.8	0.3	4.1	4.5	-7.8	3.6	3.5	-8.1	-20.9	-12.0	5.6	-34.8
2009	-11.2	-12.3	8.7	15.3	2.9	1.3	9.5	2.8	5.6	-6.9	3.0	7.9	25.2
2010	-3.7	4.4	8.0	5.6	-7.7	-7.9	6.8	-7.5	12.3	4.0	3.4	7.8	25.3
2011	-0.3	5.4	2.4	2.6	-2.0	-2.5	-3.7	-8.8	-11.4	15.0	-0.5	0.5	-5.5
2012	7.0	2.3	2.4	-1.6	-6.7	4.8	-1.4	3.2	3.1	-2.2	0.4	3.3	14.6
2013	6.2	1.0	4.4	-0.4	3.9	-0.7	6.9	-3.3	6.2	2.5	3.9	1.8	37.0
2014	-2.8	4.6	-0.8	-3.9	0.7	5.2	-6.1	4.8	-6.2	6.5	-0.02	2.7	3.5
2015	-3.3	5.8	1.6	-2.6	2.2	0.6	-1.2	-6.4	-5.1	5.6	3.1	-5.2	-5.7
2016	-8.8	-0.1	7.8	1.5	2.1	-0.2	5.9	1.6	0.9	-4.8	11.0	2.6	19.5
2017	0.3	1.8	-0.1	1.0									
TOTALS	54.0	48.2	56.0	57.0	52.0	20.9	-11.9	9.0	-20.1	-10.7	77.7	98.3	
AVG.	1.4	1.2	1.4	1.5	1.4	0.6	-0.3	0.2	-0.5	-0.3	2.0	2.6	
# Up	21	23	28	24	25	23	18	22	21	21	25	30	
# Down	18	16	11	15	13	15	20	16	17	17	13	8	

RUSSELL 2000 INDEX MONTHLY CLOSING PRICES SINCE 1979

	Jan	Feb	Mar	Apr	May	Jun	Jul	Aug	Sep	Oct	Nov	Dec
1979	44.18	42.78	46.94	48.00	47.13	49.62	51.08	55.05	54.68	48.51	52.43	55.91
1980	60.50	59.22	48.27	51.18	55.26	57.47	63.81	67.97	69.94	72.64	77.70	74.80
1981	74.33	74.52	80.25	82.25	84.72	82.56	80.41	73.94	67.55	73.06	75.14	73.67
1982	70.96	67.21	66.21	69.59	67.39	64.67	63.59	68.38	70.84	80.86	87.96	88.90
1983	95.53	101.23	103.77	111.20	118.94	124.17	120.43	115.60	117.43	109.17	114.66	112.27
1984	110.21	103.72	104.10	103.34	97.75	100.30	95.25	106.21	105.17	103.07	100.11	101.49
1985	114.77	117.54	114.92	113.35	117.26	118.38	121.56	120.10	112.65	116.73	124.62	129.87
1986	131.78	141.00	147.63	149.66	154.61	154.23	139.65	143.83	134.73	139.95	139.26	135.00
1987	150.48	162.84	166.79	161.82	161.02	164.75	169.42	174.25	170.81	118.26	111.70	120.42
1988	125.24	136.10	142.15	145.01	141.37	151.30	149.89	145.74	149.08	147.25	142.01	147.37
1989	153.84	154.56	157.89	164.68	171.53	167.42	174.50	178.20	178.21	167.47	168.17	168.30
1990	153.27	157.72	163.63	158.09	168.91	169.04	161.51	139.52	126.70	118.83	127.50	132.16
1991	144.17	160.00	171.01	170.61	178.34	167.61	172.76	179.11	180.16	185.00	176.37	189.94
1992	205.16	211.15	203.69	196.25	198.52	188.64	194.74	188.79	192.92	198.90	213.81	221.01
1993	228.10	222.41	229.21	222.68	232.19	233.35	236.46	246.19	252.95	259.18	250.41	258.59
1994	266.52	265.53	251.06	252.55	249.28	240.29	244.06	257.32	256.12	255.02	244.25	250.36
1995	246.85	256.57	260.77	266.17	270.25	283.63	299.72	305.31	310.38	296.25	308.58	315.97
1996	315.38	324.93	330.77	348.28	361.85	346.61	316.00	333.88	346.39	340.57	354.11	362.61
1997	369.45	360.05	342.56	343.00	380.76	396.37	414.48	423.43	453.82	433.26	429.92	437.02
1998	430.05	461.83	480.68	482.89	456.62	457.39	419.75	337.95	363.59	378.16	397.75	421.96
1999	427.22	392.26	397.63	432.81	438.68	457.68	444.77	427.83	427.30	428.64	454.08	504.75
2000	496.23	577.71	539.00	506.25	476.18	517.23	500.64	537.89	521.37	497.68	445.94	483.53
2001	508.34	474.37	450.53	485.32	496.50	512.64	484.78	468.56	404.87	428.17	460.78	488.50
2002	483.10	469.36	506.46	510.67	487.47	462.64	392.42	390.96	362.27	373.50	406.35	383.09
2003	372.17	360.52	364.54	398.68	441.00	448.37	476.02	497.42	487.68	528.22	546.51	556.91
2004	580.76	585.56	590.31	559.80	568.28	591.52	551.29	547.93	572.94	583.79	633.77	651.57
2005	624.02	634.06	615.07	579.38	616.71	639.66	679.75	666.51	667.80	646.61	677.29	673.22
2006	733.20	730.64	765.14	764.54	721.01	724.67	700.56	720.53	725.59	766.84	786.12	787.66
2007	800.34	793.30	800.71	814.57	847.19	833.69	776.13	792.86	805.45	828.02	767.77	766.03
2008	713.30	686.18	687.97	716.18	748.28	689.66	714.52	739.50	679.58	537.52	473.14	499.45
2009	443.53	389.02	422.75	487.56	501.58	508.28	556.71	572.07	604.28	562.77	579.73	625.39
2010	602.04	628.56	678.64	716.60	661.61	609.49	650.89	602.06	676.14	703.35	727.01	783.65
2011	781.25	823.45	843.55	865.29	848.30	827.43	797.03	726.81	644.16	741.06	737.42	740.92
2012	792.82	810.94	830.30	816.88	761.82	798.49	786.94	812.09	837.45	818.73	821.92	849.35
2013	902.09	911.11	951.54	947.46	984.14	977.48	1045.26	1010.90	1073.79	1100.15	1142.89	1163.64
2014	1130.88	1183.03	1173.04	1126.86	1134.50	1192.96	1120.07	1174.35	1101.68	1173.51	1173.23	1204.70
2015	1165.39	1233.37	1252.77	1220.13	1246.53	1253.95	1238.68	1159.45	1100.69	1161.86	1198.11	1135.89
2016	1035.38	1033.90	1114.03	1130.84	1154.79	1151.92	1219.94	1239.91	1251.65	1191.39	1322.34	1357.13
2017	1361.82	1386.68	1385.92	1400.43								

10 <u>BEST</u> DAYS BY PERCENT AND POINT

	BY PERCENT CHANGE				BY POINT CHANGE		
DAY	CLOSE	PNT CHANGE	% CHANGE	DAY	CLOSE	PNT CHANGE	% CHANGE
			DJIA 1901 to 1949				
3/15/33	62.10	8.26	15.3	10/30/29	258.47	28.40	12.3
10/6/31	99.34	12.86	14.9	11/14/29	217.28	18.59	9.4
10/30/29	258.47	28.40	12.3	10/5/29	341.36	16.19	5.0
9/21/32	75.16	7.67	11.4	10/31/29	273.51	15.04	5.8
8/3/32	58.22	5.06	9.5	10/6/31	99.34	12.86	14.9
2/11/32	78.60	6.80	9.5	11/15/29	228.73	11.45	5.3
11/14/29	217.28	18.59	9.4	6/19/30	228.97	10.13	4.6
12/18/31	80.69	6.90	9.4	9/5/39	148.12	10.03	7.3
2/13/32	85.82	7.22	9.2	11/22/28	290.34	9.81	3.5
5/6/32	59.01	4.91	9.1	10/1/30	214.14	9.24	4.5
			DJIA 1950 to APRIL 2017				
10/13/08	9387.61	936.42	11.1	10/13/08	9387.61	936.42	11.1
10/28/08	9065.12	889.35	10.9	10/28/08	9065.12	889.35	10.9
10/21/87	2027.85	186.84	10.2	8/26/15	16285.51	619.07	4.0
3/23/09	7775.86	497.48	6.8	11/13/08	8835.25	552.59	6.7
11/13/08	8835.25	552.59	6.7	3/16/00	10630.60	499.19	4.9
11/21/08	8046.42	494.13	6.5	3/23/09	7775.86	497.48	6.8
7/24/02	8191.29	488.95	6.4	11/21/08	8046.42	494.13	6.5
10/20/87	1841.01	102.27	5.9	11/30/11	12045.68	490.05	4.2
3/10/09	6926.49	379.44	5.8	7/24/02	8191.29	488.95	6.4
7/29/02	8711.88	447.49	5.4	9/30/08	10850.66	485.21	4.7
			S&P 500 1930 to APRIL 2017				
3/15/33	6.81	0.97	16.6	10/13/08	1003.35	104.13	11.6
10/6/31	9.91	1.09	12.4	10/28/08	940.51	91.59	10.8
9/21/32	8.52	0.90	11.8	8/26/15	1940.51	72.90	3.9
10/13/08	1003.35	104.13	11.6	3/16/00	1458.47	66.32	4.8
10/28/08	940.51	91.59	10.8	1/3/01	1347.56	64.29	5.0
2/16/35	10.00	0.94	10.4	9/30/08	1166.36	59.97	5.4
8/17/35	11.70	1.08	10.2	11/13/08	911.29	58.99	6.9
3/16/35	9.05	0.82	10.0	3/23/09	822.92	54.38	7.1
9/12/38	12.06	1.06	9.6	3/18/08	1330.74	54.14	4.2
9/5/39	12.64	1.11	9.6	8/9/11	1172.53	53.07	4.7
			NASDAQ 1971 to APRIL 2017				
1/3/01	2616.69	324.83	14.2	1/3/01	2616.69	324.83	14.2
10/13/08	1844.25	194.74	11.8	12/5/00	2889.80	274.05	10.5
12/5/00	2889.80	274.05	10.5	4/18/00	3793.57	254.41	7.2
10/28/08	1649.47	143.57	9.5	5/30/00	3459.48	254.37	7.9
4/5/01	1785.00	146.20	8.9	10/19/00	3418.60	247.04	7.8
4/18/01	2079.44	156.22	8.1	10/13/00	3316.77	242.09	7.9
5/30/00	3459.48	254.37	7.9	6/2/00	3813.38	230.88	6.4
10/13/00	3316.77	242.09	7.9	4/25/00	3711.23	228.75	6.6
10/19/00	3418.60	247.04	7.8	4/17/00	3539.16	217.87	6.6
5/8/02	1696.29	122.47	7.8	10/13/08	1844.25	194.74	11.8
			RUSSELL 1000 1979 to APRIL 2017				
10/13/08	542.98	56.75	11.7	10/13/08	542.98	56.75	11.7
10/28/08	503.74	47.68	10.5	10/28/08	503.74	47.68	10.5
10/21/87	135.85	11.15	8.9	8/26/15	1081.77	39.00	3.7
3/23/09	446.90	29.36	7.0	3/16/00	777.86	36.60	4.9
11/13/08	489.83	31.99	7.0	1/3/01	712.63	35.74	5.3
11/24/08	456.14	28.26	6.6	11/13/08	489.83	31.99	7.0
3/10/09	391.01	23.46	6.4	9/30/08	634.08	31.74	5.3
11/21/08	427.88	24.97	6.2	8/9/11	647.85	30.57	5.0
7/24/02	448.05	23.87	5.6	12/5/00	728.44	30.36	4.4
7/29/02	477.61	24.69	5.5	3/23/09	446.90	29.36	7.0
			RUSSELL 2000 1979 to APRIL 2017				
10/13/08	570.89	48.41	9.3	10/13/08	570.89	48.41	9.3
11/13/08	491.23	38.43	8.5	9/18/08	723.68	47.30	7.0
3/23/09	433.72	33.61	8.4	8/9/11	696.16	45.20	6.9
10/21/87	130.65	9.26	7.6	11/30/11	737.42	41.32	5.9
10/28/08	482.55	34.15	7.6	10/4/11	648.64	39.15	6.4
11/24/08	436.80	30.26	7.4	11/13/08	491.23	38.43	8.5
3/10/09	367.75	24.49	7.1	10/27/11	765.43	38.28	5.3
9/18/08	723.68	47.30	7.0	11/9/16	1232.16	37.02	3.1
8/9/11	696.16	45.20	6.9	5/10/10	689.61	36.61	5.6
10/16/08	536.57	34.46	6.9	8/11/11	695.89	35.68	5.4

10 <u>WORST</u> DAYS BY PERCENT AND POINT

	BY PERCENT CHANGE				BY POINT CHANGE		
DAY	CLOSE	PNT CHANGE	% CHANGE	DAY	CLOSE	PNT CHANGE	% CHANGE
DJIA 1901 to 1949							
10/28/29	260.64	−38.33	−12.8	10/28/29	260.64	−38.33	−12.8
10/29/29	230.07	−30.57	−11.7	10/29/29	230.07	−30.57	−11.7
11/6/29	232.13	−25.55	−9.9	11/6/29	232.13	−25.55	−9.9
8/12/32	63.11	−5.79	−8.4	10/23/29	305.85	−20.66	−6.3
3/14/07	55.84	−5.05	−8.3	11/11/29	220.39	−16.14	−6.8
7/21/33	88.71	−7.55	−7.8	11/4/29	257.68	−15.83	−5.8
10/18/37	125.73	−10.57	−7.8	12/12/29	243.14	−15.30	−5.9
2/1/17	88.52	−6.91	−7.2	10/3/29	329.95	−14.55	−4.2
10/5/32	66.07	−5.09	−7.2	6/16/30	230.05	−14.20	−5.8
9/24/31	107.79	−8.20	−7.1	8/9/29	337.99	−14.11	−4.0
DJIA 1950 to APRIL 2017							
10/19/87	1738.74	−508.00	−22.6	9/29/08	10365.45	−777.68	−7.0
10/26/87	1793.93	−156.83	−8.0	10/15/08	8577.91	−733.08	−7.9
10/15/08	8577.91	−733.08	−7.9	9/17/01	8920.70	−684.81	−7.1
12/1/08	8149.09	−679.95	−7.7	12/1/08	8149.09	−679.95	−7.7
10/9/08	8579.19	−678.91	−7.3	10/9/08	8579.19	−678.91	−7.3
10/27/97	7161.15	−554.26	−7.2	8/8/11	10809.85	−634.76	−5.6
9/17/01	8920.70	−684.81	−7.1	4/14/00	10305.77	−617.78	−5.7
9/29/08	10365.45	−777.68	−7.0	6/24/16	17400.75	−610.32	−3.4
10/13/89	2569.26	−190.58	−6.9	8/24/15	15871.35	−588.40	−3.6
1/8/88	1911.31	−140.58	−6.9	10/27/97	7161.15	−554.26	−7.2
S&P 500 1930 to APRIL 2017							
10/19/87	224.84	−57.86	−20.5	9/29/08	1106.39	−106.62	−8.8
3/18/35	8.14	−0.91	−10.1	10/15/08	907.84	−90.17	−9.0
4/16/35	8.22	−0.91	−10.0	4/14/00	1356.56	−83.95	−5.8
9/3/46	15.00	−1.65	−9.9	12/1/08	816.21	−80.03	−8.9
10/18/37	10.76	−1.10	−9.3	8/8/11	1119.46	−79.92	−6.7
10/15/08	907.84	−90.17	−9.0	8/24/15	1893.21	−77.68	−3.9
12/1/08	816.21	−80.03	−8.9	6/24/16	2037.41	−75.91	−3.6
7/20/33	10.57	−1.03	−8.9	10/9/08	909.92	−75.02	−7.6
9/29/08	1106.39	−106.62	−8.8	8/31/98	957.28	−69.86	−6.8
7/21/33	9.65	−0.92	−8.7	8/21/15	1970.89	−64.84	−3.2
NASDAQ 1971 to APRIL 2017							
10/19/87	360.21	−46.12	−11.4	4/14/00	3321.29	−355.49	−9.7
4/14/00	3321.29	−355.49	−9.7	4/3/00	4223.68	−349.15	−7.6
9/29/08	1983.73	−199.61	−9.1	4/12/00	3769.63	−286.27	−7.1
10/26/87	298.90	−29.55	−9.0	4/10/00	4188.20	−258.25	−5.8
10/20/87	327.79	−32.42	−9.0	1/4/00	3901.69	−229.46	−5.6
12/1/08	1398.07	−137.50	−9.0	6/24/16	4707.98	−202.06	−4.1
8/31/98	1499.25	−140.43	−8.6	3/14/00	4706.63	−200.61	−4.1
10/15/08	1628.33	−150.68	−8.5	5/10/00	3384.73	−200.28	−5.6
4/3/00	4223.68	−349.15	−7.6	5/23/00	3164.55	−199.66	−5.9
1/2/01	2291.86	−178.66	−7.2	9/29/08	1983.73	−199.61	−9.1
RUSSELL 1000 1979 to APRIL 2017							
10/19/87	121.04	−28.40	−19.0	9/29/08	602.34	−57.35	−8.7
10/15/08	489.71	−49.11	−9.1	10/15/08	489.71	−49.11	−9.1
12/1/08	437.75	−43.68	−9.1	4/14/00	715.20	−45.74	−6.0
9/29/08	602.34	−57.35	−8.7	8/8/11	617.28	−45.56	−6.9
10/26/87	119.45	−10.74	−8.3	12/1/08	437.75	−43.68	−9.1
10/9/08	492.13	−40.05	−7.5	8/24/15	1056.36	−43.45	−4.0
8/8/11	617.28	−45.56	−6.9	6/24/16	1128.04	−42.53	−3.6
11/20/08	402.91	−29.62	−6.9	10/9/08	492.13	−40.05	−7.5
8/31/98	496.66	−35.77	−6.7	8/31/98	496.66	−35.77	−6.7
10/27/97	465.44	−32.96	−6.6	8/21/15	1099.81	−35.07	−3.1
RUSSELL 2000 1979 to APRIL 2017							
10/19/87	133.60	−19.14	−12.5	8/8/11	650.96	−63.67	−8.9
12/1/08	417.07	−56.07	−11.9	12/1/08	417.07	−56.07	−11.9
10/15/08	502.11	−52.54	−9.5	10/15/08	502.11	−52.54	−9.5
10/26/87	110.33	−11.26	−9.3	10/9/08	499.20	−47.37	−8.7
10/20/87	121.39	−12.21	−9.1	9/29/08	657.72	−47.07	−6.7
8/8/11	650.96	−63.67	−8.9	8/4/11	726.80	−45.98	−6.0
10/9/08	499.20	−47.37	−8.7	8/24/15	1111.69	−45.10	−3.9
11/19/08	412.38	−35.13	−7.9	6/24/16	1127.54	−44.68	−3.8
4/14/00	453.72	−35.50	−7.3	8/18/11	662.51	−41.52	−5.9
11/14/08	456.52	−34.71	−7.1	9/9/16	1219.21	−39.15	−3.1

10 <u>BEST</u> WEEKS BY PERCENT AND POINT

	BY PERCENT CHANGE				BY POINT CHANGE		
WEEK ENDS	CLOSE	PNT CHANGE	% CHANGE	WEEK ENDS	CLOSE	PNT CHANGE	% CHANGE
DJIA 1901 to 1949							
8/6/32	66.56	12.30	22.7	12/7/29	263.46	24.51	10.3
6/25/38	131.94	18.71	16.5	6/25/38	131.94	18.71	16.5
2/13/32	85.82	11.37	15.3	6/27/31	156.93	17.97	12.9
4/22/33	72.24	9.36	14.9	11/22/29	245.74	17.01	7.4
10/10/31	105.61	12.84	13.8	8/17/29	360.70	15.86	4.6
7/30/32	54.26	6.42	13.4	12/22/28	285.94	15.22	5.6
6/27/31	156.93	17.97	12.9	8/24/29	375.44	14.74	4.1
9/24/32	74.83	8.39	12.6	2/21/29	310.06	14.21	4.8
8/27/32	75.61	8.43	12.6	5/10/30	272.01	13.70	5.3
3/18/33	60.56	6.72	12.5	11/15/30	186.68	13.54	7.8
DJIA 1950 to APRIL 2017							
10/11/74	658.17	73.61	12.6	11/11/16	18847.66	959.38	5.4
10/31/08	9325.01	946.06	11.3	10/31/08	9325.01	946.06	11.3
8/20/82	869.29	81.24	10.3	12/2/11	12019.42	787.64	7.0
11/28/08	8829.04	782.62	9.7	11/28/08	8829.04	782.62	9.7
3/13/09	7223.98	597.04	9.0	3/17/00	10595.23	666.41	6.7
10/8/82	986.85	79.11	8.7	3/21/03	8521.97	662.26	8.4
3/21/03	8521.97	662.26	8.4	2/6/15	17824.29	659.34	3.8
8/3/84	1202.08	87.46	7.9	7/1/11	12582.77	648.19	5.4
9/28/01	8847.56	611.75	7.4	10/9/15	17084.49	612.12	3.7
7/17/09	8743.94	597.42	7.3	9/28/01	8847.56	611.75	7.4
S&P 500 1930 to APRIL 2017							
8/6/32	7.22	1.12	18.4	6/2/00	1477.26	99.24	7.2
6/25/38	11.39	1.72	17.8	11/28/08	896.24	96.21	12.0
7/30/32	6.10	0.89	17.1	10/31/08	968.75	91.98	10.5
4/22/33	7.75	1.09	16.4	12/2/11	1244.28	85.61	7.4
10/11/74	71.14	8.80	14.1	11/11/16	2164.45	79.27	3.8
2/13/32	8.80	1.08	14.0	4/20/00	1434.54	77.98	5.8
9/24/32	8.52	1.02	13.6	10/24/14	1964.58	77.82	4.1
10/10/31	10.64	1.27	13.6	7/2/99	1391.22	75.91	5.8
8/27/32	8.57	1.01	13.4	3/3/00	1409.17	75.81	5.7
3/18/33	6.61	0.77	13.2	9/28/01	1040.94	75.14	7.8
NASDAQ 1971 to APRIL 2017							
6/2/00	3813.38	608.27	19.0	6/2/00	3813.38	608.27	19.0
4/12/01	1961.43	241.07	14.0	2/4/00	4244.14	357.07	9.2
11/28/08	1535.57	151.22	10.9	3/3/00	4914.79	324.29	7.1
10/31/08	1720.95	168.92	10.9	4/20/00	3643.88	322.59	9.7
3/13/09	1431.50	137.65	10.6	12/8/00	2917.43	272.14	10.3
4/20/01	2163.41	201.98	10.3	4/12/01	1961.43	241.07	14.0
12/8/00	2917.43	272.14	10.3	10/24/14	4483.72	225.28	5.3
4/20/00	3643.88	322.59	9.7	7/14/00	4246.18	222.98	5.5
10/11/74	60.42	5.26	9.5	1/12/01	2626.50	218.85	9.1
2/4/00	4244.14	357.07	9.2	4/28/00	3860.66	216.78	6.0
RUSSELL 1000 1979 to APRIL 2017							
11/28/08	481.43	53.55	12.5	6/2/00	785.02	57.93	8.0
10/31/08	522.47	50.94	10.8	11/28/08	481.43	53.55	12.5
3/13/09	411.10	39.88	10.7	10/31/08	522.47	50.94	10.8
8/20/82	61.51	4.83	8.5	12/2/11	687.44	47.63	7.4
6/2/00	785.02	57.93	8.0	11/11/16	1199.16	44.50	3.9
9/28/01	546.46	38.48	7.6	10/24/14	1092.59	43.55	4.2
10/16/98	546.09	38.45	7.6	4/20/00	757.32	42.12	5.9
8/3/84	87.43	6.13	7.5	3/3/00	756.41	41.55	5.8
12/2/11	687.44	47.63	7.4	3/13/09	411.10	39.88	10.7
3/21/03	474.58	32.69	7.4	7/1/11	745.21	39.46	5.6
RUSSELL 2000 1979 to APRIL 2017							
11/28/08	473.14	66.60	16.4	11/11/16	1282.38	118.94	10.2
10/31/08	537.52	66.40	14.1	12/9/16	1388.07	73.82	5.6
6/2/00	513.03	55.66	12.2	12/2/11	735.02	68.86	10.3
3/13/09	393.09	42.04	12.0	11/28/08	473.14	66.60	16.4
12/2/11	735.02	68.86	10.3	10/31/08	537.52	66.40	14.1
11/11/16	1282.38	118.94	10.2	10/14/11	712.46	56.25	8.6
10/14/11	712.46	56.25	8.6	6/2/00	513.03	55.66	12.2
7/17/09	519.22	38.24	8.0	10/31/14	1173.51	54.69	4.9
10/16/98	342.87	24.47	7.7	10/9/15	1165.36	51.24	4.6
12/18/87	116.94	8.31	7.7	10/28/11	761.00	48.58	6.8

10 <u>WORST</u> WEEKS BY PERCENT AND POINT

	BY PERCENT CHANGE				BY POINT CHANGE		
WEEK ENDS	CLOSE	PNT CHANGE	% CHANGE	WEEK ENDS	CLOSE	PNT CHANGE	% CHANGE
DJIA 1901 to 1949							
7/22/33	88.42	−17.68	−16.7	11/8/29	236.53	−36.98	−13.5
5/18/40	122.43	−22.42	−15.5	12/8/28	257.33	−33.47	−11.5
10/8/32	61.17	−10.92	−15.2	6/21/30	215.30	−28.95	−11.9
10/3/31	92.77	−14.59	−13.6	10/19/29	323.87	−28.82	−8.2
11/8/29	236.53	−36.98	−13.5	5/3/30	258.31	−27.15	−9.5
9/17/32	66.44	−10.10	−13.2	10/31/29	273.51	−25.46	−8.5
10/21/33	83.64	−11.95	−12.5	10/26/29	298.97	−24.90	−7.7
12/12/31	78.93	−11.21	−12.4	5/18/40	122.43	−22.42	−15.5
5/8/15	62.77	−8.74	−12.2	2/8/29	301.53	−18.23	−5.7
6/21/30	215.30	−28.95	−11.9	10/11/30	193.05	−18.05	−8.6
DJIA 1950 to APRIL 2017							
10/10/08	8451.19	−1874.19	−18.2	10/10/08	8451.19	−1874.19	−18.2
9/21/01	8235.81	−1369.70	−14.3	9/21/01	8235.81	−1369.70	−14.3
10/23/87	1950.76	−295.98	−13.2	1/8/16	16346.45	−1078.58	−6.2
10/16/87	2246.74	−235.47	−9.5	8/21/15	16459.75	−1017.65	−5.8
10/13/89	2569.26	−216.26	−7.8	3/16/01	9823.41	−821.21	−7.7
3/16/01	9823.41	−821.21	−7.7	10/3/08	10325.38	−817.75	−7.3
7/19/02	8019.26	−665.27	−7.7	4/14/00	10305.77	−805.71	−7.3
12/4/87	1766.74	−143.74	−7.5	9/23/11	10771.48	−737.61	−6.4
9/13/74	627.19	−50.69	−7.5	8/5/11	11444.61	−698.63	−5.8
9/12/86	1758.72	−141.03	−7.4	7/12/02	8684.53	−694.97	−7.4
S&P 500 1930 to APRIL 2017							
7/22/33	9.71	−2.20	−18.5	10/10/08	899.22	−200.01	−18.2
10/10/08	899.22	−200.01	−18.2	4/14/00	1356.56	−159.79	−10.5
5/18/40	9.75	−2.05	−17.4	9/21/01	965.80	−126.74	−11.6
10/8/32	6.77	−1.38	−16.9	1/8/16	1922.03	−121.91	−6.0
9/17/32	7.50	−1.28	−14.6	8/21/15	1970.89	−120.65	−5.8
10/21/33	8.57	−1.31	−13.3	10/3/08	1099.23	−113.78	−9.4
10/3/31	9.37	−1.36	−12.7	8/5/11	1199.38	−92.90	−7.2
10/23/87	248.22	−34.48	−12.2	10/15/99	1247.41	−88.61	−6.6
12/12/31	8.20	−1.13	−12.1	3/16/01	1150.53	−82.89	−6.7
3/26/38	9.20	−1.21	−11.6	1/28/00	1360.16	−81.20	−5.6
NASDAQ 1971 to APRIL 2017							
4/14/00	3321.29	−1125.16	−25.3	4/14/00	3321.29	−1125.16	−25.3
10/23/87	328.45	−77.88	−19.2	7/28/00	3663.00	−431.45	−10.5
9/21/01	1423.19	−272.19	−16.1	11/10/00	3028.99	−422.59	−12.2
10/10/08	1649.51	−297.88	−15.3	3/31/00	4572.83	−390.20	−7.9
11/10/00	3028.99	−422.59	−12.2	1/8/16	4643.63	−363.78	−7.3
10/3/08	1947.39	−235.95	−10.8	1/28/00	3887.07	−348.33	−8.2
7/28/00	3663.00	−431.45	−10.5	8/21/15	4706.04	−342.20	−6.8
10/24/08	1552.03	−159.26	−9.3	10/6/00	3361.01	−311.81	−8.5
12/15/00	2653.27	−264.16	−9.1	10/10/08	1649.51	−297.88	−15.3
12/1/00	2645.29	−259.09	−8.9	5/12/00	3529.06	−287.76	−7.5
RUSSELL 1000 1979 to APRIL 2017							
10/10/08	486.23	−108.31	−18.2	10/10/08	486.23	−108.31	−18.2
10/23/87	130.19	−19.25	−12.9	4/14/00	715.20	−90.39	−11.2
9/21/01	507.98	−67.59	−11.7	1/8/16	1063.55	−68.33	−6.0
4/14/00	715.20	−90.39	−11.2	9/21/01	507.98	−67.59	−11.7
10/3/08	594.54	−65.15	−9.9	8/21/15	1099.81	−66.86	−5.7
10/16/87	149.44	−14.42	−8.8	10/3/08	594.54	−65.15	−9.9
11/21/08	427.88	−41.15	−8.8	8/5/11	662.84	−54.93	−7.7
9/12/86	124.95	−10.87	−8.0	9/23/11	627.56	−45.42	−6.8
8/5/11	662.84	−54.93	−7.7	12/11/15	1114.63	−44.64	−3.9
7/19/02	450.64	−36.13	−7.4	10/15/99	646.79	−43.89	−6.4
RUSSELL 2000 1979 to APRIL 2017							
10/23/87	121.59	−31.15	−20.4	10/10/08	522.48	−96.92	−15.7
4/14/00	453.72	−89.27	−16.4	1/8/16	1046.20	−89.69	−7.9
10/10/08	522.48	−96.92	−15.7	4/14/00	453.72	−89.27	−16.4
9/21/01	378.89	−61.84	−14.0	10/3/08	619.40	−85.39	−12.1
10/3/08	619.40	−85.39	−12.1	8/5/11	714.63	−82.40	−10.3
11/21/08	406.54	−49.98	−11.0	5/7/10	653.00	−63.60	−8.9
10/24/08	471.12	−55.31	−10.5	9/23/11	652.43	−61.88	−8.7
8/5/11	714.63	−82.40	−10.3	9/21/01	378.89	−61.84	−14.0
3/6/09	351.05	−37.97	−9.8	12/11/15	1123.61	−59.79	−5.1
11/14/08	456.52	−49.27	−9.7	7/27/07	777.83	−58.61	−7.0

10 <u>BEST</u> MONTHS BY PERCENT AND POINT

	BY PERCENT CHANGE				BY POINT CHANGE		
MONTH	**CLOSE**	**PNT CHANGE**	**% CHANGE**	**MONTH**	**CLOSE**	**PNT CHANGE**	**% CHANGE**
			DJIA 1901 to 1949				
APR-1933	77.66	22.26	40.2	NOV-1928	293.38	41.22	16.3
AUG-1932	73.16	18.90	34.8	JUN-1929	333.79	36.38	12.2
JUL-1932	54.26	11.42	26.7	AUG-1929	380.33	32.63	9.4
JUN-1938	133.88	26.14	24.3	JUN-1938	133.88	26.14	24.3
APR-1915	71.78	10.95	18.0	AUG-1928	240.41	24.41	11.3
JUN-1931	150.18	21.72	16.9	APR-1933	77.66	22.26	40.2
NOV-1928	293.38	41.22	16.3	FEB-1931	189.66	22.11	13.2
NOV-1904	52.76	6.59	14.3	JUN-1931	150.18	21.72	16.9
MAY-1919	105.50	12.62	13.6	AUG-1932	73.16	18.90	34.8
SEP-1939	152.54	18.13	13.5	JAN-1930	267.14	18.66	7.5
			DJIA 1950 to APRIL 2017				
JAN-1976	975.28	122.87	14.4	OCT-2015	17663.54	1379.54	8.5
JAN-1975	703.69	87.45	14.2	MAR-2016	17685.09	1168.59	7.1
JAN-1987	2158.04	262.09	13.8	OCT-2011	11955.01	1041.63	9.5
AUG-1982	901.31	92.71	11.5	APR-1999	10789.04	1002.88	10.2
OCT-1982	991.72	95.47	10.7	NOV-2016	19123.58	981.16	5.4
OCT-2002	8397.03	805.10	10.6	FEB-2015	18132.70	967.75	5.6
APR-1978	837.32	79.96	10.6	FEB-2017	20812.24	948.15	4.8
APR-1999	10789.04	1002.88	10.2	APR-2001	10734.97	856.19	8.7
NOV-1962	649.30	59.53	10.1	OCT-2002	8397.03	805.10	10.6
NOV-1954	386.77	34.63	9.8	MAR-2000	10921.92	793.61	7.8
			S&P 500 1930 to APRIL 2017				
APR-1933	8.32	2.47	42.2	OCT-2015	2079.36	159.33	8.3
JUL-1932	6.10	1.67	37.7	MAR-2000	1498.58	132.16	9.7
AUG-1932	8.39	2.29	37.5	MAR-2016	2059.74	127.51	6.6
JUN-1938	11.56	2.29	24.7	OCT-2011	1253.30	121.88	10.8
SEP-1939	13.02	1.84	16.5	FEB-2015	2104.50	109.51	5.5
OCT-1974	73.90	10.36	16.3	SEP-2010	1141.20	91.87	8.8
MAY-1933	9.64	1.32	15.9	APR-2001	1249.46	89.13	7.7
APR-1938	9.70	1.20	14.1	AUG-2000	1517.68	86.85	6.1
JUN-1931	14.83	1.81	13.9	FEB-2017	2363.64	84.77	3.7
JAN-1987	274.08	31.91	13.2	OCT-1998	1098.67	81.66	8.0
			NASDAQ 1971 to APRIL 2017				
DEC-1999	4069.31	733.15	22.0	FEB-2000	4696.69	756.34	19.2
FEB-2000	4696.69	756.34	19.2	DEC-1999	4069.31	733.15	22.0
OCT-1974	65.23	9.56	17.2	JUN-2000	3966.11	565.20	16.6
JAN-1975	69.78	9.96	16.6	AUG-2000	4206.35	439.36	11.7
JUN-2000	3966.11	565.20	16.6	OCT-2015	5053.75	433.59	9.4
APR-2001	2116.24	275.98	15.0	NOV-1999	3336.16	369.73	12.5
JAN-1999	2505.89	313.20	14.3	FEB-2015	4963.53	328.29	7.1
NOV-2001	1930.58	240.38	14.2	JUL-2016	5162.13	319.46	6.6
OCT-2002	1329.75	157.69	13.5	JAN-1999	2505.89	313.20	14.3
OCT-1982	212.63	24.98	13.3	MAR-2016	4869.85	311.90	6.8
			RUSSELL 1000 1979 to APRIL 2017				
JAN-1987	146.48	16.48	12.7	OCT-2015	1153.55	85.09	8.0
OCT-1982	73.34	7.45	11.3	MAR-2016	1138.84	72.26	6.8
AUG-1982	65.14	6.60	11.3	OCT-2011	692.41	68.96	11.1
DEC-1991	220.61	22.15	11.2	MAR-2000	797.99	64.95	8.9
OCT-2011	692.41	68.96	11.1	FEB-2015	1173.46	61.61	5.5
AUG-1984	89.87	8.74	10.8	AUG-2000	811.17	55.60	7.4
NOV-1980	78.26	7.18	10.1	SEP-2010	629.78	52.10	9.0
APR-2009	476.84	43.17	10.0	APR-2001	658.90	48.54	8.0
SEP-2010	629.78	52.10	9.0	JUL-2013	937.16	46.49	5.2
MAY-1990	187.66	15.34	8.0	FEB-2017	1311.34	45.99	3.6
			RUSSELL 2000 1979 to APRIL 2017				
FEB-2000	577.71	81.48	16.4	NOV-2016	1322.34	130.95	11.0
APR-2009	487.56	64.81	15.3	OCT-2011	741.06	96.90	15.0
OCT-2011	741.06	96.90	15.0	FEB-2000	577.71	81.48	16.4
OCT-1982	80.86	10.02	14.1	MAR-2016	1114.03	80.13	7.8
JAN-1985	114.77	13.28	13.1	SEP-2010	676.14	74.08	12.3
SEP-2010	676.14	74.08	12.3	OCT-2014	1173.51	71.83	6.5
AUG-1984	106.21	10.96	11.5	JUL-2016	1219.94	68.02	5.9
JAN-1987	150.48	15.48	11.5	FEB-2015	1233.37	67.98	5.8
DEC-1999	504.75	50.67	11.2	JUL-2013	1045.26	67.78	6.9
JUL-1980	63.81	6.34	11.0	APR-2009	487.56	64.81	15.3

10 <u>WORST</u> MONTHS BY PERCENT AND POINT

	BY PERCENT CHANGE				BY POINT CHANGE		
MONTH	CLOSE	PNT CHANGE	% CHANGE	MONTH	CLOSE	PNT CHANGE	% CHANGE
DJIA 1901 to 1949							
SEP-1931	96.61	−42.80	−30.7	OCT-1929	273.51	−69.94	−20.4
MAR-1938	98.95	−30.69	−23.7	JUN-1930	226.34	−48.73	−17.7
APR-1932	56.11	−17.17	−23.4	SEP-1931	96.61	−42.80	−30.7
MAY-1940	116.22	−32.21	−21.7	SEP-1929	343.45	−36.88	−9.7
OCT-1929	273.51	−69.94	−20.4	SEP-1930	204.90	−35.52	−14.8
MAY-1932	44.74	−11.37	−20.3	NOV-1929	238.95	−34.56	−12.6
JUN-1930	226.34	−48.73	−17.7	MAY-1940	116.22	−32.21	−21.7
DEC-1931	77.90	−15.97	−17.0	MAR-1938	98.95	−30.69	−23.7
FEB-1933	51.39	−9.51	−15.6	SEP-1937	154.57	−22.84	−12.9
MAY-1931	128.46	−22.73	−15.0	MAY-1931	128.46	−22.73	−15.0
DJIA 1950 to APRIL 2017							
OCT-1987	1993.53	−602.75	−23.2	OCT-2008	9325.01	−1525.65	−14.1
AUG-1998	7539.07	−1344.22	−15.1	AUG-1998	7539.07	−1344.22	−15.1
OCT-2008	9325.01	−1525.65	−14.1	JUN-2008	11350.01	−1288.31	−10.2
NOV-1973	822.25	−134.33	−14.0	AUG-2015	16528.03	−1161.83	−6.6
SEP-2002	7591.93	−1071.57	−12.4	SEP-2001	8847.56	−1102.19	−11.1
FEB-2009	7062.93	−937.93	−11.7	SEP-2002	7591.93	−1071.57	−12.4
SEP-2001	8847.56	−1102.19	−11.1	JAN-2016	16466.30	−958.73	−5.5
SEP-1974	607.87	−70.71	−10.4	FEB-2009	7062.93	−937.93	−11.7
AUG-1974	678.58	−78.85	−10.4	JAN-2014	15698.85	−877.81	−5.3
JUN-2008	11350.01	−1288.31	−10.2	MAY-2010	10136.63	−871.98	−7.9
S&P 500 1930 to APRIL 2017							
SEP-1931	9.71	−4.15	−29.9	OCT-2008	968.75	−197.61	−16.9
MAR-1938	8.50	−2.84	−25.0	AUG-1998	957.28	−163.39	−14.6
MAY-1940	9.27	−2.92	−24.0	AUG-2015	1972.18	−131.66	−6.3
MAY-1932	4.47	−1.36	−23.3	FEB-2001	1239.94	−126.07	−9.2
OCT-1987	251.79	−70.04	−21.8	JUN-2008	1280.00	−120.38	−8.6
APR-1932	5.83	−1.48	−20.2	SEP-2008	1166.36	−116.47	−9.1
FEB-1933	5.66	−1.28	−18.4	NOV-2000	1314.95	−114.45	−8.0
OCT-2008	968.75	−197.61	−16.9	JAN-2016	1940.24	−103.70	−5.1
JUN-1930	20.46	−4.03	−16.5	SEP-2002	815.28	−100.79	−11.0
AUG-1998	957.28	−163.39	−14.6	MAY-2010	1089.41	−97.28	−8.2
NASDAQ 1971 to APRIL 2017							
OCT-1987	323.30	−120.99	−27.2	NOV-2000	2597.93	−771.70	−22.9
NOV-2000	2597.93	−771.70	−22.9	APR-2000	3860.66	−712.17	−15.6
FEB-2001	2151.83	−620.90	−22.4	FEB-2001	2151.83	−620.90	−22.4
AUG-1998	1499.25	−373.14	−19.9	SEP-2000	3672.82	−533.53	−12.7
OCT-2008	1720.95	−370.93	−17.7	MAY-2000	3400.91	−459.75	−11.9
MAR-1980	131.00	−27.03	−17.1	JAN-2016	4613.95	−393.46	−7.9
SEP-2001	1498.80	−306.63	−17.0	AUG-1998	1499.25	−373.14	−19.9
OCT-1978	111.12	−21.77	−16.4	OCT-2008	1720.95	−370.93	−17.7
APR-2000	3860.66	−712.17	−15.6	AUG-2015	4776.51	−351.77	−6.9
NOV-1973	93.51	−16.66	−15.1	MAR-2001	1840.26	−311.57	−14.5
RUSSELL 1000 1979 to APRIL 2017							
OCT-1987	131.89	−36.94	−21.9	OCT-2008	522.47	−111.61	−17.6
OCT-2008	522.47	−111.61	−17.6	AUG-1998	496.66	−88.31	−15.1
AUG-1998	496.66	−88.31	−15.1	AUG-2015	1100.51	−73.04	−6.2
MAR-1980	55.79	−7.28	−11.5	NOV-2000	692.40	−70.66	−9.3
SEP-2002	433.22	−52.86	−10.9	FEB-2001	654.25	−68.30	−9.5
FEB-2009	399.61	−47.71	−10.7	SEP-2008	634.08	−68.09	−9.7
SEP-2008	634.08	−68.09	−9.7	JUN-2008	703.22	−65.06	−8.5
AUG-1990	166.69	−17.63	−9.6	JAN-2016	1069.78	−62.10	−5.5
FEB-2001	654.25	−68.30	−9.5	MAY-2010	601.79	−53.27	−8.1
NOV-2000	692.40	−70.66	−9.3	SEP-2002	433.22	−52.86	−10.9
RUSSELL 2000 1979 to APRIL 2017							
OCT-1987	118.26	−52.55	−30.8	OCT-2008	537.52	−142.06	−20.9
OCT-2008	537.52	−142.06	−20.9	JAN-2016	1035.38	−100.51	−8.8
AUG-1998	337.95	−81.80	−19.5	SEP-2011	644.16	−82.65	−11.4
MAR-1980	48.27	−10.95	−18.5	AUG-1998	337.95	−81.80	−19.5
JUL-2002	392.42	−70.22	−15.2	AUG-2015	1159.45	−79.23	−6.4
AUG-1990	139.52	−21.99	−13.6	JUL-2014	1120.07	−72.89	−6.1
SEP-2001	404.87	−63.69	−13.6	SEP-2014	1101.68	−72.67	−6.2
FEB-2009	389.02	−54.51	−12.3	JUL-2002	392.42	−70.22	−15.2
NOV-2008	473.14	−64.38	−12.0	AUG-2011	726.81	−70.22	−8.8
SEP-2011	644.16	−82.65	−11.4	NOV-2008	473.14	−64.38	−12.0

10 **BEST** QUARTERS BY PERCENT AND POINT

	BY PERCENT CHANGE				BY POINT CHANGE		
QUARTER	CLOSE	PNT CHANGE	% CHANGE	QUARTER	CLOSE	PNT CHANGE	% CHANGE
DJIA 1901 to 1949							
JUN-1933	98.14	42.74	77.1	DEC-1928	300.00	60.57	25.3
SEP-1932	71.56	28.72	67.0	JUN-1933	98.14	42.74	77.1
JUN-1938	133.88	34.93	35.3	MAR-1930	286.10	37.62	15.1
SEP-1915	90.58	20.52	29.3	JUN-1938	133.88	34.93	35.3
DEC-1928	300.00	60.57	25.3	SEP-1927	197.59	31.36	18.9
DEC-1904	50.99	8.80	20.9	SEP-1928	239.43	28.88	13.7
JUN-1919	106.98	18.13	20.4	SEP-1932	71.56	28.72	67.0
SEP-1927	197.59	31.36	18.9	JUN-1929	333.79	24.94	8.1
DEC-1905	70.47	10.47	17.4	SEP-1939	152.54	21.91	16.8
JUN-1935	118.21	17.40	17.3	SEP-1915	90.58	20.52	29.3
DJIA 1950 to APRIL 2017							
MAR-1975	768.15	151.91	24.7	MAR-2013	14578.54	1474.40	11.3
MAR-1987	2304.69	408.74	21.6	DEC-2016	19762.60	1454.45	7.9
MAR-1986	1818.61	271.94	17.6	DEC-2013	16576.66	1446.99	9.6
MAR-1976	999.45	147.04	17.2	DEC-1998	9181.43	1338.81	17.1
DEC-1998	9181.43	1338.81	17.1	DEC-2011	12217.56	1304.18	12.0
DEC-1982	1046.54	150.29	16.8	SEP-2009	9712.28	1265.28	15.0
JUN-1997	7672.79	1089.31	16.5	JUN-1999	10970.80	1184.64	12.1
DEC-1985	1546.67	218.04	16.4	DEC-2003	10453.92	1178.86	12.7
SEP-2009	9712.28	1265.28	15.0	DEC-2001	10021.50	1173.94	13.3
JUN-1975	878.99	110.84	14.4	DEC-1999	11497.12	1160.17	11.2
S&P 500 1930 to APRIL 2017							
JUN-1933	10.91	5.06	86.5	DEC-1998	1229.23	212.22	20.9
SEP-1932	8.08	3.65	82.4	DEC-1999	1469.25	186.54	14.5
JUN-1938	11.56	3.06	36.0	DEC-2013	1848.36	166.81	9.9
MAR-1975	83.36	14.80	21.6	MAR-2012	1408.47	150.87	12.0
DEC-1998	1229.23	212.22	20.9	MAR-2013	1569.19	143.00	10.0
JUN-1935	10.23	1.76	20.8	SEP-2009	1057.08	137.76	15.0
MAR-1987	291.70	49.53	20.5	MAR-1998	1101.75	131.32	13.5
SEP-1939	13.02	2.16	19.9	JUN-1997	885.14	128.02	16.9
MAR-1943	11.58	1.81	18.5	DEC-2011	1257.60	126.18	11.2
MAR-1930	25.14	3.69	17.2	JUN-2003	974.50	125.32	14.8
NASDAQ 1971 to APRIL 2017							
DEC-1999	4069.31	1323.15	48.2	DEC-1999	4069.31	1323.15	48.2
DEC-2001	1950.40	451.60	30.1	MAR-2017	5911.74	528.62	9.8
DEC-1998	2192.69	498.85	29.5	MAR-2000	4572.83	503.52	12.4
MAR-1991	482.30	108.46	29.0	DEC-1998	2192.69	498.85	29.5
MAR-1975	75.66	15.84	26.5	MAR-2012	3091.57	486.42	18.7
DEC-1982	232.41	44.76	23.9	SEP-2016	5312.00	469.33	9.7
MAR-1987	430.05	80.72	23.1	DEC-2001	1950.40	451.60	30.1
JUN-2003	1622.80	281.63	21.0	DEC-2013	4176.59	405.11	10.7
JUN-1980	157.78	26.78	20.4	DEC-2015	5007.41	387.25	8.4
JUN-2009	1835.04	306.45	20.0	SEP-2013	3771.48	368.23	10.8
RUSSELL 1000 1979 to APRIL 2017							
DEC-1998	642.87	113.76	21.5	DEC-1998	642.87	113.76	21.5
MAR-1987	155.20	25.20	19.4	DEC-1999	767.97	104.14	15.7
DEC-1982	77.24	11.35	17.2	DEC-2013	1030.36	90.86	9.7
JUN-1997	462.95	64.76	16.3	MAR-2012	778.92	85.56	12.3
DEC-1985	114.39	15.64	15.8	MAR-2013	872.11	82.21	10.4
JUN-2009	502.27	68.60	15.8	SEP-2009	579.97	77.70	15.5
DEC-1999	767.97	104.14	15.7	DEC-2011	693.36	69.91	11.2
SEP-2009	579.97	77.70	15.5	JUN-2009	502.27	68.60	15.8
JUN-2003	518.94	68.59	15.2	JUN-2003	518.94	68.59	15.2
MAR-1991	196.15	24.93	14.6	MAR-2017	1310.06	68.40	5.5
RUSSELL 2000 1979 to APRIL 2017							
MAR-1991	171.01	38.85	29.4	DEC-2010	783.65	107.51	15.9
DEC-1982	88.90	18.06	25.5	DEC-2016	1357.13	105.48	8.4
MAR-1987	166.79	31.79	23.5	DEC-2014	1204.70	103.02	9.4
JUN-2003	448.37	83.83	23.0	MAR-2013	951.54	102.19	12.0
SEP-1980	69.94	12.47	21.7	SEP-2016	1251.65	99.73	8.7
DEC-2001	488.50	83.63	20.7	DEC-2011	740.92	96.76	15.0
JUN-1983	124.17	20.40	19.7	SEP-2013	1073.79	96.31	9.9
JUN-1980	57.47	9.20	19.1	SEP-2009	604.28	96.00	18.9
DEC-1999	504.75	77.45	18.1	MAR-2006	765.14	91.92	13.7
SEP-2009	604.28	96.00	18.9	DEC-2013	1163.64	89.85	8.4

10 **WORST** QUARTERS BY PERCENT AND POINT

BY PERCENT CHANGE				BY POINT CHANGE			
QUARTER	CLOSE	PNT CHANGE	% CHANGE	QUARTER	CLOSE	PNT CHANGE	% CHANGE
DJIA 1901 to 1949							
JUN-1932	42.84	−30.44	−41.5	DEC-1929	248.48	−94.97	−27.7
SEP-1931	96.61	−53.57	−35.7	JUN-1930	226.34	−59.76	−20.9
DEC-1929	248.48	−94.97	−27.7	SEP-1931	96.61	−53.57	−35.7
SEP-1903	33.55	−9.73	−22.5	DEC-1930	164.58	−40.32	−19.7
DEC-1937	120.85	−33.72	−21.8	DEC-1937	120.85	−33.72	−21.8
JUN-1930	226.34	−59.76	−20.9	SEP-1946	172.42	−33.20	−16.1
DEC-1930	164.58	−40.32	−19.7	JUN-1932	42.84	−30.44	−41.5
DEC-1931	77.90	−18.71	−19.4	JUN-1940	121.87	−26.08	−17.6
MAR-1938	98.95	−21.90	−18.1	MAR-1939	131.84	−22.92	−14.8
JUN-1940	121.87	−26.08	−17.6	JUN-1931	150.18	−22.18	−12.9
DJIA 1950 to APRIL 2017							
DEC-1987	1938.83	−657.45	−25.3	DEC-2008	8776.39	−2074.27	−19.1
SEP-1974	607.87	−194.54	−24.2	SEP-2001	8847.56	−1654.84	−15.8
JUN-1962	561.28	−145.67	−20.6	SEP-2002	7591.93	−1651.33	−17.9
DEC-2008	8776.39	−2074.27	−19.1	SEP-2011	10913.38	−1500.96	−12.1
SEP-2002	7591.93	−1651.33	−17.9	SEP-2015	16284.00	−1335.51	−7.6
SEP-2001	8847.56	−1654.84	−15.8	MAR-2009	7608.92	−1167.47	−13.3
SEP-1990	2452.48	−428.21	−14.9	JUN-2002	9243.26	−1160.68	−11.2
MAR-2009	7608.92	−1167.47	−13.3	SEP-1998	7842.62	−1109.40	−12.4
SEP-1981	849.98	−126.90	−13.0	JUN-2010	9774.02	−1082.61	−10.0
JUN-1970	683.53	−102.04	−13.0	MAR-2008	12262.89	−1001.93	−7.6
S&P 500 1930 to APRIL 2017							
JUN-1932	4.43	−2.88	−39.4	DEC-2008	903.25	−263.11	−22.6
SEP-1931	9.71	−5.12	−34.5	SEP-2011	1131.42	−189.22	−14.3
SEP-1974	63.54	−22.46	−26.1	SEP-2001	1040.94	−183.48	−15.0
DEC-1937	10.55	−3.21	−23.3	SEP-2002	815.28	−174.54	−17.6
DEC-1987	247.08	−74.75	−23.2	MAR-2001	1160.33	−159.95	−12.1
DEC-2008	903.25	−263.11	−22.6	JUN-2002	989.82	−157.57	−13.7
JUN-1962	54.75	−14.80	−21.3	MAR-2008	1322.70	−145.66	−9.9
MAR-1938	8.50	−2.05	−19.4	SEP-2015	1920.03	−143.08	−6.9
JUN-1970	72.72	−16.91	−18.9	JUN-2010	1030.71	−138.72	−11.9
SEP-1946	14.96	−3.47	−18.8	SEP-1998	1017.01	−116.83	−10.3
NASDAQ 1971 to APRIL 2017							
DEC-2000	2470.52	−1202.30	−32.7	DEC-2000	2470.52	−1202.30	−32.7
SEP-2001	1498.80	−661.74	−30.6	SEP-2001	1498.80	−661.74	−30.6
SEP-1974	55.67	−20.29	−26.7	MAR-2001	1840.26	−630.26	−25.5
DEC-1987	330.47	−113.82	−25.6	JUN-2000	3966.11	−606.72	−13.3
MAR-2001	1840.26	−630.26	−25.5	DEC-2008	1577.03	−514.85	−24.6
SEP-1990	344.51	−117.78	−25.5	JUN-2002	1463.21	−382.14	−20.7
DEC-2008	1577.03	−514.85	−24.6	MAR-2008	2279.10	−373.18	−14.1
JUN-2002	1463.21	−382.14	−20.7	SEP-2015	4620.16	−366.71	−7.4
SEP-2002	1172.06	−291.15	−19.9	SEP-2011	2415.40	−358.12	−12.9
JUN-1974	75.96	−16.31	−17.7	SEP-2000	3672.82	−293.29	−7.4
RUSSELL 1000 1979 to APRIL 2017							
DEC-2008	487.77	−146.31	−23.1	DEC-2008	487.77	−146.31	−23.1
DEC-1987	130.02	−38.81	−23.0	SEP-2011	623.45	−111.03	−15.1
SEP-2002	433.22	−90.50	−17.3	SEP-2001	546.46	−100.18	−15.5
SEP-2001	546.46	−100.18	−15.5	SEP-2002	433.22	−90.50	−17.3
SEP-1990	157.83	−28.46	−15.3	MAR-2001	610.36	−89.73	−12.8
SEP-2011	623.45	−111.03	−15.1	SEP-2015	1068.46	−84.18	−7.3
JUN-2002	523.72	−83.63	−13.8	JUN-2002	523.72	−83.63	−13.8
MAR-2001	610.36	−89.73	−12.8	MAR-2008	720.32	−79.50	−9.9
SEP-1981	64.06	−8.95	−12.3	JUN-2010	567.37	−76.42	−11.9
JUN-2010	567.37	−76.42	−11.9	DEC-2000	700.09	−72.51	−9.4
RUSSELL 2000 1979 to APRIL 2017							
DEC-1987	120.42	−50.39	−29.5	SEP-2011	644.16	−183.27	−22.1
DEC-2008	499.45	−180.13	−26.5	DEC-2008	499.45	−180.13	−26.5
SEP-1990	126.70	−42.34	−25.0	SEP-2015	1100.69	−153.26	−12.2
SEP-2011	644.16	−183.27	−22.1	SEP-2001	404.87	−107.77	−21.0
SEP-2002	362.27	−100.37	−21.7	SEP-2002	362.27	−100.37	−21.7
SEP-2001	404.87	−107.77	−21.0	SEP-1998	363.59	−93.80	−20.5
SEP-1998	363.59	−93.80	−20.5	SEP-2014	1101.68	−91.28	−7.7
SEP-1981	67.55	−15.01	−18.2	MAR-2008	687.97	−78.06	−10.2
MAR-2009	422.75	−76.70	−15.4	MAR-2009	422.75	−76.70	−15.4
MAR-1980	48.27	−7.64	−13.7	JUN-2010	609.49	−69.15	−10.2

10 **BEST** YEARS BY PERCENT AND POINT

	BY PERCENT CHANGE				BY POINT CHANGE		
YEAR	CLOSE	PNT CHANGE	% CHANGE	YEAR	CLOSE	PNT CHANGE	% CHANGE
DJIA 1901 to 1949							
1915	99.15	44.57	81.7	1928	300.00	97.60	48.2
1933	99.90	39.97	66.7	1927	202.40	45.20	28.8
1928	300.00	97.60	48.2	1915	99.15	44.57	81.7
1908	63.11	20.07	46.6	1945	192.91	40.59	26.6
1904	50.99	15.01	41.7	1935	144.13	40.09	38.5
1935	144.13	40.09	38.5	1933	99.90	39.97	66.7
1905	70.47	19.48	38.2	1925	156.66	36.15	30.0
1919	107.23	25.03	30.5	1936	179.90	35.77	24.8
1925	156.66	36.15	30.0	1938	154.76	33.91	28.1
1927	202.40	45.20	28.8	1919	107.23	25.03	30.5
DJIA 1950 to APRIL 2017							
1954	404.39	123.49	44.0	2013	16576.66	3472.52	26.5
1975	852.41	236.17	38.3	2016	19762.60	2337.57	13.4
1958	583.65	147.96	34.0	1999	11497.12	2315.69	25.2
1995	5117.12	1282.68	33.5	2003	10453.92	2112.29	25.3
1985	1546.67	335.10	27.7	2006	12463.15	1745.65	16.3
1989	2753.20	584.63	27.0	2009	10428.05	1651.66	18.8
2013	16576.66	3472.52	26.5	1997	7908.25	1459.98	22.6
1996	6448.27	1331.15	26.0	1996	6448.27	1331.15	26.0
2003	10453.92	2112.29	25.3	1995	5117.12	1282.68	33.5
1999	11497.12	2315.69	25.2	1998	9181.43	1273.18	16.1
S&P 500 1930 to APRIL 2017							
1933	10.10	3.21	46.6	2013	1848.36	422.17	29.6
1954	35.98	11.17	45.0	1998	1229.23	258.80	26.7
1935	13.43	3.93	41.4	1999	1469.25	240.02	19.5
1958	55.21	15.22	38.1	2003	1111.92	232.10	26.4
1995	615.93	156.66	34.1	1997	970.43	229.69	31.0
1975	90.19	21.63	31.5	2009	1115.10	211.85	23.5
1997	970.43	229.69	31.0	2014	2058.90	210.54	11.4
1945	17.36	4.08	30.7	2016	2238.83	194.89	9.5
2013	1848.36	422.17	29.6	2006	1418.30	170.01	13.6
1936	17.18	3.75	27.9	2012	1426.19	168.59	13.4
NASDAQ 1971 to APRIL 2017							
1999	4069.31	1876.62	85.6	1999	4069.31	1876.62	85.6
1991	586.34	212.50	56.8	2013	4176.59	1157.08	38.3
2003	2003.37	667.86	50.0	2009	2269.15	692.12	43.9
2009	2269.15	692.12	43.9	2003	2003.37	667.86	50.0
1995	1052.13	300.17	39.9	1998	2192.69	622.34	39.6
1998	2192.69	622.34	39.6	2014	4736.05	559.46	13.4
2013	4176.59	1157.08	38.3	2012	3019.51	414.36	15.9
1980	202.34	51.20	33.9	2010	2652.87	383.72	16.9
1985	324.93	77.58	31.4	2016	5383.12	375.71	7.5
1975	77.62	17.80	29.8	1995	1052.13	300.17	39.9
RUSSELL 1000 1979 to APRIL 2017							
1995	328.89	84.24	34.4	2013	1030.36	240.46	30.4
1997	513.79	120.04	30.5	1998	642.87	129.08	25.1
2013	1030.36	240.46	30.4	2003	594.56	128.38	27.5
1991	220.61	49.39	28.8	1999	767.97	125.10	19.5
2003	594.56	128.38	27.5	2009	612.01	124.24	25.5
1985	114.39	24.08	26.7	1997	513.79	120.04	30.5
1989	185.11	38.12	25.9	2014	1144.37	114.01	11.1
1980	75.20	15.33	25.6	2016	1241.66	109.78	9.7
2009	612.01	124.24	25.5	2012	789.90	96.54	13.9
1998	642.87	129.08	25.1	2006	770.08	90.66	13.3
RUSSELL 2000 1979 to APRIL 2017							
2003	556.91	173.82	45.4	2013	1163.64	314.29	37.0
1991	189.94	57.78	43.7	2016	1357.13	221.24	19.5
1979	55.91	15.39	38.0	2003	556.91	173.82	45.4
2013	1163.64	314.29	37.0	2010	783.65	158.26	25.3
1980	74.80	18.89	33.8	2009	625.39	125.94	25.2
1985	129.87	28.38	28.0	2006	787.66	114.44	17.0
1983	112.27	23.37	26.3	2012	849.35	108.43	14.6
1995	315.97	65.61	26.2	2004	651.57	94.66	17.0
2010	783.65	158.26	25.3	1999	504.75	82.79	19.6
2009	625.39	125.94	25.2	1997	437.02	74.41	20.5

10 <u>WORST</u> YEARS BY PERCENT AND POINT

	BY PERCENT CHANGE				BY POINT CHANGE		
YEAR	CLOSE	PNT CHANGE	% CHANGE	YEAR	CLOSE	PNT CHANGE	% CHANGE
			DJIA 1901 to 1949				
1931	77.90	−86.68	−52.7	1931	77.90	−86.68	−52.7
1907	43.04	−26.08	−37.7	1930	164.58	−83.90	−33.8
1930	164.58	−83.90	−33.8	1937	120.85	−59.05	−32.8
1920	71.95	−35.28	−32.9	1929	248.48	−51.52	−17.2
1937	120.85	−59.05	−32.8	1920	71.95	−35.28	−32.9
1903	35.98	−11.12	−23.6	1907	43.04	−26.08	−37.7
1932	59.93	−17.97	−23.1	1917	74.38	−20.62	−21.7
1917	74.38	−20.62	−21.7	1941	110.96	−20.17	−15.4
1910	59.60	−12.96	−17.9	1940	131.13	−19.11	−12.7
1929	248.48	−51.52	−17.2	1932	59.93	−17.97	−23.1
			DJIA 1950 to APRIL 2017				
2008	8776.39	−4488.43	−33.8	2008	8776.39	−4488.43	−33.8
1974	616.24	−234.62	−27.6	2002	8341.63	−1679.87	−16.8
1966	785.69	−183.57	−18.9	2001	10021.50	−765.35	−7.1
1977	831.17	−173.48	−17.3	2000	10786.85	−710.27	−6.2
2002	8341.63	−1679.87	−16.8	2015	17425.03	−398.04	−2.2
1973	850.86	−169.16	−16.6	1974	616.24	−234.62	−27.6
1969	800.36	−143.39	−15.2	1966	785.69	−183.57	−18.9
1957	435.69	−63.78	−12.8	1977	831.17	−173.48	−17.3
1962	652.10	−79.04	−10.8	1973	850.86	−169.16	−16.6
1960	615.89	−63.47	−9.3	1969	800.36	−143.39	−15.2
			S&P 500 1930 to APRIL 2017				
1931	8.12	−7.22	−47.1	2008	903.25	−565.11	−38.5
1937	10.55	−6.63	−38.6	2002	879.82	−268.26	−23.4
2008	903.25	−565.11	−38.5	2001	1148.08	−172.20	−13.0
1974	68.56	−28.99	−29.7	2000	1320.28	−148.97	−10.1
1930	15.34	−6.11	−28.5	1974	68.56	−28.99	−29.7
2002	879.82	−268.26	−23.4	1990	330.22	−23.18	−6.6
1941	8.69	−1.89	−17.9	1973	97.55	−20.50	−17.4
1973	97.55	−20.50	−17.4	2015	2043.94	−14.96	−0.7
1940	10.58	−1.91	−15.3	1981	122.55	−13.21	−9.7
1932	6.89	−1.23	−15.1	1977	95.10	−12.36	−11.5
			NASDAQ 1971 to APRIL 2017				
2008	1577.03	−1075.25	−40.5	2000	2470.52	−1598.79	−39.3
2000	2470.52	−1598.79	−39.3	2008	1577.03	−1075.25	−40.5
1974	59.82	−32.37	−35.1	2002	1335.51	−614.89	−31.5
2002	1335.51	−614.89	−31.5	2001	1950.40	−520.12	−21.1
1973	92.19	−41.54	−31.1	1990	373.84	−80.98	−17.8
2001	1950.40	−520.12	−21.1	2011	2605.15	−47.72	−1.8
1990	373.84	−80.98	−17.8	1973	92.19	−41.54	−31.1
1984	247.35	−31.25	−11.2	1974	59.82	−32.37	−35.1
1987	330.47	−18.86	−5.4	1984	247.35	−31.25	−11.2
1981	195.84	−6.50	−3.2	1994	751.96	−24.84	−3.2
			RUSSELL 1000 1979 to APRIL 2017				
2008	487.77	−312.05	−39.0	2008	487.77	−312.05	−39.0
2002	466.18	−138.76	−22.9	2002	466.18	−138.76	−22.9
2001	604.94	−95.15	−13.6	2001	604.94	−95.15	−13.6
1981	67.93	−7.27	−9.7	2000	700.09	−67.88	−8.8
2000	700.09	−67.88	−8.8	1990	171.22	−13.89	−7.5
1990	171.22	−13.89	−7.5	2015	1131.88	−12.49	−1.1
1994	244.65	−6.06	−2.4	1981	67.93	−7.27	−9.7
2015	1131.88	−12.49	−1.1	1994	244.65	−6.06	−2.4
2011	693.36	−3.54	−0.5	2011	693.36	−3.54	−0.5
1984	90.31	−0.07	−0.1	1984	90.31	−0.07	−0.10
			RUSSELL 2000 1979 to APRIL 2017				
2008	499.45	−266.58	−34.8	2008	499.45	−266.58	−34.8
2002	383.09	−105.41	−21.6	2002	383.09	−105.41	−21.6
1990	132.16	−36.14	−21.5	2015	1135.89	−68.81	−5.7
1987	120.42	−14.58	−10.8	2011	740.92	−42.73	−5.5
1984	101.49	−10.78	−9.6	1990	132.16	−36.14	−21.5
2015	1135.89	−68.81	−5.7	2007	766.03	−21.63	−2.7
2011	740.92	−42.73	−5.5	2000	483.53	−21.22	−4.2
2000	483.53	−21.22	−4.2	1998	421.96	−15.06	−3.4
1998	421.96	−15.06	−3.4	1987	120.42	−14.58	−10.8
1994	250.36	−8.23	−3.2	1984	101.49	−10.78	−9.6

DOW JONES INDUSTRIALS ONE-YEAR SEASONAL PATTERN CHARTS SINCE 1901

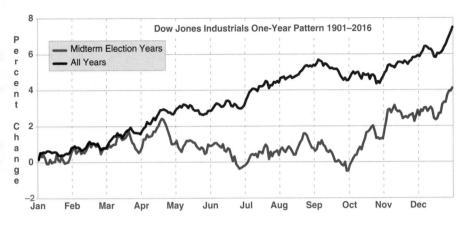

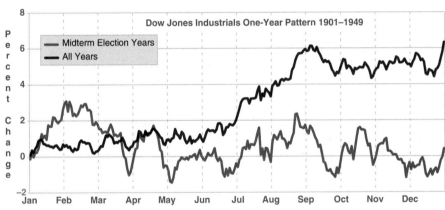

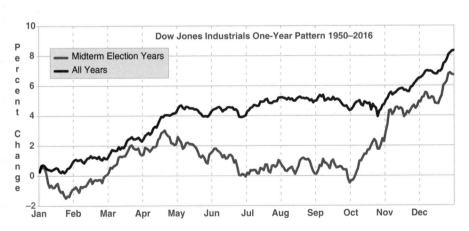

S&P 500 ONE-YEAR SEASONAL PATTERN CHARTS SINCE 1930

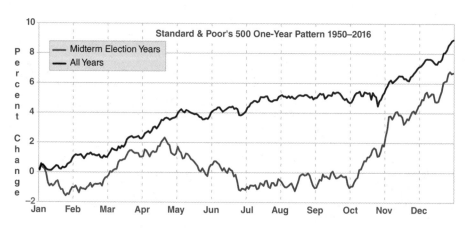

NASDAQ, RUSSELL 1000 & 2000 ONE-YEAR SEASONAL PATTERN CHARTS SINCE 1971

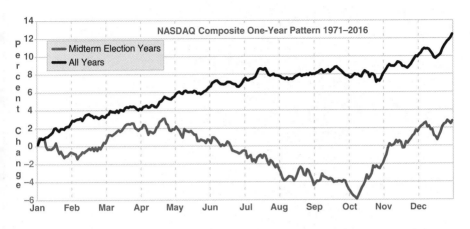

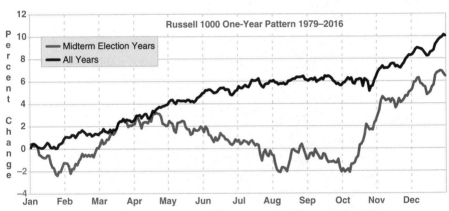

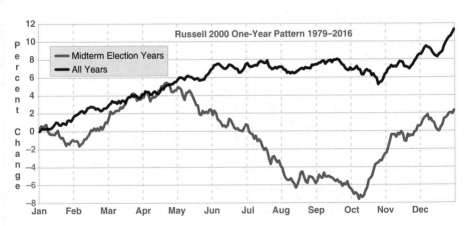

STRATEGY PLANNING AND RECORD SECTION

CONTENTS

These forms are available at our website www.stocktradersalmanac.com.

PORTFOLIO AT START OF 2018

DATE ACQUIRED	NO. OF SHARES	SECURITY	PRICE	TOTAL COST	PAPER PROFITS	PAPER LOSSES

ADDITIONAL PURCHASES

DATE ACQUIRED	NO. OF SHARES	SECURITY	PRICE	TOTAL COST	REASON FOR PURCHASE PRIME OBJECTIVE, ETC.

ADDITIONAL PURCHASES

DATE ACQUIRED	NO. OF SHARES	SECURITY	PRICE	TOTAL COST	REASON FOR PURCHASE PRIME OBJECTIVE, ETC.

SHORT-TERM TRANSACTIONS

Pages 178–181 can accompany next year's income tax return (Schedule D). Enter transactions as completed to avoid last-minute pressures.

NO. OF SHARES	SECURITY	DATE ACQUIRED	DATE SOLD	SALE PRICE	COST	LOSS	GAIN

TOTALS: Carry over to next page

SHORT-TERM TRANSACTIONS (continued)

NO. OF SHARES	SECURITY	DATE ACQUIRED	DATE SOLD	SALE PRICE	COST	LOSS	GAIN

TOTALS:

LONG-TERM TRANSACTIONS

Pages 178–181 can accompany next year's income tax return (Schedule D). Enter transactions as completed to avoid last-minute pressures.

NO. OF SHARES	SECURITY	DATE ACQUIRED	DATE SOLD	SALE PRICE	COST	LOSS	GAIN

TOTALS:

Carry over to next page

LONG-TERM TRANSACTIONS *(continued)*

NO. OF SHARES	SECURITY	DATE ACQUIRED	DATE SOLD	SALE PRICE	COST	LOSS	GAIN

TOTALS:

INTEREST/DIVIDENDS RECEIVED DURING 2018

SHARES	STOCK/BOND	FIRST QUARTER		SECOND QUARTER		THIRD QUARTER		FOURTH QUARTER	
		$		$		$		$	

BROKERAGE ACCOUNT DATA 2018

	MARGIN INTEREST	TRANSFER TAXES	CAPITAL ADDED	CAPITAL WITHDRAWN
JAN				
FEB				
MAR				
APR				
MAY				
JUN				
JUL				
AUG				
SEP				
OCT				
NOV				
DEC				

WEEKLY PORTFOLIO PRICE RECORD 2018 (FIRST HALF)

Place purchase price above stock name and weekly closes below.

STOCKS / Week Ending	1	2	3	4	5	6	7	8	9	10
5										
12										
19										
26										
2										
9										
16										
23										
2										
9										
16										
23										
30										
6										
13										
20										
27										
4										
11										
18										
25										
1										
8										
15										
22										
29										

WEEKLY PORTFOLIO PRICE RECORD 2018 (SECOND HALF)

Place purchase price above stock name and weekly closes below.

STOCKS										
Week Ending	1	2	3	4	5	6	7	8	9	10
JULY 6										
13										
20										
27										
AUGUST 3										
10										
17										
24										
31										
SEPTEMBER 7										
14										
21										
28										
OCTOBER 5										
12										
19										
26										
NOVEMBER 2										
9										
16										
23										
30										
DECEMBER 7										
14										
21										
28										

WEEKLY INDICATOR DATA 2018 (FIRST HALF)

Week Ending	Dow Jones Industrial Average	Net Change for Week	Net Change on Friday	Net Change Next Monday	S&P or NASDAQ	NYSE Ad-vances	NYSE De-clines	New Highs	New Lows	CBOE Put/Call Ratio	90-Day Treas. Rate	Moody's AAA Rate
5												
12												
19												
26												
2												
9												
16												
23												
2												
9												
16												
23												
30												
6												
13												
20												
27												
4												
11												
18												
25												
1												
8												
15												
22												
29												

WEEKLY INDICATOR DATA 2018 (SECOND HALF)

	Week Ending	Dow Jones Industrial Average	Net Change for Week	Net Change on Friday	Net Change Next Monday	S&P or NASDAQ	NYSE Ad-vances	NYSE De-clines	New Highs	New Lows	CBOE Put/Call Ratio	90-Day Treas. Rate	Moody's AAA Rate
JULY	6												
	13												
	20												
	27												
AUGUST	3												
	10												
	17												
	24												
	31												
SEPTEMBER	7												
	14												
	21												
	28												
OCTOBER	5												
	12												
	19												
	26												
NOVEMBER	2												
	9												
	16												
	23												
	30												
DECEMBER	7												
	14												
	21												
	28												

MONTHLY INDICATOR DATA 2018

	DJIA% Last 3 + 1st 2 Days	DJIA% 9th to 11th Trading Days	DJIA% Change Rest of Month	DJIA% Change Whole Month	% Change Your Stocks	Gross Domestic Product	Prime Rate	Trade Deficit $ Billion	CPI % Change	% Unem- ployment Rate
JAN										
FEB										
MAR										
APR										
MAY										
JUN										
JUL										
AUG										
SEP										
OCT										
NOV										
DEC										

INSTRUCTIONS:

Weekly Indicator Data (pages 185–186). Keeping data on several indicators may give you a better feel of the market. In addition to the closing DJIA and its net change for the week, post the net change for Friday's Dow and also the following Monday's. A series of "down Fridays" followed by "down Mondays" often precedes a downswing (see page 74). Tracking either the S&P or NASDAQ composite, and advances and declines, will help prevent the Dow from misleading you. New highs and lows and put/call ratios (www. cboe.com) are also useful indicators. All these weekly figures appear in weekend papers or *Barron's*. Data for 90-day Treasury Rate and Moody's AAA Bond Rate are quite important for tracking short- and long-term interest rates. These figures are available from:

> Weekly U.S. Financial Data
> Federal Reserve Bank of St. Louis
> P.O. Box 442
> St. Louis MO 63166
> **http://research.stlouisfed.org**

Monthly Indicator Data. The purpose of the first three columns is to enable you to track the market's bullish bias near the end, beginning, and middle of the month, which has been shifting lately (see pages 82, 145, and 146). Market direction, performance of your stocks, gross domestic product, prime rate, trade deficit, Consumer Price Index, and unemployment rate are worthwhile indicators to follow. Or, readers may wish to gauge other data.

PORTFOLIO AT END OF 2018

DATE ACQUIRED	NO. OF SHARES	SECURITY	PRICE	TOTAL COST	PAPER PROFITS	PAPER LOSSES

IF YOU DON'T PROFIT FROM YOUR INVESTMENT MISTAKES, SOMEONE ELSE WILL

No matter how much we may deny it, almost every successful person in Wall Street pays a great deal of attention to trading suggestions—especially when they come from "the right sources."

One of the hardest things to learn is to distinguish between good tips and bad ones. Usually, the best tips have a logical reason in back of them, which accompanies the tip. Poor tips usually have no reason to support them.

The important thing to remember is that the market discounts. It does not review, it does not reflect. The Street's real interest in "tips," inside information, buying and selling suggestions, and everything else of this kind emanates from a desire to find out just what the market has on hand to discount. The process of finding out involves separating the wheat from the chaff—and there is plenty of chaff.

HOW TO MAKE USE OF STOCK "TIPS"

- The source should be **reliable**. (By listing all "tips" and suggestions on a Performance Record of Recommendations, such as the form below, and then periodically evaluating the outcomes, you will soon know the "batting average" of your sources.)

- The story should make sense. Would the merger violate antitrust laws? Are there too many computers on the market already? How many years will it take to become profitable?

- The stock should not have had a recent sharp run-up. Otherwise, the story may already be discounted, and confirmation or denial in the press would most likely be accompanied by a sell-off in the stock.

PERFORMANCE RECORD OF RECOMMENDATIONS

STOCK RECOMMENDED	BY WHOM	DATE	PRICE	REASON FOR RECOMMENDATION	SUBSEQUENT ACTION OF STOCK

INDIVIDUAL RETIREMENT ACCOUNT (IRA): MOST AWESOME MASS INVESTMENT INCENTIVE EVER DEVISED

MAX IRA INVESTMENTS OF $5,500* A YEAR COMPOUNDED AT VARIOUS INTEREST RATES OF RETURN FOR DIFFERENT PERIODS

Annual Rate	5 Yrs	10 Yrs	15 Yrs	20 Yrs	25 Yrs	30 Yrs	35 Yrs	40 Yrs	45 Yrs	50 Yrs
1%	$28,336	$58,118	$89,418	$122,316	$156,891	$193,230	$231,423	$271,564	$313,752	$358,093
2%	29,195	61,428	97,016	136,308	179,690	227,587	280,469	338,855	403,318	474,490
3%	30,076	64,943	105,363	152,221	206,542	269,515	342,518	427,148	525,258	638,994
4%	30,981	68,675	114,535	170,331	238,215	320,806	421,291	543,546	692,288	873,256
5%	31,911	72,637	124,616	190,956	275,624	383,684	521,600	697,619	922,268	1,208,985
6%	32,864	76,844	135,699	214,460	319,860	460,909	649,665	902,262	1,240,295	1,692,658
7%	33,843	81,310	147,884	241,258	372,221	555,902	813,524	1,174,853	1,681,635	2,392,423
8%	34,848	86,050	161,284	271,826	434,249	672,902	1,023,562	1,538,796	2,295,843	3,408,195
9%	35,878	91,082	176,019	306,705	507,782	817,164	1,293,186	2,025,605	3,152,523	4,886,426
10%	36,936	96,421	192,224	346,514	595,000	995,189	1,639,697	2,677,685	4,349,374	7,041,647
11%	38,021	102,088	210,045	391,958	698,493	1,215,022	2,085,404	3,552,048	6,023,428	10,187,848
12%	39,134	108,100	229,643	443,843	821,337	1,486,609	2,659,047	4,725,283	8,366,697	14,784,112
13%	40,275	114,479	251,195	503,085	967,176	1,822,233	3,397,621	6,300,172	11,647,933	21,500,837
14%	41,445	121,245	274,892	570,726	1,140,330	2,237,054	4,348,701	8,414,497	16,242,841	31,315,649
15%	42,646	128,421	300,946	647,956	1,345,916	2,749,763	5,573,401	11,252,746	22,675,938	45,652,055
16%	43,876	136,031	329,588	736,123	1,589,985	3,383,389	7,150,149	15,061,631	31,678,448	66,579,439
17%	45,138	144,100	361,069	836,762	1,879,695	4,166,271	9,179,470	20,170,648	44,268,235	97,100,943
18%	46,431	152,653	395,665	951,616	2,223,497	5,133,252	11,790,069	27,019,253	61,859,935	141,566,978
19%	47,756	161,720	433,676	1,082,661	2,631,368	6,327,131	15,146,529	36,192,731	86,416,412	206,267,876
20%	49,115	171,327	475,432	1,232,141	3,115,075	7,800,418	19,459,052	48,469,462	120,656,646	300,281,459

* At Press Time, 2018 Contribution Limit will be indexed to inflation

190

G. M. LOEB'S "BATTLE PLAN" FOR INVESTMENT SURVIVAL

LIFE IS CHANGE: Nothing can ever be the same a minute from now as it was a minute ago. Everything you own is changing in price and value. You can find that last price of an active security on the stock ticker, but you cannot find the next price anywhere. The value of your money is changing. Even the value of your home is changing, though no one walks in front of it with a sandwich board consistently posting the changes.

RECOGNIZE CHANGE: Your basic objective should be to profit from change. The art of investing is being able to recognize change and to adjust investment goals accordingly.

WRITE THINGS DOWN: You will score more investment success and avoid more investment failures if you write things down. Very few investors have the drive and inclination to do this.

KEEP A CHECKLIST: If you aim to improve your investment results, get into the habit of keeping a checklist on every issue you consider buying. Before making a commitment, it will pay you to write down the answers to at least some of the basic questions—How much am I investing in this company? How much do I think I can make? How much do I have to risk? How long do I expect to take to reach my goal?

HAVE A SINGLE RULING REASON: Above all, writing things down is the best way to find "the ruling reason." When all is said and done, there is invariably a single reason that stands out above all others, why a particular security transaction can be expected to show a profit. All too often, many relatively unimportant statistics are allowed to obscure this single important point.

Any one of a dozen factors may be the point of a particular purchase or sale. It could be a technical reason—an increase in earnings or dividend not yet discounted in the market price—a change of management—a promising new product—an expected improvement in the market's valuation of earnings—or many others. But, in any given case, one of these factors will almost certainly be more important than all the rest put together.

CLOSING OUT A COMMITMENT: If you have a loss, the solution is automatic, provided you decide what to do at the time you buy. Otherwise, the question divides itself into two parts. Are we in a bull or bear market? Few of us really know until it is too late. For the sake of the record, if you think it is a bear market, just put that consideration first and sell as much as your conviction suggests and your nature allows.

If you think it is a bull market, or at least a market where some stocks move up, some mark time, and only a few decline, do not sell unless:

✓ You see a bear market ahead.

✓ You see trouble for a particular company in which you own shares.

✓ Time and circumstances have turned up a new and seemingly far better buy than the issue you like least in your list.

✓ Your shares stop going up and start going down.

A subsidiary question is, which stock to sell first? Two further observations may help:

✓ Do not sell solely because you think a stock is "overvalued."

✓ If you want to sell some of your stocks and not all, in most cases it is better to go against your emotional inclinations and sell first the issues with losses, small profits, or none at all, the weakest, the most disappointing, etc.

Mr. Loeb is the author of The Battle for Investment Survival, John Wiley & Sons.

G. M. LOEB'S INVESTMENT SURVIVAL CHECKLIST

OBJECTIVES AND RISKS

DISCARD

Security			Price	Shares	Date

"Ruling reason" for commitment	Amount of commitment
	$_____
	% of my investment capital
	_____%

Price objective	Est. time to achieve it	I will risk _____ points	Which would be $_____

TECHNICAL POSITION

Price action of stock:	Dow Jones Industrial Average
❑ Hitting new highs ❑ In a trading range	
❑ Pausing in an uptrend ❑ Moving up from low ground	Trend of market
❑ Acting stronger than market ❑ _____	

SELECTED YARDSTICKS

	Price Range		Earnings Per Share Actual or Projected	Price/Earnings Ratio Actual or Projected
	High	Low		
Current year Previous year				

Merger possibilities	Years for earnings to double in past
Comment on future	Years for market price to double in past

PERIODIC RE-CHECKS

Date	Stock Price	DJIA	Comment	Action taken, if any

COMPLETED TRANSACTIONS

Date closed	Period of time held	Profit or loss
Reason for profit or loss		

192

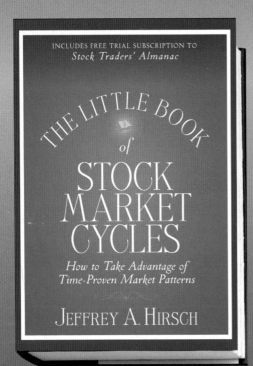